From Prairie Roots

OUR FIRST 60 YEARS

This book contains the story of a unique Canadian experience.

In 1924 a band of determined prairie farmers established Saskatchewan Wheat Pool to market their grain. By 1984 they owned and operated one of the country's largest business firms, the biggest co-operative association in Canada.

The Pool, as it came to be known, now markets grain and livestock; merchandises farm supplies; operates a publishing and printing company and a flour mill. It shares ownership in vegetable oil processing plants, fertilizer manufacturing facilities, a grain exporting firm, and an oil exploration and development company.

A well organized structure provides members with information and encourages input in directing the organization's affairs. It also provides an effective means of developing and promoting sound agricultural policies.

All these enterprises and services are devoted to improvement in the economic and social well-being of farmers for whom the Pool was started in the first place.

The Board of Directors of Saskatchewan Wheat Pool wants to share with you the record of that accomplishment.

Please accept this book with our thanks for your help through the years and our shared expectations for the future.

SASKATCHEWAN WHEAT POOL

E. K. Turner   *E.K. Turner*   President

From Prairie Roots

The Remarkable Story
of Saskatchewan Wheat Pool

by
Garry Lawrence Fairbairn

Western Producer Prairie Books
Saskatoon, Saskatchewan

Printed and bound in Canada by Modern Press ⟶1
Saskatoon, Saskatchewan

Cover design by Warren Clark

Western Producer Prairie Books publications are produced and manufactured in the middle of western Canada by a unique publishing venture owned by a group of prairie farmers who are members of Saskatchewan Wheat Pool. Our first book in 1954 was a reprint of a serial originally carried in *The Western Producer*, a weekly newspaper serving Western Canadian farmers since 1923. We continue the tradition of providing enjoyable and informative reading for all Canadians.

Canadian Cataloguing in Publication Data

Fairbairn, Garry Lawrence, 1947-
    From prairie roots

    Bibliography: p.
    Includes index.
    ISBN 0-88833-127-4

    1. Saskatchewan Wheat Pool — History.
2. Wheat — Saskatchewan — Co-operative
marketing — History. I. Title.
HD9049.W5C294 1984   334′.683311′097124

                                        C84-091108-4

Dedicated to the 45,725 original contract signers of 1923-24 whose individual acts of desperation, hope and faith combined to create an enduring co-operative empire and corporate democracy.

Contents

Foreword

Saskatchewan has never been a place for the faint of heart. In the early days above all, it was a place that demanded courage and vision from those who challenged its forbidding climate and its expanse of emptiness.

The people who accepted that challenge were a very special group, and they left a lasting mark on all of us. They learned early to be builders and to work together. They were willing to tackle almost anything, against any odds, as long as it was something in which they could believe. Because of these characteristics, they accomplished the near-impossible. What some looked upon as a wilderness, they turned into a mosaic of flourishing farmsteads and thriving communities.

The same courage and vision, the same willingness to build, to work together, to defy the odds and to fight for an ideal brought Saskatchewan Wheat Pool into existence six decades ago and made it what it is today.

On the occasion of our sixtieth anniversary, it is fitting that Western Producer Prairie Books is publishing this account of six decades that produced today's Saskatchewan Wheat Pool. It is not a dull, conventional corporate history, nor is it the sanitized product of a bureaucratic committee. Our predecessors deserved more than that. Instead, we chose an author from outside the Pool, a person experienced in history and journalism who was given free access to Pool records and personnel. A seven-person advisory committee, composed of distinguished individuals who have no direct association with Saskatchewan Wheat Pool, provided advice and reviewed the manuscript.

The product of this independent research and writing is, we feel, an appropriate tribute to those generations of members and employees who built Saskatchewan Wheat Pool. It is also a very good story — a lively and readable account suitable for both personal pleasure and historical education.

Those who ignore their past and refuse to consider their future might as well walk through life blindfolded. Within these covers readers will find material to provoke thoughts about both past and future. In some way, I hope, this history will help us to be better prepared when the future becomes the present.

E. K. TURNER
President, Saskatchewan Wheat Pool

Preface

No book can please everyone and this one does not attempt to do so. A history that tried to be pleasing to all would probably be satisfying to none. Worse, it would not be faithful to those past generations it portrays. If, for example, there are any readers searching for inspiring fairy tales, then they will not find them here. This is a book about real people, with real human failings — mistakes, confusion, jealousies, indecision. These people did not live in saintly harmony, they did not always win, and their critics at the Grain Exchange were not the epitome of evil — nor even always wrong. It is the author's contention that those same human failings make the achievements of Pool members all the greater, and demonstrate that co-operation is a practical principle, not one reserved for some unearthly paradise.

Nor is this the comprehensive, academically definitive history of Saskatchewan Wheat Pool. If that were ever to be written, it would take many volumes — volumes that would be a major contribution to historical research and to future writers, but also volumes that would be read by very few members of the general public. This is also *not* the official history of Saskatchewan Wheat Pool. In mid-1981, the Pool commissioned this work, contracting with the author for the production of "a narrative analytical history" in easily-readable style and with a text of moderate length. From the start, it was an independent project, with Pool personnel available for interviews and consultation. But the responsibility for research, selection of material, and interpretative commentary remained with the author. It was a brave and enlightened approach for the Pool to take — brave, because they were entrusting their money and their history to an outsider who had never worked for the Pool; enlightened, because by taking that approach they avoided the dead, lifeless summary that usually comes from committee-directed official histories. Whether or not the author performed well is a matter for the reader to judge — but, in any case, no blame should attach to the Pool.

Many people who have been involved in Pool history will find much missing from these pages. Short of printing long lists of names, there was simply no way to mention even a substantial fraction of the thousands of delegates, committee members, staff and others who contributed to the Pool's successes. Space constraints also prevented fuller discussion of important social, political and agricultural developments that were not a central part of Pool history. The author has tried to mitigate such omissions with periodic examples of the contributions of the many unnamed Pool members as well as providing footnotes and a bibliography for those desiring to investigate related developments. Beyond that, the author can only ask for understanding from those who would have made different choices and placed emphasis on different topics.

One other aspect of this book should be emphasized — it is a history of Saskatchewan Wheat Pool, not of the prairie-wide pool movement. In this text, "the Pool" with a capital "P" is the Saskatchewan organization. There are frequent references to the participation of Alberta Wheat Pool and Manitoba Pool Elevators in various joint endeavors, but this book does not presume to deal with their histories. Works specifically on the neighboring pools are listed in the bibliography. Saskatchewan Wheat Pool obviously did not have a monopoly on co-operative spirit or determination, and any good history of the prairie-wide pool movement would give more equal treatment to the three pools than a book about any one of them should.

So this book is not definitive, not official, not about general social history, not about the three pools; what then is it? It is one person's attempt to give others a general feeling for the six decades of co-operative effort and quiet dedication that Saskatchewan farmers have put into their organization. It is in part a means of noting certain highlights of Pool history for the historical record, and of providing an account of the past so that readers can reach their own conclusions about future policy. But it is primarily a means of commemorating what the first sixty years of Pool members and employees have achieved. Whatever merit there is in this book comes primarily from the simple fact that it reflects their story.

*   *   *

Many Saskatchewan Wheat Pool employees assisted in this project, providing everything from occasional clerical services to interviews, but there is space to name only a few. Pool research director Allan McLeod was chief liaison between the author and the Pool, providing research facilities, approving expenses, and organizing support services as well as being a valuable source of advice when requested. Librarian Elizabeth Hilts and her successor, Gwen McMillan, each tracked down several obscure publications and smilingly tolerated chaotic heaps of papers on their library table. Executive secretary Marj Dickin cheerfully made treks to the depths of the Wheat Pool building to wrestle with the cantankerous old combination lock guarding the large vault where musty records are kept.

An outside advisory committee contributed not only interviews but helpful comments on the rough draft: W. Harold Horner of Regina, former Saskatchewan deputy minister of agriculture; David Kirk of Ottawa, executive secretary of the Canadian Federation of Agriculture; John Leask of Surrey, former Saskatchewan district supervisor for the livestock branch of the federal agriculture department; Breen Melvin, former president of the Co-operative Union of Canada; W. M. Miner of Ottawa, co-ordinator of the Grains Group; Douglas H. Treleaven of Edmonton, former assistant chief commissioner of the Canadian Wheat Board; and Clarence G. Youngs of Saskatoon, former head of biotechnology for the Prairie Regional Laboratory of the National Research Council. As with the other persons here, the advisory committee members deserve a significant part of the credit for this book.

The staffs of the Saskatchewan Archives Board in Regina and Saskatoon were extremely helpful during the author's periodic visits. Also uniformly helpful were personnel at libraries used for shorter periods of time: the University of Saskatchewan, University of Regina, National Library, Public Archives of Canada, Glenbow-Alberta Institute, Thomas Fisher Rare Book Library, and the Saskatoon Public Library.

Relatives of several prominent figures in Pool history provided recollections and occasional documents through interviews and correspondence: Mary Lou Bost of Murphysboro, Illinois, for father Louis Brouillette; Hugh McPhail of North Battleford for uncle A. J. McPhail; R. A. Milliken of Regina for father R. H. Milliken; Margaret Newby of Calgary for father George Robertson; Kathleen Parker of Winnipeg for father Jack Wesson; Christine Pike of Waseca for uncle Jack Wesson; R.W.W. Robertson of Toronto for brother George Robertson; Stanley Sapiro of Encino, California, for father Aaron Sapiro; and Kenneth Steele of Ottawa for father A. J. McPhail.

People who contributed their time for interviews are listed in the bibliography at the end of the book. Even where no specific part of an interview was included in this book, the interview was usually helpful in broadening the author's understanding of past events, conditions and personalities.

Duplication services for the rough draft were provided most efficiently by the Pool's printing service department, while Deanna Harrison of the Co-operative College of Canada typed a revised draft into the college's word processing equipment. The work was greatly enhanced by the editing of Isobel Findlay.

Relevant archives, publishers and other copyright holders kindly provided permission for quotations from their material.

A very special acknowledgement is due to Lorna Bratvold, the author's wife, for not only coping with a temperamental writer and equally-temperamental one-year-old daughter in the same house, but for general support and one of the most thorough, perceptive readings of the manuscript.

Garry Lawrence Fairbairn

Saskatoon, October 1983

1
Prelude, 1900–1923

I have seen these free-born men and women of the prairies work harder and more incessantly than men can be driven in penal settlements. I have seen their lanterns glimmer around the barns before daylight, and after it. I have seen their season's effort withered by drought; have heard the machine-gun rattle of the hail; and felt the keen chill of the frost at the very threshold of harvest. I have seen the light go out of these growers' eyes, as their hopes faded.

— W. P. Davisson, 1927[1]

Some organizations, like some calves, are born with casual ease, their arrival scarcely noticed until one sunny morning finds them already routinely grazing on a gentle slope. Others come only after a raw, hard struggle, a grim rancher straining to pull the calf from a desperate cow. The birth of Saskatchewan Wheat Pool was definitely in the second category. No product of elegant theoreticians or genteel debaters, "the Pool" sprang from a clash of strong wills and stronger words among prairie-hardened farmers who were determined to let nothing block their progress toward a decent life for themselves and their families.

The dramatic 1923-24 campaigns to organize pools in Saskatchewan and neighboring prairie provinces were themselves the culmination of more than two decades of agricultural struggle. Against a turbulent backdrop of World War, massive population and cultural upheaval, general strikes, riots, influenza epidemics and political turmoil, farmers fought a continuous battle against man and nature. Even when the land was broken and a crude shelter built, even when all manner of pests, diseases and disastrous weather had been avoided and the crop was harvested, the farmer still had an uphill battle. Reminiscing about the grain growers near Abernethy, Saskatchewan, W. R. Motherwell once recalled how he and his neighbors faced a 25-mile trip to the nearest railway delivery point.[2] Even in good weather, that was then a tiresome, 50-mile round trip by plodding horse and wagon — at a time when a 50-bushel wagonload was a good-sized haul. One mile of travel on rough roads for every bushel, 5,000 miles to deliver all the grain that a moderately large farm might produce, the equivalent of a trek to Montreal and back.

And what would the farmer find waiting for him at the delivery point? Too often, his welcome would be from a smiling elevator agent who would sympathetically explain that the farmer should have been there Tuesday to catch the high wheat prices, or that the wagonload of top-grade wheat looked like a somewhat lower grade, or that a larger than expected weight would have to be deducted as dockage to allow for unwanted weeds or other grains mixed in with the wheat. And if none of these assessments were plausible, there was also the unfortunate possibility that all the elevator bins reserved for No. 1 wheat happened to be full, so that the farmer could deliver only into No. 3 bins, at No. 3 prices. As if all this were not enough, farmers had to be on guard for such other tricks as improperly-adjusted scales. One young boy who was sent to deliver wheat, John Martin, had the load weighed at a lumber yard first, then found that the elevator scales showed a suspiciously lower weight. Martin objected, and the agent reluctantly reweighed the load. Apparently presuming that a boy's word could not count against him, the agent calmly and visibly removed two rollers that had been distorting his scales.[3]

Elevator agents — the ones who kept their jobs — were not usually known for being more charitable than their colleagues at the same point, so even where the farmer had a choice of elevators he usually found a similar welcome. The collusion could at times be insultingly blatant. A farmer who decided to reject the grade offered by one agent and to go to the neighboring elevator would soon realize the futility of such effort when he saw the first agent casually stroll outside and hold up fingers to show the second agent what grade had been offered.[4] The farmer, of course, theoretically had the option of taking his wagonload home and trying the tedious round trip some other time — a choice about as realistic as storing the wheat over the winter in granaries he could not afford to build, or stalling creditors who demanded payment now and refused to accept promises that the wheat could be sold for higher prices in spring.

It was anything but surprising, then, that some talked of seizing grain elevators or blocking rail lines or even using a few bullets to attract Ottawa's attention.[5] Even if the amount of abuse by elevator companies was exaggerated, there was enough residue of fact and enough opportunity for abuse to embitter the calmest farmer.

Fortunately, there were enough volunteer leaders and concerned legislators to encourage farmers to channel that developing bitterness into constructive collective action. W. R. Motherwell, who became Saskatchewan's first agriculture minister when the province was formed in 1905, then moved in 1921 to be federal agriculture minister, first made his mark in 1901 by organizing the Territorial Grain Growers' Association and being elected its first president. "There are very few today who know how near the people were to resorting to violence at that time instead of laying the foundation of the Grain Growers' Association," Motherwell recalled some decades later.[6] The fledgling group of a dozen farmers might have had a shaky start had it not been for the fortunate combination of timely legislation and railway insensitivity. Governments had begun to show concern for prairie farmers in 1899 in the form of the first of fourteen royal commissions that were to probe the grain-handling business over the next fifteen years.[7] The landmark Manitoba Grain Act of 1900 began imposing regulations on the grain trade and a key 1902 amendment to that act required each delivery point to maintain a car order book. A farmer wishing to bypass the local elevator could put his name in the book and get a railway car delivered to that point for his own use — provided that he was fortunate enough to be among the fifty per cent or so of farmers who individually had enough of one grade of grain to fill a rail car. In law and theory, the individual farmer's order would take precedence over any cars ordered later by the local elevator. In practice, the railways saw no need to bother with such irksome details and filled farmers' orders only as an afterthought. The railways' disregard for legal niceties, however, ended abruptly after a well-publicized trial in which the Grain Growers' Association took a Sintaluta station agent to court for ignoring farmers' car orders. The symbolic fine levied on that hapless agent prompted prairie-wide obedience to the law and launched the Grain Growers' Association on its energetic and influential career.[8]

But prairie farmers were only just starting to flex their muscles, only just beginning to realize what joint action could do. Sintaluta again entered the history books when an irascible, cantankerous farmer from that area, Ed Partridge, decided that farmers could operate and profit from a grain-handling business just as well as anyone else. Partridge's decision came after a few neighbors scraped together enough money to send him to Winnipeg for a week — even a coach train ticket and a cheap hotel room required pooling pocketbooks in those days. He returned with the conviction that the hubbub of the Winnipeg Grain Exchange was just superficial sound and fury concealing decisions by five major private grain companies who dominated price-setting. In 1906 the Grain Growers' Grain Company (later renamed United Grain Growers) was created — the result of faith, a lot of hard work, and the willingness of several farmers to put all their hard-won assets at stake to back loans. Although the grain company was completely independent from the grain growers' associations, the two groups provided much mutual support. Partridge's personality proved too acerbic and uncompromising to survive long on a board of directors, but no one could take away his role in spearheading the drive for the Grain Growers' Grain Company and in becoming its first president.

While that prairie-wide farmers' company was getting started, separate provincial initiatives also cut deeply into the private world of grain elevators. Both Saskatchewan and Alberta launched co-operative elevator companies, while the Manitoba government between 1909 and 1912 bought 174 elevators to test the theory of government ownership. High purchase prices and poor selection of elevators hampered the Manitoba experiment. Perhaps more important, the Manitoba government sought to cover costs solely through storage and handling revenues instead of also using the elevator system for the more profitable activity of buying and selling grain. Mounting losses prompted the government to turn the whole system over to the Grain Growers' Grain Company, which went on to absorb the Alberta co-operative elevators in 1917. With that amalgamation came a new name, United Grain Growers, and a solid financial base that was to provide much aid to the pool-organizing campaigns. Thus Partridge's creation developed along lines different from those he had originally planned. The man from Sintaluta had sought a farmer-owned grain trading company within a system of government-owned elevators. Under his plan, prairie provincial governments would own elevators inside their individual jurisdictions while Ottawa would own the large terminal elevators at the Lakehead. Instead, the Grain Growers' Grain Company became a full-fledged elevator company after the Manitoba experiment failed.

Saskatchewan's vastly larger grain resources, coupled with generous government aid, gave the Saskatchewan Co-operative Elevator Company less incentive to consider amalgamation after its founding in 1911. In the first year it built forty elevators and bought six more; 1912 added another ninety-three and "the

Breaking first sod on the prairies, as re-enacted for The Drylanders. *So bare is the land that the farmer has no landmarks at which to aim his plow. For a straight furrow, he points the plow at the boy at left. (NFB Photo 97793)*

Co-op" was off and running.[9] Shareholders had to pay only $7.50 for a $50 share. The rest was provided as a Saskatchewan government loan, to be repaid out of company earnings. While the Grain Growers' Grain Company worked energetically to arrange co-operative buying of farm supplies for its members — everything from binder twine and fence posts to flour and sewing machines — the Saskatchewan Co-operative Elevator Company stuck to the grain business.

Farmers did not forget about political action in this busy period. Some 500 from the West joined 300 Ontario farmers in a mass demonstration on Parliament Hill in December 1910, flooding onto the floor of the House of Commons to push their demands for federally-owned grain terminal elevators at the Lakehead, a railway to Hudson Bay, and tariff reductions. In 1910, farmers were not a mere special-interest group to be blocked with iron fences and security guards. They were a majority of the population and agriculture was still the foundation of all things economic. The Toronto board of trade endorsed their demands, members of Parliament welcomed their visitors in the Commons chamber, and the 1912 Canada Grain Act came to meet several of their desires. That act established a three-man board of grain commissioners to tighten grain-trade regulation and grain inspection, as well as giving the government authority to build terminal elevators. Matching actions to words, Ottawa soon had a terminal elevator built at Port Arthur, plus inland terminals at Saskatoon,

Moose Jaw and Calgary. The eventual addition of terminals at Edmonton and Lethbridge completed the federal network.

All the progress of 1900-1915, however, proved to be inadequate. For many, disillusionment with even the farmers' elevator companies set in quickly. Neither United Grain Growers nor the Saskatchewan Co-op implemented the basic co-operative principle of patronage dividends. Rather than returning earnings to members in proportion to each member's business, they paid dividends according to capital invested in the company. Partridge and United Grain Growers had fought mightily for the legal power to pay patronage dividends, only to be frustrated by Senate refusal to put such power in the company charter and by Grain Exchange refusal to grant membership to a company that paid such dividends. By the time those obstacles were removed, the last vanishing with the new UGG charter of 1917, the company had become comfortable with the share-dividend concept.

For hard-line disciples of the fast-spreading philosophy of co-operation, there was even less excuse for the way Saskatchewan Co-operative Elevator Company was developing. Not only did its directors refuse to undertake patronage dividends, always seeing a greater need for more cash reserves and equity, but also the organization's internal democracy had several failings. Directors, once elected, were safe from the membership for three years.[10] All were elected at large instead of by district and all were elected at the annual meeting instead of in the country. With slight effort, a board could comfortably perpetuate itself for many years under those conditions, insulated from the mass of members. Farmers' experience with Co-op Elevators was, in fact, the key reason why Saskatchewan Wheat Pool was later blessed — and burdened — with an extensive democratic structure. Declining profits of Co-op Elevators, which came despite larger volumes and higher storage fees than other companies, may have also contributed to farmers' discontent with the company.[11]

Meanwhile, the Territorial Grain Growers' Association had in 1906 become the Saskatchewan Grain Growers' Association (SGGA) and was starting to suffer similar discontent. Part of the reason was overlapping leadership — for more than a decade, John A. Maharg was president of both the SGGA and the Co-op Elevator Company. For part of 1921 he even added the position of Saskatchewan agriculture minister to his duties, following four years as a federal MP. With Maharg spread so thinly, the SGGA increasingly became the creature of its central secretary, J. B. Musselman. The board of directors met rarely, Musselman-approved candidates were lined up before annual meetings, and the presence of appointed directors-at-large further insulated the

Left: *Edward Alexander Partridge, founder of the Grain Growers' Grain Company, about 1910. (SWP Collection, Saskatchewan Archives Board R-A 15,253)*
Right: *J. B. Musselman, secretary, Saskatchewan Grain Growers' Association. (Saskatchewan Archives Board R-A 8494)*

board from upsets. Fairly or unfairly, Musselman early became a symbol of all that the reformers wished to change. His image with farmers also suffered because of his influential role in the provincial Liberal party, which was trying to prevent formation of a farmers' political party. Nor did Musselman's membership in Regina's posh Assiniboia Club help his standing with farmers.[12] Whether out of misplaced loyalty to a friend or philosophical kinship, Maharg did nothing to correct the situation. The reform wing of the SGGA finally scored a breakthrough in 1922, replacing Musselman as secretary with a rigidly-idealistic farmer from the Bankend area, A. J. McPhail. Another reformer, Violet McNaughton, was elected as an SGGA director despite Musselman's blatant attempts to ignore her nominator.[13] Musselman remained influential in farm organizations, shifting to a senior position in the Co-op elevator company under Maharg. In addition to such problems, the SGGA was also suffering from a strategic weakness that it never fully appreciated. Heavily Anglo-Saxon, it made no significant special effort to bring the many non-English groups in the province into policy-making.[14] The combination of Anglo-Saxon bias and an image of comfortable conservatism opened the door in the early 1920s to a radical new rival, the Farmers' Union of Canada.

There was, however, a much more fundamental reason why farmers became dissatisfied with all the institutions they had built by 1917. Looming behind all the day-to-day trials of the farmer was the mysterious world-wide system of setting grain prices, a system that produced many rich corporate empires but few if any rich farmers, a system symbolized by the Winnipeg Grain Exchange.

The Grain Exchange System

"The Grain Exchange is a device for making agriculture profitable for those who dislike to wear overalls," commented one farmer.[15] Thousands of his colleagues would have considered that an excessively charitable description of an institution that gave a speculator with a few hundred dollars a chance to make more money off wheat in one afternoon than a farmer could from a year's labor. Just a simple walk through some sections of Winnipeg was enough to convince some people that something was drastically wrong with the system. William McKenzie Ross, a longtime Saskatchewan Wheat Pool director, recalled how he became determined to change the system as a Winnipeg school-boy, "seeing all the palatial homes on acreages facing the Assiniboine River on Wellington Crescent."[16] Members of the Grain Exchange owned those homes, "some with massive stone walls screening themselves not only from their own ilk, but also from what they considered the lesser breed." At the Exchange itself, farmers could see traders barking their buy and sell orders in the pit, acting out mysterious rituals that somehow paid for the Wellington Crescent mansions. The grain flowed fairly steadily from Canadian farms to Manchester housewives, whose patterns of consumption changed little during the year, but Exchange prices would rise and fall on a whisper or a whim. Whatever profits the Exchange traders made did not seem to come out of consumers' pockets. And it was, to say the least, a source of considerable suspicion that wheat prices seemed to hit bottom each fall, when most farmers had to sell the bulk of their grain to pay creditors.

If the Exchange had been merely a place where elevator companies sold wheat to export customers, it would never have developed the satanic reputation it did among many farmers. The trouble — and the Exchange's greatest strength — came in provisions for trading "futures." To buy a wheat future, often wrongly called an option, was simply to make a contract to acquire wheat in a certain month at a certain price — for example, buying "May wheat" at $1.25 a bushel. The superbly streamlined system did away with the need to write out a complete legal contract, substituting a simple exchange of phrases or gestures on the trading floor of the Exchange. Often, the full price of the future did not have to be paid; a deposit of ten cents a bushel with one's trading representatives was usually sufficient. Just as easily as purchases could be made, so too could sales be arranged, even sales of "paper wheat" that the seller would never have. For a $100 deposit, anyone could sell 1,000 bushels of wheat futures. On a later day the speculator could erase the transaction by buying 1,000 bushels. If he sold the original futures at $2 a bushel and bought at $1.75, he would have a $250 profit for temporarily putting up $100.

The Exchange, however, was not created solely for speculators. It also met legitimate needs of companies that actually delivered or received wheat. An elevator company or other merchant who bought wheat would not want to carry the risk of a sharp drop in prices between the time of purchase from the farmer and the time of delivery to a customer. To avoid risk the firm could hedge by immediately selling grain futures as soon as it acquired the wheat. If wheat prices fell, the firm would lose on the physical quantity of wheat, but it would balance that loss with a gain on its futures trading. With that safety net underneath the firm, banks would lend money for the firm's operations, using the hedged wheat as security. "The contribution to the efficiency of grain merchandising was considerable," grain historian C. F. Wilson wrote later: "By competition, these savings were reflected back to the producer."[17] In this context, speculators were seen as a desirable lubricant in the whole process, being willing to finance the unbalanced seasonal deliveries of grain by buying futures from elevator companies at the time of peak deliveries in fall. Even writers with impeccable farm-movement credentials were willing to concede that there was much truth in this view. Futures trading, wrote Hopkins Moorhouse, "is the balance wheel which steadies the entire grain business."[18] The first elected president of Saskatchewan Wheat Pool, A. J. McPhail, told a 1931 inquiry that the futures market offers "very useful protection" to the legitimate interests of grain merchants, millers and bankers.[19]

Some two decades later, someone finally got around to doing an intensive study of speculative profits and losses. The U.S. Commodity Exchange Authority took the records of 400,000 trades handled over nine years by a discontinued Chicago brokerage and found that 2,184 speculators had made $2 million profits in the period — but the other 6,598 speculators had lost $12 million.[20] That, some would argue, means speculators donated $10 million net to the legitimate grain trade and enabled them to pay more to farmers. In retrospect, such studies and assessments do much to qualify contemporary judgments about the Exchange system. But qualification is not the same as exoneration. It is difficult to believe that every group of speculators lost money over-all, at all times and places. It is impossible to believe that all the other middlemen involved did not make large profits between the farmer and the consumer. Of greater importance, the speculative system was not designed to give the farmer either stable income or the highest prices that consumers could fairly support. As McPhail said in 1931, "a system which may work in a satisfactory manner and provide sheltered safety to bankers, millers and grain handlers and merchants, may not, and in my opinion does not, provide the same security to the grain producers who are after all the all important group in the picture."[21] For farmers, the system meant not only unpredictable prices, but a tendency for low prices in the fall when they made their deliveries and elevator companies created great selling pressure by hedging that grain.

That lack of protection could have severe costs in human terms. Veteran journalist Wilfrid Eggleston recalled boarding with a farmer who raised 6,000 bushels of wheat in 1920.[22] Instead of delivering that immediately, the farmer agreed to a neighbor's pleas to help the neighbor thresh his crop. Six weeks of custom threshing earned the farmer $800 — but declining wheat prices in those six weeks lowered the value of that farmer's crop by $2,000.

Discing near Saskatoon, date unknown. (SWP Photo)

Losses were certainly not suffered only by careless or slow-witted farmers. Jimmy Gardiner was a farmer delivering wheat that fall of 1920.[23] He bypassed the low prices at his local elevator and shipped his own carload to the Lakehead. When it got there, prices were still low. He borrowed $600 from a bank to store the wheat at the Lakehead, but prices fell again. After renewing the bank loan twice, he finally cut his losses and sold the wheat, before going on to a successful political career as Saskatchewan premier, senior federal cabinet minister and head of the most efficient Saskatchewan political machine of the interwar years. If Jimmy Gardiner could not beat the system, no one could.

And that, in short, was what farmers were realizing in increasing numbers. Growers' associations, farmer-owned elevators and increased government regulation were all very nice, but they still operated within the Grain Exchange system. This realization, which came about the same time that the Progressive party and other innovations were launched in an effort to reform the broader political and economic system, also opened a gulf between farmers and governments. Some historians have observed that when farmers' ambitions shifted to the overthrow of the Grain Exchange, the personnel of grain-related royal commissions appointed by government changed dramatically, from farmers to establishment representatives. Farmer radicalization was evident in the 1918 "Farmer's Platform" adopted by the Canadian Council of Agriculture. The platform included calls for: extension of co-operatives over all agricultural marketing; public ownership of transportation and communications; and methods by which voters could directly initiate legislation.[24]

Farmers, meanwhile, had been given a short-lived example of an alternative marketing system, in the form of the first Canadian Wheat Board. Ironically, the experiment started in 1917 at the request of the Winnipeg Grain Exchange. Canada's wartime allies had bought huge amounts of wheat futures, but a poor-quality crop did not yield enough of the good grades specified in the futures contracts. Wheat prices skyrocketed since the allied governments had, in effect, inadvertently "cornered" the market with their futures. The Exchange closed futures trading, persuaded British agents to accept lower grades at lower prices, and then asked Ottawa for government controls to prevent a similar crisis erupting under wartime conditions. Ottawa obliged with the Board of Grain Supervisors, which fixed wartime prices and was drawn into marketing grain.

On 22 July 1919, eight months after the Armistice, the Exchange resumed business. Cash wheat — wheat sold for genuine delivery, not on a futures basis — opened that day at a fraction under $2.25. Six days later it was nearly $2.46.[25] With world wheat trade still disrupted as a result of the war, Ottawa feared out-of-control prices and moved quickly to put a lid on them. Under authority of the War Measures Act, the cabinet issued an order on 31 July to establish a Canadian Wheat Board.[26] Farmers grumbled at the swift action to put a ceiling on prices. When had government ever moved that fast to slow a price collapse? But one year of experience with the board changed many minds. Everyone got the same price, without worrying about rushing to market before the volume of neighbors' deliveries would depress prices. The board made an initial payment of $2.15 a bushel, an interim payment of another 30 cents, and a final payment of 18 cents when accounts were wound up after all the grain was sold. Cynical farmers who sold their delivery certificates for a few cents a bushel before the interim and final payments lost the extra 48 cents, but got a valuable education in pooling procedure.

The basic concept of pooling was simple — the board assumed ownership of all wheat delivered to country elevators, then sold the wheat and paid each farmer the same price per bushel. For every bushel of wheat a farmer delivered, he eventually received the average price that board salesmen obtained on domestic and world markets. The methods of implementing that concept were to vary slightly over subsequent decades, but in essence they would be the same whether pooling was operated by farmer-owned co-operatives or by later wheat boards. There would be an initial payment when a farmer delivered wheat to the local elevator, an interim payment some months later when much of the total crop had been sold and it was clear the average price would be above the initial payment, and then a final payment after all stocks were sold and the true average could be calculated. The pooling agency's operating expenses plus grain transport and handling costs would be deducted from the average sales price before farmers received their final payment for the wheat. Provided that the wheat was sold for prices averaging higher than the initial payment, no type of government subsidy would be involved, nor any financial losses by non-government pooling organizations.

To ensure that farmers received fair value for the specific kind of wheat they produced, there would be a different pool for each grade of wheat — producers of top-grade wheat in 1919-20, for example, received a total of $2.63 for it, but they and others got lesser amounts for lower grades. Similar practices were used for later pooling of oats, barley, and rapeseed in later years. Usually, all deliveries of one kind of grain in one August-to-July crop year went into the same pool, but pool periods varied from a few weeks to five years during a few periods of unusual marketing conditions. The proportion of grain going into a pool, as opposed to direct sales to elevator companies, would vary considerably depending on whether federal law required all producers to pool their grain or whether pooling was voluntary.

Abolition of the Canadian Wheat Board, 1920

By the mid-1920s, wartime disruptions had sufficiently receded that Ottawa could not constitutionally continue to use the power of the War Measures Act to compel everyone to deliver to the wheat board. Many farmers who still did not like the board at the time of its dissolution generally became converts in 1920-22, when they saw what followed it. The Winnipeg futures market re-opened on 18 August 1920 and cash wheat closed that day at $2.73. By 18 November it was $2.07.[27] A year later it was about $1.11. Those standard reference prices are for No. 1 Northern, the top grade, in store at Lakehead terminals. As in all other prices cited, the amounts are significantly more than the farmer would actually be paid. Deductions would be made from the reference price to cover transportation costs to the Lakehead, differentials for lower grades, the local elevator's handling charges and penalties for delivery in less than carload lots. The deductions would take up proportionately more of the $1.11 than they would of the $2.73, thus increasing the impact on farms of the price decline.

Prices would probably have fallen to some extent even if the wheat board had somehow been continued, but the farmers of the prairies were in no mood to quibble about pennies. All they knew was that once again they had clear — and painful — evidence that the system did not work to their advantage. From hundreds of groups, large and small, came one cry: bring back the wheat board! Federal politicians had never been enthusiastic about such drastic interference with the free-enterprise system, but they were realistic enough to know that they could not stand directly in the face of such wrath. After the December 1921 federal election, the Liberals had a minority government, with the second largest group in the Commons consisting of Progressives allied to grain-grower interests. Agriculture Minister Motherwell, despite his election slogan of "Vote for Motherwell and the Wheat Board," tried to push the idea of a voluntary wheat organization that would leave farmers free to sell via local elevators and the Exchange if they chose. But even Motherwell's respected record was not enough to make that idea fly and, on 22 June 1922, the Commons passed legislation to set up a 1919-style compulsory wheat board. The legislation, however, could apply only as far as the current concept of federal jurisdiction would carry it; for the board to become reality, at least two of the three prairie provinces would have to pass enabling legislation. And the federal powers for the board would expire in mid-1923 unless previously extended.

In a province where everyone watched the progress of crops anxiously, Saskatchewan legislators knew their duty. A special session was held in July to rush through legislation giving the proposed board every necessary power under provincial jurisdiction. Alberta followed suit, but Manitoba had problems. When Manitoba's legislature finally got around to making a decision on enabling legislation, in April 1923, it defeated the bill 24 to 21. Manitoba Premier Bracken had shown restrained support for the wheat board idea earlier, telling a farm convention that he would work for enabling legislation only on certain conditions.[28] The conditions included limiting the board to one year and having prairie governments and farm groups announce plans to set up a co-operative, non-compulsory marketing scheme for the 1924 crop. Manitoba farmers, he said, would gain less from a wheat board since they traditionally enjoyed better prices because of their earlier harvest and shorter rail haul to the Lakehead: "I am not prepared to take the responsibility of sacrificing Manitoba's interests for more than one year."

Despite Manitoba's foot-dragging and ultimate defection, the action of the other two prairie legislatures was enough to satisfy federal requirements. But it was not enough to attract capable leaders for the proposed board. Saskatchewan Premier Charles Dunning and Alberta Premier Herbert Greenfield tried everything short of conscription to find able, credible commissioners for the board, but found that virtually every candidate wanted nothing to do with a one-year board that lacked Manitoba's participation.[29] James Stewart and F. W. Riddell of the 1919 board declined to leave their posts with the Saskatchewan Co-operative Elevator Company. John I. McFarland of Alberta Pacific Grain Company and James Murray of UGG, who many years later were to become controversial heads of the wheat board, also declined. Alberta patriarch Henry Wise Wood was willing to follow the call of duty from his position as head of the United Farmers of Alberta, but he sensibly pointed out that he lacked experience in the sophisticated grain trade and would need top men to work with on any board. Another major drawback for most prospective board members seemed to be a belief that such a board could work only with the co-operation of the private grain trade, an unrealizable condition in view of the hostility emanating from the trade.

At the SGGA, a lesser-known figure was watching these proceedings with growing contempt. Alexander James McPhail was fast running out of patience with those who blocked farmers' progress. In August 1922 McPhail expressed dark suspicions about Dunning's motives, telling one correspondent "this Wheat Board business is a fizzle all through & I think things are being worked to have it so." Some months later, however, he decided that the real backroom schemers were at the Co-op elevator company.[30] The official death notice for the wheat board idea came on 22 June 1923, when Greenfield and Dunning issued a statement declaring "we have found it impossible to secure a board combining all necessary elements of experience, ability and public confidence."[31] By then, thousands of farmers were ready to give up on governments. If they wanted a new system, they would have to build it themselves.

The idea of a farmer-run wheat pool had been circulating for some time. In 1918 the Canadian Council of Agriculture, an early forerunner of the Canadian Federation of Agriculture, recommended a voluntary pool. Two years later, after committee study, it endorsed a plan for a pool based on contracts in which members would commit all their wheat acreage for five years to the pool, whose operations would not begin until sixty percent of all wheat acreage was signed up.[32] That 1920 plan was close to the one born in 1923-24, the major difference being that the Council plan did not provide for a democratic structure. But any one such plan had a host of critics and competitors; some farmers wanted small-scale pools of farmers at each delivery point; others rejected the all-or-nothing contractual approach and argued that a farmer should be free to deliver each load of wheat either inside or outside the pool, switching from day to day as he thought best. Many said a prairie-wide pool would never be able to get the massive financing needed. Many disliked the idea of a five-year commitment, arguing for lesser terms. By 1921 the Council of Agriculture had virtually abandoned its plan, concluding that there was little prospect of a sixty percent sign-up and much chance that anyone who did sign would later be tempted to break the contract.

As it became clear that efforts to re-create the wheat board were failing, new pool proposals sprouted everywhere. Premier Dunning urged the Co-op and UGG elevator companies to form a joint export company to pool wheat. In private correspondence, he pushed the idea of a co-operative organization, saying "no responsible public man or farm leader has as yet, to my knowledge, advocated a Wheat Board as a permanent measure" and predicting that no parliament would ever grant such powers on a permanent basis.[33] In another letter, marked "confidential," the premier complained that "the Farmers' movement in all three

Provinces is seething with internal intrigue," preventing joint action for a solution along co-operative lines.[34] In the spring and summer of 1923, different pool proposals came from the Co-op elevator company, UGG, the SGGA, the new Farmers' Union of Canada and various other groups. SGGA officials were acutely aware of farmer discontent. Despite the SGGA's many past accomplishments, their membership had dropped from 40,000 a year or two earlier down to 15,000 in 1922; now in 1923 the Farmers' Union was acquiring more prominence as a competing organization.[35] SGGA secretary McPhail told friends that many people felt farm organizations were "dilly-dallying in a manner that will never get the farmers anywhere". If the SGGA flatly declared its support for a farmers' co-operative wheat marketing agency, he said, "it would be the greatest boost that our Association could have." If the SGGA did not act, he warned, "the initiative is going to come from other sources."[36]

The uncertainty lessened somewhat when a 23 July Regina meeting of the SGGA, United Farmers of Alberta and United Farmers of Manitoba resolved to set up uniform provincial pools with a common central agency to handle all their sales, and identical contracts binding their members.[37] But that was just a devout wish for 1924; for the rest of 1923 there were to be more of the same uncoordinated attempts at halfway measures, measures whose success might preempt opportunity for a comprehensive contract pool, whose failure might deter farmers from such a further step. "A provincial wheat pool is too big a thing to organize and get going efficiently in a few short weeks or even months," Henry Wise Wood of Alberta told the press.[38] Hesitant farmers, disgusted with the existing system but reluctant to gamble on an untried idea promoted by people without grain trade expertise, could only be further deterred by such sights as the competing tents of the SGGA and the Farmers' Union at the 1923 Regina Exhibition, each promoting a different pool, each casting implicit aspersions on the other's sincerity and practicality.[39]

Then, into the midst of Babel, came a California lawyer.

2
Overture, 1923–24

When will you learn that you are not dealing with
wheat? What you are dealing with is human lives, what
your children will eat, what your children will wear,
how you will pay the doctor, how you will send them to
school, whether you will have taxes to pay for roads,
whether you will even have taxes enough to start and
pay off the national debt. It is not wheat at all! It is all of
your standard of life wrapped up in the doings of a little
gang of men at Winnipeg, a larger gang of men at
Chicago, and a cleverer gang of men at Liverpool.

— Aaron Sapiro, 7 August 1923.[1]

Aaron Sapiro

No one in Saskatchewan had ever seen his like before. Even
many who later saw John Diefenbaker and Tommy Douglas in
their full glory said they never again saw the equal of Aaron
Sapiro on a public platform. Samuel W. Yates was then an SGGA
official, later an historian of the pool movement. The opening
words of Yates' book left no doubt as to his view of Sapiro's
role:

In the month of August, in the year 1923, there came
to the Province of Saskatchewan a missionary . . . he
passed like a brilliant meteor from point to point,
leaving behind him, as it were, a trail of light stretching
like the tail of a comet across the heavens.[2]

Neither in Canada nor the United States did the principles of
producer-controlled commodity pools begin with Aaron Sapiro.
But then, neither were the individual Ten Commandments
unheard of before Moses. And Coca-Cola was just the hobby of
one Atlanta druggist before someone with a flair for marketing

discovered it. With Sapiro, the clashing imagery of Moses and Madison Avenue were rolled up into one dynamic force. Born to a poor Jewish family in Oakland in 1884 — poor enough that they had no home and he was delivered on an aunt's kitchen table — Aaron Leland Sapiro was out on the streets at age six, selling newspapers and matches to help support the family. When he was ten, his widowed mother put him and three other children into an orphanage because she could no longer support them. "Those years are seared into my soul," he once recalled. "I was no longer Aaron Sapiro; I was 'Number 58' — a puppet in a cold, unfeeling system that tended to squeeze the joy of living and the individuality out of any child."[3] But even then, Sapiro was beginning to make his mark, organizing a platoon of small boys to overwhelm any larger bully who tried to pick on them individually. When he later became assistant superintendent at his former orphanage, a part-time activity for the rising lawyer, he implemented a wide range of reforms. Academic brilliance and intense study rescued the young Sapiro from the crucible of poverty, leading him first to eight years of rabbinical studies and then to what he considered a more socially relevant law degree. An appointment to the California markets board staff introduced him to the theme of agricultural co-operation. Within a few years he was criss-crossing the country, organizing producers: California prune and raisin growers; Washington apple producers; cotton farmers in Arkansas, Georgia, South Carolina and Alabama; Chicago dairy producers; northwest wheat farmers; Maine potato farmers; Kentucky tobacco producers; and others. He regarded poverty with a contagious hatred. If that vehemence led him to arrange high incomes for himself in later years, it also drove him to end such scandals as the average $360 annual income of Kentucky tobacco families.[4] From every direction, word of his activities came into Canada. In 1922 they heard how 2,500 farmers followed him through the streets of Abilene, searching for a large enough hall to hear him speak. The newspapers called him the lawyer with half a million clients — the memberships of the farm groups for which he was consulting counsel actually surpassed 650,000.

Billy Sunday and Aimee Semple McPherson had the Bible as their source material; Aaron Sapiro had just a legalistic marketing bill that he co-authored and saw adopted by forty-one states; yet to prairie historian James Gray, the California lawyer far outclassed those legendary revivalists in emotional impact, compelling logic and sheer inspiration.[5] Sapiro drove himself hard, speaking virtually everywhere despite threatening letters from right-wing or anti-Jewish elements and despite his doctors' advice to take rests because of Bright's disease. In three and a half years in the early twenties, for example, he was home only thirteen weeks.[6]

Students of 1920s history, however, look in vain for biographies of Aaron Sapiro. A Sapiro biography would be an epic. His career also included: artillery sergeant-major and officer trainee in World War One; chairman of the national legislative committee of the American Legion, 1923; president of the motion picture exhibitors association, 1928; president of Journal Square National Bank, N.J., 1928; and president of the Midtown Bank, 1929. More often than not, even the passing references to him in reviews of prairie history play down his role. For many, his reputation was later tarnished by publicity about his high fees, by his legal work for a Chicago laundry-owners' association dominated by Al Capone, by his New York state disbarment on charges of tampering with witnesses, and by his later career dabbling as a middleman in the shadowy world of high finance. In addition to the bank positions, Sapiro sought to maintain the 1920s contract between the pools' central selling agency and the J. Rank milling interests of Britain. He also tried to work through Pool contacts to arrange New York financing for the Saskatchewan government.

Even in 1923 W. P. Warbasse was sceptical about Sapiro — before some of Sapiro's co-ops began collapsing. The New York magazine, *Co-operation*, edited by Warbasse, said in September 1923:

> the fact that a successful lawyer sells good services to the farmer does not make him a Co-operator. The fact that he is opposed to the farmers eliminating the middlemen, as well as the fact that he is opposed to the farmers developing their own co-operative banks, and that he would turn them over to the mercy of "high finance" after they have got their money, are indications that he would sell the farmers as well as to them.[7]

Many people, unfortunately, were led to disown Sapiro by a series of unsavory articles that U.S. auto magnate Henry Ford sponsored and published in his own Dearborn *Independent* in the 1920s, accusing Sapiro of being the agent of an international Jewish conspiracy to control the world's food production. Over 2.5 million copies of the newspaper were distributed to farm co-ops and other groups. Sapiro's 1927 libel suit against Ford was almost daily news in the New York *Times* for many months. The trial, during which Sapiro spent three weeks on the witness stand under cross-examination, ended with a ruling against Sapiro on technical grounds. Before his appeal started, Ford settled out of court, issuing an apology, paying legal costs, and agreeing to sell the *Independent*. By the time the initial trial started, Sapiro had not one client. He had dropped some to save them embarrassment or to concentrate on the trial, while others dropped him.[8]

Then a series of criminal charges came in the 1930s: indicted with Al Capone but acquitted on charges of conspiracy, bombings and restraint of trade; indicted with theatrical promoter Sam Roth but acquitted on charges of conspiracy and bribery of jurymen; disbarred in New York for improper contact with jurors. Sapiro, who had moved to New York from Chicago in 1927, retreated to Los Angeles in 1936. He then became involved with maritime unions and appeared in the famous Harry Bridges deportation hearings as a government witness, seeking to show that the rebellious union leader was a communist who should be deported. Later, Sapiro did legal work for producer Louis B. Mayer, actor John Barrymore, and composer Igor Stravinsky. He also helped organize a laundry workers' union and gave university lectures.[9]

From the viewpoint of some Saskatchewan Wheat Pool leaders, however, all this was overshadowed by what they considered his divisive 1924-29 activities, in which he championed internal critics and seemed to be constantly stirring up trouble. The Pool's distaste for Sapiro was to last for many years.[10]

Although all that was in the future in the summer of 1923, Sapiro's controversial later roles left behind him a muddied picture of precisely how and why he came to Saskatchewan, as different groups alternately tried to take credit for him or avoid being associated with him in retrospect. Two things, however, are clear — almost everyone wanted him to come sometime, and the upstart Farmers' Union of Canada was responsible for his coming when he did.[11] The chain may have started in 1920, when UGG's *Country Guide* (then called the *Grain-Growers' Guide*) did a major series of articles on Sapiro, introducing the colorful lawyer and his philosophy to Canadian farmers.[12] Ontario got a first-hand look at Sapiro in 1922, when agriculture minister Manning Doherty brought him there to help organize dairymen. Doherty's recommendation was enough for UGG leader Thomas Crerar to press provincial grain grower groups to invite Sapiro to speak on wheat marketing in January 1923. The SGGA was reluctant to change its convention schedule, but might have been persuaded if Sapiro had not in the meantime undertaken other engagements.[13] In April and May the initiative passed to the Farmers' Union, which began writing letters to Sapiro asking him to come.[14]

At the rival SGGA, secretary McPhail wanted to restore his association's declining credibility and vigor by getting it firmly behind the pool idea. Writing to other SGGA directors, he argued that "regardless of Aaron Sapiro's political views, we should do everything possible to have him visit Western Canada in the near future."[15] Ironically, the Regina *Morning Leader*, later a bitter foe of Sapiro and a critic of the wheat pool campaign, almost had the status of being his sponsor. The *Leader*'s managing editor wired an invitation to Sapiro on 12 May, agreed to Sapiro's request to line up government, farm and bank leaders to join in the invitation, then called the whole deal off in mid-June. The *Leader* said it had decided a Sapiro visit might threaten what it saw as improved prospects for a wheat board.[16]

The breakthrough came on 2 July 1923, when the Farmers' Union held its first convention and a blunt, plain-spoken former railway worker got up to deliver his presidential address. Throwing that formality aside, Louis McNamee instead declared that the most important order of business should be sending a convention invitation to Sapiro. "Motion carried," McNamee later recalled in a laboriously-scrawled account of those times. "The Element of Surprise had stood the acid test. My own old Hat colected the money to send the wire to Sanfrancisco Calf. Within 12 howers we had Aron Sapiro's answer."[17] Sapiro was ready to come on behalf of the Farmers' Union alone, so the visit was on. But he preferred a more universal invitation and some weeks were spent arranging that. Union stalwart Louis Brouillette took the lead in trying to browbeat Premier Dunning and the SGGA into joining the invitation, only to be initially shrugged off.[18] But the Union's optimism and enthusiasm was kept high by such things as Sapiro's assurances that he could, if necessary, arrange the money for a wheat pool organizing drive.[19] Sapiro eventually wired the SGGA direct, requesting an invitation, but McPhail replied that the SGGA could not organize a joint meeting with Sapiro because the SGGA had decided to move immediately to set up its own non-contract pool for the 1923 crop. As pressure from farm opinion mounted, however, the SGGA's independent position became increasingly untenable. Brouillette finally turned the tide by getting access to a 23 July meeting of the SGGA and its Alberta-Manitoba counterparts, where the Farmers' Union representative argued that Sapiro's services could be dispensed with if his proposed Saskatoon speech turned out to be unacceptable.[20]

Meanwhile, in Alberta, the enterprising Edmonton *Journal* and Calgary *Herald* were offering to sponsor a Sapiro tour, sending telegrams to him on 19 and 20 July.[21] They met reluctance from H. W. Wood of Alberta's United Farmers to co-operate in such invitations — Wood tried to shift the responsibility to the Alberta government — but editorial blasts from the two newspapers put Wood on the spot. Finally the grand tour was set, with Alberta speeches first on the itinerary as a result of complex scheduling negotiations.

Decidedly mixed feelings awaited Sapiro. As late as 30 July, Premier Dunning told the Farmers' Union he could not say whether he would be at the meeting arranged for 7 August in Saskatoon.[22] Earlier, Dunning had grumbled in a newspaper interview that Sapiro insisted on practical unanimity among farm groups before he came — a condition Dunning felt removed any need to bring in such a "high-priced marketing engineer."[23] Meanwhile, there were squabbles within the Farmers' Union over whether and when Sapiro could speak in Regina and Swift Current. Sapiro himself had to rebuke his Union allies for their changeable schedules.[24] And one Union organizer was charging that the SGGA was working with local business establishments to make Sapiro's meeting in Regina and Moose Jaw failures.[25]

No matter how many times different groups promised different types of pools for 1923 or 1924, many farmers continued to feel that progress was being made with all the speed and vigor of sleepy old men pursuing petty, droning debates in the stuffy confines of their comfortable club.

On 2 August 1923, Aaron Sapiro kicked in the door of that sleepy club, a howling fresh wind at his back. To 3,500 assembled farmers and townspeople in Calgary, he bluntly declared that prairie farmers were only a few short steps away from an organization that would give them both decent prices and control of their own destiny.[26] That, he added, would be only the start of a worldwide transformation: "I tell you that before two years are past there will be a pool of surplus wheat between the United States, Canada, Australia, and perhaps, even Russia." But by itself the Canadian pool would mean ten cents more per bushel to farmers. Who would put up the money to finance initial payments and storage costs until the proposed pool could sell the wheat? No problem, Sapiro said — Canadian banks would scramble to get shares of the financing for a soundly based pool. And if they did not, "I am authorized to say that there are American bankers who will lend you between $100,000,000 and $170,000,000." Applause from the hope-parched crowd overwhelmed his next words, erupting also as he gave a long, detailed account of how his co-operative strategy helped the tobacco growers of Kentucky break free of large tobacco corporations, become owners of their own warehouses, and raise their previously pathetic incomes by 800 percent.

It was the same story in three smaller Calgary speeches that same day, plus another three in Edmonton the next day. The magnificent orator seemed to answer every doubt, every fear in

Left: Saskatchewan Premier Charles A. Dunning. (Saskatchewan
Archives Board R-A 631 [1])
Right: Aaron Sapiro, 1927. (SWP Collection, Saskatchewan
Archives Board R-A 15,263)

listeners' minds. Alberta government representatives were impressed at a private conference on 3 August, huge crowds heard
him again on 4 August in Lacombe and Camrose. A bandwagon
was rolling, speeded by newfangled radio broadcasts of his
speeches and the through-the-night efforts of prairie newspapers
to transcribe those speeches and print them in full.

Sapiro's pooling rules were clear, simple and uncompromising.
The pool must be non-profit, non-speculative, exclusively focused
on one commodity only. "Never handle an ounce of stuff for a
non-member." There must be absolute democracy: one man, one
vote, regardless of quantities of wheat delivered or cash invested.
Directors must be chosen in geographically defined districts, to
ensure proportional representation and prevent centralized control. Every member must be bound by a written contract, more
sacred than matrimony, to deliver all his wheat for a full five-year
period. No operations would start without fifty per cent of the
wheat acreage locked up in such contracts. With such a base, the
pool would have the power and permanence to hire the best men
available and to challenge the old system. Many farmers must
have gulped as Sapiro told them not to be afraid to pay $50,000 for
a top-quality manager, but he bluntly warned that more farmers'
organizations had been wrecked by lack of managerial expertise
than any other reason. The pool should as soon as possible own its

own elevators. And, above all, there had to be an end to all the talk of overlapping and competing pools. There should be only one pool organization per province, with the three prairie provinces' pools selling all their wheat through one central sales agency to avoid duplication and competition. That would amount, in effect, to one united, powerful Canadian Wheat Pool. Cheers rang out in Edmonton as Sapiro told a farmers' conference that the pool would bring them dignity and self-respect: "You are going to stand on your own feet and you are not going to be charity wards." No obstacle could withstand united farmers: "I cannot conceive of any power on earth that can possibly stop you from going over within 30 days."

There were still some elements going in conflicting directions as the Sapiro bandwagon neared Saskatchewan, but their days were numbered. Farmers in one Alberta constituency declared their own local pool in operation, but were soon swallowed up in the province-wide movement. Vice-president J. H. Haslam of the Farmers' Union described his variant plan, which would involve organizing a pool that would use UGG and Saskatchewan Co-op elevators to handle grain while relying on the Dreyfus family of European grain merchants to sell it. But a hastily-arranged meeting of Union leaders raked Haslam over the coals for allegedly breaking ranks and later pressured him out of the organization.[27] Grain inquiry hearings in Regina on 6 August heard SGGA president John Maharg announce incorporation of the United Farmers' Wheat Pool Ltd., while Premier Dunning told the same meeting that he doubted the practicality of any pool based on five-year contracts.[28]

Maharg's pool announcement lasted precisely one day. On 7 August, Sapiro made his first Saskatchewan speech following participation in a Saskatoon conference with SGGA and Union leaders.[29] The two rival groups, caught between Sapiro's uncompromising dogma and the ever-clearer desires of the thousands of farmers already on their way to Third Avenue Methodist Church to hear Sapiro, quickly agreed. Representatives from the SGGA, Union and unorganized farmers would start setting up the machinery to organize a Sapiro-style pool for the 1923 crop.

It was time for Saskatchewan farmers to find out in person what a Sapiro speech was like. Veteran journalist Pat Waldron found no standing room within 100 feet of the large church when he arrived. He recalled that day well, even fifty years later:

> he was the most inspiring, invigorating speaker I've ever heard. He moved, he played on that audience like an artist. He controlled their emotions, they yelled and cheered. He

could do anything with them. I never saw anything to equal what Sapiro could do on a public platform.[30]

Premier Dunning gave a carefully-worded pledge as he introduced Sapiro: "the moral support of the Saskatchewan Government is assured for any sound pooling scheme having the support of the farmers of Saskatchewan."

Then it was Sapiro's turn, to repeat and embellish his themes from earlier speeches. In front of this crowd, which included many disgruntled members of the Co-op Elevator Company and the SGGA, he won heavy applause with such details as his advice on directors: "Elect them all annually, so that if they are unsatisfactory you can kick them out annually." But Sapiro also made it clear that the farmers themselves were the root of the problem — in the form of each fall's mad rush to dump all the grain in sight on the local elevators and thus on the Exchange: "The central problem of co-operative marketing, the central problem of the farm is to try to stop dumping by the farmers!" How could cash-short farmers, many of whom had minimal education, build the elevator empire needed to compete in the grain business? Not to mention create a sophisticated global sales network and hire expensive managers? No problem, said Sapiro — those same farmers were already paying for all that:

> Just remember this: Who is paying the salary of every man in the grain trade today — the grain trade of Canada? Who is paying his travellers, and his expenses, and his dividends? Who is paying the salary of his office boy, and of his clerks? Who is paying for his book-keeper? Who is paying for his stenographers? Who is paying for all his equipment? Who is paying for all his bonuses? He? No! *YOU ARE PAYING EVERY CENT OF THAT!* But you have no right to choose them; you have no right to say what they will receive; you have no right to fire them when they do not make good. You are paying their expenses, and salaries, and profits, and bonuses, and commissions, and dividends — every penny out of your pocket!

Sapiro freely threw his advice into internal details of the embryonic pool organization, insisting at a breakfast with McPhail, George Edwards and George Robertson, that McPhail must be the man in control of the organizational drive, regardless of who might be the titular head. By coincidence or otherwise, the next day McPhail wrote Violet McNaughton about Sapiro: "The more I see of this man, the more intense becomes my admiration for him." That was one of McPhail's last admiring comments, however. His strong distaste for Sapiro that became virtual hatred in the late 1920s, was to begin forming that fall and winter.[31]

More conferences and equally powerful speeches in Regina, Moose Jaw and Swift Current rounded out Sapiro's five-day Saskatchewan tour, a tour that helped change the nature of the province's society and economy. So overpowering was his presence in those five days that, in late September, the SGGA's official organ would refer to the incorporation of "Saskatchewan Co-operative Wheat Producers Ltd., which is the official incorporated name of the Saskatchewan Sapiro Wheat Pool." An enthusiastic Saskatoon lawyer who threw his entire energy into pool organization without pay, R. H. Milliken, told one audience: "All credit for the much-talked-of wheat pool is due to Aaron Sapiro, undoubtedly the clearest-thinking and most brilliant speaker who ever addressed a gathering of farmers in Saskatoon."[32]

But inspiration alone could not produce a wheat pool. The various organizations and volunteers had to buckle down to the task of organizing workers in every Saskatchewan hamlet. And someone had to provide money. The Farmers' Union had brazenly sent collect telegrams to municipal councils, asking them to donate $25 each to help organize a wheat pool, but when the "Farmers' Union Wheat Pool Account" was opened on 14 August, it was with a deposit of only $29.24.[33] The SGGA was able to borrow $10,000, which it lent to the pool campaign committee, and then was rescued from the problem of how to repay the bank loan when the Saskatchewan Co-op Elevator Company provided $15,000 to the SGGA.[34] In a significant decision, the rapidly formed organization committee decided not to copy Alberta in having the contract include a clause allowing the pool to proceed with under fifty percent of wheat acreage signed up. That decision was to have annoying repercussions in a few weeks, but it was made unanimously.[35]

Formation of Saskatchewan Wheat Pool

The next step was to form a provisional board of directors for "Saskatchewan Co-operative Wheat Producers," which even then was known informally by today's official title of Saskatchewan Wheat Pool. It took only one day for that provisional board to be torn with bitterness after it first met on 23 August.[36] On 24 August, the board resolved that directorships should not be allowed for anyone who was an MP, MLA, director of a farmers' association or director of an elevator company. That was too much for John Maharg — SGGA president, Co-op Elevator executive, and

MLA. Already annoyed once over McPhail's refusal to allow Maharg's friend Musselman on the organizing committee, Maharg angrily announced his resignation. The fiasco was complicated when Maharg used as his pretext for resigning a previous resolution limiting directors' terms to one year. And it was confused even further after the provisional board rescinded both resolutions in an attempt to remove Maharg's grounds for resigning. The whole effort ultimately produced nothing but headaches — Maharg did not play any significant role in the pool organization, nor even sign a pool contract, and later boards eventually reinstated the two policies.

That dispute, however, did not prevent the 25 August 1923 incorporation of Saskatchewan Co-operative Wheat Producers Ltd. under the province's Companies Act. A formal act of the legislature the following 25 March gave firmer status to the pool, but it was a legal entity as of that Saturday in August.[37] Shares were allotted to the men who were to be directors and on 28 August they formally constituted themselves as the first official board, although still terming themselves a provisional board since the "real" board would be elected only after the pool started operations and its tens of thousands of members could cast ballots.[38] After a close SGGA-Union contest at the provisional board's first meeting, a balanced executive of five was elected: A. E. Wilson as president, representing unorganized farmers; McPhail of the SGGA as vice-president; fellow SGGA reformist George Robertson; and Brouillette and Richard Dundas of the Farmers' Union. With Wilson fated to be largely a figurehead, the key battle was for the vice-presidency, McPhail edging Brouillette by one vote.[39]

Alfred Edwin Wilson, a little-known figure in prairie farm history despite being president of the Pool's first board, was a sensible Indian Head farmer with a background that would help inspire confidence in the new organization.[40] President of the Saskatchewan Municipal Hail Insurance Association and a former Dominion Seed Grain Commissioner, Wilson had also held various federal agriculture jobs, was an Indian Head councillor and a member of Regina's Assiniboia Club. At sixty-one the oldest of the Pool's first leaders, he had been born in England, homesteaded at Indian Head in 1892, and built up a prosperous farming operation. During the Pool's troubled organizational period, he was able to offer it a $15,000 loan. Despite his prosperous, establishment background, Farmers' Union representatives nominated him for the presidency. And despite the Union backing, McPhail and Robertson respected and liked him. When the Pool eventually became a reality, he quietly declined nomination for the first presidency of the permanent board and served as an ordinary director for several years. The Pool noted his death in its thirteenth annual report, paid tribute to his "sound business judgment," and thereafter left McPhail with the historical spotlight and the title of first president.

While the top-level organization was still being put together, the campaign was already under way in the country. Few companies before or since have enjoyed such a rousing reception as the Pool. Throughout Saskatchewan, banks, boards of trade, retail merchant associations, municipal councils and service clubs jumped into the organization drive. The provincial agriculture department prepared publicity posters, with no one complaining about use of taxpayers' money for a private organization. Some twenty life insurance companies pledged the help of their staff in collecting signed contracts from farmers.[41]

Manning Doherty, the former Ontario agriculture minister who had invited Sapiro to Ontario the year before, came to Saskatchewan to become the pool campaign's star speaker. Doherty worked a grueling pace, giving speeches every day from 21 August to 1 September. Pool organizers were even given space to fill in the

A congested scene in 1923 at Meyronne, Sask., as farmers line up to deliver the new crop. (Dept. of Regional Economic Expansion Photo 22151)

Regina *Morning Leader* and its sister papers in Regina and Saskatoon that formed the so-called "Concentrated Press" near-monopoly of urban readership. Organizers' enthusiasm occasionally threatened the bounds of propriety, as when McPhail issued a memo to Saskatchewan clergy asking them to preach sermons in support of the Pool and suggesting a text based on Hebrews leaving well-fed Egyptian slavery for independence.[42] Farmers also discovered that many of the agents for private elevator companies were genuinely sympathetic. One Inter-Ocean Grain Company agent, George Turner, let Pool recruiters use his office to buttonhole farmers delivering grain and get them to sign contracts.[43] Turner, who later became general manager of Manitoba Pool Elevators, said that if his bosses at Inter-Ocean had found out about how their office was being used, "I would have been hanged, drawn and quartered." But, he noted, many such agents helped the Pool and later became its first agents.

The formidable contracts, two legal-sized pages of lawyers' jargon in tiny print, were distributed everywhere in several languages in preparation for "Sign-up Day," the 29 August official start of the sign-up campaign. Throughout the province hundreds of eager workers jumped into long days of jolting country-road travel to bring the co-operation gospel to farmers.

The dawn of 27 August brought extra reinforcements to the Pool drive in the form of a hastily-produced, upstart newspaper entitled the *Progressive*. Renamed the *Western Producer* in 1924, the newpaper would emerge decades later as the unchallenged leader of western farm publications, with healthy profits and ambitions that soared to having farm homes receive its news via computer terminals.[44] All that, however, was science fiction in 1923. Then, the struggling paper grappled with temporary presses and irregular paper sizes to rush out its first few editions in time to help the Pool drive. Punchy slogans in large type proclaimed such things as: "At the present time the Farmer Plows in Hope, Lives on Faith, and Markets by Accident."

Surprisingly, that campaign of 1923, a campaign that seemed to become a province-wide social movement, met no open opposition. Pool organizers' speeches continually challenged audiences to name just one significant figure in farm organizations or in politics who would flatly oppose the Pool. No such individual appeared that year. But here and there, veiled forces were at work. Premier Dunning, whose delicate and diplomatic fence-sitting posture was becoming ever more uncomfortable, told a Springside meeting on 18 August that he was not advising for or against the Pool, but felt farmers should as a matter of common sense study the contract well: "before you sign it, for God's sake read it."

That was the signal for the editorial battleships of the Concentrated Press, proudly led by the *Leader*, to steam majestically into the fray with broadsides that endlessly quoted Dunning's warning without — quite — flatly condemning the Pool. The controversy finally pushed Dunning into another statement where he said: (a) those who believe in pooling should sign the contract; (b) the majority of Saskatchewan farmers appear to want the Pool; (c) thus he would like to see the campaign succeed.[45] No tiptoeing diplomat in pinstripe suit ever minced through a more delicate statement — but it was enough to scuttle the subtle campaign of the *Leader*. Deprived of the chance to hide behind the premier's supposed opposition to the Pool, the *Leader* seemingly decided to dispense with half measures and unfurl its true colors. If the Leader Publishing Company grew wheat, a 31 August editorial solemnly intoned, it "would no more consider signing than it would consider going into the combination hairbrush and mirror business with Andrew Gump and J. Ambrose Hepwing."[46] For those unfamiliar with 1920s comic-page characters, that meant the *Leader* did not think kindly of the Pool. More extreme opposition came from Edmonton, where the *Morning Bulletin* ran scathing attacks on the Pool plan — in editions that were mysteriously shipped to Saskatchewan in large quantities by an anonymous interest. "The Sapiro idea," said the *Bulletin*, amounts to "a financial dictatorship" in which unbelievable economic power would be concentrated in the hands of a few Pool directors.[47] Sapiro's orderly-marketing plan, moreover, was a trap — the smooth lawyer came here "to persuade the Canadian farmer to hold his wheat off the market in order that the United States farmer and dealer might unload last year's holdover." No one, least of all newspapers, pulled rhetorical punches in those days. The editorial blasts, however, did not prevent papers like the *Leader* from giving lengthy news-page accounts of pro-Pool speeches. The newspaper printed the full text of lengthy letters from pool disciples blasting *Leader* editorials, even letters accusing the *Leader* of seeking to kill the Pool in order to protect the newspaper's printing contracts with Co-op Elevators.

Even the one-sided editorials reflected the doubts of many Saskatchewan farmers who wondered about the legalistic contract that almost had to be taken on faith. Pool organizers could try to defuse one worry by pointing to clauses guaranteeing farmers that they could sell to local elevators and not have to sit on their wheat so long as the Pool was not yet ready to take the wheat. But when it came to the clause stating that Pool directors could order a farmer to deliver his wheat any time, any place, the farmer had to accept on faith that the directors would be reasonable persons who would only use such power in the case of miscreants who might otherwise refuse to deliver anything to the Pool. Such were the doubts and fears that circulated in the country, voiced in a thousand puzzled conversations but rarely if ever in any major public speech. "If you decide that the pool proposed is financially fundamentally sound do not allow any one to confuse you with raising obstacles," McPhail declared in an official statement as campaign manager.[48] Other spokesmen were sensitive and quick to jump on any piece of negativism. Musselman of the Co-op Elevator Company was castigated in early September when the *Manitoba Free Press* quoted him as saying "there will be no pools operating in Alberta and Saskatchewan this year." He later denied making that statement, adding also that what he told the reporter had not been for publication.

Such problems, however, seemed to be mere ripples in a fast-flowing co-operative river. From everwhere, reports of success poured in. Even the cautious Canadian Press news service reported from Regina 29 August: "Indications are the campaign will be a success." Many stories in many publications cited meetings where seventy-five percent or more of farmers had signed up.[49] Spokesmen for small elevator chains declared their willingness to sell to the Pool or handle grain for it.[50] Occasional statistics charted the Pool's progress in wheat acreage, with emphasis being given the thousands of contracts that canvassers were believed to have out in the country, where they were too busy to get them to Regina headquarters for inclusion in the statistics. Alberta officially concluded its drive on 5 September, just short of the fifty-percent mark but close enough that Alberta leaders said they would go ahead and organize the pool for the 1923 crop. A large-type, page-one editorial in the *Progressive* expressed hope that Saskatchewan farmers would not let Alberta go it alone, with "all the great mass of Saskatchewan wheat" available to the Grain Exchange to be used as a weapon to break the Alberta Pool.[51] At midnight on the night of 12-13 September, the Saskatchewan sign-up campaign drew to its planned close — in abject failure.

Despite all the support of business and professional groups, despite the most extensive propaganda effort ever mounted in the province, despite the unanimity of farm organizations, despite all the work of thousands of individuals and all the speeches of Sapiro and local politicians, on deadline night Regina head-quarters had contracts covering 3.5 million acres — only twenty-nine percent of the province's total wheat acreage. Only ten of fifty-six constituencies had passed the fifty-percent level.[52] The target had been 6.1 million, half the province's estimated wheat acreage. Alberta Pool had a clause enabling it to go ahead without fifty percent, so long as it allowed a short period for people to withdraw from their contracts. But in Saskatchewan, every single signed contract was invalid without the fifty-percent mark. Even including many contracts that trickled in after 12 September, the Pool could claim coverage of only 4.1 million acres.

In the midst of triumph and glory, any man can continue working toward a goal. Had the brief, hurried campaign of 1923 gone over the top by an easy margin, it would, in a sense, be of less interest and less value to later generations. For only in that dark, disheartening winter of 1923-24 did the true measure of the Pool organizers and contract signers emerge. Only in initial, humiliating defeat did their faith meet and pass its first severe test.

Within days of the failed deadline, Pool directors decided to continue the struggle. Everyone who had signed a contract would be asked to sign a waiver removing the deadline condition. The pool would be born when it hit fifty percent, regardless of date. A series of legal housekeeping steps followed. Since a general meeting of shareholders was required within three months of the Pool's creation, even if at this stage it was just a paper Pool, shareholders were called to a 23 November meeting in borrowed offices. The shareholders — still the same people who formed the board of directors — extended the three-month term of the provisional board and ratified the decision to continue the campaign. The Saskatchewan government provided $45,000 for further organization expenses, UGG contributed $5,000, and the shoestring Pool budget was set for another winter.[53] Sapiro, with long-distance optimism that transcended practicality, sent a telegram urging the Pool to start handling the 1923 crop, even though virtually all of it would have been sold to elevators by the time a significant number of waivers could be obtained.[54] The 23 November meeting rejected that advice.

One of the few encouraging developments was the growth of the Alberta Pool, which officially started operations on 29 October, following Alberta government guarantees to the banks that were financing that pool. It met some initial opposition from elevator companies who refused to accept wheat delivered by farmers for the pool's account. Alberta Pool officials, however, coolly instructed their members to deliver the wheat into elevators for storage only, then to send the storage receipts to pool headquarters when they had a carload accumulated. Alberta Pool would then order the wheat out, leaving elevator companies with only the handling charge of 1.75 cents a bushel, less than the pool was offering them to act as pool agents for receiving wheat. Not surprisingly, the balky elevator companies fell quickly into line.[55]

In Saskatchewan, however, it was a winter of dissent, recrimination and occasional despair. A Wynyard SGGA official issued a statement declaring that "those of you who did not join the wheat pool deprived yourselves and the rest of us of 10 cents a bushel."[56] Within the Pool organization, even at the peak of sign-up campaign optimism, there had been hard feelings between the SGGA and Farmers' Union elements. "Some of these Farmer Union men are having the time of their lives stopping at the Kitchener Hotel and just attending the meetings," McPhail complained.[57] "We are doing all the work of putting the thing over and I suppose the Farmers Union will get the credit because we came in at the last minute." Although McPhail had thrown every waking moment into the pool campaign, and earlier had led reformist forces within the SGGA, he became the target of a critical whispering campaign based on his forthright declaration that "We have no quarrel with the Grain Exchange," a statement that especially irked zealous Farmers' Union types.[58] What McPhail meant was simply that pool organizers should concentrate on the positive, constructive work of creating a wheat pool and should not waste energy in unnecessary attacks on the Exchange. Organization of the pool itself would do all that was needed to remove the Exchange as a problem. Since the moralistic McPhail saw no reason to disown a blunt statement that he sincerely believed, he doggedly kept defending it. Another SGGA official, George Edwards, resented giving expense money to Union President McNamee to help get contracts that fall. McNamee, Edwards believed, spent the money organizing Farmers' Union local lodges and sent back only one pool contract.[59]

The suspicion was not all one-sided, however — on 3 November, the Union executive resolved to have Union officials cease being Pool constituency chairmen, charging that the SGGA was using the Pool organization to do SGGA organizing.[60] Part of the problem, too, was undoubtedly a clash of personalities. The strait-laced, refined McPhail would find it extraordinarily difficult to get along with earthy types like McNamee. McNamee's style at public meetings, for example, was to give rousing speeches, pointing to his impressive medical-style bag and saying it was crammed full of statistics to prove his arguments. "In the bag usually was a pair of socks and a shirt, sometimes waiting for a laundry job," another Union offical recalled.[61] With such behavior presumably in mind, McPhail lamented to one correspondent: "The Farmers are a bunch of mutts when they will fall for the kind of men who have been organizing for the Union. . . . most of their men who have been organizing are of the cheap hot air artist type."[62] Such feelings may have made little difference while the two groups were working toward a clearly-defined common goal, but they were signs of trouble ahead once the Pool became operational and had to handle a wide range of day-to-day problems. They were also evidence, if such be needed, that people can work hard in the co-operative movement without being required to have a saintly, forgiving attitude toward colleagues.

Despite the criticisms of McPhail and other SGGA officials, the Farmers' Union had acquired new power and credibility. It entered the pool campaign with a few hundred members and came out with 10,000.[63] To many outsiders the Union appeared to be a suspicious organization, since its meetings were barred to non-members and secret passwords were needed to enter. Union "lodges" were also often in non-English areas that were unfamiliar to the SGGA's Anglo-Saxon leadership. The secrecy, however, produced exaggerated fears. One early study of the Union's board of directors found ten Liberals, six Progressives, two Conservatives, two socialists and — contrary to widespread rumors — only one lone Communist.

Pool organizers were soon caught in an annoying crossfire between the Farmers' Union and the Regina *Leader*, a crossfire made all the more irksome because the organizers partially agreed with each side. From the Union came insistent calls to bring Sapiro to Saskatchewan again to get the campaign back on the tracks. Sapiro let it be known he was willing to come, preferably with an invitation endorsed by all sides, but under Union auspices alone if necessary. McNamee issued a statement declaring that the issue was whether Sapiro would return or whether farmers "are to be guided solely by amateurs in the science of co-operative marketing."[64] The *Leader*, meanwhile, portrayed that as a sign of weakness: "A permanent, successful wheat pool cannot be formed and carried on in this province if a California lawyer has to be called in periodically to give it a shot of enthusiasm."[65] The call for Sapiro spread to the editorial columns of the *Progressive* and into SGGA ranks, where members were finally getting the opportunity to dump their old leaders. At the SGGA's annual meeting in Moose Jaw, January 1924, President J. A. Maharg took the unpopular step of criticizing "extravagant claims" concerning the benefits of centralized selling of pool wheat.[66] Delegates, also conscious that Maharg personally had not signed a pool contract, voted 264 to 198 to replace him as president with George Edwards, setting the stage for a more unified pool effort later. The same convention also resolved to send an invitation to Sapiro. A few days later the provisional Pool board's secretary, George Robertson, resigned, saying his duties as member of the Legislature would occupy his time for the next few months. Thus

Robertson, the only one of McPhail's associates to remain strongly opposed to Sapiro's return, allowed Brouillette to take over as secretary and organize the return visit. Robertson, however, returned to serve thirty-four years as Pool secretary, giving up political activities in favor of the Pool once it became operational.

Sapiro Returns

Even with the prospect of Sapiro's return, things still looked bleak that winter. "We were wondering at the *Progressive* whether we would ever re-awaken the enthusiasm which had died at the end of '23," journalist Pat Waldron recalled.[67] "And then, all of a sudden, something happened again." The "something" was a sustained series of Regina *Leader* attacks on Sapiro in February. Lurid eight-column headlines in red ink screamed from the *Leader*'s front page: "Startling Expose of Aaron Sapiro's Pool Methods" — "Fraud, Dishonesty Charges Made by Former Associate" — "Sapiro's Pet Pool Reveals Orgies of Wanton Expenses." The credibility of the *Leader* among pool supporters, however, was not enhanced when its editorial page added at the same time:

> The manner of electing directors prescribed in the contract is unfair to the landed farmer, as the tenant farmer has the same voting power as the proprietor farmer. The farmer with a quarter section has the same vote as the farmer operating ten sections.[68]

What the *Leader* saw as a wart, most farmers regarded as a beauty mark. Similarly, most farmers seemed to have faith that the "expose" of Sapiro would turn out to be wrong.

By the hundreds, farmers had to be turned away from Regina's Metropolitan Church on 20 February 1924, when an enraged Sapiro rose to slash the *Leader*'s stories to ribbons. Ever the showman, he described how his work for co-operatives brought him death threats and health problems, how he had so far received not a penny beyond expenses for his grueling 1923 prairie tour, how people who could not refute the logic of pooling turned instead to attacks on its most famous champion:

> During the war there was such a thing as "shock troops" who only got killed. They were used for that purpose. Some of us are the "shock troops" of co-operative marketing and we know just what is going to come up in those areas. We deliberately do this so long as the work goes ahead. . . . We say we are not essential; the idea is essential and we can be spared, who are only the interpreters of the idea. I am

perfectly willing to be destroyed in Saskatchewan — or
elsewhere — if it will help to reach the goal, but do not let the
Regina *Leader* or anyone else keep you from the goal by
throwing bricks at me.[69]

In addition to the emotional rhetoric, however, Sapiro also gave
a point-by-point refutation of the *Leader* charges, which basically
all came from one disgruntled former employee of the Kentucky
burley tobacco co-operative. Sapiro agreed, for example, that he
did get a $50,000 fee from the co-op — but he had let co-op
leaders name his fee, talked them down from original suggestions
of a higher figure, and in any case created an organization for
them that gave farmers benefits vastly greater than many such
fees. The fee also was unusual — Sapiro's practice was to throw
himself into organizational work with no arrangements for fees
and to collect fees later if the organization succeeded in becoming
functional. When the three prairie pools were operating, Sapiro
for two years was paid $4,000 a year as consulting counsel to the
central sales agency, the type of fee that could add up into large
figures when paid by many organizations across the continent. But
to date, his Saskatchewan work had brought him only $336.99 in
expenses and another $363.01 on account for services. After the
Pool was operational, the Union asked it to pay Sapiro $4,455, but
Pool directors decided by a seven-six vote to pay only $1,700, the
extent of their liability for the Farmers' Union costs of Sapiro's
1923 visit. The most comprehensive list of Sapiro's Canadian
earnings was given in a 25 June 1928 letter from Robertson to
Gilbert Johnson: $2,500 paid by the Pool provisional board; a
lesser amount from the Calgary *Herald*; less than $1,000 from
Manitoba Pool; $8,000 from the Central Selling Agency in
1924-25; about $3,000 over four years for Pool consultations and
the Pool share of a 1927 tour.[70]

After two years of court action by Sapiro, the *Leader* decided to
settle out of court and was induced to retract its stories and print
an apology — but in February 1924, those stories gave Sapiro and
the struggling pool organization a heaven-sent target on which to
focus farmers' wrath. Some of that wrath lasted many years. Pool
delegates at an annual meeting later passed a resolution condemning the newspaper attacks on Sapiro and declaring that
Sapiro's defence against the attacks "aroused a wave of enthusiasm for the Pool, which was largely instrumental in bringing it to
success."[71] With such hostile feelings toward the established press,
Pool delegates began a tradition of closed meetings that continued
for more than fifty years. Reporters were generally allowed into
annual meetings only to cover certain formal speeches.

In Regina, Saskatoon, Kindersley and Weyburn, thousands had to be turned away from overflowing halls for Sapiro's speeches. At Saskatoon, secretary Robert Magill of the Grain Exchange faced Sapiro on the same platform and was verbally swept into oblivion when he gave a low-key, non-controversial description of Exchange mechanics.[72] One might as well have politely offered guided tours of the Bastille to charging French revolutionary hordes. Sapiro's sermons, meanwhile, were as fiery and bold as ever. Farm leaders throughout North America, he said, expect a Canada-U.S.-Australia-New Zealand pool to be organized within three years, with a joint Liverpool sales agency that might also handle Argentine wheat. If and when such an office were set up — even one including only North American and Australian pools — "that office would name the price of wheat for the entire world production of wheat."

Even in that month there were dissenting voices to warn that such a world monopoly was unlikely and in any case would only provoke strong countermeasures from consuming nations. James Howard, former president of the American Farm Bureau Federation, brought Regina's Canadian Club that message on 23 February.[73] Howard also described in detail the fragmented state and problems of U.S. grain co-operatives and local pools. In North Battleford on 23 February Sapiro rebutted charges that he had been associated with U.S. wheat pools that had failed. Sapiro had written the Nebraska pool contract, stipulating that the pool should have twenty million bushels lined up before it started. He resigned as counsel when pool leaders went ahead with 200,000 bushels. Similarly he resigned in Kansas when that pool started with three million instead of fifty million, and he resigned in North Dakota when they started with two million instead of fifty million.[74]

If Sapiro was too much given to promising heaven on earth, people like Howard had their own feelings that Saskatchewan farmers recognized. Howard's approach of having only local pools would amount to little more than farmers averaging among themselves whatever the elevator companies were willing to give them. Given the choice of cautious tinkering with the existing system and a visionary drive to turn the system upside down, the crowds flocked to Sapiro.

But as the excitement of his second visit faded, organizers had to return to the duller, plodding work of reviving committees, printing brochures and getting canvassers circulating in the countryside once more. George Robertson was hauled before the legislature's agricultural committee to answer rumors that some pool organizers were paid large sums, rumors that were conclu-

sively disproved when pool accounts showed no more than lists of
people who had put in long days for token allowances. The
fifty-six constituency chairmen got five dollars a day, canvassers
twenty-five cents a contract.[75] The chairmen's pay in the original
signup drive had been larger, ten dollars a day including general
car use. Meals, hotel, telegraph, gasoline and similar out-of-pocket
expenses were also paid. The Pool's provisional board also had to
keep working on internal policies that would set important
precedents. Resurrecting the policies that had provoked Maharg
to resign, they decreed that directors should be elected for terms of
only one year and that no director could be an MP, MLA or
director of another grain company or farm organization.

By 15 March, more than seven months after Sapiro's first visit
launched the initial pool campaign, the provisional pool had only
3,094,006 acres of wheat under contract, barely a quarter of the
provincial total.[76] Ominously, the total was considerably less than
was achieved in the first sign-up campaign before that campaign's
initial contracts were invalidated through failure to meet the
fifty-percent goal by the deadline. Efforts to revalidate those
contracts by having people sign waivers had fallen short. Despite
all Sapiro's contributions, the key to success would remain that
patient, determined and largely-anonymous army of workers who
"talked pool" over a million cups of coffee. The truism that
co-operative organization must rest on a solid educational base
was perhaps never so thoroughly proved. The farmers again
gained useful help from the business community. Saskatoon's
board of trade, for example, set up seven routes, ranging as far as
Melfort and usually involving overnight stays, for its members to
follow in getting contract signers.[77] The board, the wholesalers'
association and retail merchants also contributed a series of
half-page newspaper advertisements.

As spring swept over the prairies. the pool's acreage totals rose
steadily: 4.3 million 12 April, 5.15 million 13 May. There was
mixed news from Manitoba, where a sign-up campaign ended on
1 April with less than thirty percent of that province's acreage. But
Manitoba organizers decided to go ahead anyway to set up a pool
for the 1924 crop. In Alberta, the pool was operating profitably
and could provide the heartening statistic that eighty percent of its
wheat was being sold direct to export customers, bypassing the
Winnipeg Grain Exchange completely. The pools' opponents were
still scoring points on occasion, as when the latest royal
commission drew Sapiro to Winnipeg on 28 April, delivering him
into the hands of Grain Exchange lawyers for cross-examination.
Sapiro was indeed forced to recant controversial statements that
Alberta pool members were getting eight cents a bushel more than

their neighbors and that the Alberta pool was making a mistake selling even twenty percent of its wheat through the Exchange.[78] He also admitted that a Canadian wheat pool by itself would not be able to control world prices. The cross-examination, however, did not shake his basic arguments for the benefits of a pool. The same royal commission had, a few days earlier, given a good boost to the pool campaign when it provided a forum for a terminal elevator manager to describe mixing practices in Port Arthur.[79] The manager noted that his terminal shipped out 1.8 million bushels more No. 1 wheat than it received — a reminder of the profitable practice of mixing grain to produce a combination that would barely meet standards for the top grade. Needless to say, the extra profits made by "promoting" No. 2 to No. 1 stayed with the elevator company.

As May ended, the tempo of Pool organization picked up. McPhail and Robertson sat down one evening and divided the province into sixteen districts, each with ten subdistricts, for delegate elections;[80] nomination papers were distributed; interprovincial conferences agreed on the last details of the central selling agency; and publicists geared themselves up for an all-out burst of rhetoric:

> The preliminary skirmishing has been done: the enemy has been silenced: the advancing forces are equipped and ready: the Zero hour has struck. OVER THE TOP, YOU MEN OF SASKATCHEWAN!
> — Farmers' Union advertisement

> Every additional contract signed above the minimum required is another nail in the coffin of the speculative system of grain marketing.
> — Saskatchewan Wheat Pool advertisement

> Co-operative marketing is on trial in this province on a scale that, if it succeeds, will take the distribution and merchandising of wheat out of the hands of private and speculative interests forever. If it fails, they will be entrenched as they have never been entrenched before. The eyes of the world are upon Saskatchewan.
> — Pool president A. E. Wilson[81]

Once again, the urban centres of Saskatchewan responded to the appeal. Many town councils declared the tenth of June official sign-up day, to be a civic holiday so citizens could devote themselves to pool work. After the year-long effort, it was anticlimactic for the weary McPhail to scribble in his diary on 16 June: "Wheat Pool over the top today."

Pool Democratic Structure

With the long-elusive fifty-percent target finally reached, the provisional directors met on 26 June, 1924, to declare the pool operational — backed by 45,725 contract signers and 6,433,779 acres of wheat.[82] For the last time the directors met in their capacity as the total shareholders of Saskatchewan Wheat Pool and ratified details of voting procedure; henceforth the shareholder body would be numbered in the scores of thousands and would elect delegates to represent them at annual meetings. By 30 June, all 45,725 ballots were in the mail — in itself a mammoth task in those pre-computer days. The mailed-in ballots, totalling 27,227, were counted on 14 July; delegates met within each district on 22 July to elect the first sixteen directors of the Pool's permanent board; and the first permanent board met on 25 July to elect McPhail president and Brouillette vice-president. With the Pool in operation, McPhail resigned as SGGA secretary on 16 August. One anomaly is worth noting — two directors of the first board, A. E. Wilson and Harry Marsh, were not delegates. Wilson had been

Saskatchewan Wheat Pool's original contracts, 1924. From Left: George Robertson, R. B. Evans, Fred Pragnell, A. E. Wilson, J. A. Watson, A. J. McPhail. (SWP files)

defeated in delegate elections and Marsh was apparently too busy to get nominated. By the time the Pool's bylaws stipulated that each director must be chosen from elected delegates, Wilson and Marsh had become delegates. Despite the turnover in presidents and directors, the five-person executive committee of the Pool board was remarkably unchanged. McPhail, Brouillette, Wilson, and Dundas served on the executive committee on both boards. Robertson was the fifth executive member of the provisional board, being replaced by Harry Marsh when the elected board took over but remaining influential as Pool secretary.[83]

The battle for control of Saskatchewan Wheat Pool was under way from the start of this historic period.[84] The same day that McPhail scribbled his terse, triumphant diary note, Farmers' Union central secretary N. H. Schwarz was issuing secret Circular Letter No. 37 to Union lodges, exhorting them to put all their votes behind one candidate in each Pool delegate election.[85] A disgruntled Union member sent the letter to the Regina *Leader* early in July, unleashing a wave of SGGA protests against the Farmers' Union attempt to get pro-Union delegates elected. An editorial in the *Progressive* blasted the circular as "the exact negation of co-operation," but a second editorial put the matter in more perspective: "When the sparks are flying there is ground for hope that something worth while may be wrought."

Whatever else it did, the Farmers' Union campaign of July 1924 made clear that Pool directors would not be spared the discomforts of democracy, that the Pool itself was too important for its policies to avoid vigorous public debate. Union president McNamee attacked the principle of equal provincial representation on the planned central sales agency, saying that would be unfair to the more numerous Saskatchewan farmers. The bulk of initial Union effort, however, was reserved for electing sympathetic delegates and for a campaign to move Pool headquarters to Saskatoon, away from the influence of the SGGA, Co-op Elevator and government establishment in Regina. Although he was consulting attorney for the Pool, Sapiro participated in the fight by long distance, sending the Union a letter that the Union lost no time in publishing:

> I hope that I will some day have the privilege of appearing before the Canadian wheat growers to remind them that the Farmers' Union of Canada took hold of their problems when the other organizations had failed either to see the difficulty or to accomplish a means of curing the ills of Canada.[86]

McPhail's forces, however, maintained control by slim margins. They first sidetracked Union demands to have Sapiro brief the permanent board on its first meeting day, symbolically rescheduling Sapiro for the second day. To McPhail that gesture was important. Telling Violet McNaughton about the demands to have Sapiro present on day one, McPhail had written that "we have to come to a show-down with these men who are continually interfering with the business of the organization." McPhail would also have been miffed on 3 July when the Pool executive decided to send two representatives to Chicago to consult Sapiro on the interprovincial agreement setting up the Central Selling Agency.[87]

A proposed resolution to move head office to Saskatoon was amended to one stating that it should remain in Regina for the time being — deferring that battle until 1925. Brouillette, whom McPhail was coming to dislike intensely, could not be denied the vice-presidency, but was defeated in his bid for the top spot and in his effort to be elected as one Pool representative on the board of the central selling agency. The agency, under the formal title of Canadian Co-operative Wheat Producers Ltd., a title retained to this day, was organized at a 29 July interprovincial meeting in Regina. Contrary to McNamee's view, each pool had an equal share of directorships in the agency, which became commonly known by the abbreviation for its informal title (CSA).

A flurry of major personnel decisions were made, notably the appointment of George Robertson as secretary — incidentally, another victory for the SGGA forces. R. H. Milliken, the energetic Saskatoon lawyer, became counsel, beginning an association with the Pool that he and his son would continue to the present day. Donald MacRae, a traveling superintendent with the Co-op Elevator company, was hired as first manager of the Pool and immediately horrified the board by insisting on having an office manager too, rather than doing both jobs himself.[88] Despite Sapiro's exhortation to pay big salaries to get big men, the first permanent Pool board took a more conservative approach: MacRae's salary was set at $8,500 a year, while Robertson got $3,600 and McPhail himself took only $4,000.[89] With its organization and managers in place, Saskatchewan Wheat Pool was finally ready for business.

Ready, that is, except for all the physical and financial arrangements necessary to handle an ocean of grain. The first board meeting had to quickly authorize two directors to run out and buy twenty chairs for everyone to sit on.[90] Then a head office was located — the first floor of the Union Bank building at 1822 Scarth Street. Milliken later marvelled at the incongruity of it all — one of the world's largest grain enterprises being created overnight, starting with one year already gone on the first five-year contract:

They did not possess another asset in the world but they did owe some $40,000. . . . They did not possess an elevator anywhere and must, in addition to all their difficulties, enter into an agreement with the elevator companies then in existence, to handle their grain.[91]

3
Triumph, 1924–29

We speak of the romance of war, of the Crusades, of daring deeds on land and sea and air, but what of the romance of quiet, plain, ordinary men and women facing anew each day the perplexing, and so often discouraging problems of life and living; men and women with no prospect of better things to come, with no prospect of relief from the haunting fear of poverty in old age, yet who go bravely on, facing each day with patience and courage?

— A. J. McPhail, 1929[1]

All the money it had was borrowed and all the grain it hoped to handle would have to move through facilities owned by others. Yet Saskatchewan Wheat Pool in the summer of 1924 had assets that transcended such conventional items as cash reserves and elevators. The Pool had the faith and hope of tens of thousands of people scattered across the farms of Saskatchewan, people who were relying on this new, untested organization as their tool for escaping from the suffocating trap of being without economic power. The initial triumph of Saskatchewan Wheat Pool and its sister organizations came from the determined support of these tens of thousands of members and their families. Comparatively few of their stories were ever recorded, for history is better designed to handle the tales of generals and kings than it is to report the lives of common people.

But, here and there, archives record examples of what was happening in the country, examples that should be remembered while perusing the voluminous records of what directors and presidents were doing. One such episode began near Sintaluta, when war veteran Frank Boss arrived at the local elevator with a load of wheat. The local agent happily pronounced it No. 1 grade

— but when Boss announced that the wheat was being delivered to the new Pool account, the agent reconsidered and said he could give only a No. 2 grade in that case. Sintaluta farmers, it seemed, had a clear choice: they could break their Pool contracts and sell to the elevator for a good grade, or they could take a grade loss that would provide extra profit for the elevator. For Boss and his friends, the choice was unacceptable. They joined together that winter for many backbreaking hours of loading cars they ordered themselves, moving the wheat across the platform, one shovelful at a time. That winter they loaded more cars by shovel than were filled by the elevator. Even dedicated men could not keep that pace up forever, but one farmer came to the rescue by buying a machine to blow the wheat out of the wagons and into the railway cars. That, however, brought in the railway company. Noting that the farmer was charging five dollars a carload to recover the machine's cost, the railway declared that such business enterprises were not allowed on railway property. The farmers, with the help of a sympathetic lawyer, replied with a little co-operative ingenuity. The next time the car-loading crew showed up, they filed with the agent an official bill of sale showing that the machine had been sold to the wheat's owner for one dollar. The machine's original owner, meanwhile, was technically just hired help, being paid five dollars a car to operate the machine. The next day brought a different farmer's wheat, and another bill of sale showing that he was the machine's new owner. All the railway agent could do was sit back and watch the bills of sale pile up in his office. Perhaps he had time to ponder the lesson that one of those farmers, future Pool director Warden Burgess, drew from the story: "Big companies can't beat the little people if the little people join together. They're not little when they get together."[2]

Over at Bulyea, which the next year became the site of Pool elevator No. 1, there was a similar story in 1924 as seventy-five farmers put up eleven dollars each for a scale and small office to handle shipments over the platform. By 11 October, they had loaded fifteen cars and twenty-two more were on order. Decades later, a commemorative brochure on that first Pool elevator and the men who had worked to get the Pool grain flowing at that point truly called the elevator "symbolic of the zeal and the determination of a whole generation of grain producers."[3]

Such popular support was harnessed and coordinated by an ambitious democratic structure that made the Pool far more than a grain-selling operation. At virtually every delivery point, an advisory committee was elected by farmers to supervise local operations, discuss the large issues of the day, and receive accountings from the delegates and directors. Their input into

Pool policy was valuable, but perhaps more important initially was their function as promoters of the Pool. In effect, the new organization quickly had more than 10,000 public relations agents across Saskatchewan, in the form of the committee members. The heaviest workload, of course, fell on the elected delegates and directors who had to make corporate decisions, spend several weeks a year in general meetings in Regina, attend district meetings and consult almost continuously with committees and individual farmers. Little is known of the original 160 delegates, but their contribution was important. For the 160, plus two directors who temporarily were not delegates, Pool records list only twenty-four birthplaces and twenty-one ages. If those are even a roughly representative sample, it would appear that the first delegates were largely foreign-born and were old enough to have made good progress developing their farms and families. Of the twenty-four, nine were born in Canada (none in Saskatchewan itself), eight in Britain, four in the United States and three in other foreign countries. Their average age was a shade over forty-two, only one of the twenty-one being under thirty-seven. Names by themselves are unreliable guides to ethnic origin, but the names were overwhelmingly British, with a heavy sprinkling of German and Scandinavian surnames and virtually nothing else. That, probably, reflected the fact that those groups had been established longer, had been able to develop their farms and families to the point where they could spare time for Pool business, had had time to acquire community standing, and were more articulate in English.

Alexander James McPhail

Much more, fortunately, is known about the two men who dominated the Pool board of directors from 1923 to 1931, Alexander James McPhail and Louis C. Brouillette. McPhail's impact within Pool history came not just from his status as first elected Pool president, but even more from his own character:

> No man who ever met him or heard him failed to be impressed by his almost awe-inspiring integrity. It shone out of his eyes, it was implicit in his bearing — in his every word and gesture. There were great personalities in western Canada in those days but in his rock-ribbed integrity McPhail towered over them all. Against it, the efforts to spread doubt and distrust and fear broke into vain and futile spume.[4]

An early neighbor had similar impressions, remembering McPhail as not physically impressive but impressive in character:

Left: A. J. McPhail, SWP president. (SWP Collection, Saskatchewan Archives Board R-A 15,243)
Right: Louis Brouillette, SWP president. (SWP files)

"You could tell that he was a real good man. You could tell that he was a co-operator through and through."[5] A longtime colleague put it in somewhat different terms, calling McPhail "almost offensively honest and straight-forward."[6]

McPhail's background was certainly one that could have been designed to produce an unusually heavy sense of duty and responsibility.[7] Born 23 December 1883 in Ontario, he was not quite six when his parents moved to a Manitoba farm. By the time he was nineteen, both parents had died of disease and Alex McPhail was head of a family of eight — five younger brothers and three younger sisters. They worked hard to stay together as a family and moved to Saskatchewan in 1906, settling in the Bankend district near Elfros. As his brothers and sisters grew up, McPhail was able to undertake new activities: a winter at Manitoba Agricultural College; a provincial government job as agricultural inspector; and, in 1915, enlistment in the army. Rather than being sent overseas, he was transferred to the militia and commissioned a lieutenant.[8] After the war he returned to farming, with much emphasis on buying and selling livestock.

At the close-knit homes of the McPhail clan, the intellectual world often took precedence over physical comforts. Little attention was paid to furniture, but much to studying the Bible, Shakespeare and Scottish poet Robert Burns. A young family member recalls the style as "plain living and high thinking," with perhaps a tendency to be too critical of those who did not measure up to McPhail standards.[9] Although historically Conservative, the family were strong supporters of the Progressive movement when that started in the 1920s. Originally Presbyterian in Scotland, the McPhails became Baptists in Ontario when no Presbyterian church was available in their area. The strong sense of propriety involved with such a background caused Alex McPhail discomfort on at least one occasion. On his way to church in his mid-teens, McPhail was given a lift by a neighbor and the neighbor's daughter, whom McPhail had a crush on at the time. Before getting in the buggy, the polite teenager swallowed the tobacco he had been chewing.[10] Although in many ways a plain, straightforward person, McPhail at times showed an almost poetical, romantic streak. Fittingly for someone whose favorite historical character was Abraham Lincoln,[11] this streak occasionally showed itself in bursts of eloquence in otherwise-simple speeches, as when McPhail defined co-operation:

> It is as the sun, sending its warm and healing rays wherever there is trouble and inequality among men. Its ultimate result, if given freedom of action, will be to quietly, peacefully, and effectively displace the old ruthless, coercive, competitive system, which has brought so much suffering to mankind.[12]

Described by a nephew as "sort of the last Puritan," McPhail's sense of propriety was strict.[13] After marrying one of the Pool's best secretaries, Marion Baird, he insisted that she leave the Pool, lest there be a conflict of interest or a seeming conflict with him as president.[14] McPhail admitted once that he had denied deserved promotions to R. C. Steele simply because Steele was his brother-in-law.[15] Fortunately, Steele moved to the Central Selling Agency in Winnipeg and eventually became general manager of Manitoba Pool Elevators, winning wide respect for his talent. McPhail's sense of duty also produced a well-known stinginess concerning salaries. In 1922 he wrote: "when we are paying a man $3500 we have a right to all his time."[16] Nor, despite Sapiro's call for big salaries for big men, did McPhail feel that senior managers should expect much: "Seven thousand a year should be enough for any man if his heart is in the work."[17] Such views were, however, only partially due to McPhail's own convictions. They were also based on a strong feeling that farm organizations must bend over backwards to avoid the appearance of being concerned with good incomes for their leaders. The farmers, he said, could be wrong in their suspicions, "but they pay the bill, and it is on them we have to depend for an organization if we are to have any."

When the Pool started and McPhail took a salary of only $4,000, it was roughly equivalent to what he could have made farming that year. His tax assessments show net income of $987 in 1921, rising to $2,209 in 1922 and $3,259 in 1923.[18]

As he became involved with Progressive party organization and the SGGA, McPhail quickly was confronted with the need to learn how to compromise and how to tolerate working with people with lesser intellects or simply different convictions. By 1931 he had succeeded in becoming what Central Sales Agency treasurer R. C. Findlay termed "the type of man the world needs today, the practical idealist."[19] But it was a hard, sometimes painful, adjustment process. Soon after becoming SGGA secretary in 1922, he declared that he would not take the job if he had the choice to make over again.[20] After a few more months, he firmly believed that it was "much easier to be independent and a free lance and much harder and perhaps more difficult to have to put up with the things a man in this position very often is compelled to put up with."[21] But he was at the same time starting to take a more patient approach: "Perhaps a man in a position of this kind can gradually shape things in the right direction by a process of winding and bending rather than direct action." After becoming Pool president in 1924, he wrote that he was keeping himself psychologically prepared to return to his farm: "at any time I feel I could have to compromise to keep from going there."[22] But, even while declaring that he would not compromise basic principles, he tried to avoid considering his own views as all-important. Daily life, he wrote, goes much better if "we can always keep before us the fact that we are only here for a passing moment, and that the world would go on just the same if we passed out at any moment, even our own little world, where we may think we cut quite a figure for the time being."

As the Pool developed, McPhail was confronted with two major conflicts between his strongly-held views and the need to compromise, when the majority of delegates and farmers rejected his position on buying the Co-op Elevator company and on seeking compulsory pooling legislation. Although he bitterly opposed the decisions ultimately taken, McPhail worked hard to implement those decisions. They had gone against his view of co-operative principles, but, more important, to refuse to carry out those decisions would have violated the principle of majority farmer control. McPhail believed strongly that personal feelings should be submerged in one's commitment to serve the common good:

> Further, desire for personal notice and reward is not the kind of service which makes possible great forward move-

ments in the interest of the people; rather, it is the work which is carried on by men and women, here and there, who, without too much thought of personal reward, give heart and life to these movements.[23]

One safety valve for McPhail was his private diary; another was confidential correspondence with Violet McNaughton, another SGGA activist. In those writings, he vented feelings that he restrained even at Pool board meetings. Of Louis Brouillette, who was to be McPhail's successor as Pool president, McPhail wrote: "He is a fanatic and is apt to do things that a more balanced man would not do."[24] On another occasion, McPhail criticized Brouillette's "underground methods" and pronounced him "quite useless in an office."[25] Such comments could say as much about the strain McPhail felt as about the person being criticized.

Personal factors also contributed to the tension in McPhail's life. Bothered occasionally by spells of biliousness, on at least one occasion he had an attack so bad that he had to bow out of a scheduled meeting with three premiers.[26] Even his 1926 courtship was a major source of tension. McPhail and Marion Baird were to have been married on 18 August 1926, but she became emotionally disturbed shortly before then, suffering from hallucinations and fits of depression. On several occasions in August and September, she made seeming attempts at suicide. Through it all, McPhail stuck by her and quietly helped pay for her care in hospitals and retreats. She recovered and they were married on 3 January 1927.[27] Three days after the marriage, he was off on an eleven-day business trip to New York, Toronto, Ottawa and Winnipeg. But it would be a mistake to consider his life as one unrelieved period of tension. He did find pleasure in marriage, a son, friends, and the Pool. His public impression of austerity and reserve relaxed with certain intimate friends, with whom he could be congenial, companionable and even a practical jokester.[28] He died in 1931, amid bad times for the Pool, but neither the tension nor overwork involved in Pool affairs killed him. He was in good spirits after an apparently-successful operation, before a chance complication developed that caused his death. Although McPhail thus did not literally give his life for the Pool, there is much truth in Harold Innis's epitaph on McPhail: "McPhail's contribution was the preservation of unity. To that end he was willing to sacrifice his opinions again and again and eventually his life."[29]

Louis C. Brouillette

If McPhail helped hold the Pool together against internal convulsions and external attack, Louis Brouillette provided much of the drive that prevented the Pool from being too cautious or excessively concerned with reaching slow consensuses. "For his outstanding quality was tenacity — a grim, stubborn, sometimes frightening tenacity," Pat Waldron wrote. "He allowed nothing to daunt him or divert him from his purpose."[30] That tenacity became useful for simple survival when Brouillette was president in the troubled 1930s, while in the 1920s it was the driving force behind several key policies.

Born on 16 November 1885 in Illinois, Brouillette took auctioneering courses in Chicago and moved to Canada, settling at Landis, Saskatchewan, and building up a large farm there. His family remembers him as a devoted but strict husband and father, who liked obedience and never changed his mind after saying "No".[31] Praying nightly for wisdom and guidance, Brouillette in 1923 credited divine forces as helping him in his Farmers' Union and other work: "I feel that surely God is helping us out, for I know that many things and thoughts have occured to me that no doubt is His work."[32] Like McPhail, Brouillette came to have an overwhelming emotional commitment to the Pool. His *Western Producer* obituary in 1937 commented:

> He did not possess that veneer of cynicism or that detachment which is so useful in the hurly-burly of public life. He held the cause too dear and seemed to suffer a physical reaction when the fortunes of the farmers' movement were subjected to the buffeting of stormy seas.[33]

Salvation for the farmers lay in Sapiro's philosophy, Brouillette felt, and he used all his tenacity to support the Sapiro position on issues like buying elevators and compulsory pooling. When the Brouillettes' fifth and last child was born during the Pool organization period, he was named Louis Sapiro Brouillette. Sapiro in turn reciprocated that respect, writing in 1937: "Without Brouillette the Wheat Pools of Canada would never have been formed and without the Wheat Pools the Canadian Prairies would have been utterly helpless and desolate."[34]

Although very different from McPhail in personality and style, Brouillette too demanded dedication from employees. When Depression forced staff cuts in the 1930s, Brouillette was clear on who should go:

> There was an excuse at first, when we were assembling men and women for these large-scale cooperatives, for not having time to determine whether or not they were cooperatively-minded. But there will be no excuse if we continue to keep in our service those who continue to look upon their work as a job — merely as a means of earning wages and salary.[35]

Not a polished speaker, Brouillette nevertheless was able to leave an impact on audiences through sheer force and sincerity. In the rough-and-tumble of Pool business and other debates, he held strong feelings and "could be very rough indeed" on those who stood in his way: "For those who did cross him he had a long memory and did not easily forgive. But when peace was reached all was forgotten."[36] In social gatherings, even persons associated with the McPhail faction remember him as a delightful, well-mannered person.[37] Brouillette's French background included ancestors who were early settlers in Quebec, but Louis himself grew up in an English-speaking environment in Illinois and spoke no French.[38] He died on 22 April 1937, after only six years as Pool president and after several years of failing health. Despite occasional rhetoric to the contrary, Brouillette's death (like McPhail's) was not the result of overwork or excessive worry about the Pool. He died of cancer, although the cancer was not discovered until after his death.[39] Like provisional president A. E. Wilson, he was destined to be left in the shadows of history because of all the attention given McPhail as first elected president and because of the mass of diaries and letters that McPhail left.

With McPhail and Brouillette in that early Pool leadership were several other strong personalities who also deserve note. John H. (Jack) Wesson, who was to succeed Brouillette as president, deserves a book to himself and is described in chapter six. He

Home of Pool delegate A. McEwen, near Riverhurst, 1928. (SWP Photo 53)

played an increasingly important role on the board in the 1920s, but others who were more in the limelight then included the irrepressible, colorful Avery Fenton Sproule and Harry Marsh. McPhail grumbled in his diary that those two talked too much at board meetings,[40] but there is no doubt their speaking skills were invaluable in the country. Sproule in particular "had the ability to light fires under young people," recalled one person who heard him in the 1930s.[41] He could also handle the hecklers who were a standard feature in the lively country-hall meetings of the 1920s. At times he dared them with flashing eyes and combative stance to try coming on stage if they seemed to be out to disrupt the meeting.[42] For normal hecklers, a few salty phrases were sufficient — one in a Jewish community was squelched when Fen Sproule suggested the wrong part had been thrown away after the heckler's circumcision. Sproule was a trial to prim, proper elements like secretary George Robertson, who tried to restrain his outspokenness, but he was also a popular drawing card for farmers' gatherings. Perhaps more important, he too had one of those solidly-good characters that inspired confidence in enterprises he joined. Travelling by wagon in the spring of 1912, he and some friends befriended a young couple who were caught in a pouring rain, with no tent and the wife about to give birth. Sproule made his tent available and was joined by a healthy baby boy by the time the husband returned with a doctor. Sproule continued on his journey, leaving the tent and blankets with the couple, and the incident was all but forgotten for thirteen years, until he was in the Willow Bunch area on one of his countless tours persuading farmers to sign the Pool contract. At one farm he found the couple he had befriended on that stormy night and was quickly recognized by the woman, who firmly declared that her husband and all his brothers would sign contracts for the Pool. "When they have men like you in it, it cannot be the bad thing some people have been telling us," she said. "People who would help us without even asking where we lived, can be trusted to sell our wheat."[43] Although he opposed McPhail's position in the tough fight over compulsory pooling legislation, a controversy where McPhail felt particularly strongly against those who disagreed with him, Sproule received a letter from McPhail praising his co-operative attitude in helping work out a solution.[44] A. F. Sproule died in 1953, after nearly thirty years as a Pool director, including a period as vice-president. He once told an associate: "I fear neither God nor man. The only thing I'm afraid of is that I will let the wheat pool down sometime."[45]

Harry Marsh, meanwhile, was a director only for the Pool's first seven years, but continued as a delegate for another thirty-one

years. An apprentice stonemason in England, he moved to
Canada to escape the health effect of stone dust, then found
temporary jobs taming wild horses and repairing chimneys before

*John Maharg (right) and Harry Marsh, presumably in the years
both were active in the Saskatchewan Grain Growers' Association.
Maharg went on to head the Saskatchewan Co-operative Elevator
Company; Marsh became an original director of Saskatchewan
Wheat Pool. (SWP Collection, Saskatchewan Archives Board R-A
15,247 [2])*

becoming a farmer. He carried the bronc-busting spirit with him into agricultural affairs and public meetings, handling Jimmy Gardiner so roughly in one 1921 debate that the politician would not speak to him for ten years afterward.[46] Although a Farmers' Union member, Marsh opposed many ideas he considered radical and used his membership mainly for access to Union meetings so he could learn about and oppose such ideas. Marsh, however, was far from being an establishment type and in 1927 got into trouble with both the Pool hierarchy and the Board of Grain Commissioners for his unproved public accusations that grain was being improperly mixed at Lakehead terminals. Being raked over the coals so much for that incident, he recalled later, led him eventually to quit being a director.[47] But he remained prominent at annual meetings, acting as chairman for his last twenty-six years as a delegate and taking satisfaction in the fact that his huge, booming voice never needed a microphone even in the largest halls. He died in 1981, aged ninety-four.

Working quietly behind these strong, sometimes flamboyant, personalities for more than three decades was one of the most influential employees the Pool ever had, George Robertson. Ironically, in view of his quiet background role, Robertson was one of the most prominent original leaders of the Pool through his status as a member of the legislature. Born 1889 in Scotland, he worked briefly for a Scottish grain merchant before coming to Canada. He settled on a farm near Mozart in 1914, became an SGGA director in 1918, and was elected to the legislature in 1921. Although Robertson was a member of the Progressive party's Saskatchewan executive, he sat as an Independent since the Progressives were then formally active only on the federal level.[48] In 1924 he resigned from the legislature to become Pool secretary fulltime. With Robertson, the job was actually more than fulltime. His daughter Margaret recalled frequent weekend trips to Pool headquarters to take meals to her father: "he would go to work Saturday morning and would emerge for Church Sunday at eleven."[49] Except for one occasion he always found time to chat with his daughter when she dropped in for a visit — the one exception was when she dropped in while he was starting the first of three scheduled appointments with representatives of three different Saskatchewan political parties — each of which was inviting him to run for them and be agriculture minister after the coming election.[50] Mitchell Sharp, who worked with many grain-industry leaders in his years with the trade department, considered Robertson "the most subtle of the characters I knew" — the philosopher of the pool movement, always at the president's side at major meetings, always effective.[51] A believer in unity and public decorum, Robertson was distressed when an edited version of the McPhail diaries was published in 1940, complete with McPhail's caustic comments about his colleagues.[52] A close associate of McPhail's, the closest Robertson ever came to criticizing Brouillette was when he privately told his daughter the Brouillette period "was no bed of roses." One of his methods of coping with human obstacles, expressed in another context, was: "If you can't get rid of somebody, you build fences around him."[53] With the clashing personalities on the early Pool boards, a fence-builder — or fence-mender — was handy to have around. Government officials, colleagues, and other observers also noted his impressive administrative skill, which was most visibly demonstrated in organizing petition campaigns.[54]

Yet Robertson was far more than a man concerned with the exercise of bureaucratic power or the company of important persons. On one country tour he was not heard from for a few days. It later transpired that Robertson, who had been trained in the Presbyterian ministry, came across a church and congregation that had been lacking a minister for some time, so he filled in.[55] Despite world travels to wheat conferences and formal diplomatic receptions, his heart remained with the simple prairies. One Qu'Appelle Valley community so struck him that, on regarding beautiful scenery thousands of miles away, he was apt to declare it "as pretty as Lumsden."[56]

George Robertson's sense of humor showed up subtly in his Pool duties. A speechwriter for both Brouillette and Wesson, — McPhail always wrote his own speeches — Robertson used to insert a few key phrases in Wesson's texts, one example being "in the final analysis," to let a faraway daughter know he had written them.[57] But that in-joke was about as close as he went to the edge of propriety. After signing himself "George Wilson Robertson" for most of his life, he ultra-correctly dropped the "Wilson" after discovering no middle name had been registered on his birth certificate. He was also one of the most active of Pool leaders in non-Pool community affairs. Before dying in 1963, he had been a Regina public school trustee, member of the University of Saskatchewan board of governors, chairman of the board of managers for First Presbyterian Church in Regina, chairman of the advisory board to a Catholic hospital, president of Regina Rotary, and national head of the Sons of Scotland.

Soon after it started operations in 1924, Saskatchewan Wheat Pool found it had need of all the varied talents and determination of its directors, delegates, employees and membership. The over-riding problems and the strongest initial controversy centred on the issue of elevator facilities to handle the rivers of wheat flowing into the Wheat Pool. There was no trouble about the Pool's very first grain-handling facility, an old warehouse at Scobey, Montana, that was bought for $2,280 in September 1924. Although closed the next March, it served as a temporary delivery point for Pool members near the border who had no convenient Canadian elevators. But in the years until the Pool could build or buy its own network of elevators, there was no alternative to the frustrating task of hammering out handling agreements with existing elevator companies:

> Not only the first year, but each year thereafter, no matter how early in the season the organization undertook to get the next year's contract entered into, grain was practically ready to move before the Pool had completed an agreement with the elevator companies. It is of interest to note that the elevator companies received 5¢ per bushel for handling the top three grades and 6¢ per bushel for handling the lower grades, for the same work which the elevator companies now do for the Wheat Board for 3¢ per bushel.[58]

United Grain Growers was the only exception to the general lack of co-operation, signing an agreement with the Pool by 24 August 1924. Negotiations with the Saskatchewan Co-operative Elevator Company went so poorly that the Pool decided to seek an agreement with the privately owned elevator companies first. (The

Platform and elevators at Davidson, date unknown. (SWP Photo)

private elevator chains were commonly called "line elevator companies," referring to the days when they began by building a series of elevators along particular railway lines, along which each company often had an initial monopoly.) With an agreement covering the line elevators completed by 4 September, Pool leaders could put the pressure on Co-op Elevator leaders, whom McPhail believed were counting on the line companies not to agree to a better deal than the one the Co-op had proposed. To save face, the Co-op took the position that no formal contract was necessary after all, and they handled Pool wheat in 1924-25 on the basis of a letter of agreement.[59]

But that was only the start of a thorny relationship between the two organizations, which as co-operatives might have been expected to work together closely. The Pool board accepted a co-op letter, 11 September, as the basis for their handling arrangements, then by 9 October were compelled to protest Co-op actions in charging one cent a bushel more on stored and special-bin wheat than the line elevators did.[60] Although that charge was not spelled out in the letter of agreement, the Pool felt it violated the spirit of the agreement, that the Co-op would handle grain as the line companies did. One day after issuing that protest, the Pool board resolved on the motion of A. F. Sproule to put "an elevator or elevators" of its own in place for the 1925 crop. Brouillette and Pool manager Donald MacRae went to Chicago to consult Sapiro on elevator policy, returning with the firm advice that "you must ultimately own, in absolute right, all of your necessary physical facilities." In a 31 October 1924 memo on elevator policy Sapiro insisted, "every system, which enables the farmer or encourages the farmer to handle wheat in another way, is against the Pool." The Pool board approved Sapiro's strategy on 13 November, a day after they had issued yet another protest against Co-op actions, this time against a special one cent a bushel commission the Co-op was charging for handling carlots of Pool wheat. The battle soon moved into the country, where Co-op members were electing delegates to their next annual meeting and where Pool activists campaigned to have farmers elect delegates sympathetic to the Pool. Brouillette told one country meeting that several Co-op directors had not yet signed a Pool contract: "he who is not with us is against us."[61] The elections ultimately resulted in a few sympathetic directors being placed on the Co-op board, but its top leadership remained unchanged.

Reluctant to enter into wasteful construction that would duplicate the Co-op's extensive network, and unsure about undertaking the heavy financial load of buying the Co-op outright, Pool leaders began exploring possible half-way measures. Pursuing a suggestion by Alberta Premier Brownlee, the Pool suggested that it be given managerial control of Co-op elevators.[62] The elevators would be transferred to a Co-op subsidiary on which the Pool would have half the directorships. The Co-op, however, said it could not accept the idea of having to bargain with such a subsidiary for the use of its own elevators to carry on its own business. Joint meetings were held between the three prairie pools, UGG and the Co-op to try to find some way of meeting the pools' desires for greater control over their grain movement. Suggestions included joint advisory committees, handling pool grain at cost, and having elevator agents also act as pool agents, with instructions direct from the pools' head offices. McPhail complained that the Co-op leaders — J. A. Maharg, J. B. Musselman and F. W. Riddell — were obstructing talks with "fencing and ferreting and stalling."[63] But the major reason for the breakdown of talks was the pools' demand that UGG and the Co-op drastically reduce service to farmers who were not pool members. Expressing fears that close links between the pools and the two farmer-owned companies would cause line companies to complain about preference being given to the two, the pools insisted that UGG and the Co-op should buy wheat from non-pool farmers only in carlots. With about half the grain being sold to elevators in smaller amounts, that would mean both UGG and the Co-op would have to bar some of their farmer-owners from using their own facilities. Both the companies refused the demand. The pools' first attempt to wield the power of their wheat thus failed when they went too far in their demands, seeking to transform the two long-established companies into virtual puppets of the pooling system. It also cost the pools points in the public-relations contest, as Co-op directors loudly announced their resolve to provide "public facilities for the use of all farmers without discrimination."[64]

Meanwhile, Pool directors had resolved to have the Pool build its own elevators as quickly as possible, making full use of a key clause in members' contracts permitting deductions for that purpose. The elevator-deduction clause authorized the Pool to retain up to two cents from the price obtained for every bushel of wheat sold, and to use those funds for building and buying grainhandling facilities. The money was in effect an indefinite loan from members, who received certificates recording the amounts they were owed. As stressed by Sapiro and other speakers, the deduction system was essential to the Pool's growth, because as a co-operative it did not have access to investors' capital beyond the one dollar paid by each member for a share. After the board's decision to make the maximum deductions

The Pool's first elected board: Front row, from left: George Robertson (secretary); Harry Marsh; L. C. Brouillette; A. J. McPhail; A. E. Wilson; R. S. Dundas. Middle row: Brooks Catton; Donald MacRae (general manager); J. H. Robson; A. F. Sproule; Herbert Smyth; Allan Lefebvre. Back row: R. H. Milliken (counsel); J. H. Wesson; A. E. Bye; C. W. Coates; Thomas Bibby; R. J. Moffat; J. D. Read (treasurer); E. B. Ramsay absent.

permitted under the Pool contract, Saskatchewan Pool Elevators Ltd. was incorporated as a subsidiary 24 February 1925. The issue of how aggressively to build Pool elevators dominated the Pool's first general meeting of delegates in February. Hard-liners succeeded in passing resolutions urging construction or purchase of an elevator "at each of the heaviest contract shipping points in Saskatchewan" and seeking "complete unity at the earliest possible moment" with farmer-owned companies. But the moderates also scored, with an amendment saying that elevators should be acquired with regard to a previously approved policy "of refraining as far as possible from competing with farmer owned elevators."

The matter was thus left largely in the hands of a divided board of directors. Brouillette had been fighting strongly for a policy of competing with farmer-owned companies just as strongly as with the line companies. McPhail, seemingly believing that directors should present a united front before delegates, felt that Brouillette "double crossed the board in advocating his own viewpoint" in the general meeting.[65] And he later clashed with Brouillette in interpreting the delegates' resolution, Brouillette arguing that it left the board free to acquire elevators at any point, regardless of the presence of UGG or Co-op elevators. McPhail was also trying to restrain public attacks on the Co-op, advocating instead a policy of "peaceful penetration."[66]

Central Selling Agency

Meanwhile, a tense drama was unfolding at the Central Selling Agency, a drama that both threatened the existence of the pools and injected new bitterness into Saskatchewan's debate over elevator policy. The problem centred on the CSA's inescapable dealings with the Winnipeg Grain Exchange. Although the agency was trying to sell as much wheat as possible directly to export customers and domestic mills, bypassing the Exchange in those transactions, it had to sell large quantities on the Exchange also. And customers who dealt directly with the agency often wanted to pay for pool wheat by giving the agency futures that the customers had bought earlier. Price-related decisions on when to sell wheat and futures on the Exchange put the Central Selling Agency into the thick of the speculative process. As early as 3 November, sales agent D. L. Smith was suggesting that the CSA should occasionally *buy* wheat futures to slow sharp price declines.[67] On 24 January 1925, Smith also advised that higher prices were coming, there would "hardly be enough wheat to go around," and the CSA should in the meantime make only moderate sales.[68]

McPhail, as head of the agency, was willing to accept very limited use of such tactics as part of good selling procedure, but he emphatically insisted that the business of the pools was to keep wheat moving toward consumers, not to undertake speculative operations on a large scale in hopes of making large profits through speculation. Whenever the pools tried to get above-average prices, he felt, they risked ending up with less than the year's average. That view put him into early conflict with Henry Wise Wood of Alberta, who at a tense 31 January CSA directors' meeting argued strenuously for buying May futures. "I fought it and would have resigned if they had insisted on putting it into practice," McPhail noted.[69] But "for the sake of harmony" he reluctantly agreed to one temporary restriction on sales efforts — direct sales to specific customers would continue, but the agency would not indirectly sell wheat by selling May futures. Whereas Wood did not want to sell wheat for less than $2 a bushel, by 7 March the Exchange prices had fallen to $1.88. Instead of lowering agency selling prices to move wheat, Wood wanted to buy wheat futures in anticipation of a profit as the price rose.

"Absolute nonsense and exceedingly dangerous," McPhail wrote in his diary.[70] By 31 March prices were fluctuating in the $1.41 to $1.48 range and it was clear that buying futures at $1.88 would have been disastrous. But worse prices and an even graver threat were on the way. Prices fell to $1.38 on 3 April, just three cents above the amount the pools had already paid out to farmers — $1 initial payment and 35 cents interim payment. "If the pool is smashed there is only one man to blame," McPhail wrote in a caustic comment on Wood.[71] For a few days, the future of the pools was hanging by a thread. Without a 10-cent spread between current prices and what had been paid to producers, there was a chance that the banks who had lent money for the producer payments would insist on drastic reductions in the wheat stocks the central agency was carrying. Such forced dumping of large quantities of wheat in a short time could in turn cause even lower prices.

In the midst of all this, McPhail noted widespread rumors that the unexpected drop in Exchange prices had been engineered by leaders of the Saskatchewan Co-operative Elevator Company: "They must be fiends if it is true."[72] The market seemed to be dominated by "bear" interests who were selling wheat futures in anticipation of more price declines, while potential "bull" influences who might have bought futures in hopes of a price rise were deterred by fear that the pools would start dumping their wheat. The course of action for McPhail was both distasteful and clear:

> The pool appears to be the only organization that can go in and change the trend of the market and to do it we must take steps which we would not under ordinary circumstances take. But we must fight the devil with his own weapons.[73]

Starting on 4 April 1925 the Central Selling Agency thus became a speculative buying agency for six weeks. It bought 3.2 million bushels of wheat futures, as well as juggling another 605,000 bushels by simultaneously buying that amount of futures on the Winnipeg Exchange and selling the same amount on the slightly higher Chicago Exchange. The Winnipeg price quickly rose to $1.69 — an indication that it may well have been artificially depressed earlier — and the agency made a profit of $486,508 or 11 cents a bushel on its futures trading.[74] The Canadian Wheat Pool had been saved, speculators had been taught that the pools could defend themselves, and the Saskatchewan Pool had new reason for bitterness against Co-op leaders.

Back in the continuing elevator policy debate, Brouillette was pushing for an invitation for Sapiro to come and discuss elevator policy. The Pool board agreed, to stop Brouillette from resigning, but it turned out that Sapiro could not come at that time.[75] "I was very glad for I consider it the veriest nonsense to be depending on the advice of a man 1,000 or more miles away," McPhail wrote.[76] A long telegram of advice from Sapiro, urging immediate purchase of the Co-op elevator system, provoked another confrontation on 9 April when the Pool board rejected a Brouillette motion to buy the system. McPhail felt that the board majority was strongly in favor of slower, pay-as-you-go progress, especially in view of the lesson of the pools' vulnerability to price drops and the need to build up a strong cash reserve.[77] But influential directors like A. F. Sproule and Jack Wesson had voted for Brouillette's motion and the battle was not over. Farmers' Union leaders bluntly told Pool executives that the Union would use "sledge hammer" tactics if necessary to get Pool delegates to back the Sapiro-Brouillette position.[78] A flurry of resolutions came in from farmers in Brouillette's district accusing other directors of misinterpreting delegates' views on elevator policy and declaring support for Brouillette, who was threatening to resign from the board's elevator committee. The struggle on the Pool board continued that summer, with McPhail forces succeeding in maintaining the policy that no Pool elevator would be acquired at a point that already had a Co-op elevator unless there were more than 30,000 acres of wheat under contract to the Pool at the point.[79]

All factions, however, had grounds for celebration on 1 July 1925, when Pool elevator No. 1 was opened at Bulyea. Amid cheers, Pool delegate P. B. Thompson delivered fifty-seven bushels of No. 2 wheat, receiving a voucher for $65.55. With tongue in cheek, Donald MacRae received the load and declared: "I'd give you 2 for this, Thompson, only unfortunately our bins are mostly filled and you'll have to take a 3."[80] Generations of prairie farmers had had to swallow serious comments like that, but on that sunny Dominion Day it was cause only for laughter. By the time the Pool's first annual report was released in October, there were eighty-six Pool elevators, built or bought on a cash basis. Directors noted that fifty-two had to be built: "it was found exceedingly difficult to purchase existing elevators from Line Companies at a price in keeping with the valuation placed on them by our Inspectors." Pool handling charges of four cents a bushel on top grades were a cent lower than any other company except UGG.

But eighty-six elevators were still only a tiny start and once again the Pool had to work out handling agreements with other companies for most of the harvest. The Co-op again proved

Elevator No. 1, Bulyea, opened 1925. (SWP Collection, Saskatchewan Archives Board R-A 15,202) Photo taken about 1926–27.

difficult, leading the Pool to advertise on 15 October that no agreement had yet been reached with the Co-op. The Co-op then counter-advertised, to prevent lost business, that it was accepting grain for the Pool at cost even though no agreement was signed.

Delays in reaching handling agreements meant more than just administrative headaches for Pool headquarters — they often represented very real losses for farmers, particularly on less desirable grades. When no facilities were available to handle Pool wheat, farmers could either go without income or sell to local elevators. William McKenzie Ross took his first crop in that fall, a load of frozen wheat, and was offered 12.5 cents a bushel for it. He refused, managed to hang on until a handling agreement was in place, and delivered the wheat to the Pool's account early in the new year. His initial, interim and final payments for that wheat eventually added up to seventy-two cents a bushel, almost six times the elevator's offer. "I vowed then a Line Company would never get a bushel of wheat from me," Ross said.[81]

Meanwhile, the Pool and Co-op were arguing over whether the Co-op's profits on handling Pool wheat would be paid directly to farmers by the Co-op or whether they would be paid in a lump sum to the Pool as the Pool wanted. The Pool won that one, but its membership was getting increasingly fed up with such protracted wrangling. At the Pool's first annual meeting — the February meeting was for policy debate, not to consider the formal first annual report — delegates voted to authorize the board to buy the Co-op system at an arbitrated price and to start negotiations with other pools to buy UGG's elevators.

Saskatchewan Co-operative Elevator Company Purchase

On 12 November 1925, Co-op directors sidestepped a Pool proposal to buy the Co-op system at an arbitrated price, saying they had no power to discuss such purchase proposals. That set the scene for a stormy session from 16 to 18 December, when Co-op delegates gathered for their annual meeting. Co-op president Maharg took the offensive against the Pool, blasting it for trying to deny use of elevators to non-members: "The Pool has no right to say where any non-pool farmer will sell his grain."[82] Other speakers said talk of arranging a world wheat pool could bring disaster on farmers: "the people that eat bread throughout the world will rise in their might against us." And Co-op general manager F. W. Riddell declared that the Co-op was buying farmers' wheat at higher prices than the Pool would provide. The Co-op leaders, however, soon found themselves on the defensive against delegates who demanded to know why relations were so bad with the Pool, why the Co-op had never got around to the co-operative practice of paying patronage dividends, why there were cases of non-farmers owning Co-op shares, and why Union president L. P. McNamee was denied the right to buy a Co-op share. The Co-op leaders replied by claiming that much malicious propaganda was being spread. Riddell declared that "there are different kinds of co-operation, and there is no one who has a right to say that they have the only kind in existence." Secretary W. C. Mills said McNamee was "an avowed enemy of this Institution" and wanted a share only to qualify as a delegate and come to the annual meeting to make trouble.

All such defences and explanations, however, were swept aside by the Co-op delegates when they voted on 17 December to call a special meeting within two months to consider the Pool's purchase offer. Two minutes of pandemonium erupted, with the cheers of delegates and visitors startling passers-by outside. It had taken two years for the general membership to overcome rules that slowed replacement of directors and other reforms, but the decision was irrevocably made. UGG had earlier decided at its annual meeting to remain in existence as an alternative to the pools, but acquisition of the Co-op system would make Saskatchewan Wheat Pool predominant in the province.

With the majority of both Pool and Co-op delegates on record in favor of a takeover, the next developments might have been expected to go smoothly. McPhail, however, launched a last-ditch effort to head off the purchase. "We all think it would not be in the interest of the pool to buy out the Co-op. e. Co. now that the board is friendly to the pool," he wrote after a talk with allies on the Co-op board. "So long as we can safeguard the interests of the pool, we would be foolish to take on the heavy financial responsibility at this stage."[83] McPhail was bolstered when Premier Dunning privately suggested a compromise plan whereby the Pool would get half the Co-op directorships in return for paying the Co-op's $2.4 million debt to the government and giving the Co-op $1 million equity in Pool Elevators.[84] But whereas McPhail was acutely conscious of the pool's potential vulnerability in its wheat sales, the opposing camp felt equally strongly that the Pool could never be secure without physical assets and a presence at delivery points. Sapiro tried, unsuccessfully, to persuade McPhail directly that: "The absolute acquisition by purchase and ownership of these properties will be your greatest single achievement toward the permanency of your pool and the ultimate success of all your great efforts."[85] The Pool board was now behind Brouillette, but McPhail managed to win consent for a special general meeting of delegates, 17 to 19 February 1926, to reconsider the elevator issue. On the opening day he declared that "this is, perhaps, as important a meeting as the Delegates of this Pool will have, even if the Pool is in existence for 50 years."[86] Agreeing on the desirability of an eventual takeover, he warned that such a takeover should be deferred while the Pool mustered all its resources to defend against attempts to destroy it. Business and public confidence in the Pool, he said, must not be endangered by assuming large debts to buy elevators. The tense debate ended, however, with delegates approving the purchase offer 98 votes to 46, just one vote above the two-thirds margin needed for approval. Although a strong contest preceded the vote, the meeting then made it a unanimous decision. McPhail had said before the vote that if delegates decided to proceed despite his opposition, "no one will hear any more from me against it." True to his word, he thereafter worked dutifully to implement the decision. And he was philosophic about defeat, writing to a friend that only trouble would result if thirty-five percent of delegates were able to block the will of the majority:

> the man or men who try to set themselves up against the majority wish of the people are very apt to get steam rollered out of existence. The people today are different to what they were 8 or 10 or 25 years ago. They are more widely awake.

They are doing more thinking for themselves than ever before. Perhaps some wrong thinking but that does not matter so much. . . . We never know for sure if we are absolutely right. The sale at this time *may* be the best thing after all. At any rate the vast bulk of farmers want it and I am inclined to think a great deal more harm than good would be done by trying to balk them.[87]

In one of his rare surviving personal letters, Brouillette, meanwhile, confessed great personal relief to his mother after being vindicated in the final vote, following a year of struggle in a minority position of the board: "right (as you always taught) is might."[88]

Events moved quickly after the February 1926 Pool meeting. The special Co-op meeting voted 366 to 77 on 10 April to accept the Pool's offer. The arbitrators' report on 26 July set a value of $11.06 million on Co-op properties and on 2 August 1926 the Pool's elevator subsidiary grew suddenly by 451 country elevators, two Lakehead terminals, and a transfer terminal at Buffalo. It also inherited a lease on a third Lakehead terminal. Co-op shareholders did well from the deal, particularly the original shareholders.[89] They had paid $7.50 cash for each share and had watched company dividends pay the remainder of the $50 nominal value of the share. For each $7.50 investment, they received $155.84 after the sale.

From 89 operating elevators in 1925-26, the Pool quickly grew to 586 in 1926-27, 727 the next year, and 970 in 1928-29. During 1926-27, its first crop year to include the Co-op elevators, the Pool system handled more than 90 million bushels — "the greatest quantity of grain ever handled by a single organization through its own facilities in any country in the world."[90] After a brief experiment with Central Selling Agency operation of some terminals, the Saskatchewan Wheat Pool by 1928 controlled five terminals at the Lakehead, totalling more than 26 million bushels of storage capacity. That included the newly-built Terminal Seven, featuring storage of 7.2 million bushels, five automatic car dumpers and the reputation of being the most modern terminal in the world.

As the elevator and terminal system was mushrooming, Saskatchewan Pool joined with its neighboring pools in late 1926 for another try at buying UGG elevators. The UGG annual meeting in December turned down the idea by a decisive 4-1 ratio, but unanimously agreed to lease or sell individual elevators as necessary to prevent undesirable duplication of UGG-pool facilities. That, however, was not enough to avoid competition,

The Saskatchewan Wheat Pool's first facility — a grain dump at Scobey, Montana, purchased to serve Saskatchewan farmers who had no nearby Canadian railway. Photo taken about 1927. (SWP Collection, Saskatchewan Archives Board R–B 7511)

since a year later Pool delegates voted to provide facilities at every shipping point in Saskatchewan. Relations between UGG and the rest of the co-operative movement became strained in the late 1920s by what UGG officials considered a "routine of petty persecution," largely emanating from Saskatchewan co-op leaders who considered UGG not a "real" co-operative, and from consumer co-op representatives who disliked UGG's role as a purchasing service for farmers.[91] The pressure succeeded in causing UGG to leave the Co-operative Union of Canada in 1929.

Meanwhile, the acquisition of an elevator system confronted Saskatchewan Wheat Pool with more difficult policy questions, chief among them the issue of whether to pay patronage dividends to elevator customers. All Pool members were paying to build the elevator system, but patronage dividends would go only to those members who happened to have a Pool elevator within delivery range. At the 1925 annual meeting the majority of delegates approved the board's policy of distributing the elevator company's surplus direct to those members who delivered to Pool elevators. But the debate continued over the next few years, despite McPhail's explanations to correspondents that patronage dividends "bring home to the minds of all Pool farmers as forcibly as possible the value of putting their grain through their own elevator."[92] Those members who took the trouble to go to Pool elevators, and to wait for space in Pool elevators if necessary, would be disaffected if they saw the elevator subsidiary's earnings spread among farmers who did not take such trouble. After an initial year of paying cash dividends — two cents a bushel on wheat, one cent on coarse grains — Pool delegates decided to use elevator surplus earnings to make payments on the debt incurred to buy Co-op Elevators and to expand the Pool elevator system. Patronage dividends would still be allocated to members delivering grain to Pool elevators, but instead of those dividends being paid in cash, they would remain as credits to the farmer's account, to be paid at some unspecified future date. The elevator system's dividends would thus be handled like the two-cent-a-bushel elevator deduction or the one-percent commercial reserve deduction, which were being taken off the selling price of grain but remained on the books as credits to individual producers.

But one year after starting that system, delegates voted to change it. Under the new policy, members delivering to Pool elevators would get a cash dividend of 1.75 cents on a bushel, while those delivering elsewhere would get one cent. A large minority at that 1927 meeting called for the radical step of having Pool elevators handle grain exactly at cost, with no charges being levied until the year's final costs were determined. As if Pool bookkeepers did not have enough work already with more than 50,000 member accounts, the Pool was also paying interest at six percent on the elevator reserve and five percent on the commercial reserve. That too caused some debate, since some held that the commercial reserve was a cost of doing business, not a fund of money borrowed from members for capital projects, and thus should not earn interest for members. Pool leaders, in fact, were confronted with a host of precedent-setting problems in the early years. In one case, however, they made a precedent-reversing decision, organizing a coarse grains pool in 1925 despite failing to meet their goals of signing up a third of oats and barley acreage and half of flax and rye acreage. Even with lower initial figures, the coarse grains pool worked well, adding more volume to Pool elevators while giving members assurance of average prices.

Pool Enforces Contracts

One of the most frustrating types of problems was enforcing Pool contracts, trying to steer a middle course between the dangers of being too punitive and of being too lax. The magnitude of the problem was evident in a few basic statistics: after its first year of operation, the Pool had contracts covering almost seventy-two percent of Saskatchewan's wheat acreage; but from 1925 to 1928, each year the Pool marketed only fifty-six to fifty-eight percent of the wheat. In 1925, Pool directors said deliveries were "quite satisfactory," considering that much wheat was marketed before the Pool could accept deliveries at the start of the 1924-25 crop year, and that crop failures were particularly bad in areas of heavy Pool membership. A year later, however, such excuses were no longer applicable and things had not improved. Directors then noted the probability of some contract violations, but said most of the problem was caused by loan companies, landlords and other parties taking part of a farmer's crop and selling it on the open market. Directors said the Pool was trying to sign contracts with such creditors so that they too would deliver to the Pool. As for "leakage" of Pool grain through members selling on the open market in violation of their contracts, directors said in their second annual report: "The responsibility for checking such evasions must of necessity devolve upon the Growers themselves." At one point, committee members were enlisted in a mass campaign to try to educate farmers in one basic legal aspect of the contract — a Pool member was allowed to mortgage or otherwise pledge his wheat as security for a loan, but only on condition that the creditor would deliver the wheat to the Pool if he took possession.

Enforcing the contract was not just a matter for education, moral pressure or even communication in many languages, difficult as those tasks were. Several key court battles and many routine ones had to be fought. A lawsuit against Leon R. Zurowski of Southey for non-delivery eventually confirmed the legality of the Pool contract, but only after an initial decision against the Pool.[93] One key element was a clause in the Pool contract providing for a penalty of twenty-five cents a bushel penalty for delivering wheat outside the pool. Without such a clause it would be hard to make a non-deliverer pay any penalty since any one particular non-delivery would not cause the Pool measurable damage. The validity of the penalty clause was confirmed, but the Zurowski case uncovered another weakness in the pool system — no one had ever formally notified the first block of members that their applications for a share of Pool stock had been approved. Thus members could argue that their contracts were not yet operative. To take care of that technicality, the corporate secretary had to mail an official letter of acceptance in late 1925 to each of about 46,000 persons.[94]

Other thorny problems for counsel R. H. Milliken and Pool directors included provincial laws obliging certain creditors, including threshers, to sell on the open market any grain they seized to pay off debts. The Pool could have obtained an amendment to the legislation to have grain sold to the Pool, but since Pool initial payments were generally lower than the open market's once-and-for-all cash payment, that would mean the creditors would have to seize larger amounts of wheat to cover the debts. Judging that the organization could afford to forgo the small amounts of grain in question rather than cause hardship to some producers, Pool leaders left that situation as it was.

More often, it was a matter for patient explanation rather than courtroom work. Many farmers had, with or without the advice of line elevator agents, come to believe wrongly that they could sell wheat ouside the pool in the name of a wife or child, or that acreage put in wheat after signing the contract was not covered. In four years of operations with 80,000 members, only 150 cases were referred to Pool solicitors. Of those, Milliken estimated that 100 contract violations were due to misunderstanding and 30 to "stress of financial circumstances," leaving only 20 cases of willful contract violation.[95]

Member loyalty to the Pool was also demonstrated in the comparative ease with which the second contract found signers. The first contract expired 31 July 1928, but more than a year earlier the Pool had enough 1928-33 contracts signed to ensure continued operations. Without exception, every working day brought new contracts into Pool head office. As with all other developments, the contract-renewal campaign brought more legal work and study. Milliken, for example, determined that the Pool was not obliged to refund elevator reserve deductions to persons who failed to sign new contracts, unless the Pool cancelled their shares.

Fortunately, the Pool had an invaluable force working for it in its efforts to sort out the hundreds of confusing problems that arose in the early years. This was the legendary group of "field men" who fanned out across Saskatchewan, buttonholing farmers, organizing meetings, helping delegates, investigating complaints, boosting allied organizations and generally undertaking a super-human workload. The seventeen fieldmen of 1925-26 — one for each Pool district, plus one for "non-English sections" — held 800 meetings that year, with an average 300 farmers at each meeting. They also visited 24,069 farmers individually, made 3,000 elevator visits and obtained twelve percent of the year's new contracts, not to mention selling *Western Producer* subscriptions.[96] They had to soothe conservative school boards that considered the Pool to be linked with the Bolshevik movement and that refused to allow Pool meetings in the schools.[97] Some, like fieldman John Stratychuk, had to contend with discrimination against Ukrainians even though, as one farmer recalled, Stratychuk "could tell you more in a few minutes than the average fellow could in a half hour." One committee chairman told the Pool fieldman "this committee doesn't have to accept any advice from any bohunk." Another time, half the audience walked out when he rose to speak. Some of those who walked out criticized their delegate for subjecting them "to a goddamn foreigner telling them about the affairs of their own organization." That particularly galled Stratychuk, since he was born in Canada while twenty-three of the twenty-six who walked out were born elsewhere. In 1940 Stratychuk returned to the same hall, urging an audience of about 350 to buy victory bonds, and one man moved a vote of thanks, apologizing for having walked out eleven years earlier.[98] Thus patience and perseverance eventually overcame such prejudice, as well as helping defeat the occasional delegate's resolution calling for disbanding the field staff on the grounds that it cost too much. Other public relations initiatives included mailing materials in Ukrainian, German, French, Hungarian, and Rumanian, and starting a weekly radio broadcast from Pool head office. The hour-long program included commentary and entertainment by members of head office staff, broadcasting under the call letters CJBR — "Co-operation Justified By Results".

By the time CJBR came along in 1927, the Pool had finally resolved the old issue of where its head office should be. Back in July 1924, the first permanent board had deferred the question, but it was re-opened in February 1925 when office space was getting short and a move of some sort was imminent. Moose Jaw's board of trade presented a brief inviting the Pool to move there, noting that Moose Jaw was the northern terminus of the Soo railway line to Chicago and thus the logical point for wheat exports to the United States once U.S. tariffs on wheat were lowered. Even in 1925 the idea of selling wheat to the United States in any substantial quantity was far from practical, but the city could also list several agricultural and milling operations to give its pitch credibility. Directors, however, were totally absorbed in the choice between Regina and Saskatoon, deciding in an argumentative board meeting on 24 February 1925 by a one-vote margin, to stick with Regina. The issue simmered through 1925 and 1926 before delegates voted 88 to 44 at the 1926 annual meeting to stay in Regina. The Farmers' Union had by then been absorbed into the new United Farmers of Canada, but their views were still strongly held and one UFC meeting, where all present were Pool members, unanimously passed a resolution urging reconsideration of the decision to stay in "the nefarious political atmosphere of Regina":

> Remembering that practically all champions of the farmers' cause previously sent to Regina seem to have had short

memories of those left behind, every unbiased pool member should agree that Saskatoon will prove a safer home for our pool than Regina. . . . Many pool members have not forgotten and never will forgive the hostility shown by Regina to our Wheat Pool at its birth.[99]

The hostility of such institutions as the Regina *Morning Leader*, however, caused less day-to-day inconvenience for Pool staff than did their initial cramped quarters. Filing cabinets stuffed full of contracts filled every available space. One bathroom in a suite of offices became a corridor between offices, traversed by putting one foot in the bathtub and stepping over it. The temptation was too much for office boy Jimmy Langford and filing clerk Susie Mitchell to resist in those high-spirited days — a succession of Pool executives soon found themselves putting one foot into a bathtub that was half filled with water.[100] By May 1925, the Pool had eased its space problem, moving into the former Sherwood department store building that it still occupies. Built in 1912, the three-storey structure served as a military supply depot and garage before being transformed into the Saskatchewan Wheat Pool Building. The Pool reduced costs by renting ground-floor space to a car dealership, indoor miniature golf operation, government offices and the Bank of Montreal, with the bank remaining as a tenant to the present day. Purchase price was a reasonable $200,000.

SWP head office, about 1927. (SWP Collection, Saskatchewan Archives Board R-A 15,295)

Among other secondary — but important — activities, lobbying government for legislative changes quickly became a continuing Pool function. With the aid of the Progressive faction in the Commons, the three pools were able to score such successes as the 1927 Campbell Amendment, which gave farmers the right to designate which terminal would receive their grain. That was particularly important for the pools, who wanted their terminals to receive pool grain that had been delivered to line elevators. Nothing, however, ever seemed to be settled that simply. Within months after passage of that amendment, some elevator companies were giving farmers a new form of storage ticket that the companies said entitled them to send pool grain to the companies' terminals. When deliveries were light, farmers could insist on getting the regular storage ticket approved by the Board of Grain Commissioners and their grain would go to pool terminals — but when deliveries were heavy and elevators full, only the non-standard tickets were available.[101] Wherever laws or regulations were being considered or reviewed, the pools were present. Lawyer R. H. Milliken found himself making lengthy trips to Ottawa, but he had the satisfaction of frequent successes, as when the Exchequer Court ruled in 1929 that pool elevator and commercial reserve deductions were not taxable as income. A brief telegram to Pool secretary George Robertson announced: "Income tax judgment issued complete victory for us." Robertson replied with even greater brevity: "Three hearty British cheers."

The Pool's electoral structure was shaken up in 1928 as district and subdistrict boundaries were revised to reflect the distribution of cultivated acres, rather than just the distribution of 1924 contract signers. But the number of districts and directors stayed at sixteen, despite McPhail's private complaints that sixteen was too large and unwieldy a number.[102] The Manitoba and Alberta pools each had only seven directors and academic observer Harold Innis has suggested that the Saskatchewan Pool would have operated more efficiently with less emphasis on democracy. Also, Innis said, "McPhail and Brouillette might have been alive."[103] Pool delegates, however, firmly believed that administrative headaches were a small price to pay for a broadly based democratic structure. And the emphasis on contact with committees and farmers meant that Saskatchewan, with its greater farm population, could use more elected officials than its neighbors.

The 1925-29 period also saw greater than usual attention to personnel choices since they became a centre of intrigue both within Saskatchewan Wheat Pool and among the three pools. The Central Selling Agency executive tried to get Alberta Premier Brownlee as their general manager and almost succeeded, but in the end turned to Edward B. Ramsay, who had become a farmer near Fillmore, Saskatchewan, when his health declined after a banking career that included spells in London, Bangkok, Glasgow, New York, and Seattle. Opposition to Ramsay's appointment came mainly from the Brouillette group, who wanted McPhail to become CSA manager — a move that would have left the Pool presidency open for Brouillette.[104] There were also problems with the CSA's top grain salesman, David L. Smith, who had trouble getting along with Ramsay. CSA director H. W. Wood of Alberta took the opportunity of McPhail's absence on a long trip to fire Smith, telling him: "You may be the best wheat salesman in Canada but you are not a co-operator."[105] Smith had also had a more cautious sales policy than Wood, believing that a third of expected wheat handlings should be hedged by selling them in the futures market. After McPhail's return, Smith was rehired at a higher salary to operate the CSA's new London office. Despite such conflicts, the pools were fortunate in their personnel — of the five CSA salesmen in 1926, three later became wheat board commissioners (Smith, W. C. Folliott, and George McIvor). Ramsay went on to head the Board of Grain Commissioners, starting in 1929.

Although the Pool was technically completely separate from the Saskatchewan Grain Growers' Association and the Farmers' Union of Canada, its leaders helped encourage the 1926 amalgamation of those hostile organizations into the awkwardly-named "United Farmers of Canada (Saskatchewan Section) Ltd."[106] Pool delegates urged union at their first annual meeting and the SGGA-Union amalgamation convention was held in Saskatoon nine months later. Aaron Sapiro was brought in to preside over the union and give another round of speeches. Saskatoon city council hailed him as "the most inspiring organizer of co-operative farm enterprises" in a special resolution on 7 July, then formally granted him the freedom of the city and presented him with a case of sterling silver.[107] But Sapiro's presence was distasteful to McPhail: "Some of his remarks were very petty and others very misleading, but he seemed to put them all over. I am convinced he is one of the most dangerous men, perhaps the most dangerous, to the Co-operative movement."[108] Sapiro in this period was directing much of his criticism at the Alberta Pool, accusing it of being a puppet of the United Farmers of Alberta, but McPhail heard enough second-hand stories about Sapiro criticizing Saskatchewan Pool leaders to keep his dislike high. For McPhail, perhaps the gravest charge against Sapiro was his friendliness with Brouillette, whom McPhail called the "snake in the grass" among Pool directors.[109] McPhail's forces succeeded in defeating a board motion to make Sapiro consulting counsel for the Pool, but the Sapiro-Brouillette forces were clearly winning the contest for control of the new United Farmers.

Campaign for "100 percent Pool"

All the simmering personality clashes and philosophical differences that had marked SGGA-Union and McPhail-Brouillette relations finally erupted in the traumatic "100 percent Pool" campaign. Launched by Sapiro in a series of July 1927 speeches, the campaign was aimed at getting legislation to force every Saskatchewan farmer to deliver his wheat to the Pool. So long as a sizeable minority of farmers remained outside the Pool, Sapiro argued, their wheat could be used as an economic weapon to damage the interests of the majority. At the same time, the minority was receiving benefits from Pool efforts to raise wheat prices and reform grainhandling, without contributing anything to Pool costs. Opponents, meanwhile, charged that any such action would be undemocratic. Pool delegates reacted initially with mixed feelings, passing a resolution in November 1927 saying only that the United Farmers should ensure a thorough, province-wide discussion of the issue so that all farmers could be well informed. United Farmers delegates approved the idea in February 1928, but by so slim a margin that their divided executive did not feel it had a mandate to take any position.

McPhail's reaction was uncompromising: "I think the idea is out of the question when mentioned in the same day as co-operation."[110] Convinced that the campaign could only arouse a wave of antagonism against pooling itself, he told a Regina conference that non-pool farmers are not the greatest enemies of either pooling or the Pool: "it is not the opponents of democratic institutions who are its greatest menace, but its members. No one can really hurt or impede the progress of a great organization, or a great cause, or a great principle, as much as the members or supporters themselves."[111]

But the tide was running against McPhail. Just as Sapiro's success in organizing tobacco and other pools had helped inspire creation of Saskatchewan Wheat Pool, so too did the collapse of several U.S. Sapiro pools seem to demonstrate that a non-pool minority of famers could wreck a pool. The June 1928 meeting of Pool delegates sidestepped a direct vote on the issue, but passed votes of thanks to Sapiro and the UFC for promoting discussion of the topic. The November annual meeting expressed confidence in the current system of contract pooling, but resolved to co-operate with the UFC in gettting farmers' views. "It will kill the organization if it becomes the policy of the pool to seek compulsory legislation," McPhail feared.[112] When the UFC convention in February 1929 voted decisively to seek compulsory pooling legislation, the real battle was on.

By a margin of about 120 to 25, Pool delegates rejected the compulsion principle on 21 June 1929, but directors like Jack Wesson had joined the pro-compulsion forces.[113] The Pool board decided that no director should officially accompany Sapiro on his next Saskatchewan tour — but eight directors went to Saskatoon ten days later to meet Sapiro.[114] Sapiro's speaking tour in June and July of 1929 was one of his most strenuous, frequently leaving him hoarse and voiceless. It was also virtually free, as he charged the UFC only $300 for expenses.[115]

A provincial royal commission on grain delivered a report in early September condemning the compulsory pool idea, but Sapiro was back in Saskatchewan later that month to redress the balance, scoring points with many pool supporters as he ridiculed "the Umbrella Man," the non-pool farmer who would sneak under the pool umbrella in bad weather but would not help hold the umbrella up. At Kerrobert on 20 September, Sapiro took dead aim at McPhail and certain other Pool leaders, saying they were hesitant about starting the pool in 1923 and they opposed aggressive elevator acquisition: "Each great step forward that you have made — you have achieved in spite of them."[116] At Humboldt, he said a compulsory pool should put an end to use of Grain Exchange facilities: "if 100% control is obtained and the pool then went on to the exchange, they ought to be shot." One Pool fieldman, Osborn Upper, argued with Sapiro at the Humboldt meeting, saying that the pool would have to operate under government supervision if non-members were forced to sell their wheat through it. Also, Upper said, "if we had every kernel of wheat in the world in the final analysis international finance will tell you what you will get for it."[117] Sapiro responded that any Pool employee with such views should be fired. That exchange was a small sample of the stormy meetings that were sparked by the compulsory pooling issue — some featured thrown eggs and one saw Pool delegate Jim Whiteman, who was nearly seventy at the time, put a hammerlock on one drunken heckler and run him out of the hall.[118]

McPhail and his allies, meanwhile, had decided "the time for aggressive action has come to combat the insidious campaign being carried on by the U.F.C. which is being directed by a Wheat Pool board member against the policy of the W. P. organizations."[119] The action included a heavy schedule of country speeches by McPhail throughout October, leading up to the Pool's November annual meeting. McPhail and other critics of compul-

"Portable elevator" operating at Radville, 1928. (SWP Collection, Saskatchewan Archives Board R-A 15,067 [3])

sion hammered particularly hard at the fact that the 1929 compulsion plan would not give a vote in the Pool to the non-members who were to be forced to join. If the government wanted compulsion, McPhail said, it should set up a new agency to pool wheat that was not going to Saskatchewan Wheat Pool. The Pool annual meeting, however, deferred most resolutions on the issue until the next June, except for passing Jack Wesson's motion that each delegate "be allowed individually to use his own discretion" in speaking about the issue until June. The resolution, in effect, undercut McPhail's position that Brouillette and his allies were acting improperly. The arguments continued throughout the winter, with McPhail writing to one delegate: "You would have a much stronger organization in any line of ten men who were free, voluntary and enthusiastic members of the organization than if you increased that ten to fifteen by forcing the last five into the organization."[120] The disunity problems involved in acquiring those last five members, he argued, would seriously dissipate Pool energies.

Resolution of the compulsion controversy had to wait until later, when the pools and the nation found themselves in vastly different economic and social circumstances. In the meantime, despite the importance of such activities as policy debates, contract enforcement and lobbying, the fate of pooling was being decided in sales strategy and international developments.

In their first annual report, Pool directors had noted preparations for a conference of Canadian, U.S. and Australian wheat growers' associations, declaring: "It is vitally important to the success of our organization that some understanding should be developed between these three countries at the earliest moment." But when the first International Wheat Pool Conference was held, 16 to 18 February 1926, in St. Paul, Minnesota, little progress was made. The three Canadian pools, four Australian pools, ten U.S. pools and two Soviet Union observers basically agreed only to hold another meeting in 1927. The conference, however, did result in several of the U.S. organizations considering an experiment with a central selling agency, while Canadian representatives were invited to Australia to advise on possible reorganization of pools there. The conference was notable for strong advocacy of price control by two Central Selling Agency directors, H. W. Wood of Alberta and W. G. A. Gourlay of Manitoba. "I feel there are too many men who are somehow ashamed to admit that the object of this pool is to raise the price of wheat," declared Gourlay.[121] Wood predicted that "these three great English-speaking countries, United States, Canada, and Australia, can raise the price of wheat at least fifty percent above the level of the price that has been maintained through the old system without the assistance of any other country in the world."[122] Between that conference and the next, Sapiro came up with a suggestion that the Canadian pools' agency should act as seller for surplus U.S. wheat when U.S. farmers became properly organized.

By the time of the second international pool conference, May 1927 in Kansas City, advocates of price control were on the defensive, perhaps partly because of critical overseas reaction to the previous year's casual talk of boosting prices fifty percent. Brouillette told the conference, "you will have an international pool if you want to have it," but he spent much of his emotional energy blasting the conference for not inviting Sapiro to speak, and for what he called the virtual crucifixion of "one who has done wonders for you in the United States to save you from financial destruction."[123] Salesman D. L. Smith of the Central Selling Agency had sent a paper contending that the pools had created a new situation in Canada where "the price is fixed to a large extent by the owner." But Smith's arguments were overwhelmed by a speech McPhail made in person to the conference, warning of the dangers of trying to push up commodity prices unduly. Any such attempt, whether through current power or "larger combinations" of pools, McPhail said, could produce hostile reactions in consuming nations: "it would only be a temporary gain which would almost inevitably result in defeating our own ends." Even H. W. Wood stated that it would be impractical to merge the world's wheat pools into one centrally managed unit. Saskatchewan Pool secretary George Robertson said a world pool would be too remote from members and Saskatchewan farmers could not pledge their wheat to it. Robertson also noted a recent Rome meeting called by Mussolini to discuss ways of dealing with the prospect of a world wheat pool and of raising European wheat production. The best that could be done, Robertson suggested, was to set up a small international bureau to promote the general idea of pooling and to try to discourage excessive competition between grain-selling co-operatives.

When the third International Wheat Pool Conference met in Regina in June 1928, it was clear that Sapiro's 1923-24 vision of a giant world pool could not be realized. Not only were there growing doubts about any attempt at price control, but people had virtually given up hope that the fragmented U.S. co-operative scene would ever produce a unified pool sales agency like Canada's. Agricultural economist J. F. Booth listed six major differences between Canada and the U.S. that had combined to produce the united Canadian Wheat Pool: Canadian emphasis on large elevator networks instead of locally-owned elevators; overwhelming Western Canadian reliance on one crop; greater Canadian uniformity of grainhandling routes and facilities; a much heavier Canadian export orientation, which encouraged larger organizations; favorable Canadian experience with a wheat board; and a strong, united national banking system.[124]

Even as the idea of world co-operation was withering, the Canadian pools were daily getting new experience and confidence in what they could do by themselves. One key victory for the pools had been won at the start without a struggle, thanks to the effort of a sympathetic banker. Jackson Dodds, senior western official of the Bank of Montreal in 1924, argued strongly within a committee of banks handling pool financing that the pools should not be compelled to hedge wheat through sale of futures on the Exchange: "It is not our job to say how the wheat in this part of Canada should be marketed. Our job is to finance its marketing and we should be very careful that no action should be taken that would drive the Wheat Pools into the hands of the government."[125] If other banks did not want a share of pool financing on that basis, Dodds told the committee, he would recommend that the Bank of Montreal take a greater share. Thus the pools were left free to pursue their goal of direct export sales, bypassing the Exchange as much as possible and relying for financial security on keeping their initial payments to farmers below the open-market price. Technically, observers commented, that meant the pools were "engaged in a stupendous speculation in cash wheat,"[126] but that vulnerability was generally agreed to be of academic interest only. The pools' convincing 1925 defence of wheat prices against an Exchange "bear raid" had shown how their strength could work in practice.

The pools expanded on all fronts, arranging in 1927 to include Ontario pooled wheat in Central Selling Agency duties and setting up a CSA London office the same year for direct sales that would bypass European traders as well as the Winnipeg exchange and Canadian traders. The reaction of the Birmingham *Gazette* to the new CSA office, however, was not encouraging: "Housewives Will Not Benefit," read one headline over a story saying that any savings from direct sales would not be passed on to British consumers.[127] Nor was that ominous reaction confined to sensationalist newspapers or the British grain trade. The British co-operative movement, recalled Canadian co-operative statesman George Keen, was suspicious of the Canadian pools from the start: "They seemed to regard them as food trusts organized to oppress the consumer."[128] Keen, the general secretary of the Co-operative Union of Canada, worked hard to soothe such suspicions and persuade the British groups that Canada's producer co-operatives were legitimate partners for the largely consumer-oriented general co-operative movement. The Pool, in fact, joined and supported the Co-operative Union of Canada. But all the work of people like Keen was at least partly undercut every time a pool official spoke of price-control possibilities or boasted of how the pools had kept prices up. In a notable 1928 speech, wheat buyer A. H. Hobley of the English Co-operative Wholesale Society appealed to the Canadian pools for firm statistics to demonstrate that farmers were getting only a reasonable margin over their production costs:

> We welcome the prosperity of the Canadian farmer, but we ask him, as a brother in the Great British Empire, to consider the needs of the working and poorer classes of the people in the United Kingdom, and other parts of Europe....
> It is no use complaining that capitalists organize themselves to get all the profits they possibly can, if we are only out for the same thing.[129]

Central Selling Agency directors seemed, nevertheless, to have little concerns that year, stating in their annual report: "What little

adverse propaganda has appeared in the public press has been
-ignored."[130]

While public relations problems were simmering in consuming
nations, the pools were also running into commercial problems. As
one influential British periodical noted, the pools' decision to sell
direct to European mills, bypassing traditional middlemen,
carried a heavy price:

> The effect of this was simple and instantaneous. It turned
> Canada's former agents into competitors, and competitors
> who knew that business thoroughly, who had been in it in
> some cases for generations and who were able to divert a
> great deal of the trade formerly enjoyed by Canada to
> others.[131]

Even as early as the summer of 1928, CSA salesman D. R.
McIntyre warned in an internal report that European millers
believed the Canadian pools had kept wheat prices significantly
higher than they would have been otherwise.[132] Since the millers
were then having financial problems and suffering from excess
capacity, McIntyre said, they tended to blame the Canadian pools
for much of their problems: "This might, if we try and keep our
wheat too high, result in a disaster for us in a year when there is
even a small surplus."

One specific problem concerned the powerful English milling
company, J. Rank Ltd., with which the pools had had a direct

*First SWP information tent at a provincial fair, Weyburn, 1927.
(SWP Collection, Saskatchewan Archives Board R-A 15,029 [2])*

sales contract since 1924. McIntyre recommended ending the contract since the Rank firm had the lowest selling price in Britain, other British millers believed Rank was getting preferential treatment from the pools, and Rank was thought to have ambitions to control the British milling industry, a possibility that if realized would give Rank great buyer power over wheat prices. Before McPhail could end the Rank contract, however, he had to fend off pressure from Sapiro to continue the contract. There is no indication whether Sapiro was acting as a paid agent in this or other representations he made over British sales arrangements, but the suspicious McPhail thought Sapiro was trying to find ways to pay for his heavy expenses in the lawsuit against Henry Ford.[133]

All such problems, however, seemed slight beside the basic impressive fact of the Canadian Wheat Pool's existence. In a few short years, it had emerged as one of Canada's most prominent and most economically important institutions. The first commercial telephone call from England to Winnipeg was to Central Selling Agency offices, fifty-one dollars for three minutes to order 3,000 tons of No. 3 wheat. British newspapers may have concentrated upon the pools' effect on British bread prices, but Canadian journalists found a good outlet for purple prose about "This infant prodigy, sprung from the dreams of prairie farmers, whose sire was disgust and whose dam was a fighting spirit."[134] The prairie pools' organization was described in a *MacLean's* article as "the colossus of the prairies" and their joint elevator system was "a veritable Gargantua, the like of which mankind has never seen." The article also declared that the pools' system of paying moderate initial prices and seeking a good average in their sales was "as nearly fool-proof as any commercial machine can be."[135] With pool wheat accounting for a fifth of world wheat trade, "in five years the pool has made the Man Behind the Plow the mightiest merchant in this Dominion."

There was also, however, a different kind of publicity with which pool leaders had to contend. In books, articles, speeches and pamphlets, supporters of the Exchange system of selling grain attacked almost all the basic principles of the pools. "Orderly marketing . . . is one of the popular catch phrases of the co-operative charlatan," grumbled one author.[136] He and grain trade spokesmen argued that there were legitimate reasons for the unbalanced seasonal flows of grain. Among others, Canadian grain was wanted by the world soon after the Canadian harvest, when harvests in other regions had not yet started; to hold back the bulk of Canadian wheat would risk losing sales to those other regions. It would also mean that more Canadian wheat would be burdened with winter storage charges. Pool defenders conceded that traditional middlemen had done a fairly good job of meeting such export demands in as orderly a manner as possible — but emphasized that the old system did not provide orderly marketing at the farmer's level, where there was heavy pressure for the farmer to sell all his crop right after harvest.

The most controversial and involved arguments, however, came over whether or not the farmer could get a higher net price from the pools than from the open market. The war of statistics opened in October 1925, when the pools reported that their first year's activities produced a price of $1.66 a bushel for top-grade wheat, delivered to Fort William at the Lakehead. More than fifty-five percent of the wheat was sold "outside of the regular Exchange channels," Saskatchewan Pool directors noted. The exchange, however, was ready with an impressive array of figures, based on a Price, Waterhouse and Company audit of fifteen elevator companies.[137] This study, said the Exchange, proved that non-pool farmers received 5.1 cents per bushel more than pool members for No.1 wheat from 15 September 1924 to 5 July 1925. Out of twenty-nine other grades, the non-pool farmer was said to have received more for twenty-five grades than his pool counterpart.

Outraged pool spokesmen, however, pointed out several gaps in the Exchange's case. The 4.3 cents in elevator and commercial reserve deductions retained by the pools had not been counted as a benefit realized by the pool members, even though it was credited to them in pool accounts for later payment. The fifteen companies surveyed also may have accounted for only a twentieth of non-pool wheat handlings and thus may not have been a representative sample. More important, the prices paid to non-pool farmers were those paid for wheat in store at the Lakehead. To get those top prices, the farmers would have to be among the fifty percent who had enough wheat of the same grade to deliver it into a special bin and have it shipped by the carload for sale at the Lakehead. Fifty percent of non-pool farmers were not in that category and had to take lower "street" prices for the wheat they sold to the local elevator. Also, those who did sell at the terminals might have had to wait weeks or months to get an acceptable price and thus might have paid five to ten cents a bushel in storage fees. The pools' final price, meanwhile, was the net result after such storage costs had been paid. The Exchange counter-attacked by saying that the pools' selling performance was even worse than the first set of figures alleged, since some of the final realized price would come from terminal profits and from interest earned on the amounts of money not paid to the farmers at time of delivery but deferred to the interim or final payments.

Such back-and-forth arguments continued vigorously throughout the life of pooling, with the masses of statistics building up to the point where the average farmer could decide between them only on faith and intuition. Charts from the Exchange periodically showed the Exchange's cash closing prices as being higher than the pools' price for most days of the year, but the pools retorted that such comparisons were meaningless. In periods when farmers were delivering virtually no wheat, high Exchange prices were of no benefit to them. Any attempt to sell large quantities in such a period would have immediately depressed the prices. In an attempt to find a true average of prices received by farmers on the open market, the Pool compared private elevators' daily prices for street wheat with monthly deliveries to country elevators. The Pool concluded that its competitors paid an average of nearly $1.04 a bushel for No. 3 street wheat in Saskatchewan during 1927-28, while the Pool paid slightly over $1.06. The Pool price included 3.2 cents in commercial and elevator reserve deductions, but did not include elevator patronage dividends.

Although the pools got some academic support for their side of the argument and many farmers were doubtless happy to have a mechanism for getting average prices, pool assertions of gains ranging from two to four cents above Exchange prices did little to satisfy those who had higher hopes for pooling. One historian concluded: "In retrospect it is fair to say that the achievements of the pools in the early years were such as should have satisfied all reasonable expectations. At the time, however, the expectations of pool members were by no means entirely reasonable."[138] One Manitoba Pool director, for example, had declared, only partly in jest, that "We are going to put fur coats and silk stockings on every farm woman in the Province of Manitoba."[139] Many farmers would also remember Aaron Sapiro's 1923 predictions of a gain of at least ten cents a bushel and the 1927-30 campaign for a compulsory 100 percent pool that was supposed to boost prices. The pools' case in price comparisons was also weakened by the fact that any successful efforts to get higher prices for farmers would tend to boost the prices received by non-pool farmers as well as pool members. Much of the benefits of pooling would thus be overlooked in simple price comparisons.

The pools were also struggling with increasingly difficult crop and marketing conditions as the 1920s drew toward their close. The $1.66 total pool price for No. 1 wheat in 1924-25 declined to $1.42 in 1927-28. The 1927 crop was judged "perhaps a crop of the lowest relative quality that Canada has ever produced,"[140] with a high proportion of tough and damp grain and low protein content. Ocean freight rates were up 200 percent for part of that year because of heavy coal shipments to Britain to make up for a

British coal strike. Economic damage caused by that same strike also interfered with sales in Canada's largest wheat market. But aggressive selling and efforts to persuade British millers to use more tough wheat enabled the pools to end the 1927-28 crop year with no carryover. Erroneous reports of large pool carryovers depressed prices for a while in combination with predictions of a huge 1928 crop, but such problems seemed to have been sorted out when the new crop year began on 1 August 1928. Just over three weeks later, disastrous frosts swept the West, presenting an even graver challenge to the pools. With a large U.S. crop being harvested and large Argentine-Australian crops on the way, Canada's farmers and business community would have been severely hurt by "complete and utter demoralization of the market" had it not been for the pools, directors of the Central Selling Agency said a year later. Saskatchewan Wheat Pool, meanwhile, initiated a farm storage plan in the fall of 1928, seeking to hold grain back on farms by promising extra payments of a cent a bushel for February deliveries, two cents for March, and three cents for April or later. Despite the challenges facing the pools with the poor-quality, large 1928 crop, pool leaders were confident they would meet the new test as they had met earlier ones. The pools' expertise, membership, world sales network, financial reserves, and elevator systems were all greater than they had ever been. In November 1928 Saskatchewan Wheat Pool directors were optimistic enough to report that "the outlook for the continued success of the co-operative marketing movement is brighter than at any time in the Agricultural history of the Province of Saskatchewan." Outside Saskatchewan, however, massive economic forces were starting to move, forces that would crush the prairie prosperity of 1928 as surely as a steamroller.

4
Collapse, 1929–31

Were it to dissolve into thin air tomorrow, it would still remain in the memory of man as one of the world's greatest monuments to the co-operative ideal.

— W. A. Irwin, 1929[1]

1929 Overpayment

At the Central Selling Agency of the three prairie pools, the fateful year 1929 opened quietly. A problem seemed to be arising with heavy shipments of low-priced Argentine wheat, which was displacing Canadian wheat in European markets. But speculators on the Winnipeg Grain Exchange were propping up Exchange prices and the CSA's experienced salesmen thought satisfactory sales could be maintained even during the presumably temporary period of strong Argentine competition. Although the pools were philosophically committed to selling as much wheat as possible direct to domestic mills and overseas consumers, CSA general sales manager George McIvor recommended on 14 February that they compromise their ideals and sell more wheat in the form of futures on the Exchange so long as prices remained higher there.[2] The agency, however, carefully limited such sales so as not to depress Exchange prices. By 7 May, McIvor was able to report to the CSA board that Argentine sales were easing, their prices had moved up to a more moderate margin under the higher-quality Canadian wheat, and CSA sales were rising again.

That same day, however, saw what McIvor termed "probably the most drastic break in wheat prices since the Spring of 1925." Exchange prices for wheat dropped eight cents a bushel in that one day, following speculation that the United States was going to take aggressive action to sell its growing wheat surplus. At President Hoover's request, western U.S. railways lowered their freight rates for export wheat 7 May, providing fresh evidence for such speculation.³ At about the same time it was becoming clear that Argentina still had a good supply of wheat and that January storms in Russia and the United States had not appreciably damaged crops in those countries. But the price break on 7 May — a date known as "Black Tuesday" until an even blacker Tuesday came in October — was not considered wholly legitimate at the Central Selling Agency. The market, McIvor said, was "being unduly depressed by interested parties." By normal commercial standards the Central Selling Agency was then in a good position — it had sold seventeen million bushels of wheat futures on the Exchange, creating a large "short" position that speculators would have envied at a time of falling prices. Unlike speculative interests, however, the agency's prime purpose was to get maximum prices for the farmer, not to make profits in declining markets. As it had done in similar circumstances in 1925, the CSA began buying wheat futures to slow the price decline. As in 1925, the strategy worked — at a profit. About six million bushels were bought at an average price of $1.14, producing a profit of $537,000 when they were sold for an average $1.23 after prices rose again.⁴ The Central Selling Agency seemed amply justified in its 11 May public statement that denied financial difficulties and asserted that increased 1928-29 wheat production had been offset by increased consumption.

Although farmers could rejoice in the pools' defence of their prices, the CSA action aroused strong antagonism elsewhere. "Wheat Pools Cheat World of Cheaper Bread," declared a British newspaper headline above a story that said: "The general public is being cheated of the bounty of nature. The great trusts are hoarding the world's grain."⁵ Defenders of the Exchange system of setting prices also quarrelled with the pools' manipulations. The May 1929 prices that the pools considered inadequate would have returned $18.59 an acre to the average Saskatchewan farmer, after deducting transportation costs and allowing for the average grade and quality of wheat in the 1928 crop, one such defender said.⁶ By contrast, the $1.66 pool price for the 1924 crop, a price listed by the pools as a worthwhile accomplishment, gave the average farmer only $14.57 an acre on the same basis, largely because 1924 yields were half those of 1928. The comparison was flawed, in that May 1929 prices would not have held up had the pools in fact tried to sell large amounts of wheat then. But the figures are nevertheless a useful illustration of the importance of maintaining sales volumes, not just prices.

The flaw in the pools' May 1929 price-support success was that prices had been held up only by forgoing possible sales and accumulating a backlog of wheat. By the time of McIvor's 9 July report to the CSA board, market prices were up again and the CSA was back in the selling business, having disposed of the wheat futures it bought in May. The trouble was that overseas customers did not want to pay the Winnipeg market's prices: "Unfortunately the man on the other side is still buying cheaper wheat elsewhere but we cannot believe that this situation will maintain itself indefinitely."[7] With drought reducing Canada's forecast wheat crop and world statisticians predicting tighter supplies in fall, the general consensus was that foreign customers would soon realize the necessity to pay higher prices.

With such optimistic forecasts for prices, representatives of the three pools on the Central Selling Agency considered they were being quite conservative when they met on 11 July and set an initial price of $1 a bushel for the coming 1929 crop. Even in retrospect, more than a year later, McPhail wrote: "We could not have paid any less. Our difficulty in that fall of 1929 was to withstand the pressure to increase the initial payment."[8] Farm opinion called for an even higher initial payment, with Winnipeg Exchange cash prices that day above $1.44. Any lower initial payment would have seemed totally unwarranted, might have panicked speculators and might have set off a wave of sales to private elevators by farmers in violation of pool contracts. As it was, McPhail commented: "A great deal of bootlegging being done. More than ever before."[9] And that bootlegging, in turn, would have given a boost to the continuing campaign for a compulsory pool.

For several weeks more, that $1 initial payment continued to seem like a perfectly sound decision. The Exchange's cash price rose to a 27 July peak of $1.78 and U.S. developments provided additional grounds for optimism as the U.S. government began allocating hundreds of millions of dollars for new agencies that were to stabilize commodity marketing. By August, however, CSA salesman were expressing puzzlement that the overseas buyers continued to avoid large puchases and that wheat prices were declining moderately. The world wheat carryover was expected to be up 93 million bushels, McIvor wrote, but 1929-30 production would be down 593 million. Once threshing returns started coming in, he felt, the overseas customers would begin to recognize reality. British wheat stocks in particular were "dangerously low" and "the Englishmen cannot remain out of the market very much longer." The U.S. agriculture department and private statisticians were similarly forecasting that demand could exceed supply, but European customers did not seem to be listening. Germany, France and Italy, in fact, had been imposing new duties on wheat imports in attempts to encourage their domestic producers. While waiting for the trend to change, the Central Selling Agency was also watching its debts grow to record levels.[10] On 31 August the CSA owed $68.2 million to banks and $6.7 million to the three pools, while the unsold wheat in its possession was valued at $105.3 million — at 31 August prices.

The growing wheat surplus, in fact, was becoming embarrassingly visible. Newspapers reported in mid-August that Montreal's storage facilities, rated at 15 million bushels capacity, were almost full with 12.6 million bushels on hand but shipping orders for only 315,078 bushels. Meanwhile, thirty-six lake boats were waiting to unload more grain, the new harvest was starting, and there were rumors that the pools had 100 million bushels of the 1928 crop still in western elevators. "The Pool is the cause of it all; there is no doubt about that," one grain trader was quoted as saying: "It is simply a case of gambling in prices."[11] The reports, rumors and concern reached all the way to the British cabinet, which sent Lord Privy Seal J. H. Thomas to Winnipeg in early September.

Fortunately, the pools were able to convince the visiting cabinet minister that — by Grain Exchange standards — they had indeed been trying to sell wheat instead of hoarding it.[12] As evidence given to a later royal commission showed, the Central Selling Agency offered wheat for export sale at prices below those on the Winnipeg exchange for forty-seven of the seventy-six business days in July, August, and September 1929.[13] The CSA offering price matched the Exchange price on five days and was above it on sixteen days, while CSA made no offers eight days. Also, the pools' carryover of the 1928 crop was less than rumors said. On 31 July 1929 the pools and CSA had 84.6 million bushels on hand. That represented 66.51 percent of the total Canadian carryover in a year when the pools received 52.15 percent of the wheat which farmers brought to elevators. The carryover statistics, representing wheat not *delivered* to customers, may have exaggerated the pools' actual share of wheat not *sold*. Of the 84.6 million bushels of carryover wheat in the hands of the pools, 5.8 million was held under open sales contracts and was on its way to specific buyers. The pools also had a net 26.7 million bushels in futures sales and could choose to close out those futures by delivering the wheat rather than by buying futures. On this basis, the pools could count themselves as having net unsold stocks of only 52.1 million bushels. To realize that net figure, however, the pools would have had, in effect, to deliver the 26.7 million bushels to people who had bought the corresponding amount of futures. Except for the small proportion of those people who actually wanted physical possession of wheat, the futures holders would have scrambled for

Left: SWP Secretary George Robertson, about 1958. (SWP Collection, Saskatchewan Archives Board R-A 15,527, photo by West's Studio, Regina)
Right: *George McIvor, general sales manager of Central Selling Agency. (SWP files)*

safety, cutting their losses by selling futures or cash wheat, and the high Winnipeg prices would have collapsed.

That, in short, was the pools' dilemma: only by initiating a massive collapse of Winnipeg Grain Exchange prices could they get wheat moving overseas again in large volumes. The situation was so skewed that throughout the fall of 1929 the Winnipeg Exchange's prices were 5.6 to 8.1 cents a bushel higher than the Liverpool exchange's futures, despite all the costs of transporting wheat from Winnipeg to Liverpool, costs that normally made Liverpool prices higher.[14] Faltering economic conditions were making European speculators pessimistic, while European mills were cutting their inventories to minimum amounts. Also, some European importers who were taking Argentine wheat were using the Winnipeg Exchange for their hedging, selling Winnipeg futures when they bought the Argentine wheat and then buying Winnipeg futures when they resold the Argentine wheat. So long as Winnipeg prices rose or fell in rough step with other world prices, the importers were protected, regardless of how much Winnipeg prices were above the rest of the world. Their use of the Winnipeg Exchange, meanwhile, would help support Winnipeg speculative activity and thus Winnipeg prices.

Caught in this squeeze, the Central Selling Agency maintained its position with increasing nervousness. In August, it passed a week with no offers, waiting for Europeans to give up and raise their prices. For another three days it offered wheat at prices slightly above the Winnipeg Exchange. Then, starting on 16 August, it went thirty-two straight business days with offers ranging from a fraction of a cent to 5.25 cents under Winnipeg Exchange prices, except for two days of identical prices. But even that was not enough to attract European buyers. "We have never witnessed a period in which it had been so impossible to obtain export business," McIvor told the CSA board on 10 September. The European buyer "is stubbornly contesting every inch of the ground and reducing his purchases to a minimum." The Argentine supply situation was mysterious: Argentine exports were continuing at heavy levels and low prices; there was no sign that the Argentine volumes would be sharply reduced, as had been expected for some time; reports still estimated that Argentina's growing crop would be 100 million bushels less than the previous one; but reports of bad crop conditions there might have been exaggerated; and the CSA's observer in Argentina had been on leave for some time. Meanwhile, CSA statistician Andrew Cairns' latest estimate was that world production would be down 568 million bushels from the previous year and total net exports from all countries would be only 710 million bushels, compared with import demand of 800 million. In such circumstances, McIvor found comfort in the fact that Canada had storage facilities enabling it to hold back up to 350 million bushels, an action that would probably "have a very noticeable effect on the attitude of the foreigner and the United Kingdom in regard to our wheat."

While newspapers and magazines were increasingly portraying the situation as a test of will between Canadian wheat salesmen and European buyers, one prominent figure at least declared that the Canadians — the pools in particular — had already won. In a 20 September Regina speech, Aaron Sapiro declared: "You can thank your stars that wheat fell this year to one dollar because your pool had to carry the wheat over. A shortage on this year's crop threw the price up and the carry over of last year will be sold at a magnificent price with a profit."[15] Sapiro turned out to be partially right — the 1928 crop carryover was eventually sold without significant loss. But the days of "magnificent" wheat prices were not to return in that generation, and the 1929 crop was piling up while the 1928 carryover was being sold. Sapiro's bitter enemy, A. J. McPhail, had a much clearer picture of what was happening. As chairman of the CSA board, McPhail was paying close attention to ominous warnings from CSA London representative D. L. Smith and was becoming increasingly convinced that basic world conditions were changing for the worse. CSA treasurer R. C. Findlay recalled that the agency's sales experts had "a tendency to smile a little" at McPhail's caution, but McPhail's influence kept sales efforts stronger than they would otherwise have been.[16]

By 7 October, the impasse seemed about to break wide open. The Central Selling Agency sold a million bushels that day, its best export day for six months. The next day McIvor concluded:

> The long period of waiting is at an end. We feel that with the drying up of the Argentine shipments, which will take place shortly and the lessened supplies of domestic wheats, that the foreigner and the Englishman will have to turn to Canada and the United States.

Cairns, meanwhile, had been revising his statistics in view of general increases in production forecasts and decreases in demand forecasts. The new predictions were for 760 million bushels available for exports, compared with 800 million for import demand. Cairns noted a British expert's forecast of 744 million bushels demand, but said the expert was "invariably too low." For the moment, there were still grounds for optimism. The Central Selling Agency's debt was up to $74.3 million, compared with only $4 million a year earlier, but its wheat stocks were valued at $111 million.

Market Collapses on "Black Tuesday"

Then came 1929's real "Black Tuesday" — 29 October — and worldwide financial chaos. Stock market prices dropped disastrously, banks collapsed and fortunes were lost. Yet, for a while, the pools and the commodity exchanges seemed to be riding out the storm. The 13 November assessment of the CSA sales department was that the stock market collapse prevented what might have been a good increase in wheat prices, since speculators had to sell their wheat holdings to cover stock market losses: "It seems very much as if we are required to maintain our present position until such time as the stock situation and financial conditions right themselves." In view of the shaky situation, the department said, CSA salesmen were refraining from making sales offers other than on some unsold wheat that had already been shipped from the Pacific coast.

Saskatchewan Wheat Pool directors reported that month to the Pool's annual meeting that operations generally were "very satisfactory" in view of world conditions. A decision on entering the flour industry by building a large new mill had been deferred and the elevator construction program had been trimmed due to light crops, but the Pool still enjoyed a $1.9 million surplus. And Saskatchewan Pool directors were determined to keep fighting:

> we have arrayed against us in our fight for better conditions on the Canadian farm, every force in Europe, which requires to purchase our products. . . . Our wheats are the finest in the World, are relished by all bread eaters, and they are entitled to a fair price or they are not worth growing.

Optimism and faith were also still in control at the Central Selling Agency, where officials calculated that only 52 million bushels remained to be shipped from Argentina, compared with 180 million a year earlier. The CSA agent in Argentina, W. J. Jackman, had estimated the coming Argentine crop at 238 million bushels but revised that to 187 million when CSA headquarters cabled him that the first estimate was far too high. Meanwhile, U.S. grain magnate Julius Barnes told a Senate committee he had only one criticism of the CSA — that it had been undermining buyers' confidence by selling wheat below Winnipeg Exchange prices.[17] Despite such prestigious but misguided advice, McPhail's concerns were growing. "There appears to be every reason to believe that our wheat is needed but still the foreigner does not buy," he wrote in his diary on 10 January. The CSA department was at the same time finally losing its confidence, noting that lack of sales was preventing the pools from reducing debt and making a final payment of the 1928 crop: "we cannot maintain the present position indefinitely and if buyers do not meet us we must give consideration to a change of policy." The department's advice, however, was weakened when it added that large sales on the high-priced Winnipeg market would demoralize it and all other markets, as well as possibly leading U.S. authorities to abandon their new price support policies. With so much at stake, the department said, the CSA should await reports from a committee being sent to investigate European conditions firsthand: "the situation is exceedingly difficult and puzzling."

Two days after that mournful estimate of the situation, Canadian newspapers printed an upbeat special article by J. F. B. Livesay, general manager of Canadian Press:

> the wheat pool is run by hard-headed canny Scots who know the business through and through and whose policy has the approval of the banks and financial houses as well as their own membership. It begins to look as though they were right for a world wheat shortage is now admitted and the wheat holdings of the pool are no more today than they were just a year ago.[18]

But there were many hostile voices to offset that sympathetic assessment. In the U.S., *Barron's* magazine condemned the pools for "this most audacious and most gigantic speculation in the history of the grain trade."[19] An even harsher verdict came from Winnipeg mayor Ralph Webb, who told a Winnipeg conference on unemployment that the fast-growing problem was due to pool actions:

> Hundreds of thousands of men have been laid off by the railways as a result of the pool's holding policy. . . .
> The real unemployment trouble started this year when the agricultural interests began to dictate to the Old Country buyers what they should be paid for their wheat. The result is that the growers have not yet been paid for their 1928 crop, nor the 1929 crop, and that has been responsible for the unemployment this year, much more than the New York stock crash.[20]

More threatening comments came 29 January 1930, when a Central Sales Agency delegation consulted the chairman of the bank committee dealing with the pools, seeking assurance that the banks would not "embarrass the Pool" by demanding rapid sale of wheat stocks if prices declined further. The banker, S. L. Cork, noted that the pools had agreed with the banks to keep a fifteen-percent margin between the level of payments to growers and current wheat prices. If wheat prices fell to within fifteen percent of initial prices being paid to farmers, the banks would indeed want liquidation of wheat stocks.[21] CSA officials interpreted that as an ultimatum — though more senior bank officials later denied any intention to issue an ultimatum — and were thus alarmed when coincidental developments threatened to drive wheat prices down further. Several provincial governments had seized the accounts of certain grain brokerage firms, prompting speculation that those firms' clients would soon have to dump large amounts of wheat futures onto an already-weak market. To restore confidence among the banks and the public, the government investigators released the accounts of such clients, enabling them to maintain their futures by keeping up margin payments, while the three prairie provincial governments declared that they would guarantee the pools' fifteen-percent margin. The rapid governmental action avoided the possibility of the pools' being forced to unload large amounts of wheat — and once again the increasingly inevitable price collapse was deferred. A statement issued by the Central Selling Agency on 7 February explained the situation, denied that there was any occasion for alarm and declared that there was "not the remotest likelihood" of the pools' wheat being sold for an average price less than the one dollar initial payment to farmers. The president of the Canadian Bankers' Association declared the same day that continued orderly marketing of pool wheat stocks was assured.[22]

During the hectic period of bank consultation and government guarantees, McPhail had since mid-January been on an intensive thirty-eight-day European tour, piling up evidence that a change in sales strategy and attitudes was imperative. He took time to assure a committee of the Empire Parliamentary Association that the pools were not trying to fix high prices, although at times they could "have a steadying and stabilizing influence on the market by not pressing when there is no demand."[23] In private cables during the next few days, however, he made it clear that this was not the time to avoid pressing sales. Saying that there was no indication of European demand picking up, he urged the CSA to sell on all markets near $1.25 — then amended that the next day to urge sales "at this or lower levels."[24] About the same time, CSA treasurer R. C. Findlay was sounding the alarm in Winnipeg,

Central Selling Agency directors, June 1927. Seated, left to right: Colin H. Burnell of Manitoba Wheat Pool; A. J. McPhail of Saskatchewan Wheat Pool; Henry Wise Wood of Alberta Wheat Pool. Standing, from left: R. A. McPherson of Alberta; W. G. A. Gourlay of Manitoba; Stuart Gellie of Manitoba; E. B. Ramsay of Saskatchewan; C. Jensen of Alberta. R. S. Dundas of Saskatchewan is absent. (SWP files, photo by Robson Studio, Winnipeg)

stating in one memo: "each time we 'stabilize' prices we defeat our own object since the apparent reason for the lack of sales is that the consumer says the prices are too high for him."[25] Advances in European milling practices, Findlay noted, meant they need a smaller percentage of high-quality Canadian wheat and thus Canada's bargaining power has declined.

McPhail, meanwhile, had come close to salvaging part of the situation when he worked out a tentative plan with British cabinet minister J. H. Thomas to trade Canadian wheat for British coal.[26] That plan, however, foundered within days when Nova Scotia coal interests let it be known they would undersell any British coal sent to Canada. Despite that frustrating failure, McPhail did succeed with British officials' help in disproving erroneous reports that some British bakers were proudly advertising they did not use Canadian wheat or flour — it turned out that the rumors started when some British bakers advertised that they were not using cheap flour from outside the Empire that was hurting British farmers' prices.

On his return to Winnipeg, McPhail was mildly depressed to find some fellow CSA directors still willing to hold wheat and believing that the pessimism in McPhail's cables was the result of the pessimistic German mood:

> Some of them did not realize that I am not much influenced by any atmosphere. I have never been unduly influenced by the market going either up or down. I have always said sell wheat, especially if it is going up. They were still prepared to take a stand that conditions would not justify wheat going below a certain level. If we were to do so and acted accordingly, the net result might easily be to simply load ourselves up with more wheat.[27]

McPhail's fears began coming true on 12 March 1930, when the Central Selling Agency board again tried buying wheat. By one perspective, it seemed to be another straightforward case of correcting an abnormally weak market — Winnipeg Exchange prices had dropped to seven cents under Chicago prices instead of the usual level of three to four cents above Chicago. The trouble for the pools was that both Chicago and Winnipeg prices were still above what customers wanted to pay.

Initially, the pools' price-support activities seemed to work well. The CSA was careful to advise the new U.S. Farm Loan Board of its strategy. In a 15 March meeting between McPhail and U.S. board chairman Alexander Legge, the two leaders tentatively discussed co-operation in restricting sales and in encouraging reductions in North American wheat acreage.[28] Finally, it seemed, the old hope of coordinated U.S.-Canadian selling strategies was in sight. The prospect did not go unnoticed in Britain, where the London *Daily Herald* on 20 March 1930 published an article on how "one of the most ruthless world wars in commercial history" was being fought, with the National Association of British Millers fighting "the price-fixing attempts of the American and Canadian Pools." In major speeches in Regina and Winnipeg, McPhail sought to explain the pools' position, saying they would have just touched off a disastrous price war and market collapse if they had tried to match Argentina's low prices.

McPhail's efforts, however, were offset by surprising and unpleasant news reports from California, where Aaron Sapiro told a university audience that the Canadian pools were guilty of speculation.[29] Sapiro, who had recently been rebuffed when his agents tried to act as go-betweens in contacts with the pools and U.S. Farm Loan Board, said the pools should have lowered prices ten to fifteen cents a bushel if necessary to sell more wheat. It was a radical shift for a man who had been the champion of those who had felt the pools could prop up prices and perhaps even control prices. Even more ironically, the same day Sapiro's charges were being published, the long-critical *Manitoba Free Press* jumped to the pools' defence, declaring the pools to be victims of "a campaign of innuendo, calumny, mendacity and bluff" throughout the world. If the pools had dumped wheat, the *Free Press* said, prices would have plummeted to the unthinkable seventy-cent level.

Meanwhile, McPhail was continuing his battle against the Central Selling Agency's sometimes ostrich-like attitudes. In a report to the CSA board, 10 April 1930, he noted that when the CSA decided to support wheat prices by refusing to make sales offers for short periods, the agency carried the no-sales policy to the extreme of turning away buyers who were approaching the agency.[30] The board of the English Co-op Wholesale Society, he said, "have been very greatly irritated at different times when they wanted to buy wheat and we refused to offer or sell." The CSA, McPhail added, had also been blind to developing conditions in Europe — a reference to declining demand there for wheat imports — and should have sent observers sooner.

By 8 May 1930, McPhail felt he had finally converted the rest of the CSA board to his views: "They are all convinced at last that our greatest problem is to *sell* our wheat and have given up all idea of sticking for a certain price."[31] Markets continued to decline, but the pools were launched at last on an aggressive sales policy. For many farmers, the first real impact of changed world market conditions came on 10 July 1930 when the pools decided on initial payments of only seventy cents a bushel for wheat — and twenty-five for barley, thirty for oats and thirty-five for rye. The Exchange cash price that day was only ninety-five cents for wheat, but in the minds of farmers like those who threw eggs at one Saskatchewan Pool delegate, that was no excuse for the pools' price.[32] But worse was to come — the seventy-cent price was barely in effect before it was cut to sixty cents, largely because of pressure from CSA treasurer R. C. Findlay, who threatened to resign if any higher figure was chosen.[33]

Then, on 31 July, the pools got their real taste of the unpleasant surprises that could come from the banks with which they had done business for six years. In late afternoon, CSA officials were summoned to a meeting to be told that no more money would be forthcoming from the banks.[34] Provincial guarantees covering the 1929-30 crop pool were to expire at midnight that night and the banks had decided that the guarantees did not clearly include all the grain that had been delivered into the 1929-30 pool but not yet moved to terminal elevators. By 10:00 P.M., however, the banks relented — credit would be continued if they could have the additional security of warehouse receipts for grain transferred to them, by midnight. Frantically, pool and CSA officials got to work, delivering receipts to bankers in Calgary, Regina and Winnipeg.

The first day of August and the new crop year dawned with a weary "Canadian Wheat Pool" still staving off bankruptcy and carrying 64.6 million bushels of old-crop wheat. That carryover, however, was only 50.9 percent of the total Canadian carryover and the pools had handled 51.2 percent of Canadian wheat deliveries. This time, the pools were proportionately no more responsible for the carryover than the private grain trade. But they were still in a shaky financial position and had to call in the three prairie premiers to help them negotiate new arrangements with the banks in the first days of August. The urgency and informality of the situation was illustrated in Alberta Premier Brownlee's recollection of one expedition with McPhail and Manitoba Premier Bracken:

> I will never forget my wife and I had made all plans to go east for a holiday and to spend the time going around to the various homes that we both knew as Ontario people and we landed in Winnipeg and were going to stay off a day there. And as I stepped off the train there was Mr. McPhail and Mr. Bracken waiting for me with the news that after two days they weren't going to honor any more checks. So, instead of being able to do what I wanted to that day, I went right up

with Bracken to his office, got on the long distance with the banks in Toronto and Montreal and finally got them to postpone action until we could get down there and Bracken put on his best bib and tucker along with myself and we went down together and for a solid month instead of having a holiday I was back and forth between Toronto and Montreal working out that problem of the pool indebtedness.[35]

But there was a limit to how far even provincial governments could go, with weak wheat prices making it clearer every day that the pools would take a substantial loss when they finally sold the wheat left over from the 1929-30 pool, and that they could even have trouble covering the initial payment on the 1930-31 pool. Within hours of R. B. Bennett's new government being sworn in, the three premiers and McPhail were in the prime minister's Ottawa office, seeking federal guarantees. Meetings continued for a week without success, as Bennett believed the provinces and banks could handle the problem by themselves. Complex negotiations between the pools and the banks dragged on from 16 to 25 August. A new agreement signed on the 26th provided for some continued provincial quarantees, bank financing for the 60-cent initial payment, a fifteen percent margin to be maintained between the initial payment and current wheat prices, and current sales to be divided fifty-fifty between the new crop and the old crop that had been guaranteed by the provinces. McPhail had been highly suspicious when the banks at one point suggested the initial payment be 70 cents, with a twenty percent margin to be kept between that and current wheat prices. Wheat was then selling for about 90 cents and if it fell to less than 85 the pools' margin would be inadequate, leaving the pools again subject to new bank conditions. McPhail wrote:

> Several things have happened which would indicate a conspiracy in high quarters to manoeuvre the pool into a position where it would no longer be a free agent and where, in fact, it would be completely at the mercy of the banks. I do not know that the banks themselves are a part of this. We do know that a number of them are quite indifferent to say the least about the welfare of the pool.[36]

After a relatively quiet September, Winnipeg cash prices lurched down to about 72 cents in mid-October, forcing the pools to reduce their initial payment to 55 cents. Within a month, Winnipeg prices were at 68 cents and the initial payment had to be cut further, to 50 cents — but the pools had been buying wheat for two months at 60 cents and for a month at 55.

The final phase of the long nightmare began about 14 November, when McPhail noted in his diary: "Everything is tottering." The market fell again, requiring the Central Selling Agency to provide another $211,000 to the Grain Exchange as a deposit on seven million bushels of wheat futures that the CSA had held. Because the CSA was two hours late with the cheque, a delay that sparked fears for its financial viability, the Exchange called for another $350,000. From midnight to 1:30 A.M. that night, pool officials, bankers and premiers conferred. With a new provincial guarantee, the banks finally agreed to finance deposits on the futures position for a few more days — but McPhail also had to sign an agreement to appoint someone acceptable to the banks to the position of CSA general manager, which had been left vacant when Ramsay left to join the Board of Grain Commissioners.[37] On 15 November, when still more money was needed to maintain the futures position, the banks were given additional protection through an agreement to allocate all cash sales for a month to the 1930 crop that the banks were financing, rather than the 1929 crop that the provinces had guaranteed.

Although bank officials in Winnipeg were satisfied for the moment, their eastern head offices were getting increasingly nervous, calling for an end to financing futures and for a $10-million federal guarantee. Wearily, McPhail and the three premiers went straight from the Winnipeg talks onto the train east. McPhail noted: "I never went on a trip so reluctantly. I was tired to death."[38] In the east, the delegation found Ottawa reluctant to intervene and the banks talking of taking over all the pools' wheat and selling it quickly. Private grain firms, McPhail heard, were already volunteering to sell the wheat for the banks: "The vultures are gathering."[39] From talks with grain traders, the banks were coming to the conclusion that European prejudice against Canadian wheat could be removed as soon as the Central Selling Agency of the pools was out of business. McPhail made little impression when he argued that "there was no mysterious manner by which the wheat could be sold and there would not be a demand for one bu. more or one bu. less whether the pool was in business or not."[40]

Central Selling Agency

Prime Minister Bennett, who was at a London conference throughout this crisis, was finally persuaded to wire approval for Ottawa to guarantee half of any bank loss up to $10 million. Perhaps of even greater importance for the banks was McPhail's reluctant decision to accept veteran grain trader John I. McFarland as CSA general manager:

The Bankers are not particulary interested in anything pool officials have to say. They are only interested just now in anything that will help to get the Federal Gov't to protect them against loss. Hence the reason they are so set on McFarland becoming G.M. They know he is one of, if not the most intimate friend of, Bennett's and that if he can be got into the pool it will probably do more than anything else to get the Dominion Gov't to do something.[41]

Even before McFarland's appointment, McPhail had lamented having to appoint him — "It is gall and wormwood to have to do as you are told by a bunch of bankers who are quite ignorant of the biz."[42] When McFarland's first major action as general manager was to close all CSA offices abroad and revert to the system of selling through private intermediaries, McPhail became even more irate, accusing McFarland of becoming a dictator. Neither the pools nor McPhail, however, had any rational alternative to accepting McFarland's decisions — he was the only figure standing between the pools and bankruptcy.

Within a few years McFarland would be a hero to most farmers in the pool movement, just as he would be proved right in his 29 November 1930 public statement that declared: "The only possible permanent solution of the depression in the world wheat situation is a proportionate reduction of acreage by all wheat producing countries." But, for the moment, McFarland was distrusted by many pool leaders and his call for production cuts was widely attacked.

The pools' Central Selling Agency, meanwhile, had ceased to be under the pools' control and was virtually a government agency. Pool leaders were left in the dark as McFarland consulted with Bennett in December 1930 and had to be content with Bennett's general assurance that CSA wheat stocks would be marketed in an orderly fashion instead of being dumped at low prices. Influential friends of Bennett like CPR president Edward Beatty were calling for federal aid to the West, including federal responsibility for selling the 1929 and 1930 crops. To deny government financing for orderly marketing, moreover, would have been politically disastrous. Even with Bennett's 22 December assurance of orderly marketing, prices for top-quality wheat fell to a heart-breaking 50 cents a bushel four days later, a record low. After Bennett reaffirmed federal guarantees that wheat stocks would not be forcibly liquidated, prices recovered only to 53.5 cents by year-end.

As far as the Central Selling Agency was concerned, the year 1931 became simply a matter of cleaning up loose ends and going out of business. The ill-advised 1930 purchases of wheat futures were closed out, with a final loss of more than $2 million — almost double the profits made in 1925 and 1929 through similar price-support attempts. Banks made it clear they would never again finance any organization carrying 100 million bushels of unhedged wheat.[43] Alberta Wheat Pool became the first formally to write off the CSA, sending official notice in March of its intention to withdraw from its contract to provide wheat to the CSA. The Alberta withdrawal, of course, made no real difference by then; but it was the occasion for further Alberta-Saskatchewan irritation. Alberta Pool president H. W. Wood said the Saskatchewan Pool board consisted of "too many agitators who were inclined to chase rabbits." McPhail, on the other hand, wrote in his diary 29 March 1931 that Alberta's withdrawal was a disappointment but no surprise: "Alberta and especially Wood is extremely provincial-minded. They have no vision and do not see much beyond the boundaries of Alberta."[44]

On 12 June, the CSA board decided to dismiss all CSA employees — "a very disheartening business," McPhail wrote. As far as certain British politicians and grain traders were concerned, the story of the Canadian Wheat Pool was over. As one told the press after a North American tour: "I take it that it is the last time in the lifetime of any present Canadian that any attempt will be made to form a wheat pool, or for the Government to interfere in any way with the normal supply and demand of wheat."[45]

There were, however, a few significant lingering traces of the once-proud Central Selling Agency. Although its pooling function was over and that informal title was no longer applicable, although it had virtually no employees, it remained in existence as a legal entity, Canadian Co-operative Wheat Producers Ltd. Under McFarland that paper corporation would in effect be a powerful government agency, the precursor of the wheat board. And later, when control of CCWP returned to the prairie pools, it would be a useful vehicle for their co-operation.

In the meantime, the three pools went their separate ways, basically becoming elevator companies who bought wheat from farmers and sold it immediately in the form of futures on the Exchange to avoid the risk of carrying unsold wheat.[46] Saskatchewan Wheat Pool continued some small-scale pooling for those members who were able and willing to take the tiny initial payments that were possible, but that was a minor percentage of Pool business. Pool members were freed from their contractual obligations to deliver wheat for sale on a pooling basis and the vast majority sold their wheat for immediate cash. With their elevator assets pledged to the hilt as security for 1929-30 pooling debts, the pools began to grope for ways to pay off those debts in the middle of economic depression.

As the tragedy of the Central Selling Agency unfolded in 1930 and 1931, Saskatchewan Wheat Pool had simultaneously been involved in the dramatic resolution of the campaign for a 100 percent compulsory pool. That campaign was revitalized in the spring of 1930, when United Farmers policy was changed to call for full membership rights in the proposed compulsory pool for those who would be forced by law to join it. To McPhail that change made the plan "much more palatable and feasible" than the previous proposal to deny such conscripted members a vote, but he maintained his opposition to compulsion.[47] That opposition put McPhail in a delicate position, since the majority of his fellow Pool delegates in the district were in favor of compulsion.[48] If those delegates had not continued to elect McPhail as a director, the Pool would have had a new president and McPhail would have been unavailable to act as chairman of the Central Selling Agency, since he would not be a Pool director. That in turn would probably have meant less CSA effort to sell wheat, much greater resulting losses, and perhaps even losses big enough to drag the provincial pools down with the CSA. The restraint and common sense of a handful of Pool delegates may thus have avoided an even greater disaster.

Meanwhile, it became clear that the United Farmers policy change had won over a majority of Pool delegates and members.

Sharks cartoon, 1930. (SWP files)

At the June 1930 general meeting, delegates resolved to poll the membership on the issue, with a favorable vote committing the Pool to push for a compulsory pool for all Saskatchewan grain. The compulsory pool would be created provided that two-thirds of all grain growers in the province voted in favor of it, the pool would be entirely under farmer control, and all farmers would have an equal voice in its operations. Almost 59 percent of Pool members returned ballots, with 71 percent of those ballots supporting the proposal and thus setting the stage for the proposed province-wide vote. McPhail continued to worry that the compulsion campaign would alienate farmers and hurt the Pool's next contract-signing campaign, but in accordance with member desires the Pool executive asked the provincial government for the necessary legislation. Within a few months the Saskatchewan government was organizing a referendum to see whether the idea had two-thirds support and various anti-compulsion organizations had sprung up to enter the referendum campaign. Amid charges that compulsion would be communistic, the campaign began. McPhail's fears were confirmed when anti-compulsion leaflets took aim at the Pool itself:

> The Wheat Pool has unlimited resources and does not hesitate to utilize every possible means to spread propaganda throughout Saskatchewan. . . . Despite the Depression and their bankrupt condition they are spending the farmers' money like drunken sailors to force the rest of the agriculturalists to come under their dominion.[49]

Among other problems the Saskatchewan Pool leaders had to contend with the well-publicized anti-compulsion views of Alberta Pool leader H. W. Wood. In an attempt to gloss over their differences, McPhail wrote to Wood in March, expressing concern over the use of Wood's name in anti-compulsion propaganda and asking whether Pool spokesmen could tell people that Wood's opposition was to the earlier compulsion proposal, not the latest one. That drew a rebuke from Wood, who said he had no interest in anything but voluntary pooling: "the only advice I can give you is to go straight ahead in meeting your problems and responsibilities just as frankly as you would if the name were a blank. . . . That is the only thing I can advise you to do, because it is the only thing you have a right to do."[50]

For once, the moralistic McPhail had been out-moralized. Still smarting from that chastisement, McPhail also had to cope with renouncing the principles of voluntary pooling that he had so long defended. On 4 April 1931 he issued a circular proclaiming his total support for compulsory pooling, saying that the current proposal "differs entirely in principle" from the previous year's plan, which would have denied all farmers an equal voice. McPhail's conversion, however, was not as sudden as it may have appeared in public. In a 2 July 1930 letter to D. L. Smith he noted he still opposed compulsion but felt "The really vicious principles in the former proposal are eliminated."[51] McPhail's change of mind, however, may not have come solely from the desire to maintain unity within the Pool and to implement majority decisions. He had by this time had bitter experience with trying to operate a pool that had only half Canada's wheat, and he noted in the circular that a 100 percent pool would make it easier for Canada to co-operate with similar control bodies in other countries.

Among other Pool spokesmen that April, director J. H. Wesson was prominent in declaring his support for compulsion: "The whole structure of our civilization is built upon democracy. That simply means the conversion of a large majority of the people to an idea and then compelling a minority to agree to that idea through legislation."[52]

Meanwhile, Aaron Sapiro, who had offered money to one Regina newspaper writer the previous year to write pro-compulsion propaganda,[53] contributed a statement in which he said a 100 percent Canadian pool was necessary for co-operation with other wheat-exporting nations. So strongly did he support the 100 percent idea, Sapiro said, that he would favor it even if he knew that archfoe McPhail would head the compulsory pool. To R.B. Evans he commented: "I do not think much of McPhail. He is honest but wholly lacks constructive imagination and the ability to do strong bold things for the farmers when crises require such action."[54]

The whole campaign, however, suddenly became academic on 27 April 1931 when the Saskatchewan Court of Appeal ruled that it was beyond the powers of a provincial government to set up a compulsory pool. The Saskatchewan government saw no grounds on which to appeal the decision and the Pool's plans to appeal were thwarted by a disaffected member, W. A. Scott of Salvador. Scott, who had been sued by the Pool for breach of contract, went to the courts and got an injunction preventing the Pool from spending members' money on either a pro-compulsion campaign or on an appeal of the 27 April decision. Suddenly the whole compulsion campaign was over, before Saskatchewan farmers could vote on it.[55]

Prairie premiers, pool leaders and other farm representatives met in Regina, 4 May 1931, to assess the situation. They decided unanimously — including even the leaders of anti-compulsion groups — that the next step was to press Ottawa for a wheat board.[56] As McPhail reported in a radio speech the next day, they agreed "no arrangement short of one organization with control over the sale of all the wheat in Canada can give reasonable hope of being able to cope with present day world-wide marketing conditions."[57] Prime Minister Bennett, however, told the premiers that legal and other difficulties ruled out a wheat board. Briefly, the three pools considered a plan to hedge and sell wheat through their central agency, using it more or less as a trading corporation instead of as a wheat pool, but the idea was shot down by McFarland. In McPhail's words: "He lost his temper completely and was quite insulting, using the terms subterfuge, impractical, it won't work, childish, trying to hide your real purpose behind a screen."[58]

The dream of a Canadian wheat pool, owned and controlled by the farmers it served, was dead. In its place came an 11 August statement by the three prairie premiers, announcing that the three pool organizations will "function in exactly the same manner as privately owned enterprises" except for some small-scale pooling — with a safe initial payment of only 35 cents a bushel for No. 1 wheat entering the pools. Even that pitiful initial payment was not considered risk-free, McPhail noted: "As usual the banks want to get their hands on all the security they can think of. They would want our souls if they were worth anything."[59] The Saskatchewan government also felt constrained to supervise and restrict the Pool's capital spending and dividend payments, to protect the government's loans. An era had ended, and with it also ended the 47-year life of Alexander James McPhail. When he died on 21 October 1931,[60] after seven years of heading one of Canada's largest businesses, he left an estate that provided only $400 a year to his widow and child.[61] But, even amid the failure of wheat pooling, he also left behind him an example of determination and dedication. In thousands of farm homes, they read and approved the minister's comments at McPhail's funeral: "He took upon his own shoulders the burdens and problems of the farmers of these prairies, and the load was too great. Like our Lord, he would save others, himself he could not save."[62]

Meanwhile, when all the accountants' ink had dried, Saskatchewan Wheat Pool was burdened with a $13.3 million debt, its share of the Central Selling Agency's total $22.1 million loss. One of the few consolations for the pools was that their loss was a temporary gain for the farmers of 1929-30, since the bulk of the loss came from overpaying the farmers. Except for about $2 million lost in futures trading, pool members in effect borrowed the money from their future. But that consideration did little to deter economic and political arguments over whether the pools were to blame for their and Canada's misfortunes, nor did it stop the search for lessons to be learned from the collapse of pooling.

One of the basic lessons, which McPhail and others knew from the start, was the futility of trying to control world market prices. Contemporary writers made much of the fact that the pools "controlled" a tenth of world wheat trade — half of Canada's one-fifth share — and could thus influence prices. But that "control" was an illusion, since it could only be exercised by not offering wheat for sale. Unless supplies were extraordinarily tight, such a holdback would simply allow foreign and domestic competitors to take over more of the market, reducing the pools' share far below a tenth. Temporary price-support actions could smooth out sudden and artificial price drops, but any long run of high prices would encourage both excess production and a consumer switch to other foods. A government could use legislation to set prices for wheat consumed domestically, and international agreements between governments could in theory control prices, but it was clearly shown that a private organization should not hope to succeed in such ambitious tasks.

A second historical lesson, one that received less publicity than the dramatic collapse of pooling, was that the private organizations and individuals trading on the Winnipeg Grain Exchange did no better, collectively, than the pools. Virtually every criticism of the pools' pricing and selling decisions applied with equal or greater force to the rest of the Canadian grain trade. At the end of the crucial 1929-30 crop year, the pools held no more than their proportionate share of the Canadian wheat carryover, indicating that they were no slower to move the wheat overseas than was the rest of the trade. One of the most important obstacles to selling Canadian wheat, in fact, was the high level of speculative prices on the Winnipeg Exchange. The contemporary verdict of Stanford University's food research institute was that pool and non-pool organizations alike over-estimated Europe's need for wheat imports:

> In the sense that the maintenance of high prices in the face of unusually slow movement of wheat may be regarded as a holding policy, there was a holding policy participated in by practically all factors trading in Canadian wheat, but most significantly by traders in Winnipeg wheat futures.[63]

But to say that the pools did no worse than the rest of the trade is far from praise. There were many occasions when they could have sold more wheat and, in retrospect, it is evident that their last major venture in buying wheat futures to support the market was unwise. The most controversial and important question about the pools' actions, however, is whether they were negligent in not exercising their power to lower the high Winnipeg prices. Just as they had the power to block an attempt in 1925 artificially to lower prices, in 1929-30 they had the power to end artificially-high prices. There were many understandable reasons for not taking such action — not least of them the natural reluctance of farmers, elected by other farmers to represent farmers' interests, to take action to lower wheat prices. Those leaders who took such action would risk being defeated in elections and the pools themselves would risk mass defections by disgruntled members. Yet the pools had had clear warnings that such action might be necessary. Back in July 1927, Alberta Premier J. E. Brownlee toured Europe on behalf of the Central Selling Agency and reported that the pools could have made more sales if they lowered their prices five or six cents. Instead, Brownlee felt, the pools' CSA was relying too much on Exchange prices:

> No object can be gained by allowing high prices to be established on the Exchange, if wheat cannot be sold at that price. . . .
> Should the Winnipeg Grain Exchange, as it has done in the last two years, force prices beyond a proper export level, the Pool should force sales on the Exchange, either benefitting by the high price or forcing the price to a proper level.[64]

Salesmen D. R. McIntyre and George McIvor made similar comments before the disaster,[65] while people like Saskatchewan Pool director J. H. Wesson and CSA treasurer R. C. Findlay said in retrospect that the selling agency made a mistake in not selling futures in August 1929 to cover the coming crop.[66] An economic historian has said such strategy would not have left the grain trade as a whole any better off, but the pool could "have confounded its most bitter critics by leaving them holding the unwanted baby."[67]

But even if such action had been humanly possible, even if the farmer-directors of the pools could have been so unquestioningly certain of coming lower prices that they could have initiated the price drop themselves — the action might have been largely futile anyway. Winnipeg Exchange prices would have rapidly dropped if the pools began selling large volumes of wheat on the futures market, so only limited gains would have been possible there. The only hope remaining would be that the new lower prices would result in substantially more export sales. That would be an unlikely hope, in view of Argentina's clear determination to sell its wheat at any price. In a period of surplus world production, the pools simply could not match Argentina in a price war. The unorganized Argentine farmers could be made to endure far lower standards of living than their Canadian counterparts and Argentina had traditionally rushed all its wheat to market since it lacked extensive storage facilities. Much Argentine wheat, in fact, was not sold on the Liverpool Exchange until it had already been put on ships bound for Britain, a practice that removed much of the sellers' bargaining power.

Nor was Argentina the only obstacle to Canadian sales. The Soviet Union exported only 5.7 million bushels of wheat in 1929-30, but then squeezed its granaries dry to raise money in 1930-31 by exporting 92.5 million bushels, at prices as much as 15 cents a bushel less than even No. 3 Canadian wheat. Meanwhile, Canadian wheat could not even compete effectively with that grown in western Europe, since several major consuming nations imposed tariffs that amounted to as much as $1.62 a bushel on imported wheat. The initial, moderate tariffs may or may not have been a reaction to high wheat prices in the mid-1920s — one pool salesman thought they were[68] — but the later, higher tariffs seemed clearly designed to protect European farmers against an inflow of cheap wheat. In any case, the expanded domestic European production, sheltered behind tariffs, slashed Canadian market opportunities even more surely than did Argentina's fire-sale prices.

One theoretical solution to that problem of protectionism was to find a sheltered market for Canadian wheat — in other words, the "Imperial Preference" concept of having Britain set up tariff barriers to commodities from outside the Empire — or Commonwealth, as it would shortly be known. McPhail, in effect, tried unsuccessfully to promote such arrangements with his Canadian-wheat-for-British-coal idea. But there were insuperable obstacles in the way of Imperial Preference: deep-rooted British reluctance to put duties on food imports; the unwillingness of Canada and other former colonies to buy massive amounts of British goods in exchange; and British reluctance to offend non-Empire countries like Argentina. There were almost as many miles of British-owned railways in Argentina as in Britain itself, with equipment supplied from Britain — a lucrative connection that one British diplomat said outweighed any advantages in Imperial Preference: "if we blindly put a duty on foreign foodstuffs we shall do grave injury to these gigantic British interests in Argentina, reduce the dividends of thousands of British shareholders, and put British workmen out of work just when we most particularly want to employ them."[69] The increasingly centralized British milling industry was also a powerful influence for continuing cheap wheat imports. Canadian farmers would thus find no salvation in British tariff policy, just as they would not be rescued by new Asian markets for several decades, despite some initial Central Selling Agency ventures into Asia.

For an organization trying to serve farmers by selling their wheat, the period 1929-31 was thus an impossible trap. The Central Selling Agency could have lightened its own losses by selling a few more million bushels here and there, and by not buying as many futures as it did. But that would only have hastened the arrival of 50-cent wheat, and the arrival of 50-cent wheat in any form would be fatal to pooling. Few if any farmers could afford to exist on the initial payments a pool could afford to make when wheat prices were 50 cents for top-grade wheat. If it had not collapsed so suddenly, pooling would have withered away in another year or two in any case as economic circumstances forced farmers to desert the pools in favor of sales to elevators for maximum immediate cash.

The "Canadian Wheat Pool" had to die, although wiser board decisions could have given it another year or two of life, perhaps also the chance to wind up its affairs without such crippling debts. Presumably that would have made little if any difference in prairie farmers' realization that only a universal government agency could handle pooling with security. But a lingering death for the Canadian Wheat Pool might have made a huge difference in how the national government reacted. By collapsing with mountains of both unsold wheat and bank debts, the Canadian Wheat Pool virtually forced Ottawa to intervene and to run the former selling agency as a stabilization agency backed by massive federal financial guarantees. As later events make clear, without that involvement it is questionable whether the federal government of the 1930s could have been convinced of the need to create the Canadian Wheat Board. Even in the humiliating, near-bankrupt manner of its death, the Canadian Wheat Pool left a worthwhile legacy.

5
Depression, 1931–39

I recall in the thirties when our Fieldman, Wilson
Parker, put on picture shows at evening meetings. These
meetings were highlights for our members and their
families. On one particular occasion Wilson put on a
show at an inland school house some fifteen miles from
town. After the show, I was accompanying him in his
car, we caught up to a girl and a boy in their late teens,
walking home. Wilson asked them if they would like a
ride. They said they would with such enthusiasm that
I'm sure that was a treat for them. After we got going
again just to make conversation I asked them how they
liked the show. The girl spoke up. She said — "Oh, It
was just Wonderful". She hesitated a moment then said,
"You know that is the first picture show I have ever
seen".

I realized then and there the Pool was more than a
commercial organization.

— William McKenzie Ross.[1]

For Saskatchewan Wheat Pool, 1931 marked more than the end
of one era and the start of another. The collapse of pooling
brought an abrupt change to the activities and even the basic
purpose of the Pool. The informal title of Saskatchewan Wheat
Pool remained, but — with minor exceptions — the Pool was no
longer a pool. The formal title of "Saskatchewan Co-operative
Wheat Producers Ltd." was a more accurate name for an
organization whose major activity was operating elevators. The
nature of the Saskatchewan Wheat Pool story also changed
radically with that bleak year. Once, the Pool had been the core of
a worldwide marketing organization whose day-to-day decisions
were watched closely by businessmen in world capitals, whose
selling strategy was important enough to bring a British cabinet

minister to Winnipeg. Now, the Pool was a Saskatchewan elevator company struggling to cope with a $13-million debt. Its broad world view had shrunk as the organization concentrated on the provincial situation. The tense urgency of day-to-day decisions involving the sale of many millions of bushels of wheat had been transformed into a slower-paced evolution of policies and corporate strategies to deal with less dramatic problems.

Behind all the Pool's troubles in the 1930s lay one unspoken question: had all the farmers' effort of the 1920s been for nothing? Saskatchewan farmers had a large, farmer-owned elevator company when the Pool was formed in 1924 to sell members' wheat and give every member the average price realized. The Pool quickly swallowed up the Saskatchewan Co-operative Elevator Company and now, as a commercial organization, was little more than an elevator company itself. Why not simply have left things the way they were in 1924?

The Pool's unspoken search for an answer to that question was made amid social and economic devastation, sometimes under skies black with blowing dirt, sometimes in the midst of grasshopper plagues of Biblical proportions. The Great Depression brought poverty and heartbreak to many lands, but its effect was magnified on the prairies by simultaneous drought and crop failure. The real story of the Depression on the prairies lies in millions of individual struggles whose intensity can only be hinted at by statistics. Those statistics, however, are grim in themselves. Caught in a squeeze between poor yields and record low prices, the value of prairie wheat production went from $424 million in the 1928-29 crop year to $112 million in 1931-32. Not until the last year of World War Two did it recover fully. The all-time low price for No. 1 wheat came on 16 December 1932 — 38 cents a bushel. And that was the price at the Lakehead; farmers in northwest Saskatchewan would get only about 22 cents after transportation and handling charges were deducted. If, as was more common, the crop was No 2 feed oats, a 100-bushel wagonload might bring the farmer only $2.50 in cash. "There weren't many farm boys or girls went to University that year," George Robertson recalled later.[2]

Many farmers who had borrowed to buy equipment or land in the 1920s met disaster in the 1930s. Whereas it took 233 bushels of wheat to pay $300 in interest charges in 1927, it took 620 bushels in 1930 to pay the same amount of interest.[3] While some farmers found themselves driven off the land by financial pressure, others saw their land literally leave them. The erosion and topsoil loss of the 1930s was symbolized by the great North American dust storm of 12 May 1934, in which perhaps 300 million tons of topsoil was airborne.[4] Drought and grasshoppers were also problems that year, followed by drought, hail, frost, and stem rust the next. Year by year, the troubles piled up. Debt relief legislation may have eased the debt burden slightly, but farmers found buildings, equipment and even clothes wearing out with no money for repair or replacement. For crops, the worst year came in 1937, when wheat crops averaged 2.8 bushels an acre, a small fraction of the longterm average of 16.5 bushels. The Pool's annual report noted that rust, grasshoppers and scattered drought combined to produce "the greatest disaster which Saskatchewan farmers and their families have been called upon to face in any year since this province was first settled." The next year, 1938, looked better — until hail, rust, and insects arrived. Regina storm sewers were plugged by the "worst grasshopper blizzard within the memory of man,"[5] and farmers lost more than twenty-three percent of their expected crops to the grasshoppers and sawflies.[6] By the end of 1938, prices recovered to a still-inadequate 80 cents a bushel for No. 1 wheat.

The economic strains brought social disruptions — riots in Estevan and Regina, legions of sullen young men in relief camps, thousands of hopeless and jobless people riding freight trains. There were scattered calls for western secession from Canada,[7] but the poverty-stricken prairies were too clearly dependent on eastern charity and Ottawa's aid programs for any serious attempt to be made at secession. Politically, discontent manifested itself in the formation of the Co-operative Commonwealth Federation (CCF)

1930s drought turns farmyard into sea of sand. (SWP Collection, Saskatchewan Archives Board R-A 15,077 [1])

in Saskatchewan. With the CCF gaining more than twenty-one percent of votes in the 1938 Saskatchewan election, and the radical Social Credit party forming the Alberta government in 1935, voters were clearly ready to try new ideas.

For the nearly bankrupt Saskatchewan Wheat Pool, however, the era of bold new ventures had been replaced by an era in which mere survival as an elevator company would be tough enough. Operating expenses were slashed ruthlessly in 1931, with many jobs being eliminated and the surviving employees taking pay cuts of ten to fifteen percent. Radio broadcasts were halted, advertising was sharply curtailed, there were no Pool exhibits at Provincial fairs and no Pool calendar was printed for 1931-32. Delegates also cut their daily pay to $4 from $5, with an identical $1 reduction in the $5 maximum daily sustenance allowance. Elevator construction at new points was halted, as was the practice of holding two general meetings of delegates each year. The July 1931 general meeting was the last such meeting for almost four decades; only the formal annual meeting in November of each year was maintained. Altogether, the austerity drive reduced total net operating expenses to $403,182 from $723,171.

Despite their financial troubles, delegates appeared determined to work as a united organization. One resolution proposed by a country meeting called for the directors' resignations, but delegates at the July 1931 meeting instead gave the board a unanimous standing vote of confidence. Later that year, delegates also resolved to re-enter the export grain business as soon as possible. By 1932 the Pool was selling some grain direct to the British and Scottish co-operative wholesale societies. The amounts were token ones compared with the 1920s, and the wheat was handed over at the Lakehead instead of being handled by the Pool all the way to Britain, but Saskatchewan Wheat Pool at least demonstrated that it was not tamely surrendering to the Grain Exchange system.

With pooling virtually ended, the Pool also had to set up a new basis for membership. Directors in 1932 suggested having farmers sign a new contract, promising to market their wheat through the Pool, on a pooling basis, as soon as seventy-five percent of the wheat acreage was signed up. That proposed new contract would probably never have become operational with such a high percentage sign-up required and delegates decided to take the simpler course of enlisting new members by allowing them to buy a one-dollar share each. Those farmers who had signed the first Pool contract but not the second had their memberships reinstated, since they were still entitled to one-dollar shares from the first contract. The 82,893 signers of operative wheat contracts in 1930 were thus transformed into 105,001 shareholders by 1935.

The biggest headache, however, came in accounting for the 1929-30 overpayments. Basically the Pool was caught between two irreconcilable views: many farmers who received overpayments felt they were in no way to blame for the Pool's deficit and should not be called upon to repay the sums individually; other farmers who did not get overpayments or were not Pool members at the time of the overpayment felt they should not have to pay for the first group's excess receipts. Whichever way the Pool turned, it would risk losing actual or potential members. In 1930 general manager J. D. Read proposed that the entire overpayment be treated as a company loss and that an all-out effort be made to pay off the debt in three years.[8] Trying to collect from individuals in any way, he warned, would arouse resentment and affect their deliveries to Pool elevators.[9] If successful, his plan would have settled the issue at the cost of discouraging new members for three years — but what he could not know was that grain volumes would be so reduced by drought in coming years that the Pool's elevator revenues had no chance of paying off the debt that quickly. Delegates, in any case, rejected his advice and decided to keep the overpayments as debits to individual members' accounts. It would be impossible to launch thousands of lawsuits to make the farmers pay back the money directly — even if they had any spare cash — but, in theory, repayment would be made gradually from patronage dividends credited to the members. In the meantime, those members would not be able to benefit from the equity they had built up through elevator fund deductions or commercial reserve deductions. Interest on the overpayments, however, would be paid by the Pool as a whole.

Slowly, the Pool began to make progress in tidying up its financial obligations. One initial problem was that the $13.3 million debt guaranteed by the government was composed of two items, a $15 million loss on the 1929-30 pooling of Saskatchewan wheat and $1.7 million surplus in 1928-29 pooling. After negotiations with the banks and the government, the government guarantee was modified so that the Pool could distribute the 1928-29 surplus in August 1932. Only those farmers who had no 1929-30 overpayments actually received cash — a total of $175,000 was mailed out — while the rest had the 1928-29 surplus credited against their overpayments.

And in 1933, the Pool made its final payments on the purchase of the Saskatchewan Co-operative Elevator Company — $1.45 million to the Company's liquidator and $630,450 to the Saskatchewan government for remaining debts owed to it by the Company. In the same year the Pool managed to make its first repayment of principal in the overpayment debt — $448,086 — as well as an interest payment of $680,502. And fifteen country elevators were bought from UGG for $110,000. The Pool was finally able to stand on its own feet, dispensing in 1933 with the government guarantees that had been necessary for its elevator subsidiary to get bank credit in the previous two years. Another milestone was reached in April 1936, when final payments were made on the 1930-31 pool. McFarland's lengthy stabilization operations, using unsold wheat from the 1930 crop, had finally ended when the Canadian Wheat Board was formed in 1935 and the wheat transferred to it at an arbitrary price that permitted equalization of payments to farmers. Those who received that first initial price of 60 cents a bushel in 1930 got nothing extra, but those who delivered wheat for later and lower initial payments received final payments that boosted their return to 60 cents also.

The only problem with the Pool's progress in repaying the debt left from the 1929-30 repayment was that it was too slow. Pool leaders had originally hoped to repay the debt in six to ten years, but by 1938 it was clear that grainhandling volumes were too low to permit that and the full twenty-year repayment term provided for in agreements with the provincial government would probably have to be used. Treasurer William Riddel advised delegates that the long time needed for repayment would mean that many 1929 farmers would retire from farming, cease delivering grain to Pool elevators, and thus never be able to redeem their liability and restore the value of their share of the elevator reserve fund.[10] Those farmers whose equity in the elevator reserve was higher than their overpayment liability were also barred from realizing any of the net benefit. Throughout 1931-38 the Pool received almost daily requests for full or partial refunds of the elevator and commercial reserves, sometimes from farmers who needed the money for food or medical attention.[11] But the equity held by older farmers could not be transferred to new ones so long as overpayments remained outstanding to the older farmers. The result of all this, Riddel said, was that many farmers felt they had no real stake left in the Pool "and have lost all desire to improve their position by active participation in patronizing the facilities of the Organization." Also, many farmers continued to firmly believe they should not have any liability for 1929-30 overpayments since 1929-30 open market prices were generally higher than the amounts they received from the Pool: "whether or not it can be overcome, the fact remains that some of these growers are refusing on these grounds and will continue in their refusal to give their fullest patronage and support to the Company."

Finally, on the first day of August 1938, the 1929-30 overpayment became a company liability. The indebtedness of individual members was only partially paid by erasing their credits for elevator patronage dividends they had earned before 1 August 1938. In the vast majority of cases the accumulated dividends were far short of the individual liabilities. The collective shortfall, about $10 million, was left to be borne by the Pool as a whole, but that would in large part have happened anyway since many of those members would be unable or unwilling to make further repayments. Thus, almost a decade after the disastrous overpayment was made, Pool members' slates were finally wiped clean. The Pool as a whole would continue making repayment for almost another decade, but individual members could once more watch their equity grow through patronage dividends, occasionally enjoy some dividends paid in cash, and more easily realize that equity when they retired. With the resolution of this frustrating accounting problem, many alienated members began returning to Pool elevators and the Pool could concentrate on building a more vigorous membership base. The long overpayment headache was over, even though the financial burden remained.

Among other adjustments in the 1930s, the Pool had to learn to co-operate with private elevator companies, and they with it. The transition was difficult for both parties, but especially for the farmer-owned pool, which in 1932 found itself in the awkward position of urging the private companies to give farmers worse grades. That came at a Swift Current conference of fourteen elevator companies, called by the Pool to discuss recent aggressive competition for the province's declining grain volumes.[12] Some private companies had been overgrading to get more business and the Pool had retaliated by offering more than the elevator companies' daily list of prices for the various grades. The conference agreed unanimously to end both overgrading and overlist pricing. After the conference, the Pool worked to enforce the agreement, sending protest telegrams to other companies when it heard instances of overgrading or too little allowance for dockage. Clearly the days of war between the pools and the private sector were over. Under pressure from delegates' resolutions, however, Pool directors and managers swung back to a more aggressive and independent policy in seeking deliveries to their elevators, although still avoiding cut-throat competition. A 1937 Pool bylaw provided that farmers who delivered grain to non-Pool elevators when a Pool elevator was available to them would not be eligible to be delegates or directors.[13] The more assertive approach seemingly had some effect in stabilizing Pool elevators' share of the Saskatchewan wheat crop — from handling nearly 46 percent of the province's wheat in 1930-31, the Pool elevator system declined to just under 41 percent in 1931-32, then rose to hover above 43 percent for the next few years. With widespread crop failure in areas where Pool elevators were particularly dominant, only 894 out of the Pool's 1,068 country elevators had actually been in operation in 1931-32, but virtually all were active in the next year. The 43 percent share of grainhandling was considerably less than the Pool's potential, since Pool members at this time produced 68 percent of the province's grain. The Pool, however, had only a third of the number of elevators in the province and only 36 percent of elevator capacity. With above-average handlings in relation to its number and capacity of elevators, the Pool was able to undertake modest expansion, growing to a system of 1,085 elevators in 1936 serving 91.6 percent of Saskatchewan delivery points. Meanwhile, terminal operations were trimmed by leasing the Buffalo, N.Y., terminal to Cargill Grain Company in 1933 and by giving up Pool Terminal No. 8 at the Lakehead, which had been leased from the CPR. The near-total crop failure of 1937 hit the Pool system hard, slashing volume to less than a quarter of a normal year and producing a $1.3 million loss. For both 1936-37 and 1937-38, the Pool was unable to allow anything for depreciation on its elevator system. The last year of peacetime saw the Pool struggle back to net earnings of $4,947 on the elevator and terminal system, with provision for token depreciation of one percent.

All these financial troubles and administrative headaches, however, were not enough to crush Saskatchewan Wheat Pool's determination to be more than just an elevator company. It would have been easy and understandable for delegates and directors to focus all their efforts on money-making activities, to think of nothing except regaining financial health so that the Pool could at some later date resume its social and political roles. Had the Pool's directors been businessmen in a far-away head office, obliged to put the financial position of their shareholders above all other considerations, perhaps that is what they would have done. But each director was a delegate and each delegate was an ordinary farmer elected by his neighbors to work for their general interests. Perhaps at no other time in the Pool's first sixty years was its democratic, grassroots structure so crucial in determining the role the Pool would play in Saskatchewan society. Because of that structure, the Pool chose to go beyond narrow commercial activities, to launch itself toward the goal of serving the more general and basic needs of rural Saskatchewan. The province's farm families needed champions to fight on their behalf in government offices from Regina to Ottawa; the Pool became one such champion. They needed to band together in co-ops and credit unions to obtain basic services at cost; the Pool was there with every form of organizational help. They desperately needed to understand what was going on in a world where every force of economics and nature opposed them; the Pool provided everything from discussion groups to a full-scale newspaper. Above all, the farm families of Saskatchewan needed hope — and, for many, Pool personnel brought that hope.

Pool Fieldmen: Agents of Change

Almost every Pool employee, delegate and committee member was, in one way or another, a vehicle for such social activity. But the grassroots leaders were a small, unique band of exceptional individuals who formed the Pool's field staff. Never more than eighteen at a time, plus one or two supervisors, they crisscrossed the countryside in fourteen-hour days and every imaginable type of ground conveyance. At various times, they were called everthing from country organizers to district representatives, but for the most part they were simply "field men." It was impossible to define their function precisely, so no one really tried — the unspoken obligation was to be everywhere and help with everything. They have yet to be discovered by those who make movies or television serials, but their story was an epic one and their names were known throughout their large districts.

In the 1920s fieldmen were essential to the Pool's commercial success — persuading farmers to sign contracts to pool their wheat and coarse grains, investigating cases of contract violation through non-delivery and helping smooth over local disputes. The end of pooling also meant the end of their primary functions, but in the 1930s Saskatchewan Wheat Pool fieldmen shaped a new role for themselves as guardians of the Pool's democratic structure and communication channels. They were on the road ceaselessly, organizing meetings, giving speeches and consulting local groups. In the 1937-38 fiscal year, for example, the sixteen fieldmen were at: 372 Pool district or subdistrict conventions; 1,788 general public meetings; 1,138 Pool film shows; and 747 Pool committee meetings. On average, that meant the small field staff was holding 11 meetings every day of the week. All told, they were at meetings attended by 223,919 people — and in addition made visits to 16,275 farmers, 6,028 businessmen and 4,909 elevators. They received no overtime pay and only on rare occasions did they stop to count their hours, as fieldman Oliver Olson did once: "I remember the census-taker coming to our house and filling out the papers. And she wanted to know how many hours I'd worked the week before. I figured it out and told her it was seventy-two hours.

I don't know whether she believed me or not, but that was the actual figure.[14]

Promoting and explaining Pool policies, however, took up a minority of their time. They became agents for general social change, helping organize and promote both producers' and consumers' co-operatives and credit unions. Fieldman Everett Baker chalked up twenty credit unions that he helped organize in eight and a half years.[15] John Stratychuk played a major role in arranging a three-day co-operative school in 1939, the first of a long series of such schools that taught the philosophy and practice of co-operative organizations, while Tom Bentley worked with local Pool committees to provide a municipally hired doctor in one area.[16] When the Saskatchewan Co-operative Wholesale Society needed more communities to set up local co-ops to order and receive farm supplies in bulk, Society leaders asked the Pool for help. Fieldmen fanned out across the province, enlisting delegates and committee members to help promote the idea. Within five months, 419 such co-ops were organized.[17] Wherever rural groups worked together for a worthwhile purpose, it seemed a Pool fieldman was there.

There were also the much-remembered Pool movie shows, often the only such form of entertainment for isolated communities in an era when there was little spare cash for radios or even batteries. Although there was continuing clamor for pure entertainment, the Pool concentrated on serious films about co-operatives at work, preceded or followed by speeches and discussion — but there were almost always one or two cartoons too. Traveling over poorly-maintained roads in all types of weather, carrying with them a bulky electric generator, fieldmen would set up their movie gear in a succession of country schools, often long distances from the nearest town, and for one night bring a touch of modern technology and entertainment to people who were otherwise sadly lacking such luxuries. Often, public health nurses and other government extension workers would come with the fieldman, using his drawing power to bring people in for their talks.[18] With their well-thumbed "black books" listing virtually every community group leader, businessman, teacher and prominent personality in their area, the fieldmen were valuable sources of information, advice and introductions for such extension workers.

Appreciation for the fieldman's services transcended ethnic and other differences. Abel Toupin recalled his days as the Pool's only Francophone fieldman, attending Pool committee meetings held in Orange Lodges, where committee members would absent-mindedly refer to each other by the titles they held in the local

Lodge. No one, however, treated Toupin as an intruder: "It didn't matter, I was a Wheat Pool fieldman, I was all right."[19]

With such close grassroots contact, the fieldmen were also able to keep Pool head office well informed on the feelings and problems of the countryside. The zest with which they approached their jobs ensured, however, that the reports would be more than dull summaries of meetings attended — as when Alfred Himsl reported that rain stopped him from getting to Moose Jaw: "Yes, rain, wonderful rain. It came in drops — but the drops kept coming all afternooon till it came in streams down the street and filled holes and ditches. It washed the worry off the faces of men and women, and it seems that even now the grass is more green."[20] Himsl, tragically, was the field staff's first casualty, being killed in a 1944 car-train collision after giving a movie show and then making a small detour to give an elderly couple a ride past a muddy spot. "He died as he lived, doing kindness to his fellows," supervisor R. B. Evans wrote.[21]

The automobile, in fact, was one of the basic reasons why Pool fieldmen played such a major role in rural Saskatchewan affairs in the 1930s. In an age when few people could afford the operating costs and license fees of a car, the Pool fieldman with his company car and expense account had unusual mobility. Similarly, the regular paycheques of Pool elevator agents made them prominent figures in their areas. As an agent at Bures, Don Sinclair had the only licensed car in the countryside. Everyone else with a car used it "Bennett Buggy" style, drawn by horses, but Sinclair's $50-a-month salary enabled him to live on $10 and spend $40 for his six-cylinder DeSoto coupe.[22] The only drawback was that Sinclair's coupe became transportation for every pregnant woman in the area when the time came to go to hospital — although, fortunately for Sinclair, all the babies waited until arrival at the hospital before being born.

In later decades the Pool's dominant role in rural society would recede, with competition from prosperity, better roads, more cars, radio, television, spreading government services and the growth of co-operatives that the Pool originally helped launch. But in the 1930s, when the countryside was poverty-stricken and isolated to an extent that later generations can barely imagine, the Pool loomed large. Although Pool personnel generally tried their best to remain non-partisan, all their efforts to get people thinking and talking about economic problems inevitably had an effect on political development, as did the Pool's provision of a committee and delegate structure in which people could gain speaking skills. The result was unusually-close links between Pool activists and those who formed the early Co-operative Commonwealth Federation. Of 431 rural delegates to the CCF's 1946 convention, sixty percent had been members of a Pool committee and ten percent had been Pool delegates.[23] A survey of Pool delegates at the same time showed that eighty-five percent supported the CCF.

The broad, active Pool role in policy and education, however, left little room for the United Farmers of Canada, whose prime purpose was to fulfill those functions. In a sense, the UFC left a vacuum for the Pool to fill since poor UFC finances and its involvement in helping form the CCF left the UFC with few resources for the types of activities the Pool undertook. But the Pool could have provided money for the UFC if Pool delegates had chosen to do so. The UFC's financial trouble, in fact, started with the Pool's 1929-30 troubles. Previously, farmers had paid their UFC dues by authorizing the Pool to deduct the money from Pool interim payments, thus assuring the UFC of a convenient and steady income. But there were no Pool interim payments for 1930-31 and thus no deductions. After considering its precarious position, the Pool decided not to continue the UFC deductions in its later dealings with members, even though many farmers' authorizations for the UFC deducations were still valid. The Pool feared that any more deductions would discourage member patronage, but UFC secretary Frank Eliason angrily accused the Pool of seeking to "ask us to co-operate with you in destroying this organization."[24] From the Pool's viewpoint, it had done all it could for the UFC. Some $10,000 had been advanced to the UFC in expectation of 1930-31 deductions and should theoretically have been repaid by the UFC. Hamstrung by a court injunction, obtained by a disgruntled member seeking to stop the Pool from funding the UFC-inspired compulsory pooling campaign, Pool directors could not legally give gifts to the UFC and were personally liable for the debt.[25] But, in response to UFC pleas for debt writeoff, they indicated that they would never seek to collect the debt unless government handling of the leftover 1930-31 crop produced extra payments from which deductions could be made. The UFC also objected to a 1937 agreement whereby the Pool's 18 fieldmen would work part-time on behalf of a co-operative wholesale society, a livestock pool, a dairy pool and a poultry pool. The UFC felt it should handle educational services on behalf of such organizations; but the Pool already had the network of fieldmen in place and was the obvious choice. Such disagreements helped foster suspicion and distrust that were to color relations between the Pool and the UFC's successor, the Saskatchewan Farmers' Union. One UFC loyalist described Saskatchewan Wheat Pool actions this way:

For the sake of satisfying their human hunger for the three major ambitions — security, prestige and power — many people reach out and grasp these things, regardless of the consequences or the cost to their neighbours. Some even revert to the barbarous practice of devouring their own parents in order to achieve their ambitions.[26]

Despite such strong criticism, Saskatchewan Wheat Pool's problem — then and now — was that it could not give up its policy and educational activities without becoming a radically different organization. It had created an elaborate structure of committees, delegates and extension workers to ensure that farmers had the opportunity to be well informed and to exercise real control over the province's largest agricultural enterprise. There was no practical way to stop those farmers from exercising their basic right to use that structure to develop and promote policy. And even if the farmers and their elected representatives voluntarily left all policy issues to the UFC, there would still be questions about whether Pool directors could legitimately hand over large sums of members' money to a completely separate and independent organization, one to which many Pool members did not belong. Pool leaders had to represent all their members, not just those who also held UFC memberships.

The Western Producer

Even without all the effort of the fieldmen and similar part-time work by elevator agents and delegates, the Pool would have had a major influence on Saskatchewan rural society solely through a unique prairie institution, the *Western Producer*. The newspaper was a small part of Pool business affairs, but it played a major role in the Pool's social impact on rural Saskatchewan. The *Producer*'s contributions went far beyond even the important task of providing news, commentary and advertisements to a rural audience. Sections of the newspaper and individual columnists became institutions in themselves, providing farm families with everything from sewing patterns to the latest agricultural techniques. Generations of eager children found pen pals and outlets for poetical ambitions in the Young Co-operators' pages. Fierce debates raged in Open Forum, possibly Canada's most vigorous and least edited letters section. Advertisements by people seeking spouses became legendary, although it is probably an exaggeration to say that a farmer once advertised for a bride with a new tractor and asked for photographs — of the tractor.

From its birth the *Producer* was closely linked to Saskatchewan Wheat Pool. Under its initial title of the *Progressive*, the newspaper was rushed into print on 27 August 1923 to provide a major publicity organ for the initial pool sign-up campaign. In a sense the origins of the *Progressive* go back to the horrors of World War One. Harris Turner, badly wounded and blinded in the battle of Ypres, was convalescing in a Saskatoon hospital when he met Pat Waldron, a casualty of the Somme battles. From their similar experiences and growing friendship came a determination to do something to improve the society around them. In 1922, Turner and his partners found the cause and allies they needed. Rural discontent with the old wheat-marketing system was growing and an activist reform group within the SGGA saw the need for a friendly, farm-oriented weekly to voice their demands for change. Turner and his partners owned a printing plant and were available, but the SGGA leadership did not want to offend Saskatoon *Star* publisher W. F. Herman, whose newpaper gave valuable support to the Progressive political movement. When Herman sold to less friendly parties, the way was clear for the SGGA to endorse Turner's planned weekly and to provide more than $7,000 in loans.[27]

The *Progressive*'s mission was clear — in the words of Pat Waldron, the newspaper was "started purely and simply as a propagandist organ for the farmers' movement, a rather general term, and particularly for the Saskatchewan Grain Growers Association." From the start, it was clear that the newspapermen were aiming more at service than personal gain. Under a 1923 agreement, the SGGA could nominate three persons to the five-person editorial board and would have a friendly publicity organ that it could buy outright at any time for a sum equal to one year's average profits. In exchange, the SGGA would encourage members to subscribe to the newspaper, arranging at least 5,000 subscriptions at two dollars each to launch the enterprise.[28] The *Progressive*, however, would not just parrot what SGGA officials said. An early meeting of the SGGA-controlled editorial board agreed to provide space in the newspaper for the rival Farmers' Union — though the board also noted that such content would mean "peaceful penetration" of Union homes with the remainder of the newspaper.[29] The same meeting also declared that the *Progressive* and its editors "should be as free as possible to take an absolutely independent stand on any public question — provincial or federal — having regard only for the best interests of the agricultural community of this province."

With the creation of Saskatchewan Wheat Pool, the *Progressive*'s owners sought to have the Pool become their new sponsors and a formal agreement was reached in August 1924. In return for the Pool's encouraging its members to subscribe, the *Progressive* undertook to: change its name to avoid confusion with the Progressive political party; remain generally non-partisan in politics; support co-operative marketing; and provide a space for "authentic news of the Wheat Pool supplied by the officials of the Pool."[30] Beyond those general requirements — which matched Turner's own views — the newspaper would have editorial independence. Thus the *Western Producer* was born, its first issue under that name appearing on 18 September 1924.

Only two pages of the newspaper were directly under Pool control — the SGGA and Farmers' Union also had space allocated to them — but the Pool vigorously promoted the newspaper with an early $3,000 loan and 5,393 subscriptions obtained by the field staff alone. Turner's political activities became a minor embarrassment to Pool leaders, since he was not only an MLA but by this time had succeeded J. A. Maharg as leader of the Progressive-related opposition in the legislature, which in 1924 included many Independent farmer representatives. When the Progressives decided in 1925 to formally enter provincial politics, Turner became head of the Saskatchewan Progressive association. Turner's position prompted Liberal strongman Jimmy Gardiner to accuse the Pool of indirect political activity. And McPhail confided to Violet McNaughton: "so long as Harris Turner is leader of the opposition and editor of the paper it is going to be difficult and perhaps harm the pool."[31] Alberta Premier Brownlee, a close ally of the pool movement, was urging that the pool movement start its own newspaper on a prairie-wide basis, but Saskatchewan Wheat Pool leaders decided to continue their arrangements with the *Producer*. McPhail noted: "We are not sure enough of the success of the paper to ask him to resign his position in the legislature." As the newpaper gained a solid footing and the Progressives faded politically, however, Turner became a full-time publisher.

Early in 1925, the *Producer* made one of the most fortunate hiring decisions in the history of Canadian journalism, persuading Violet McNaughton to become Women's Page editor. As with several other figures in Pool history, McNaughton deserves a book to herself. A tiny woman — once denied a British civil service position because she was a half inch short of the five-foot height requirement — she played a large role in prairie social history. After two years as a social worker in British slums and several years of teaching, she moved to Harris, Saskatchewan, in 1909 at the age of thirty to join her father and brother. Their one-room house was a rude introduction to the prairies, although she had the luxury of a partitioned-off section whenever the section was not wholly occupied by wheat. With her husband John — whom she

Left: Violet McNaughton, Western Producer *women's editor.*
Western Producer *photo)*
Right: John I. McFarland, general manager of the Central Selling
Agency. (SWP files, photo by Curlette's Studio, Calgary)

married in 1910 — she soon became involved in farm organizations and began writing for the *Saturday Press,* which became
Turner's Weekly after Turner and Waldron acquired it. Even in
that male-dominated age, no one could deny her zeal and ability;
she became not only president of the SGGA women's auxiliary,
but a full board member of the SGGA itself, playing a major role
in the reform movement. Her wisdom and common sense were
highly valued on a personal as well as an organizational level —
McPhail confided his innermost feelings to her in letters that
commented on Pool personalities only slightly less frankly than
his diary did. Noting that she was the only one he felt able to
consult on such personal matters, McPhail even sought
McNaughton's advice on his fiancee's emotional problems.[32]
     One of the three SGGA representatives on the *Progressive's*
editorial board, McNaughton helped arrange the transition into
the *Western Producer.* As she worked for women's rights, regional
hospitals, schools for the deaf and a hundred other causes, she
built up a network of correspondents and fans that amounted to
an invisible social-reform movement and included virtually every
prominent figure in prairie social reform. The superhuman scope
of her activities won her the Order of the British Empire in 1934
and feature treatment in *MacLean's* magazine in an article
entitled "Mothering the Prairie." Understandably, "her name was

a tower of strength to us," Waldron recalled some years after her death in 1968. More important, she was a source of practical information and inspiration to generations of farm women and ensured that the *Producer* would serve all members of the farm family.

With such people on staff, the *Producer* became an invaluable part of Pool activities, so much so that a veteran Pool employee declared: "Probably the *Western Producer* has done more for Saskatchewan Wheat Pool than any other single factor."[33] The Pool reciprocated, directing all fieldmen one winter to work two weeks exclusively on getting *Producer* subscriptions, then on two other occasions subsidizing distribution of 10,000 copies of the *Producer* to non-pool farmers. But the *Producer* was not linked only to the Pool in this period. After the United Farmers of Canada were formed, the *Producer* received a $6,984 UFC loan and gave the UFC the option to buy the *Producer* for an arbitrated price.[34] Growth and change came steadily — in 1927, the *Producer* acquired new premises in Saskatoon, the Modern Press Building, named after the owners' corporate name. And today's tabloid format was started in 1928.

The Depression, however, almost brought disaster to the newspaper. Like the UFC, the *Producer* had relied on deductions from Pool interim payments for its income, with most subscribers paying by authorizing those deductions. The end of pooling meant the end of that form of income. General economic troubles made the outlook even bleaker. At a meeting on 15 November 1930, Pool delegates rejected a resolution to buy the newpaper, but two days later authorized directors "to finance the Western Producer on a safe basis". By then, the Pool had made more than $60,000 in advances to the newspaper on authorized deductions that apparently would now not be made. To protect Pool funds, Pool directors felt obliged to put a mortgage on *Producer* assets — an action that ended the newspaper's bank credit and left the Pool financing everything.[35] As Pat Waldron commented: "Here was the Pool with this squalling baby in its lap, which it couldn't afford to let die and which it didn't know on earth what to do with."[36] By May 1931, Pool advances totalled more than $82,000 and the *Producer*'s owners said they would have to close shop unless the Pool took over. An appraisal listed assets of $128,344 versus liabilities of $119,383, close enough that the Pool acquired ownership by simply assuming the liabilities. With only a slight name change — "The" was dropped from "The Modern Press Ltd." — the operation became a Pool subsidiary.

For Harris Turner, it was a disappointing time. His years of effort had produced nothing financially and he was in poor health.[37] He bowed out of the operation after eight years as president of the company, returning only to write "The Southeast Corner" column in later years. Turner's other partners stayed with the newspaper as employees, Waldron as editor. Pool publicity director H. S. Fry became Modern Press manager. The Pool was undertaking a heavy burden, just at the time of its most serious financial troubles. With the Pool's very existence dependent on provincial government guarantees, Pool leaders had to consult the cabinet before the takeover.[38] But regardless of short-term financial problems the Pool was determined to maintain the newspaper.

Even without a Depression the task of rebuilding *Producer* circulation would have been hard. Out of 31,000 subscribers at the time of the 1 June 1931 takeover, 27,000 were unpaid. Without paid subscriptions, the newspaper's mailing privileges would end on 1 November. In a successful effort to build up paid subscribers, subscription rates were halved to $1 a year, with special rates of $2 for three years and 50 cents a year for subscriptions ordered in bulk. Pool fieldmen began showing movies — the origin of the famous Pool picture shows — to boost circulation, offering free admission to families with paid subscriptions. That gimmick had to be stopped when the Audit Bureau of Circulations demanded verified paid subscriptions for the protection of advertisers, not a form of movie tickets.[39] Attempts to get Pool elevator agents to sell subscriptions also met obstacles in the form of reluctant managerial staff,[40] but within a year the newspaper nevertheless reached 48,000 paid-up subscribers. The loss that first year was $37,152, initiating a long tradition of *Western Producer* deficits, but at least the newspaper was saved. Among other things, it meant the survival of the only printing establishment in Saskatchewan that carried a union label on its work.

By mid-1936 circulation edged past the 100,000 mark, including 21,268 in Alberta and 11,318 in Manitoba, but the annual deficit had risen to $58,590. As editor, Waldron had to fight suggestions from the United Farmers of Canada to cut costs by eliminating editorial material and relying on farm organizations to contribute text. Waldron insisted that newspapers invariably failed when they did that. *Producer* manager H. S. Fry suggested that farm organizations could pay for advertisements instead of getting free space, but UFC secretary Frank Eliason replied that the UFC could not afford that; it would have to drop its publicity pages if the space had to be paid for.[41] Fortunately, Waldron had the support of Pool delegates, who declared in a 1936 resolution: "the value of the Western Producer cannot be gauged in dollars and cents."

Waldron also successfully launched another tradition that was to last even longer than the tradition of losing money — despite Pool ownership and having to get a Pool subsidy each year, he remained largely independent. When Pool secretary George Robertson suggested once that the Pool should have one of its own people associated with the *Producer*'s editorial staff to ensure the Pool got adequate space and coverage, Waldron bluntly called Robertson an "unreasonable bugger".[42] The two, however, remained friends and later co-operated in persuading Pool directors to provide money for printing plant expansion. Waldron successfully fought for an enlightened view of the *Producer*'s role, establishing it as first of all a credible newpaper. He rejected the concept of sermon-like appeals to support the co-operative movement in favor of fair, professional coverage of such matters. If the word "co-operation" were never to be printed in the newspaper but its news reports helped establish confidence in such movements, Waldron said, more progress would be made than by continually preaching co-operation directly.[43]

Waldron's great degree of independence, however, was bounded by two types of considerations. First were the publisher's legitimate strategic directives: to serve the needs of prairie farm families; to continue support for co-operatives and orderly marketing; and to do all this within the limits of approved budgets. The second type of consideration was responding to the enthusiastic, sometimes naive, suggestions of Pool delegates who considered the *Producer* "our paper." Except for a few emotional topics like banning liquor advertisements, the editor could usually treat the delegates' resolutions as suggestions, gently putting any impractical ones aside. More important, however, was that almost every meeting also passed resolutions commending the newspaper over-all.

The turbulent politics of the 1930s, with radical new movements challenging traditional parties, had some repercussions on the *Western Producer*. In 1933, Pool directors noted that there had been accusations of *Producer* bias "from all political parties now in the field," a situation the directors said probably meant the *Producer* was being fair. Before the 1935 Alberta election that gave Canada its first Social Credit government, however, editor Pat Waldron had singled out the Social Credit theory for extra publicity. He later recalled: "I don't think that up to that time there was a paper in Canada that espoused the Social Credit doctrine. We were more or less responsible for bringing it to the attention of the general public."[44] Waldron, however, had no great liking for the way politicians simplified Social Credit. He also doubted that the theory could be applied by a provincial government and saw publicity of Social Credit as a way to get people thinking about monetary issues.

While *Producer* editorials annoyed various politicians from time to time, its financing bothered the United Farmers of Canada. The UFC had lent the *Producer* $6,000 before the Pool takeover and objected when the Pool cancelled that debt by writing off $6,000 in Pool advances to the UFC. Despite UFC protests, the Pool also refused to write off a $3,400 UFC debt to the *Producer* in 1935, apparently owed for printing services or subscriptions for local lodges in years past. To make matters worse, the Pool took a $20 advertisement in a UFC handbook and did not pay cash but simply deducted $20 from the $3,400. UFC president G. R. Bickerton complained: "with our financial position as it is at the present time, even $20 is quite an item."[45] Pool delegates, meanwhile, had directed that space should not be set aside for other organizations to fill unless those organizations paid for the space. UFC secretary Frank Eliason tried to reverse that policy, urging the editorial board in 1937 to allocate a page for the UFC, plus one each for every other farmers' educational organization. Waldron, supported by Pool director Jack Wesson, said the newspaper would continue to provide news, not publicity notices. Eliason had the satisfaction of the last word — "it would improve the paper" — but no other success.

The *Western Producer*'s deficits and its Saskatchewan base, meanwhile, deterred the Alberta and Manitoba pools from accepting 1936 Saskatchewan Wheat Pool offers to share ownership of the newspaper.[46] The *Producer* won support from Manitoba Pool president Paul Bredt, who said his organization would promote the newspaper and would even fold the *Manitoba Co-operator* when *Producer* circulation in Manitoba was somewhat higher. Alberta Pool directors, however, declined to have their agents sell subscriptions, saying the *Producer* already had salesmen in Alberta and compliance with the request would mean pressure from Alberta farm publications to do the same for them. Like it or not, Saskatchewan Wheat Pool was on its own as proprietor of a prairie-wide newspaper.

Pool services, of course, went beyond the fieldmen's organizing skills or movies or the newspaper. Starting in 1930, the Pool's library lent books to members by mail, building up to a circulation of 11,000 books annually ten years later. Boxes of books were also rotated among elevator agents for lending in their local communities. The library-by-mail service ended in 1969, after other library services had become accessible to virtually all farm families, but for the 1930s the service was highly valued by borrowers. Weekly radio broadcasts were resumed in 1934 in the form of fifteen-minute commentaries by officials of the three prairie pools. In 1939 radio activities were expanded to include a Sunday newscast, using British United Press reports, and capsule histories of Saskatchewan villages. Broadcasts of provincial hockey games, with low-key Pool commentary between periods, were added shortly afterward. By then the Pool's crop-condition reports were established as a major item of provincial news. Other activities ranged from university scholarships to publication of a book on farm co-operatives and associations. Technical services included a laboratory that did tens of thousands of germination and moisture tests annually for members, plus widespread grain cleaners to allow farmers to save their screenings for livestock feed. In co-operation with the Saskatoon college of agriculture, the Pool also operated a variety test program that helped crop research while providing a worthwhile activity for the hundreds of farm children who cared for the test plots.

The Pool also became tentatively involved in the distribution of farm supplies, having elevator agents act as agents of the Saskatchewan Co-operative Wholesale Society for such supplies as binder twine. Amendment of the Pool charter for authority to distribute bulk supplies, however, touched off a wave of protest from Saskatchewan retail merchants, who said they were already stretched to the breaking point carrying customers' debts.[47] There was also concern about the effect on fledgling co-operatives and on the Pool's still-shaky financial reserves, so the issue was deferred to trouble a later generation of Pool delegates. The issue of Pool sales to farmers also came up in 1937, when the company's act of incorporation was being amended to allow it to engage in co-operative or "fraternal" business. A 29 March 1937 memo from George Robertson to delegates and committees said there had been "considerable opposition" to the idea. Opposition from vested business interests could be dismissed as being "the type of opposition always directed against co-operative development wherever found," while the reluctance of some farmers to see the Pool have more powers "can only be ascribed to lack of knowledge of our democratic set-up." Pool assistant secretary R. B. Evans said in a 29 June 1937 letter to R. G. Rothwell that some businessmen were creating unfounded fears of chains of Pool retail stores: "It has not been our intention, and is not at present to launch into any undertaking that might dissipate our commercial reserve."[48]

With the UFC financially crippled, the Pool also became the chief spokesman for Saskatchewan farmers in government circles, winning the honor of having one provincial cabinet minister call Saskatchewan Wheat Pool "the agricultural Parliament of the province of Saskatchewan."[49] The lapse of the old Canadian Council of Agriculture left a void in the 1930s that the Pool helped fill, as it played a major role in the 1935 creation of the Canadian Chamber of Agriculture, which a few years later was renamed the Canadian Federation of Agriculture, a name retained to the present day. Jack Wesson, a Pool vice-president in 1935, was chosen as the federation's first president and remained in that capacity for five years even though he acquired a heavier workload by becoming Pool president in 1937. As well, the three prairie pools worked together through Canadian Co-operative Wheat Producers in many representations to government. Whether the topic was shipping regulations that might add costs to grain movement on the Great Lakes, or co-operative taxation technicalities, the Pool was involved. In one major initiative, the opening of Churchill as an export port, Saskatchewan Wheat Pool was able to back up its policy resolutions with its commercial strength, providing eighty-six percent of the wheat shipped through the port in its first three years and chartering most of the ships.

Nor did Pool delegates restrict themselves to exclusively agricultural matters. Their resolutions urged such reforms as a national bank, with sole power to control the supply of currency. On the provincial level they helped win debt adjustment legislation and promoted teaching co-operation in schools. Many of the things they were working for involved greater government regulation and control — a theme that was to trouble some Pool leaders in later generations — but the directors of all three prairie pools saw that danger in 1935. To them the solution was formation of more co-operatives: "As the State assumes a greater control of business it must in turn arrange facilities for the extension of control by the people. This is the only assurance we have for equity, justice and security — it is co-operation."[50]

Struggle for the Canadian Wheat Board

Although the Pool was influential in the whole spectrum of government policies affecting rural Saskatchewan, its other contributions are overshadowed by the historic struggle to create the Canadian Wheat Board. Other issues were important, but this one was at the heart of Pool principles. In effect the question was whether the old Central Selling Agency would disappear without trace, or whether it would be reincarnated in better form. The answer to that question would determine whether wheat remained a speculator's plaything or was marketed in orderly fashion for the benefit of producers. At first the outlook for Pool policies was discouraging. Prime Minister Bennett's chief wheat advisor, John

McFarland, was in control of the remnant of the pools' former Central Selling Agency and was dead set against such measures as a wheat board. McFarland, a former president of the Alberta Pacific Grain Co., wrote his old friend Bennett in 1931: "if you abolish the Futures Market, then there is only one thing left and that is Government Monopoly, and that would be too horrible to contemplate."[51] But there was equal conviction among Pool leaders that anything but government monopoly would be unacceptable.[52] Soon they had the three prairie premiers and their neighboring pools lined up with them in demanding a board — although Alberta Pool directors were less than enthusiastic. McPhail noted in his diary, 28 May 1931, that it took considerable persuasion to get Alberta Pool president H. W. Wood and others to give lukewarm suport to the idea: "Mr. Wood put it on the grounds of agreeing to it because Sask. wanted it and it wouldn't hurt Alta."

For the next four years it became a matter of keeping ceaseless pressure on the government while evidence accumulated that there was no alternative to a wheat board. The voluntary, non-contract pooling operated by Saskatchewan Wheat Pool limped along with low volumes — only 1.08 million bushels in 1931-32 pooling, 6.5 million 1932-33 and 1.3 million 1933-34. With initial payments of 35 cents a bushel in the first two years and 50 cents in the third, the pools were financially safe but few farmers could afford to take such low initial payments. In 1932 Pool directors argued for at least a temporary board, to last "until some measure of economic stability has been attained." The next year they spelled out a more detailed plan for an agency that would operate with delivery quotas for individual farmers and be headed by a majority of producer representatives.

The call for delivery quotas reflected growing worldwide consensus that there had to be a system of controls to discourage overproduction — an argument that McFarland had been one of the first to make in Canada. Events on the international scene were moving with surprising swiftness toward the historic first International Wheat Agreement, starting with tentative talks at a 1931 London conference on wheat marketing. The same Depression that radicalized many prairie farmers and sent them to new political movements was also having its effect on diplomats and bureaucrats, driving them to reconsider ideas that once seemed impractical. Even Imperial Preference was realized in a form at the Imperial Economic Conference in Ottawa in 1932. Britain allowed Canada a six-cent-a-bushel tariff advantage on wheat coming into Britain. The move, however, was made over the objections of the three pools, who told Bennett that such a step might cause retaliation and jeopardize Canada's access to other markets. After their bitter experience with continental Europe's tariff barriers, the pools saw clearly that the key to recovery would be tearing down such obstacles to trade, not building new ones. Among their recommendations to Ottawa was that Canadian tariffs on manufactured goods used by farmers be lowered so Canada's grain producers could better compete with other nations. The pools had more success, however, in asking Ottawa to push for an international wheat conference. "It is unthinkable that existing conditions should be allowed to force wheat growers the world over back under the domination of the old jungle law of the survival of the fittest," Saskatchewan Pool directors declared.

With Canada's prime minister presiding, a thirty-nation wheat conference opened on 21 August 1933 in London, England. Within four days, twenty-two nations signed the first International Wheat Agreement. A half century later, the ideals of that first agreement have still not been fully realized, but it was a landmark step toward international co-operation, one that at least set standards for later behavior in matters affecting the wheat trade. Importing nations basically agreed to reduce artificial incentives to domestic wheat production while exporting nations agreed to limit their production. Canada, which had an average 35.6 percent of world wheat trade in the 1920s, was allocated 35.7 percent of the trade for 1933-34. Gaps in the agreement were apparent from the start — Russia, for example, agreed to limit its wheat exports but would not name a specific amount or percentage of world trade. Canada, Argentina, Australia and the United States initialled an agreement to cut wheat acreage by 15 percent, but Australia backed out of that commitment and the final agreement just called for lower exports. Other nations noted that Canada's wheat acreage jumped from an average 9.9 million acres in 1910-14 to 27.2 million acres in 1932 but that Canada was not prepared to take effective measures to slash that acreage. Within a year the first IWA had effectively collapsed as Argentina persisted in exporting more than its quota, seeking to justify its breach of the agreement by saying Canada and others were not reducing their acreage. Despite at least one telegram to Bennett in which Pool directors endorsed the idea of bringing production into line with consumption, such spokesmen as vice-president Jack Wesson and secretary George Robertson spoke out against the idea of acreage or production cuts.[53] In a speech to the Pool's 1933 annual meeting, McFarland bluntly declared that there was no real choice:

> If the importing countries now require 200,000,000 (bushels) less than heretofore, what power have we to compel them

to eat more than they want? . . . We live in a changing world, and if we refuse to adapt ourselves to the change which has already taken place in the wheat world, then we must expect to pay the penalty.

The next year, however, McFarland noted that the issue was temporarily irrelevant because of "an unprecedented destruction of production as a result of unparalleled adverse weather conditons."[54] Drought and disease would eventually remove the mammoth current wheat surplus and nations would have more time to plan ways to stop overproduction occurring in normal crop conditions, he said. The first International Wheat Agreement had failed, but it had pointed the way toward possible solutions and in doing so had given wheat board advocates a forceful argument — that a board, with delivery quotas, was almost essential to enable Canada to participate in formal or informal agreements to limit production.

Meanwhile domestic considerations were also pushing John McFarland and Bennett toward the wheat board concept. Theoretically McFarland was supposed to be selling the pools' 1930-31 wheat stocks, but the pools' wheat and their agency became tools for government stabilization measures. McFarland's belief in free enterprise did not stop him from realizing that there was not enough speculative activity to support Grain Exchange prices — the Chicago and Winnipeg Exchanges, he wrote Bennett, were no longer real markets: "they are now nothing more than 'slaughter houses'."[55] In late 1932 he reported to the pools that there had not yet been any time when wheat prices were strong enough for the wheat stocks to be sold for an amount that would repay bank advances on those stocks. The next year he noted that Canadian farmers were receiving "many many millions of dollars" extra for current crops because his government-financed agency was refraining from dumping its wheat and depressing prices. He added, however, that such success would not have been possible if the United States had not been holding its huge wheat surplus off the market in the same period.[56]

At about this point, officials of the Winnipeg Grain Exchange made one of the worst public-relations blunders in grain trade history, issuing a statement declaring that their free-market system had worked "smoothly" in the last abnormal few years. And McFarland, up to his ears in unsold wheat and struggling to support prices while feeling that Exchange members were speculating on price drops, blew his top. In a letter to Bennett on 30 October 1933, McFarland ridiculed the Exchange's claim: "The only way it functions smoothly is when it is going down. Most things run pretty well downhill, and it is one of them."[57] Bennett responded with a 2 November letter to the Exchange, calling their statement "an insult to the intelligence of those who read it" and adding: "it is the strongest argument that has yet been presented to me for the creation of a wheat board at the earliest possible moment." The prime minister also noted that he was asking government lawyers for a memo on how to set up such a board.

By that time McFarland had built his agency's wheat holdings up to such an extent that he almost had a monopoly on Canadian wheat anyway. In a 12 December 1933 note to Bennett, McFarland reported that he had 210 million bushels out of Canada's total visible supply of 242 million.[58] With an estimated 10 million to 15 million bushels still on farms, that left only 17 million to 22 million in the hands of the entire grain trade and speculators. Not only had McFarland not been selling the 1930-31 pool wheat, but he had bought almost double that amount in wheat futures, seeking to support prices. His powerful independent role in wheat policy was underlined in one excerpt from a telephone conversation with Prime Minister Bennett, who thought a temporary price rise offered an opportunity to get rid of some wheat:

> B: How about selling some wheat, John?
> M: No, I don't think so.
> B: Why?
> M: Well, those people over there have been skinning us alive for three years; now the shoe is on the other foot and we are going to make the bastards pay.
> B: John, I think you should sell.
> M: No, I will not sell.
> B: I order you to sell.
> M: All right, I'll resign.
> B: John, I do not want you to do that, but you must sell.[59]

Eventually, McFarland was persuaded to sell a little wheat — but quickly bought more than he sold. By 2 June 1934 McFarland was ready to give up his efforts to support wheat prices and wait for wheat to start being sold through the Exchange's trading pit:

> I am therefore putting it up to you as to the advisability of seriously considering a national wheat board. Brouillette and his followers want it and will not rest until they succeed. Indeed I am not sure they may be right. The Pit operations are a sham, and have been for several years. The registered price represents only the value of that portion of the supplies

which we do not own, and as you fully realize that has been but a small percentage of the available supplies. . . .

. . . you think I am against a Board, and it is true I have been, but from here on I have no argument against it.[60]

The next year brought even more evidence that a futures system was unable to carry large volumes of wheat at adequate prices. Over the winter the futures system carried from one to fourteen percent of Canada's wheat. By July 1935 McFarland's agency owned 29 million bushels more wheat than Canada had,[61] indicating that Exchange traders had made massive sales of futures, speculating on price declines and thus creating pressure to reduce prices.

Meanwhile the Bennett government's first step toward reform of agricultural marketing was to pass the Natural Products Marketing Act of 1934, enabling marketing of a commodity through one agency whenever two-thirds of producers voted in favor of such a step. Saskatchewan Wheat Pool lawyer R.H. Milliken spent weeks in Ottawa lobbying for the bill and trying with other agriculture representatives to help sort out a confused situation. In one private consultation he asked Agriculture Minister Robert Weir why an early draft did not clearly state that an agency could have exclusive marketing powers. In reply Weir provided "the astounding explanation that he hoped to get the bill through the House without the House knowing that it possessed such power" and Weir complained that farm lobbyists had spoiled that plan.[62] Wheat, however, demanded its own legislation and Bill 98 to establish a Canadian Wheat Board was introduced on 10 June 1935, receiving royal assent on 5 July. Farmers wishing to sell through the wheat board could deliver their wheat to the board and receive the average pooled price, while the federal treasury would cover losses in any year that the average selling price was less than initial payments.

For a brief time, it seemed that the highest goal of the prairie pool movement had almost been reached and that the frustrating loose ends of earlier years were being cleaned up. The 1930-31 wheat supplies were formally transferred to the new board, opening the way for formal settlement of the 1930-31 pool. Saskatchewan Wheat Pool ended its 1934-35 pooling with a gross selling price of 80.5 cents a bushel and a total of 1.6 million bushels of wheat pooled, then for the first time in its eleven-year history was not involved in pooling at all. McFarland was appointed to head the three-man board, which also included Henry G. Grant and former pool salesman D. L. Smith. The prairie pools also had four of the seven spots on the producer advisory committee to the board.[63] Prime Minister Bennett announced a wheat board initial price of 87.5 cents a bushel for top-grade wheat, more than current open-market prices. In their 1935 annual report, Pool directors said: "We regard our record as a grain marketing organization with that sense of utmost satisfaction which comes from the achievement of a life-long goal."

By the time those words reached print, however, Bennett's government had been defeated in the 14 October 1935 general election. The Liberal government of W. L. Mackenzie King quickly moved to abolish the producer advisory committee and to dismiss all the commissioners appointed by Bennett.[64] The board's new chief commissioner, J. R. Murray, was soon nicknamed Fire-Sale Murray because of indications that the Liberal government wanted him to quickly get rid of the 1930-31 wheat stocks inherited from McFarland. Fortunately for Canadian wheat prices, the Argentine government startled the world by boosting its minimum wheat price to 90 cents from 55 cents. That was good news for those who wanted to see the Canadian surplus sold at reasonable prices, but many observers were worried by Canadian Wheat Board actions in allowing grain traders to escape being caught short by the jump. In a public statement, McFarland declared: "it is evident that instead of a board operating in the interests of the producers of wheat, it is to be a board dominated by the Winnipeg Grain Exchange."[65]

Worse was to come, as the pools slowly learned that the Liberal government had no intention of allowing the wheat board to become a normal part of wheat marketing, let alone be the sole marketing agency. In July 1936 a delegation of the three pools met the cabinet's wheat committee to press for higher initial payments — which were, in effect, government-guaranteed minimum prices — and noted university studies showing that the cost of producing a bushel of wheat and shipping it to the Lakehead was more than $1. Canadian and world carryovers by that time were back to normal levels and prices were strengthening. The cabinet, however, kept the board's initial payment at 87.5 cents — and passed an order prohibiting any deliveries to the board so long as open-market prices remained above 90 cents. With one stroke they had made the board irrelevant unless another price collapse came. Pool leaders kept pressing their case on Ottawa for the next two years — with Jack Wesson inheriting the Saskatchewan leadership after Brouillette's death on 22 April 1937 — but with little success. Large world crops brought a change in 1938, lowering over-all prices and bringing the Canadian Wheat Board into operation again, this time with an initial payment of 80 cents a bushel, a low level that still resulted in a $61.5 million loss to the federal treasury.

Still seeking a way to get out of wheat marketing, the Liberal government sought to persuade the pools to resume their pooling operations.[66] New legislation in May 1939, passed despite vigorous western protests, provided for wheat board minimum payments of 70 cents a bushel, limited farmers to delivering no more than 5,000 bushels each to the board, and repealed earlier provisions giving the cabinet power to have the board also sell feed grains. Other legislation allowed the government to guarantee initial payments of 56 cents a bushel and administrative costs of four cents for any pools run by producer organizations or private elevator companies. Reluctantly, Saskatchewan Wheat Pool operated a small 1939-40 pool for Saskatchewan and Manitoba wheat that could not be delivered to the board because of the 5,000-bushel limit. Once that limit was removed in 1940, under wartime pressures, the Pool again stepped out of pooling and concentrated on forcing Ottawa to assume its responsibilities in grain marketing. The pools had learned a hard lesson in the years immediately following creation of the wheat board — not even an Act of Parliament could prevent farmers' gains from being erased. To preserve and revive the wheat board would take ceaseless vigilance, determined lobbying and continued public-education campaigns. So long as the 1930s were fresh in their minds, Pool members and leaders would remember that lesson.

6
War and Wheat, 1940–51

No civilized world country, no matter how strongly attached to the doctrine of free enterprise, will or can let domestic agriculture be nakedly subjected to the ups and downs of the world market.

— President Dwight D. Eisenhower[1]

When Nazi German tanks swept through Polish cavalry in September 1939, shock waves were sent around the world. An era of total war was starting, one that would bring massive social and economic changes everywhere. It was even to push the Liberals in Ottawa into giving the Canadian Wheat Board full powers. Such an overdue basic reform, however, was now of secondary concern. Throughout the farms of Saskatchewan, the return of war meant apprehensive farewells to sons and daughters who marched away in uniform. For those who stayed, the war meant an all-out effort to respond to demands for grain and livestock while coping with shortages of everything from labor to spare parts. But, behind the first priority of maintaining the war effort, there was still a need to work for equity in agricultural pricing, to help plan a better international system for post-war years, and generally to make prairie agriculture a sound industry that could help feed nations starved by years of ruthless warfare.

John Henry Wesson

In playing its part in these basic tasks, Saskatchewan Wheat Pool had the leadership of John Henry (Jack) Wesson, perhaps the most influential Pool president of all. Unlike his predecessors, Wesson did not have his influence continually recorded in handy written form. He left no published diary spelling out his role in day-to-day decisions and he was not one to draw bitter battle-lines whereby historians could easily view his victories or defeats. Wesson's role was also further obscured by a change in the very nature of Pool policymaking, a shift from the clear-cut public battles of McPhail and Brouillette to a slower, more anonymous process of making decisions through evolving a consensus. After being a battleground for SGGA and Farmers' Union factions throughout the 1920s, the Pool had seen a new unity forged amid its 1930s struggle for survival, a unity over which Jack Wesson was well suited to preside. But even though his influence was thus not clearly defined in written records, it shines through the recollections of those who knew him. At international conferences and in the corridors of Ottawa bureaucracy, he was a liked and trusted figure, always involved in major agricultural developments. In rural Saskatchewan he inspired one of the most devoted followings of any farm leader. One Pool figure, visiting a farmer's old log house in the bush north of Turtleford, found only two pictures on the crude walls — the Queen and Jack Wesson.

The man who inspired such affection was born in England Aug. 24, 1887, oldest boy among ten children. By the age of fourteen, he was helping manage the family's dairy farm near Sherwood Forest. His schooling ended for lack of money with grade eight, but he continued studies at night with the help of the local teacher.[2] His ability to learn quickly and instinctively was most marked in music. He taught himself the violin at age seven and the cornet at nine, then played organ in chapel at eleven. From his tenant-farming, Methodist background, Jack brought to Canada a thorough respect for British practices. In later years, his daughter recalled, Wesson was to be very disappointed at British behavior concerning a controversial wheat agreement — "he felt a British man's word was as good as gold."[3] Wesson, at any rate, lived up to that standard.

When he came to Canada in 1907, settling near Maidstone, Saskatchewan, the young Englishman stepped off the train into a cold Saskatchewan winter. Friends had come to pick him up, but to keep warm he jogged behind the sleigh — in low oxfords, no overshoes, stiff collar, light overcoat with velvet trim, bowler hat and a walking stick under his arm. His wife-to-be, Laura Pike, watched the apparition and later recalled: "I never in all God's own world thought I would ever marry that cocky little Englishman." Laura was a major help to her husband throughout his career. As a niece wrote later: "Her feet were firmly planted on the good earth and because of this she often kept Uncle Jack from floating away over the treetops." Wesson appreciated this and told one story to illustrate it. One day he asked his wife how many really great men she thought there were in the world. "One less than you think," she replied.[4]

Wesson, however, proved to be the opposite of an English dandy and buckled down to the task of being a pioneer. A fancy frock coat he brought with him became a plowing coat since he could wrap the tails around his hands to protect them from mosquitoes while he was holding the plow.[5] He built his own log house from trees he chopped himself and then hauled with a team of horses. At one time, he worked laying cement sidewalks and tile in Saskatoon. Very mechanically minded, he bought one of the first automobiles in the Maidstone area and immediately disassembled it to learn how it worked and how he could repair it.[6] Whether the job was butchering livestock or cutting his family's hair at home on Sunday, Wesson worked cheerfully.

From his early twenties, Jack Wesson found himself in demand as a public speaker at farm meetings and soon became active in the Saskatchewan Grain Growers' Association, being elected a director in 1918. Five years later, when the provisional Pool board was formed, he was on it, beginning thirty-seven years of directorship. He seems to have been little touched by the McPhail-Brouillette feuds, generally following a middle, independent course. In 1925 McPhail noted how Wesson was one of the few Pool directors to support Brouillette often and added: "I cannot understand Jack for I know he is a supporter of mine as well."[7] At the Pool's first permanent board meeting, Wesson nominated someone else for the vice-presidency, in opposition to Brouillette, but later took Brouillette's side in the controversial compulsory-pool issue. He was indeed hard to allocate to any faction, perhaps simply because he put the Pool's welfare and his principles ahead of personal likes or dislikes. When McPhail died, several board members suggested that Wesson should be the next president instead of vice-president Brouillette, but Wesson insisted that the vice-president should move up, a decision that probably prevented some hard feelings.[8] With Brouillette in ill health for much of his presidential term, Wesson as vice-president carried many extra responsibilities even before he started his 1937-1960 reign as Pool president.

With his active role in the new Canadian Federation of Agriculture, a role that included becoming the Federation's first president, as well as his Pool leadership, Wesson soon became unofficial spokesman for Saskatchewan agriculture. Powerful cabinet minister Jimmy Gardiner frequently consulted Wesson before bringing recommendations to cabinet.[9] Wesson, however, was careful to remain politically neutral — all three major parties asked him to be a candidate, but he always declined and not even his family knew for sure how he voted.[10] Nor did his strongly-held views curb his instinctive good-natured fellowship. In radio debates, he would rip into Major H. G. L. Strange of Searle Grain Company, but then sit down with him over a bottle of scotch afterward. He enjoyed praise, was proud to be named a Commander of the British Empire in 1946 for his contributions to the war effort, and moved easily in diplomatic gatherings. But none of that stopped him from relating to every human being as an equal wherever he was — whether playing the piano to entertain maids and porters at a Swiss hotel or telling a junior Pool clerk: "Call me Jack, I'm just a farmer." In many ways, fieldman Don Sinclair recalled, "he was really a very simple sort of man — he loved praise and he loved people."

Those pleasures came in abundance when Wesson made twice-yearly visits back to his home area.[11] When "Uncle Jack" came home, Sinclair recalled, "it was always a kind of triumphal procession." In his huge, throne-like armchair, he would be the centre of attention of the cluster of three Wesson households and all their visitors, presiding at family feasts and movie shows that Sinclair would put on. Before those festivities, there would be a standard routine of a Pool district convention in North Battleford, lunch with relatives at Maidstone and the annual meeting of a Pool committee in Waseca. "He liked everything done to a pattern and he didn't like to change the pattern." Even when retired and

Jack Wesson (wearing hat) with family, North Battleford, 1938. A note on the original photo states that they all rode into town in one car. (SWP Collection, Saskatchewan Archives Board R-A 15,274)

too old to operate a combine, Jack Wesson still had to be involved in his unpretentious, helpful way, insisting on riding the combine all day in a lashed-on chair, getting caked with dust and pushing grain apart when it bunched up. By the time he died in 1965, aged seventy-eight, he had many times over proved himself able to meet the standard of quality set by a British poet of his childhood — to walk with kings and yet keep the common touch.

Wesson's leadership gifts were definitely needed in the early years of his presidency. As the 1930s ended, there were signs that the organization was becoming tired, perhaps worn down from the strain of coping with Depression, locusts and Liberals. The 1939 annual meeting resolved to encourage Pool elevator agents to do more to promote the co-operative spirit since "there is a growing indifference amongst the Pool membership toward the Pool organization as a militant force to secure economic justice for the producer." Apathy was spreading and many members could not even be bothered returning the convenient mail-in ballots for Pool elections. At least one delegate discovered that the way to get elected was to visit acquaintances, collect the ballots from them, and mail them in himself.[12] The Pool's first line of defence against such apathy was its field staff, whose monthly report in November 1940 urged removal of "dead-wood" and "hostile members" from Pool committees. Fieldmen were to do their utmost — "within the framework of democracy" — to encourage election of new and younger people.[13] After a five-day staff conference, supervisor R. B. (Buck) Evans concluded in a 10 January 1941 memo that there was a general "tendency to discouragement and defeatism". He said committees were not spreading information among farmers and delegates were spending too much time rehashing directors' debates rather than working on country organization:

> The greatest hurdle to effective organization is the fact that most of our delegates are not acquainted with the structure of their organization. Very few of them have ever studied their Act of Incorporation, their Articles of Association; their Delegates' Bylaws; fewer still seem to understand the meaning and purpose of the Wheat Pool committee by-laws.[14]

Over the next decade or two, that analysis was to lead to a marked change of role for fieldmen; instead of being organizers and speech-makers in their own right, they would become support staff for delegates, training and prodding delegates to be the Pool's front-line spokesmen. But there were inhibitions limiting what fieldmen could do — they could recruit promising people to run for vacant delegate positions, but they generally refrained from encouraging other candidates against a delegate who was standing for re-election. Sometimes they were in the position of having "to warp democracy" in the Pool's interest, one official recalled.[15] Fieldmen might not be able to directly recruit candidates against a delegate, but they could and did prompt members to bring delegates into line. At a meeting with one committee, fieldman H. A. Wagner was told that the Pool's educational wing had assured the success of a mass demonstration in Ottawa: "I was waiting for just such an opportunity. I pointed out that their delegate believed the educational part of the organization should be done away with."[16] Committee members then took the delegate to task. Most of the fieldmen's work in revitalizing the delegate body, however, was done in the more straightforward fashion of recruiting people for vacancies. They left few prospects untouched in their search for candidates and often went to unusual lengths to get people. Fieldman Wilf MacLeod remembered one wartime episode where he gingerly drove his car over rubbery, waving ice to reach one recruit, since MacLeod did not have ration coupons to get enough gasoline to drive around the frozen lake.[17] Despite such efforts, the fieldmen and the Pool generally were still passing up about half the population, since rural Saskatchewan was not yet ready to cope with the idea of having women as Pool delegates. It would be 1981 before the first woman delegate arrived at a Pool annual meeting. From 1945 to 1953 Lilyholme school district had an all-woman Pool committee, a unique situation in Pool history caused partly by the small number of district farms and lack of a delivery point there.[18]

Pool staff, meanwhile, were slowly getting more benefits as Pool finances and employment standards improved. But it was still far from being a soft life, as the wartime staff at the Pool's Winnipeg office would testify. In one twelve-month period, they worked 265 nights until 11:00 P.M. after their regular day's work, handling paperwork for the flow of grain cars to Montreal. They received no overtime pay and their 75 cents supper money was suspended at one point after supervisors discovered one man used his 75 cents to bowl on his break instead of eating.[19] By the standards of the day, however, the Pool was a good employer. "Sweetpea" — Saskatchewan Wheat Pool Employees' Association, founded in 1937 and forerunner of today's Grain Services Union — needed just two years of lobbying to persuade delegates to authorize a pension plan.[20] It had taken the delegates themselves four years to get directors to move the Pool's annual meeting from Regina's Labour Temple to the more comfortable atmosphere of the Hotel Saskatchewan, where the annual meeting was to be held like clockwork for more than four decades.

The various internal measures to improve or maintain the

morale and enthusiasm of delegates and staff, however, could not have succeeded by themselves. The Pool also had to be visibly working for worthwhile purposes and having some effect on behalf of the farmer. Saskatchewan Wheat Pool's opportunity to do just that came in the first years of the war, when government officials were preoccupied with wartime pressures and found it all too easy to give insufficient attention to farm needs. When Nazi conquest removed western Europe as a wheat market, prices dropped sharply to about 60 cents a bushel. At Ottawa's request the Grain Exchange quickly imposed an artificial price peg of just over 70 cents a bushel — a helpful step, but considered inadequate by farm groups.[21] When Ottawa announced a comprehensive wheat policy 24 July 1940, there was more improvement: the wheat board would again buy all the grain that farmers delivered to it, with no 5,000-bushel limit; the advisory committee was recreated; and a storage allowance would be paid for grain kept on the farms. But the wheat board's initial payment would be only 70 cents. In August, the wheat board announced its first delivery quotas — five bushels for each seeded acre — and began distributing the first board permit books, in which each farmer's deliveries would be recorded to ensure he did not exceed his quota. With little effect, the Pool called for higher prices and a system of cash advances on farm-stored grain. In January 1941 the Canadian Federation of Agriculture made its first annual submission to the cabinet, again with little effect so far as prairie grain farmers were concerned. In March 1941, Ottawa came up with a new policy statement that infuriated farmers who were already irate about growing wheat at a loss. The federal government announced a 230-million-bushel limit on deliveries to the wheat board in 1941-42, plus measures designed to take wheat acreage out of production. Stocks on hand at 31 July would be carried as a wartime reserve, but the government wanted no part of more "excess" production. Quotas would be based upon an authorized wheat acreage equal to sixty-five per cent of 1940 acreage, four dollars an acre would be paid for wheat land switched to summerfallow and two dollars an acre would be paid for wheat land switched to coarse grains or grass. Farmers recognized that traditional wheat markets had been disrupted by war, but they also knew that there were millions of people in that war-ravaged world who would need food whenever it could be sent to them. Many of those millions would not get that food if Ottawa's low prices, delivery limits and non-production incentives became permanent. The prairie farmer's call for higher prices had a natural base in human self-interest, but that was not his sole motive, nor his primary justification for the request.

Thus the pools pushed strongly for a $1 initial payment instead of the 70 cents announced in the government's March 1941 policy statement. Without a higher initial payment, the pools warned, western farm income from wheat would drop to $98 million in 1941-42 from $239 million the previous year. Even with $20 million in payments for reduced wheat acreage, farmers' incomes would be halved. But again western farmers got almost the opposite of what they were seeking — on 18 October 1941 the government announced comprehensive price controls, forbidding sale of goods or services at prices higher than the maximum charged in the previous four weeks. For wheat producers, that meant the 77-cent peak Exchange price for wheat in that period. Workers' pay was frozen at levels that were higher than any since 1926, while farmers were being told to take one of the lowest price levels in twenty years. For purchasing power equal to 1926-29, Saskatchewan Wheat Pool calculated, farmers would have to have a wheat price of $1.41 — yet Ottawa would not even provide $1. Something had to be done to shake up Ottawa, and Saskatchewan Wheat Pool was getting ready to do just that. "Canada cannot continue to exist half slave and half free", Pool directors declared in their November 1941 annual report with considerable exaggeration, but also firm conviction.

March On Ottawa, 1942

The Pool's strategy — a mass protest march on Ottawa — actually sprang directly from the grassroots. One of the first calls for such an act came at a March 1941 protest meeting in Abernethy, where former agriculture minister and Liberal back-bencher W. R. Motherwell was the guiding spirit.[22] In November, Pool members in Pelly sent a telegram to the Pool annual meeting, calling on Saskatchewan Wheat Pool to send a trainload of farmers to Ottawa, and delegates formally decided to organize the March on Ottawa. Even before that decision the Pool had been mobilizing farm opinion through a series of mass meetings. As always, the ubiquitous fieldmen were on hand to assess the rural mood. P. A. Jensen reported that "not in many years have so many people talked so much about the Wheat Pool, all over the country."[23] And P. B. Thompson observed: "It seems some of our original supporters who have been luke warm and very critical for years, are back to us again with their full support through these meetings."[24] The Saskatchewan campaign quickly won endorsement and imitation from the other pools, who held similar meetings in their provinces. But the core of the campaign was in Saskatchewan, where Pool fieldmen, delegates and volunteers spent the winter combing the province for 25-cent donations and signatures on a mass petition that the delegation would take to Ottawa. Heavy snowfalls led many to travel by horse and foot, virtually recreating the province-wide sign-up campaigns of 1923-24. Participation spanned all sectors of society — in each Pool subdistrict, hastily-organized groups of Pool committee members and local businessmen were formed to select three community representatives for the delegation. Meanwhile, some newspapers were accusing farmers of "cluttering up the transportation system" with the planned expedition and predicting that it would do nothing but antagonize easterners. Indeed, delegates on the trains were urged "not to behave like wild and woolly westerners."[25]

But when the two special trains with a total of 400 Saskatchewan representatives steamed into Ottawa early Sunday morning, 1 February 1942, any apprehension that capital residents might have felt soon vanished in face of the delegation's calm, business-like approach. By 2:00 P.M., the well-organized group was at work in a general assembly, electing Harry Marsh as their chairman and Pool president Jack Wesson as their spokesman to government, then approving detailed briefs and agendas. Six Alberta and two Manitoba representatives were also present to endorse the Saskatchewan delegation's work. At noon the next day, Prime Minister King led nine cabinet ministers to the Chateau Laurier convention hall to hear the Saskatchewan representatives and receive the signed petition for higher wheat prices — complete with 185,000 signatures. A succession of farmers, mayors, school trustees and clergymen politely but firmly spelled out how low wheat prices were allowing Saskatchewan rural communities to deteriorate, denying funds needed for farm equipment, roads, schools and other services. Reverend Maurice Baudoux of Prudhomme declared: "the rural home, which is recognized by all religious leaders as the most suitable environment for the practice of virtue — the rural home, which is recognized by all students in political economy as the cornerstone of nations — is rapidly crumbling under the weight of economic maladjustments."[26] Father Baudoux's plea was bluntly supported by United Church minister Allan Martin of Davidson: "We do not want a peasant class in Saskatchewan." Grudgingly impressed, Prime Minister King termed the presentations "convincing in many respects" and Agriculture Minister Jimmy Gardiner agreed that wheat growers were suffering in comparison with the rest of Canadian industry.

Over the next day and a half the Saskatchewan delegation exchanged dinners with MPs, heard and questioned a succession of civil servants, and split into smaller groups for meetings with individual MPs. Never before had Saskatchewan's problems been so thoroughly impressed on Ottawa in such orderly fashion. Of the delegation's major demands, however, none was granted soon or as a direct result of the demonstration — the government decided the time was not yet right for a one-dollar initial payment, nor for a crop insurance plan, nor for wheat prices that would provide 1926-29 purchasing power. But the wheat board initial payment was boosted to 90 cents, with Ottawa paying domestic millers a subsidy equal to the difference between 90 cents and the former price-freeze level of 77 cents. More important, the delegation had thoroughly impressed on all levels of the national government that Saskatchewan farm problems must be given greater and continual consideration in future policymaking. Pool secretary George Robertson wrote afterward:

> Much of the doubt and suspicion which undoubtedly existed at Ottawa as to the objective of the delegation, was washed away. A great deal of misunderstanding in Eastern Canada as to the actual economic situation in this province was cleared up. Members of the Cabinet from the Eastern and Maritime Provinces were deeply impressed by the sincerity and determination of the delegation that immediate action was necessary to enable Saskatchewan to play her full part in the difficult days that lie immediately ahead. Support was given to our Saskatchewan Members of Parliament in their efforts to secure economic redress. And what is possibly just as important as any of these, it brought together a splendid group of people from all walks of life in a united effort to improve living conditions in our farm homes, which will also mean better conditions in our towns and cities.[27]

Meanwhile the Pool organization had added war work to its list of activities in rural society. Committees were asked to do their utmost to convince people to vote for conscription in the 1942 plebiscite,[28] elevator agents bought 27,000 tons of scrap metal on behalf of the government, and fieldmen showed National Film Board movies to help Victory Loan drives and other wartime efforts.

Wartime extension of government regulation brought a host of practical problems for the Pool and other elevator companies, notably in the area of railway car allocation. With surplus grain accumulating, elevator throughput was determined more by the number of cars available at each elevator rather than farmers' preferences in where they delivered. From handling 44 percent of grain in 1939-40, Pool elevators fell to 40 percent in 1940-41. When the supply situation became less tight in the first seven months of 1942 — partly because of diversion to livestock feeding, partly because much British-bound grain was sent to the sea bottom by U-boats — the Pool percentage jumped to more than 48 percent. Perhaps thanks to greater understanding in Ottawa of Saskatchewan conditions, resulting from the 1942 delegation, the pools were able to persuade authorities in 1943 to allocate cars according to percentages of grain handled in 1938-40, before car restrictions distorted the pattern of farmers' deliveries.

An even more fundamental victory came on 27 September 1943, when Ottawa ordered an end to wheat trading on the Winnipeg Grain Exchange and gave the Canadian Wheat Board a monopoly. Although some farm groups had mixed feelings about the action, since wartime pressures were sending wheat prices shooting up, the three pools hailed the move as "a complete vindication of the attitude of the organized farmers."[29] In reality, the action owed more to the government's resolve to protect its anti-inflation policy, to put a lid on loans to Britain for wheat purchases, and to reduce subsidies being paid to millers.[30] The more crucial decision came as the war ended, when Ottawa had the choice of continuing the wheat board's monopoly or reverting to the pre-war system. Agriculture Minister Gardiner, who had been cultivating close ties with the pools and their supporters, received a strong warning in June 1945 that his Saskatchewan constituents were watching him closely. Although the Liberals were comfortably re-elected nationally, Gardiner won only by a 28-vote margin in his Melville constituency, after a recount. As the official historian of federal wheat policy commented: "In his near defeat, Gardiner recognized the need of doing something spectacular on behalf of producers in order to regain his popularity."[31] Not only was the wheat board monopoly on wheat preserved, but in 1948 additional legislation added oats and barley to the board's jurisdiction. By then, the pools had gained a second powerful ally in the cabinet, Trade Minister C. D. Howe. From the first year they were formed, Howe had had close relations with the pools as his Port Arthur engineering firm designed most of their terminal elevators.[32] Even with an expanded view of federal power and designation of wheat as an industry of national interest, Ottawa's jurisdiction in 1948 could not be unilaterally stretched to include the two feed grains, which were mostly fed to animals within the provinces of origin. But supporting legislation was passed by the prairie provinces, enabling the wheat board to start receiving oats and barley in 1949 and thus establishing its basic powers for a quarter-century. The grain exchange helpfully — though not intentionally — gave farmers a reminder in 1948 of the violent price swings that an open market could produce, as No. 2 rye fell from $4.79 in May to $1.40 in September.

SWP secretary George Robertson, president J. H. Wesson, director A. F. Sproule. (SWP files)

Just as the modern wheat board had been created in 1935 in conjunction with a movement toward international wheat co-operation, so too did the board's powers grow in the 1940s as nations worked toward another International Wheat Agreement. Tentative agreements among exporting nations in 1942 paved the way for a comprehensive post-war conference in 1947. The three pools not only played an influential role in persuading Ottawa to push hard for international agreement, but also had their leaders present at preparatory talks and the London conference itself. Saskatchewan Wheat Pool brought president Jack Wesson, secretary George Robertson and technical experts like the Pool's flour mill manager. Although diplomats handled public negotiations, the pools' representatives were busy lobbying their counterparts in other delegations and telling the diplomats what maximum and minimum price levels prairie farmers could accept.[33] It proved to be a frustrating task: the 1947 conference could not reach precise agreement; a 1948 agreement fell apart when the U.S. Congress failed to ratify it in time. But a 41-nation agreement was finally reached in 1949, providing for four exporting nations to move 525 million bushels in 1949-50 to 37 importing nations. Exporters were entitled to require importers to buy their full quota at the $1.50 minimum price while importers could demand that exporters sell their full quota at the $1.80 maximum price. Each group had security for both price and volume — the exporters were protected against price drops and the importers against price increases. At the end of the IWA's first year of operations, the three pools termed it "an historic achievement of tremendous potential for the future welfare of mankind."[34]

By then, however, prairie farmers had had less happy experience with a separate international agreement, the controversial 1946-50 Canada-Britain wheat agreement. Signed on 24 July 1946, the agreement provided for two years of wheat sales to Britain at $1.55 a bushel. In negotiating prices for the third and fourth years, British officials promised to "have regard to" any difference between the $1.55 and general world prices in the first two years. The deal, a pet project of Agriculture Minister Gardiner, also involved creation of a special five-year pool for wheat delivered to the Canadian Wheat Board, so that farmers delivering in the first two years would get any "have regard to" benefits that came later. Initial payments were to be $1.35 for each of the five years, although domestic wheat prices would be frozen at $1.25 with a further government subsidy to millers. Initially, most groups welcomed the British contract as valuable protection against price and market collapse similar to that which followed the First World War. The 1946 Pool annual meeting unanimously endorsed the agreement as "a first step toward securing that degree of stability and security essential to Saskatchewan agriculture as well as to the whole provincial economy." Another unanimous resolution in 1947 urged more such long-term agreements.

Trouble, however, came when world wheat prices rose steeply instead of repeating the drop of 1920. In late 1946 Pool directors noted that Canada's other exports were averaging $2.12 a bushel for No. 1 wheat, 57 cents more than exports to Britain. Even worse, Ottawa set a price of only $1.25 to farmers for each bushel of wheat used domestically. After wide farm protest, the domestic price received by farmers was boosted by 30 cents. Many farmers, however, continued to feel that they were heavily subsidizing both Canadian and British consumers. Their anger increased when, in October 1947, it became clear that the notorious "have regard to" clause was hollow. British representatives agreed to pay only $2 a bushel for wheat in 1948-49, a price that would do little or nothing to make up for farmers' losses during two years of sales at $1.55. Some areas with populations of largely British origin were philosophical, feeling that war-devastated Britain needed aid, even if farmers bore most of the cost.[35] Others, however, sourly compared their $1.35 initial payments with $2-plus world prices and blamed Saskatchewan Wheat Pool for its support of the agreement. After touring non-British areas, fieldman O. S. Olson commented: "To these people the British Wheat Agreement, the $1.35 and the Pool are the same."[36] Initial payments were raised to $1.55 in 1948 and $1.75 in 1949, slightly easing rural discontent, but then at the end of the five-year pool the board announced that its final payment would be no more than four cents a bushel unless Ottawa provided extra funds. A Canadian government delegation, including Jack Wesson, went to Britain with a final request for extra payments under the "have regard to" clause and returned empty-handed. Ottawa provided a largely-token extra payment of $65 million in 1951, adding another four cents to the final payment, and the controversy slowly wound down amid farmers' unsuccessful calls for more compensation for the substantial benefits enjoyed by British and Canadian consumers.

Fortunately the pools enjoyed greater success on another battlefield, defending their co-operative financial structure against criticism from private elevator companies. The struggle over tax treatment of co-operatives was launched in May 1940, when the Northwest Line Elevator Association urged Ottawa to investigate the pools' liability for income tax. According to co-operative theory, organizations like the pools by definition never made a profit and thus were not liable to taxation — any surplus left over at the end of the year represented excess charges that members had paid beyond the actual cost of service and the excess would eventually be returned to the members. But the private companies that made up the Line Elevator Association complained that the pools enjoyed an unfair advantage by hanging on to such untaxed surpluses for years. The focus of the mostly-technical argument was a section of 1930 legislation exempting certain co-operatives from taxation. The issue had simmered in the 1930s without serious study, but the sharp jump in corporate income tax during wartime gave the pools' private competitors a much-increased incentive to raise the issue. Even though federal officials decided in mid-1941 that the 1930 legislation did not in fact give the pools exemption from income tax, the pools continued for several years to refrain from paying income tax, while they pursued appeals to the ministerial level and then to the Exchequer Court. Meanwhile the pools were infuriating their private competitors by paying dividends for elevator patronage and cutting elevator charges below what the private companies charged. The largest cut came at a September 1944 meeting of the three pools' boards, where handling charges for wheat were dropped to one quarter of a cent per bushel, a seventh of the former rate. Confronted with an increasingly muddled situation that held serious financial implications for all co-operatives and for federal revenues, Ottawa appointed a royal commission to study the whole situation and suspended tax action while the commission looked at the issues in 1944 and 1945. The commission clarified much, but in effect tossed the central question affecting the pools right back at the cabinet. The pools were not given tax-exempt status under the 1930 legislation, the commission concluded. But it added that the legislation was ambiguous and that "co-operative associations have so conducted their affairs that great hardship would result should our recommendations be made to apply retroactively."[37]

The prospect of the pools' getting off scot-free drew even stronger representations from the Line Elevator Association, which in a 1946 statement criticized the government's seeming ability "to confer political and/or personal favours upon a preferred few at the expense of the competitors of that few and of the Dominion Treasury."[38] The association contended that the pools owed more than $25 million in back taxes, plus penalties and interest, and noted that pool auditors had been warning since 1940 that no provision was being made for possible tax liabilities. Any hardships from having to pay back taxes would be hardships the pools consciously brought upon themselves, the association argued. Intense lobbying by the pools and other members of the Co-operative Union of Canada, however, ultimately produced a favorable compromise in 1946 legislation. Under the new law, past technical omissions would be largely ignored and henceforth there would be no tax payable on surplus earnings that were distributed as patronage dividends within twelve months. Distribution would be deemed to include allocation of dividends to members while retaining the money in elevator or commercial reserves. If dividends were paid to members only, however, there would be tax payable on whatever part of the surplus came from non-member business. And in any case, there would be a three-per-cent tax payable on capital used in the co-operative enterprise. There would also be a three-year tax exemption period for new co-operatives. There would again be complaints from time to time that co-operatives enjoyed an unfair tax advantage, but the landmark 1946 law did much to regularize the situation. And since it also made patronage dividends tax deductible for private corporations as well as for co-ops, the co-operative movement had a blunt answer to future complaints: private corporations could escape tax too if they simply returned all their profits to their customers and asked their customers to lend them capital at minimal interest. With the 1946 resolution of the tax controversy, the whole co-op movement was freed to make dynamic progress in the post-war years. Saskatchewan Wheat Pool, for its part, was able to clean up three years of suspended patronage dividends — paying $6.25 million out in cash to cover two years and using the third year's dividend allocation to transfer equity from retired members to current members. The transfer meant that retired members, or the estates of those who had died, realized their equity in cash and that control of the Pool was maintained in the hands of active patrons.

The large dividend payment authorized in late 1946 also helped ease some of the resentment that the United Farmers of Canada had aroused against the Pool earlier that year. The UFC had been trying for some time to revitalize itself, a task made difficult in Saskatchewan by the Pool's overpowering presence in every field of farm policy. Initially the UFC had tried to get Pool committees to form UFC locals but few if any did, despite UFC secretary Frank Eliason's call for a farmers' organization that would be "free from political and commercial entanglements."[39]

When the Alberta Farmers' Union launched an ambitious farmers' strike in September 1946, in support of demands for parity prices, the UFC (Saskatchewan Section) quickly followed suit, not stopping to have its members ratify the decision. Some Saskatchewan Wheat Pool committees endorsed the strike and urged closure of their local Pool elevators, but the Pool's leadership remained firmly against the strike. In the Pool view, their elevators were obliged by their licenses to continue providing service to all. Pool leaders also believed the strike was a harmful

The Pool's Saskatoon flour mill, 1956. (SWP Collection, Saskatchewan Archives Board R-A 15,040 [2])

challenge to the whole Canadian Federation of Agriculture structure. And, in any case, they felt it was useless to demand parity prices without specifying important details — primarily a base period when prices were some desired amount above farm costs, and a system for calculating how much costs had risen since then. At the Pool's annual meeting in November, delegates overwhelmingly endorsed the directors' actions, despite blunt UFC appeals to the meeting to reorganize the "postponed" strike. UFC president Frank Appleby told Pool delegates: "I think it is high time that we all combined and let the east realize we are not all bohunks. . . . have you no backbone that you are not taking up this thing? Even a worm will turn its head if stepped on." Although several rural municipal councils in Saskatchewan supported the strike, both the Canadian Federation of Agriculture and the United Farmers of Alberta declined to endorse it.[40] By a vote of 131 to 21 Pool delegates said they would defend farmers' legal right to strike by holding back their produce, but opposed exercise of that right when it would interfere with the flow of food to still-suffering Europe, when consultative methods had not been fully tried, or when there was no prospect of getting beneficial results. In the last judgment, Pool delegates had the agreement of old Farmers' Union of Canada firebrand L. P. McNamee, who wrote later that the abortive non-delivery strike, which lasted from 6 September to 6 October, "appeared to me as a piece of criminal folly" because farmers were not educated and prepared for it.[41] But regardless of the rightness of the Pool position, the Pool's refusal to support strike action helped lead a more radical minority of farmers into concentrating their energies into rebuilding the UFC(SS) and its renamed successors, the Saskatchewan Farmers' Union and then the Saskatchewan section of the National Farmers' Union. Whereas once the radical and moderate wings of the farm movement had argued within the Pool organization, henceforward their debates would increasingly take the form of debates between two separate organizations, the Farmers' Union and the Pool.

As the 1940s came to a close, conditions were ripe for growing discontent. Despite losses under the British wheat deal, farmers had benefitted from wartime controls on their input costs and the purchasing power of a bushel of wheat in 1945 was higher than it had been since 1919. By comparison with 1926-29, prairie farmers had more than parity. But that prosperity was slipping away. The purchasing power of a bushel of wheat peaked in 1945, dropped by more than a third by 1949 and continued sliding throughout the 1950s.[42] A whole new category of major concerns was opened in 1948, when railways were given a twenty-one percent increase in freight rates, then an additional fifteen percent interim increase. The decisions, which did not affect most grain freight rates, nevertheless increased the cost of shipping needed goods to farmers as well as other groups. And the decisions launched a decade of rate-increase applications and controversy that included tentative challenges even to the statutory Crowsnest Pass freight rates on export grain. The rates had been enshrined in federal legislation in the 1920s, a quarter-century after their origin in an agreement between Ottawa and the Canadian Pacific Railway to run track through the Crowsnest Pass. For Saskatchewan Wheat Pool's first twenty-five years, the "Crow rate" was so much taken for granted that delegates did not even bother passing a resolution on the topic. That changed on 10 November 1949, when delegates gave unanimous approval to a Percy Simmonds motion declaring that the Crow rate was meant to stand "for all time" and should so stand. The resolution spelled out the basic principles that would guide Pool spokesmen for the next thirty years: that the grain economy of the West was founded on the assumption of permanent Crow rates; that the Crow was designed to counterbalance geographic and marketing disadvantages that still existed; and that "any increase in freight rates on grain and flour would have a disastrous effect on the Saskatchewan economy and would endanger the economy of all Canada." In 1949 there was no way that the West would tolerate tampering with the Crow — but just the fact that delegates felt the need to defend it was an ominous sign of trouble to come.

Expansion, 1944-49

In the five brief years from 1944 to 1949, Saskatchewan Wheat Pool dived headfirst into an unprecedented surge of commercial expansion and diversification, leaving behind the financial stagnation of the 1930s. The company that could not afford to print its traditional calendar in 1931-32 suddenly became owner of a new flour mill, a crushing-processing plant for vegetable oil, and a greatly-expanded printing operation, among other ventures. By the time those five decisive years were over, a new pattern had been created for Pool development and the organization was on course toward today's comprehensive, large-scale agribusiness operations. The first major step came in 1944, when the Pool merged with financially-troubled Saskatchewan Co-operative Livestock Producers Ltd.[43] The seventeen-year-old livestock co-op's name and functions survived in the form of a Pool subsidiary, while the two organizations' overlapping memberships were combined. In a statement, Pool secretary George Robertson declared that the purpose of the amalgamation was to strengthen the livestock operation throughout the province: "We believe that a strong producer organization, in which producers combine the movement and marketing of their stock, is likely to give a degree of stability to the live stock market greater than anything else offered at the present time."[44]

With the new responsibilities extending beyond grain, it was also time for the Pool to change its formal title. Thus "Saskatchewan Co-operative Wheat Producers Ltd." became simply "Saskatchewan Co-operative Producers Ltd." — although its members and patrons continued to call it Saskatchewan Wheat Pool. Over the next five years the Pool opened livestock sales yards at Swift Current, Yorkton and North Battleford, bringing more convenient selling facilities to livestock producers. At the same time the Pool encouraged the growing trend toward selling cattle by auction instead of the old "treaty" method of private negotiations between buyers and sellers. By 1949 co-operative marketing accounted for 40 percent of Saskatchewan cattle and calves, 36 percent of hogs and 35 percent of sheep and lambs.

While thus broadening its rural base, the Pool was also starting its climb up the ladder of vertical integration, launching its industrial division in 1947 with the vegetable oil plant, followed by the flour mill in 1949. From the start, Pool industrial development was a topic for some mild controversy. The Saskatchewan Co-operative Wholesale Society had operated a small, struggling flour mill at Outlook throughout the war, hampered by considerable variations in quality of output, with resulting complaints from housewives.[45] When Saskatchewan Wheat Pool decided in 1944 to build its own mill in Saskatoon, a modern $3 million plant, the consumer co-op movement was effectively shouldered aside, with some resulting hard feelings.[46] The co-operative principle of service at cost would in effect operate to the benefit of wheat producers, not bread consumers, so long as the farmers' organization owned the flour mill. But that was, in the final analysis, a theoretical problem of co-operative philosophy. In practice, only Saskatchewan Wheat Pool had the financial strength to launch the project and then endure the heavy losses that plagued the industrial division for years. The vegetable oil plant got off to a good start, earning a surplus of $61,578 after depreciation in its first 143 days of operation, producing linseed oil and linseed oilcake meal. Within two years, however, it was experiencing losses. The flour mill, meanwhile, was a heavy loser from the first — losses totalled $162,551 for its initial five months in 1948-49, followed by losses totalling nearly $600,000 over the next three years. Loss years, in fact, would be frequent throughout the 1950s and 1960s and only the 1970s would bring consistent surpluses. Pool delegates and members were to get an expensive lesson in the difficulty of breaking into an established industry and having to cope with tough competition while acquiring management and technical expertise. By standards of return on investment, the industrial development would be a failure for many years. As a co-operative, however, the Pool could afford to take a broader view — the industrial division would add to co-ops' economic control, provide a valuable window onto the food industry, and help ensure fair treatment of farmers who sold to that industry. For the generations of Pool delegates who maintained support for industrial ventures, it would be a matter more of faith than accounting.

The same was true of the *Western Producer*, which consistently managed to lose more money than the Modern Press printing operations made. The only exception, before modern days, came in the three fiscal years ending in 1946, when wartime price control kept *Producer* costs steady and permitted three moderate surpluses, while circulation rose above 110,000. But, rather than

A 1950s chat between Jock Brown (left), president of Canadian Co-operative Implements Ltd., and Western Producer *editor Pat Waldron.*

trying to squeeze more surpluses out of the newspaper, Pool delegates chose instead to pump more money into it to improve its quality. By 1948, a new printing press and a two-storey addition to the Modern Press building were in place. It had been a frustrating period, as expansion was long delayed by wartime economic controls, then by postwar newsprint rationing and shortages of labor and materials. Even when the first color comics and magazine section rolled off the presses for the issue of 19 August 1948, editors were "far from satisfied with the type of paper being turned out at present."[47] But the Pool's commitment to maintain a top-quality newspaper had been made clear. In various resolutions, delegates called for more space fot national, international, financial, economics, co-operative and Pool news. Many an editor would welcome such shareholder support in asking for more money. Delegates' traditional interest in all the details of *Producer* operations was also demonstrated by one resolution in which the assembled representatives of more than 100,000 Saskatchewan farmers urged addition of a few new categories to the classified section so readers could more easily find the specific types of farm machinery they wanted to buy. Not all Pool personnel, however, regarded the money-losing ventures with favor. Hugh McPhail, nephew of the first elected Pool president, was a Pool fieldman in this expansionist era. In 1982, he grumbled:

> They used to call them their herd of white elephants. They had the flour mill and they had the crushing plant and they had Modern Press . . . they lost a bundle of money every year on that white elephant herd they had. I don't know whether they are making a profit yet.[48]

Fortunately for the care and feeding of the "herd of white elephants," both the Pool and Saskatchewan farmers generally were enjoying a period of long-overdue prosperity. Grain was flowing fast to export markets and even the artificially-low prices under the British wheat agreement were considerably higher than they had been in the previous decade. Saskatchewan Wheat Pool's elevators had an increasing share of that flow, rising rapidly from 43 percent of Saskatchewan grain in 1943-44 to a record 51 percent in 1946-47. Surpluses for both the country elevator division and the terminal elevator division were in the millions most years. Also, Pool members as a whole could afford to leave much of the surplus earnings with the Pool, either to increase Pool assets or finance new ventures. The 1946 prairie census found that Saskatchewan farmers' mortgage debt had dropped 60 percent over the previous five years. The province's farms had had only $86 million in cash income from sales of their products in 1937, but 1947 brought them more than $428 million. In each of 1944, 1948, and 1949, the total was over $500 million.

With the Pool's new financial power and the improved incomes of its members, conditions were right for yet another major venture. This time, however, Pool funds were to be used to launch a whole new field of co-operative services, in which the entire co-op movement would share control. In May 1945 Co-operative Life was established as a mutual company under the Saskatchewan insurance act, to provide general life insurance services and carry forward the tradition that had begun in the 1920s, when the three prairie pools formed their own insurance companies to cover their grain and elevators. The initial push for Co-op Life came from Pool director H. A. Crofford, who formally proposed the idea to the board of directors in July 1944. Strong support came immediately from lawyer R. H. Milliken and directors A. F. Sproule and Tom Bobier,[49] making the venture one of the first major Pool initiatives to be the product of director and employee partnership instead of grassroots pressure. The first board of Co-op Life and its first senior officials were all Pool figures, and initially the company's sales staff consisted of Pool fieldmen, working without commissions. On his way home from the first organizational meeting for sales staff, fieldman Wilf MacLeod sold the first Co-op Life policy and within two weeks the field staff added 157 more.[50] Their enthusiasm was coupled with informality and near-total lack of bureaucracy — no medical examinations were required of the first group of policyholders. Fieldmen made their own judgments and collected a urine sample on the spot for later laboratory analysis.[51] Within two years of its founding, Co-op Life was registered federally and seeking national business, in response to repeated requests from co-operative leaders in other provinces for service for their members. As it grew and merged with other co-operative insurance services, Co-op Life acquired its own staff and independent identity. Long before it became a key part of today's organization, The Co-operators, Co-op Life was under the direction of a wide range of co-ops, with the Pool's role declining to being one among many shareholders. There was a price to be paid for such organization, since patrons did not have the same direct control over Co-op Life that they could have over their local consumer co-ops. Several layers of organizations and boards might lie between them and the directors of such a federation of co-ops. But if co-operative economic power and co-operative ethics were to expand, they would have to do so in the form of ever-larger organizations that would be built on top of the financial resources of existing co-ops. The days of running co-operative services with slices of Pool fieldmen's time and corners of Pool elevator agents' desks should and did give way to a less colorful but healthier era in which co-ops handled all their own needs themselves. Saskatchewan Wheat Pool would still be there, one among many, to share financial and leadership responsibilities in various joint ventures. But its onetime dependants would henceforth manage their own affairs.

The Pool, of course, could not afford to let its basic services lapse, even in this period of launching new ventures. The number of Pool elevators grew only modestly, from 1,135 in 1945 to 1,162 in 1949, but many were modernized under a far-reaching program of rebuilding and adding annexes. Similar improvements were made in the terminal elevator division, where new structures replaced older ones. The money-losing terminal at Buffalo, N.Y., was finally sold in 1945 and the leased terminal No. 6 at the Lakehead was handed back to the CNR in 1948. The wave of modernization, however, came too late to save Pool Terminal No. 5 and the twenty-two men who died when the building exploded

Final payment of Saskatchewan Wheat Pool's debt to the provincial government, 1949. From left: SWP secretary George Robertson, SWP president J. H. Wesson, provincial treasurer Clarence Fines, Thomas Lax. (Saskatchewan Archives Board R-B 7586, Saskatchewan Dept. of Education, visual education branch photo by James J. Walters)

on 7 August 1945. An inquiry into the tragedy was told that the massive explosion and fire may have been caused by the explosion of an unshielded electric light bulb in an atmosphere thick with grain dust. The Pool had acquired the terminal nineteen years earlier when it took over the old Co-op Elevator company. Pool employees and other people nearby did their best at rescue efforts and reports paid particular tribute to an army private, Bruce Cudmore, who swung hand over hand along an untested rope link from the top of a nearby building to reach injured men on top of Terminal No. 5. But no amount of courage could make up for the lack of better dust removal equipment and grounding to prevent static electricity, two measures that a coroner's jury recommended be taken at all terminal elevators. With that tragic lesson in mind, designers gave extra attention to safety features as the Pool in 1946-49 added a $1.45 million new workhouse, designated Terminal No. 4B, and built an extra two million bushels storage capacity for Terminal No. 7, which already had the largest annual volume of any Lakehead terminal.

As Saskatchewan Wheat Pool moved into the promising postwar era with bold new business ventures under way, it passed a psychological and financial milestone at which it had been aiming for eighteen years. On 15 September 1949 the Pool handed a $465,169.77 cheque to the Saskatchewan government, ending the long struggle to clear the $13.3 million debt for 1929-30 overpayments to farmers.[52] The once crippling debt was removed two years ahead of schedule, with payment in full of more than $8 million in interest over the eighteen years, and Saskatchewan Wheat Pool was finally free to devote its full attention and resources to investing in the future.

7
Reorganization, 1949–69

There is no organization in the world quite like the
Saskatchewan Wheat Pool.

— *Time,* 6 January 1961

In the 1940s Saskatchewan Wheat Pool won its long battles for
an effective wheat board, for expansion of co-operative economic·
power, and for its own financial security. In the 1950s and 1960s,
the Pool found that it was poorly prepared to cope with its own
successes and with the changing world that it had helped create. It
had grown to be a multi-faceted business, active in a dozen
different fields and responsible for huge new capital spending
projects. Yet, for most of this period, the Pool's various divisions
functioned with only sporadic efforts at co-ordination and with a
woeful lack of detailed financial planning capability. In a world
that was daily growing more complex — through growing
government regulation, tightening cost-price squeezes, more
convoluted diplomacy, and increasingly volatile labor relations —
the Pool was without a professional research department and had
few employees with university degrees of any sort. Nor did the
internal contradictions end there. Saskatchewan Wheat Pool's
tradition was one of championing progressive, almost radical,
reform on behalf of the downtrodden farmers who were its
members. But that membership was changing markedly as farms
became larger, more capital-intensive, more reliant on expensive
machinery and chemicals. Farmers were still farmers — but they
were also increasingly sophisticated businessmen, investors, herbi-
cide technicians, and mechanics. Many Pool members were now
livestock producers, yet the Pool seemed to have near-total
concentration on the needs of grain farmers. Trucks could cover in
an hour the distance that horse-drawn wagons took a day to travel,

165

but the pattern of grain elevators was little changed. A new generation of farmers was taking over the land, with new problems and needs to which the Pool had to respond. From almost 139,000 farms in 1941, averaging 432 acres each, the province went to 79,366 farms in 1966 with an average 807 acres, reflecting fundamental changes in rural society.

To its credit, Saskatchewan Wheat Pool recognized the need for both internal reform and new approaches to farm problems. Fittingly, the Pool acquired two new presidents to lead the way — Charles W. Gibbings from 1960 to 1969, then E. K. (Ted) Turner after Gibbings was appointed a wheat board commissioner. Both were Saskatchewan-born and from the second generation of Pool families. With the Pool's consensus-style policymaking, the leadership changes brought no radical reversals of policy. But Wesson was seventy-three in 1960 when he retired, and both he and the Pool were ready to see presidential responsibilities pass to younger, more vigorous hands.[1] Similar changes were already under way on the employee side, where George Robertson retired in 1958 at the age of sixty-nine.

Meanwhile, as the decades rolled by, Saskatchewan Wheat Pool had acquired a tradition of giving heavy responsibilities in specific areas to its vice-presidents, particularly the duty of representing the Pool in international forums. By some accounts, that tradition started or was confirmed at least partly because one vice-president, Louis Boileau, was a French-speaking rapeseed grower and was the natural choice for technical missions to France on that subject.[2] An earlier vice-president, Wes Ball, was also heavily involved with the International Federation of Agricultural Producers. In addition, Ball played a role in strengthening the credit union system, responding to the 1951 misfortunes of one tiny credit union. When the Arran credit union discovered $71,000 missing from its accounts, some depositors were threatened with the loss of their life savings. Ball pulled out $100 to deposit in the credit union as a gesture of confidence, then with help from Pool secretary George Robertson and field staff director Les Stutt began encouraging credit unions to organize a mutual aid fund. Eventually, the Arran credit union was able to continue, with no loss of money by its member-depositors.[3] Among other vice-presidents, Bill Marshall brought a livestock background to that sphere of Pool policy, E. A. (Ted) Boden participated in industry-government studies of the rail car allocation system, and Don Lockwood represented the Pool in a host of co-operative organizations.

Although the main effort at internal reorganization came under Gibbings, two formal steps were taken during Wesson's presidency. The first, in 1952, was to lease virtually all assets to the

parent company — "Saskatchewan Co-operative Producers Ltd."
— for operating purposes. This transformed subsidiary companies
into paper holding companies, while the Pool became the sole
operating company for all activities. Among other benefits, the
simplified organization prevented possible tax complications.
Before the change the Pool elevator subsidiary was paying
patronage dividends to Pool shareholders, but not to its sole
shareholder — the Pool — and there was doubt about whether
such procedure qualified for tax exemptions for patronage
dividends.[4] Nor did the subsidiaries serve any purpose in limiting
possible losses, since lenders required any large loans to be
guaranteed by the Pool as a whole, not just the subsidiary. The
second step took effect 1 August 1953: the Pool's formal corporate
title became Saskatchewan Wheat Pool. Everyone had been
calling it that for thirty years except lawyers and taxmen, and the
name had acquired a familiarity that overrode other considerations. The Pool had not been a pool, even in token form, for
fourteen years. Its base had not been exclusively wheat since
coarse grains pooling was started in the mid-twenties. And much
of its physical assets had been outside Saskatchewan since the
same era. But, to friend and foe alike, it was known as "the
Pool."

The changes, however, did not pass without scattered objections
from Pool managers.[5] C. S. Fisher, manager of the industrial
division and flour mill, wrote to head office that overseas buyers
were suspicious of any change in lettering on flour bags; he
warned that flour exports might suffer if the old "Saskatchewan
Co-operative Producers Ltd." was removed. G. E. Northcott,
manager of Saskatchewan Co-operative Livestock Producers Ltd.,
generally known as "Saskatchewan Livestock Pool," opposed any
change in either of those well-known and trusted names. And T.
R. Melville-Ness, soon to be head of Modern Press and the
Western Producer, said it would be hard for Modern Press's
salesmen to ask for business for the printing division of the Pool.
Some customers, he said, were averse to dealing with co-operatives
and would not like to be reminded of Modern Press's parentage.
Of the three, only Melville-Ness was successful in maintaining use
of the old subsidiary's name when operations were moved under a
Pool division. But more fundamental changes were to come under
a new president.

A New Generation Takes Command: Charles Gibbings

Gibbings came to the presidency in 1960 with thorough Pool
and academic experience, plus first-hand knowledge of Depression farming conditions. Born 10 August 1916 in Rosetown, he

was only eleven when his father, an early Pool delegate, was killed in a farm accident. Gibbings and a fifteen-year-old brother took over responsibility for running the farm. Despite that heavy load, he completed high school in 1934 and went on to university agriculture studies in 1938, the same year he started farming on his own. Along the way, he raised money by selling Fuller brushes near Lloydminster in 1937, becoming the company's top Manitoba-Saskatchewan salesman that year.[6] At university Gibbings initially had no intention of returning to farming, "but my observations were that the boys who were attending the University from farms seemed to be much better off financially than those who were sons of fathers who were working in other occupations."[7] When he received his agriculture degree in 1942, the wheat economy was moving up. His energy, however, could not be confined within the bounds of a farm and he also served in the 1940s as a youth training instructor and as a teacher at the University of Saskatchewan agriculture school.

In 1946 he became one of the young farmers caught by the Pool's talent-recruiting program. Before fieldman Noel Craddock and retiring delegate Bob Cowan arrived at his farmyard to ask him to stand for office, Gibbings had never attended a Pool meeting of any sort.[8] But, once elected a delegate that year, he learned fast. Within six years he was on the board of directors, and three years after that he became vice-president. In his delegate days Gibbings made his mark early as a spokesman for the younger, more aggressive group of delegates, notably with a speech about 1950 pushing for vigorous terminal expansion.[9] As Pool vice-president, he also served as a commissioner on the provincial royal commission on agriculture and rural life, winning praise for his contributions to that study.

Gibbings entered the Pool presidency with fairly well defined goals. For one, he said then that he intended to remain no more than ten years, so that younger men would not be discouraged by lack of opportunities to advance. He had also urged more attention for livestock activities and was an advocate of increased co-operation among the three pools. Perhaps more important than any single policy was his general determination to re-awaken the Pool's dynamism and to transform the company into a modern, efficient operation. The Pool, at times, literally needed awakening — some older directors used to doze off during afternoon board meetings. Once, Gibbings was mortified to notice three directors asleep when a government guest was attending a board meeting.[10] The new president's businesslike and assertive approach, as well as his policy of developing a farm supply business that competed with local co-ops, could rub some fellow directors the wrong way.

Left: SWP secretary Arthur R. Stevens. *(SWP Collection, Saskatchewan Archives Board R-A 15,269)*
Right: SWP President Charles W. Gibbings. *(SWP Collection, Saskatchewan Archives Board R-A 15,239)*

One veteran director thought Gibbings had too much emphasis on profitability, too little on the co-operative tradition of providing services at cost.[11] For many Pool activities, however, someone needed to be tough and profit-minded. Gibbings believed, for example, that longer-established firms in the flour business were resolved to take all the competitive steps necessary to ensure the Pool's flour mill venture never became financially attractive. An even greater financial bloodbath might have resulted if the Pool had jumped into the meat-packing business. After several studies of that proposed venture, Gibbings became convinced that an isolated packing plant would encounter cut-throat local competition that would drain the Pool treasury.[12] But, although he took a hard look at financial prospects, Gibbings was not exclusively concerned with profitability. He had a similar firm grasp of co-operative principles, stating that the Pool would enter the packing business only if such entry would improve producers' bargaining power. His personal conclusion was that the economic bargaining power once enjoyed by packing plants had been lost to chain-store meat buyers. The Pool, however, might have tried something in the meat-packing line if Manitoba Pool had not first jumped into the business and encountered problems.[13]

Gibbings also brought new vigor to the Pool's public relations. The age of lengthy oratory was over, and Gibbings' buoyant, effusive speeches were more suited to modern audiences. With wit and light-hearted comments, he could make listeners remember his points. His predecessor had direct ties with cabinet ministers and apparently felt little need to educate non-agricultural businessmen about farmers' needs, but Gibbings realized the Pool had to strengthen its ties with the general business community[14] — in the new age, farm organizations would need support and understanding wherever they could get it. Gibbings devoted more time to speaking to non-agricultural business groups and his outside directorships included the Royal Bank, Canadian Exporters' Association, Banff School of Advanced Management, and Great Lakes Waterways Development Association, as well as a position on the University of Saskatchewan Senate. Yet farm traditions remained part of him. While Pool president, he looked forward to breaks when he could get back to his farm, saying: "It's the best therapy I know of. There's no place in the world where you can think more clearly than on a tractor seat."[15] Gibbings had a clear sense of the Pool's basic priorities:

> It isn't necessarily so that what is good for General Motors is good for the country; and it isn't necessarily so that what is good for the Saskatchewan Wheat Pool is good for the farmer; but what is good for the farmer is good for the Saskatchewan Wheat Pool.[16]

Among 1960s changes presided over by Gibbings, the Pool's authorized share capital was boosted first from $200,000 to $35 million, then to $50 million. Instead of members' equity being awkwardly stated as a single $1 share plus their share of elevator and commercial reserves, all those amounts were consolidated into share capital. Shareholders were thus permitted to build up an unlimited number of shares through allocation of patronage dividends into share capital, but each shareholder would continue to have no more than one vote in Pool affairs. In keeping with the co-operative principle of dividing profits by patronage rather than by money invested, interest or dividends totalling more than five per cent on share capital were barred.

Meanwhile, efforts were under way to bring more modern techniques into Pool management. Delegates unanimously voted in 1958 to establish a research department under a qualified economist, and in 1960 the position was filled by R. H. D. (Bob) Phillips. The newcomer found himself in a small band of Pool staff who had post-secondary degrees — less than a dozen. Allan McLeod, another degree-holder and Phillips' successor as research director, agreed that Gibbings brought a new attitude; previously, "you almost had to apologize for having a degree, whereas Charlie turned that right around."[17] But times were changing. Auditor Bill Purslow took over as treasurer, the first chartered accountant on Pool staff, and acquired assistants who were knowledgeable about budgeting and the exotic new devices called computers. In 1961 a staff training program was launched, and a scientific personnel policy began to form. Outside consultants — more concerned with efficiency than with loyalty to co-operative principles — were brought in to evaluate jobs, employees, procedures and salaries. The experience was traumatic for many staff members, until assurances were given that reorganization and computerization would not mean firing.[18]

By early 1964 the first computer installation was complete and mindless machines took over the numbing task of processing hundreds of thousands of grain tickets, freeing staff for more rewarding duties. The next year, computer systems specialist J. M. Fair was hired to manage the system and, as it turned out, to start his climb up the corporate ladder to the position of chief executive officer. The massive volume of Pool paperwork in pre-computer days was illustrated by one 1960 episode, recalled by fieldman Bert Lee as "the time we went looking for lost souls."[19] In that laborious effort to prune obsolete entries from the Pool's mailing list, Lee found one former member whose mail had been being returned ever since 1928 — a man who was in 1960 working in the Pool's head office.

Saskatchewan Wheat Pool Reorganizes, 1967

One major change, in both an administrative and psychological sense, came in 1967 as Ira K. Mumford was appointed the Pool's first general manager. Instead of each operating division being tied separately and independently to the board of directors, all would now come under Mumford's supervision. There were qualms among the board over whether they were giving up control by creating such a position, but the tentative consensus was that the Pool was getting so big that some such step was necessary if they were to maintain control. Mumford, who received the title of chief executive officer a dozen years later, was a reassuring choice for those who wanted the Pool to maintain its philosophical tradition amid modernization. Raised on a Saskatchewan farm during the Depression, Mumford had started work with the Pool in 1938 as a head-office messenger boy. He had been trained as a teacher but found that the Pool's fifty-dollar monthly salary for messenger service was more than many teachers could get in cash.[20] After wartime service in the air force, Mumford returned to the Pool, supervising the variety test program. Significantly, he worked his way up through the publicity department and the secretary's staff, rather than in commercial operations, ensuring thorough familiarity with the Pool's democratic and policy side. For two years he was Pool secretary.

Pool directors carefully maintained two key practices to ensure that as much control as possible stayed with elected officials. First was the practice of having division managers appear regularly before the board for reports and questioning, even though they were under Mumford's day-to-day supervision. Second was to keep the social and political wing of the Pool separate from commercial operations. Such related operations as the field staff, public relations, member relations, delegate support, and policy research were supervised by the secretary, who reported to the board with status equal to the general manager of commercial operations. Despite such emphasis on the Pool's policy and member relations side, some Pool veterans thought the change meant slightly less attention would be paid to current membership opinion, since the head of field staff now reported to the secretary. Previously, field staff head R. L. (Les) Stutt had reported to the board directly.

After George Robertson's lengthy tenure, the secretary's post was filled for six years by Arthur R. Stevens, a former schoolteacher and Regina *Leader-Post* editorial writer who worked his way up through the Pool's publicity department. Mumford took over as secretary for 1964-66, after Stevens retired, then was followed by James O. Wright, a former Tisdale farmer who had been a Pool delegate for nine years before joining Pool staff as a fieldman in 1957.

On both the commercial and democratic sides of the company, reorganization came barely in time to meet perplexing new problems. By late 1967 all divisions were using capital spending budgets and more extensive financial planning, while the Pool was already in the middle of a record capital construction program, one that required $10 million in outside loans. At the same time general manager Mumford outlined a long list of areas in which five- and ten-year planning was required to cope with shifting economic circumstances. Two years later, as the 1960s were ending, the need for careful management and planning was dramatically underlined by a $298,812 loss on overall Pool operations, compared with net earnings of $2.3 million and $10.2 million in the two preceding years. Sluggish grain movement, rising interest rates and a generally weak economy had hit Pool revenues hard and Mumford bluntly gave delegates some provocative advice in November 1969: "emphasis must be shifted to profit orientation and there must be a cutback on non-earning services."[21]

Pool delegates, meanwhile, were still concerned lest the board and management acquire too much independence. In the past, the delegate body had occasionally overruled their directors, as when they voted in 1953 to double the amount of cash patronage dividends planned by a cautious board. But in the 1960s there were concerted efforts to check unilateral board-management decisions. After directors decided to donate $250,000 over five years to the University of Saskatchewan's building fund, delegates imposed a $10,000 limit on donations that did not have prior delegate authorization.[22] And the board's 1967 decision to start construction on a $2-million, seven-storey addition to head office drew a resolution urging that the Pool membership be consulted before such major projects were begun. Despite such wrist-slapping, the Pool's consensus system continued to hold together. Policy resolutions continued to be advisory and not formally binding on the board, which kept the basic confidence of delegates. And an analysis of recorded votes for 1964-67 found no visible factions at annual meetings who tended to vote together either for or against board recommendations.[23]

A more serious problem on the democratic side, one that was to remain throughout the 1970s as well, was a growing lack of candidates for delegate positions. In the 1920s the Pool had averaged 106 elections each year, with the rest of the subdistricts having just one candidate each. By 1954 there were only 14 elections compared with 152 acclamations, and thus only 3,834 Pool members got to cast ballots that year.[24] That low figure became lower in the early 1960s, when elections averaged nine per year. In one sense the lack of candidates was an indication of members' confidence in the comfortable Pool system of having fieldmen and retiring delegates invite people to stand for office. But it was also an ominous sign of possible apathy among the membership, carrying with it the danger that the delegate body would not reflect all sections of farm opinion. With so few elections, there also seemed little reason to continue the tradition of one-year terms, even though Aaron Sapiro had insisted that such terms were essential to allow members' feelings to be reflected promptly. Thus, starting in 1965, each year only half the subdistricts were up for possible election and delegates all had two-year terms.[25] Even with the relative lack of candidates, the Pool retained strict loyalty standards, passing a bylaw in 1968 requiring all members to have shipped all their grain and livestock through Pool facilities for three years before being eligible to be delegates. Exceptions were allowed only for farm-to-farm sales and in cases where Pool facilities were not available.

Meanwhile the duties of a delegate were largely unchanged.

Participation remained high at annual meetings, with one detailed study of the 1967 meeting finding that only 18.6 percent of delegates did not speak.[26] The average delegate spoke six times, for two and a half minutes each time. During general discussions and debates, directors did proportionately slightly more listening than talking, speaking five times each on average. In the country, Pool delegates were not the prominent figures they once had been, but they were still active and well known. One survey, a fifth of whose respondents were not Pool members, found that forty-six percent of rural people could name their subdistrict's delegate.[27] To many farmers, the Pool delegate was primarily the man to see about local issues. Frank Schweitzer, for example, found one of his first chores was to deal with an elevator agent who, farmers said, spent his time in the billiard hall and made people wait while he finished his game. Schweitzer, like other delegates, had no formal authority over Pool personnel, but his influence as a delegate was enough to get the agent transferred.[28] Later, he successfully used that influence in reverse, retaining an agent whom local farmers liked but who was about to be transferred. As always, delegates

Saskatchewan Wheat Pool fieldmen and supervisors, 1954. Standing, from left: J. A. Toupin; R. L. Stutt; J. L. Buckley; J. D. Stratychuk; H. A. Wagner. Seated: B. K. Lee; C. L. Pyett; Everett Baker; O. S. Olson; T. J. Nyhus; Gilbert H. Wesson; Phil Rothery; M. C. Lambie; J. C. Manning; Ivan J. McDonald; Wilson Parker; W. J. Forsyth; C. J. Finucane; H. M. Tyler; John Pavelick; Don Sinclair.

had the frustrating chore of dealing face to face with every kind of complaint or criticism from farmers who held them personally accountable for everything the Pool did, big or small. "Some days you'd feel like tramping on your hat after a session in the country," recalled Gordon South, "but next day you'd get a bright light and you'd be off again."[29] Communication skills and techniques improved as delegates received increasing coaching and support from the field staff. And, about 1960, modern slides and flip charts finally retired "the old horseblanket" — a canvas full of statistics that delegates used to drag from hall to hall and hang up to show highlights of the Pool's latest annual report.[30] Later, in an attempt to give members more immediate input into the policymaking process, delegates concentrated more on consulting their committees before each annual meeting, instead of reporting to the committees after the annual meeting.

Staff pay and benefits continued to improve with changing times, although the innate financial conservatism of farmer-delegates ruled out anything resembling excessive generosity. The 1966 meeting, for example, turned down a proposal to pay full pensions to agents who retired because of ill health after 20 years' service. For many employees, however, such failures were balanced by the Pool's traditional human, understanding approach to its staff. Don Sinclair's son was three years old when Sinclair told supervisor R. L. (Les) Stutt that he would like a Saskatoon posting when his son was university age. Stutt said that would be done, but over the next fifteen years he retired and even Sinclair forgot about the promise — until head office, at the appropriate time, called him up to say the transfer was all set if he still wanted it.[31]

International Wheat Agreements 1949-71

The world, of course, did not stand still while Saskatchewan Wheat Pool completed its various reorganizations and modernizations. While those were taking place in the 1950s and 1960s, far-reaching changes were under way both nationally and globally. In the international sphere the decades-old dream of comprehensive international co-operation slowly faded away through a succession of ever-weaker international wheat agreements.[32] The 1949 IWA basically stood for ten years, with revisions in 1953 and 1956, although the United Kingdom dropped out for the last six years. With the resumption of Liverpool wheat futures trading, British leaders felt they could get wheat more cheaply than the $1.55 to $2.05 price range set in 1953, or the $1.50 to $2.00 range of 1956. The United Kingdom returned for the 1959-62 IWA, with a $1.50 to $1.90 price range, but requirements for importing nations had been relaxed. Instead of being obliged to take set amounts at the floor price in case of a price collapse, they were supposed to try to arrange a certain percentage of purchases within the price range. The system, however, continued during another IWA in 1962-67, with everthing holding together largely because prices more or less naturally stayed in the target ranges. Close Canada-U.S. consultations also helped prevent price breaks. Disaster came after a new type of agreement in 1967, the International Grains Arrangement. Among other details, it changed the basic reference price from Canadian wheat at Thunder Bay to U.S. wheat at Gulf ports. Its minimum and maximum price structure collapsed within a year as world prices fell, with both importers and exporters disregarding the floor price. Despite large and widespread surpluses, exporting nations were able to take some steps to stabilize prices — but well below those set in 1967. Canadian authorities and their advisors in the pools and elsewhere reluctantly came to the conclusion that rigid, detailed IWAs were not practical — and that Canada had been sacrificing its own interests by making increasing concessions to persuade the United States to come along.[33] When a replacement agreement was reached in 1971, it thus had no minimum-maximum prices and consisted of little more than general pledges to retain the spirit of orderly marketing. The future, it seemed, would lie more in loose, informal consultation among exporting nations than in comprehensive exporter-importer agreements.

One gradual effect of the erosion of formal international agreements was to reinforce an existing tendency to look to Ottawa for help in the form of domestic aid programs. Farmers had ridden a wave of prosperity into the 1950s, freeing themselves by 1951 of eighty percent of the mortgage load that they carried in 1937. Even when a large wheat carryover accumulated in 1953, there were grounds for optimism. Pool directors said the situation was far different from the days of sawdust prices, since farmers of the 1950s in Canada, Australia and the United States had government boards or agencies who could hold wheat or otherwise prevent fire sales: "it is evident that the wheat is in strong hands, and is not subject to raids by speculative bears."[34] But there were limits to what existing government programs could do. While falling grain prices in that surplus period drove 1955 Saskatchewan farm cash income down almost to the level of 1946, farm costs rose to be fifty-three percent above 1946. The Pool did what it could, including an innovative program of helping communities build hockey and curling rinks — for grain storage. The rink at Abernethy, for example, was completed in mid-1956 with local funds and labor, then used to store 90,000 bushels of surplus grain for the next five and a half years, with storage fees paying for money spent to build the rink.[35]

Such measures were helpful, but only in dealing with minor side effects of the fundamental problem. As its basic solution, the Pool started in 1956 to promote the concept of "deficiency payments," arguing that Ottawa should make such payments to farmers whenever farmers' revenues fell below their fair share of the national income. Two federal election campaigns in 1957-58, with a stormy minority government in between, disrupted Ottawa's ability to respond to the Pool lobby, but in 1958 the three prairie pools began making progress. Their initial request that year was for deficiency payments of 22 cents a bushel on 1955-56 deliveries and 30 cents on 1956-57, the latter figure later being revised to 36 cents. As part of its campaign, Saskatchewan Wheat Pool made its first major use of television, producing five programs that were used on all four Saskatchewan stations of the day. In August 1958 the Diefenbaker government's response included promises of a comprehensive crop insurance program and increased agricultural credit, plus special payments of $1 an acre to farmers, up to a maximum $200 per farm.

Pool delegates in turn reacted by terming the new programs inadequate and calling on the Pool to organize a mass delegation to Ottawa. In the thirty days from 15 December 1958 to 15 January 1959, more than 1,000 meetings were held throughout the province to mobilize farm opinion and to prepare for the new expedition.[36] The capital's memories of the orderly 1942 March on Ottawa seem to have faded, for extensive security precautions were taken. "The fear in Ottawa was that they were a bunch of hayseed barbarians coming with pitchforks," recalled fieldman Ted Nyhus.[37] The March 1959 event was peaceful, however, with nearly 1,100 delegates arriving with a 302,000-name petition urging deficiency payments. Once again, as in 1942, Pool president Jack Wesson was chief spokesman. Unlike 1942, the 1959 delegation was a prairie-wide effort, co-sponsored by the other pools, the three prairie provinces' farm unions, the three federations of agriculture, and United Grain Growers. Despite all the signatures and groups involved, results were disappointing — there were to be no deficiency payments, just a 1960 repeat of the dollar-an-acre payment. Prime Minister Diefenbaker also declined the pools' request for a two-price wheat system whereby domestic consumers would pay more than the export price.

Worldwide Efforts Boost Grain Sales

Salvation — or at least a temporary respite from price-depressing surpluses — was to come from another direction. Since the

1950s the Canadian Wheat Board had been discreetly working on ways to get wheat exports flowing again. One major problem had been U.S. passage in 1954 of Public Law 480, authorizing government exports of surplus grain on such easy terms that the exports were almost giveaways. The countries that "bought" the grain immediately had their money lent back to them for development projects. Canadian Wheat Board commissioner Doug Treleaven noted that top officials of the pools were consulted as board and other government officials worked "extremely quietly" to negotiate with officials of the United States and other nations to curb market-disrupting programs involving cheap credit or low prices. Prairie farmers had little if any idea of the delicate efforts being made on their behalf, but the efforts ultimately helped curb P. L. 480 grain shipments that were severely disrupting normal trade patterns.

Wheat board officials also played a major role in the historic 1958-61 launching of large wheat sales to China, a trade breakthrough that brought an increasingly westward orientation to Canadian grain exports. Indeed, Treleaven has argued:

> the Board was *totally* responsible for this breakthrough, as it was with the institution of grain business in a number of other areas. Board personnel had started going into the Peoples' Republic in about 1958 — among the very first business men from the western world — and indeed had had contact with Chinese officials through Hong Kong as early as 1954. They had sought to develop a trading relationship with the communist regime, and their efforts resulted in the 'test' shipments of 1958. It was the Board which encouraged the government to grant visas to a Chinese trade delegation in early 1961, and which negotiated with them, in great secrecy in a hotel room in Toronto, the first major wheat and barley sale on strictly commercial terms. And it was the same personnel who realized, in talks related to that sale, that there was a great potential for massive business with China, if acceptable terms could be agreed, and who subsequently set about persuading the government to authorize and guarantee the extension of credit. With the agreement of government on credit terms, the Board officials then returned to Hong Kong and Peking (a first) for seven weeks of highly secret negotiations which ultimately culminated in the first long term agreement which led to the millions of tons of business which continues in volume today.[38]

Initial cargoes to China were shipped in 1958, with Trade Minister Gordon Churchill holding formal responsibility for the wheat board, while large-scale shipments came in 1961 with Argiculture Minister Alvin Hamilton in charge of the board.[39] The advantages of having a government board controlling wheat exports showed clearly in the large 1961 sales, which required Ottawa to provide a $100-million line of credit to a communist government it did not officially recognize. Two years later it was the Soviet Union's turn to become a customer, with a $500-million purchase of Canadian wheat. One U.S. senator branded the Soviet-Canadian deal as "an inexcusable case of trading with the enemy, for the enemy's benefit, in our cold war with the Soviet Union,"[40] but within a few weeks the U.S. government was following Canada's lead by authorizing its own wheat exports to the Soviet Union.

The new markets came just in time for Saskatchewan farmers, who had seen their net income collapse to $100 million in 1961, less than a quarter of what it was five years earlier. Things were brighter the next year, when both revenues and crops improved, and there was an open delivery quota on all grains for the first time in ten years. Even as the depressing surpluses were easing, the three pools were looking ahead to the next oversupply period. In 1964 they published a jointly-sponsored study that ruled out use of food aid programs to get rid of surpluses.[41] The study concluded that aid programs should be stable, permanent commitments, not on-again, off-again shipments depending on whether Canada had a surplus. Government and farmers would have to plan on periodic surpluses being an inevitable cost of agricultural production. Thus the Pool resumed its push for domestic wheat subsidies, two-price wheat and more government payments for storage. In 1966 the Pool goal was a federally-guaranteed price of $2.75 a bushel for top-grade wheat at the Lakehead, but the best the government could do was $1.95. Ottawa did, however, pass 1967 legislation making the wheat board formally a permanent institution, ending the practice of renewing board powers for only five years at a time. With farm costs up sixty-six percent since 1949 and prices up only nine percent, Pool delegates in 1967 called for a guaranteed price of $2.12, plus another $1 on wheat consumed domestically.

Once again, the Pool turned to innovative measures to bring its case to federal attention. Pool members meeting at Indian Head in late 1968 resolved that the entire Commons agricultural committee should be brought to Saskatchewan, a suggestion that was enthusiastically promoted by fieldman Jim Forrest and dubbed "Forrest's Folly."[42] Despite the joking nickname, the plan won approval from the Pool's annual meeting. In April 1969, committee members toured Saskatchewan farms, consulted farm leaders

Left: Preparations for the 1939 royal visit. (SWP Collection, Saskatchewan Archives Board R-A 15,061, photo by Ken Liddell of the Regina Leader-Post)

Right: Prime Minister Diefenbaker looks over petitions presented by the 1959 mass delegation to Ottawa. (SWP files, photo by Newton, Ottawa)

and split up to have MPs at twenty-four farm meetings attended by a total of more than 18,000 persons. The next month, the committee called for a two-price system, an emergency floor price on export wheat, and efforts to boost exports.

By that time burdensome surpluses were back. The 629-million-bushel 1969 crop combined with a 666-million carryover to produce a record wheat supply of 1.3 billion, much of that being undesirable high-moisture wheat. Many farmers despaired of ever finding solutions to recurring problems that had defied twenty years of lobbying and small-scale tinkering with federal programs. Reflecting that frustration, Pool delegates passed a provocative resolution on 21 November 1969, declaring: "that if the federal government does not give due consideration to the problems of Western Canada, we should consider the implications of seceding from the rest of the nation." As originally proposed, the resolution had called flatly for secession, but it was amended to weaker form. One analyst termed that motion the most notable western expression of alarm at grain markets' downhill slide,[43] and it drew wide attention. Saskatchewan Wheat Pool's reputation for well-considered policies, however, was not helped, nor was the resolution representative of serious prairie opinion. Newly-elected president Ted Turner responded with constructive firmness, emphasizing to the news media that the resolution was an expression of legitimate frustration, but that he could not accept it literally as directing the Pool down a separatist path: "The whole philosophy of the co-operative movement and my own personal philosophy has been to unite and strengthen through co-operation. This, of course, implies the very opposite to separatism."[44]

The Newest Recruit: E. K. (Ted) Turner

With Turner's election as president in 1969, the Pool's recruitment program scored another success. Turner had thought of perhaps trying to become a delegate sometime in his forties, but he was just thirty in 1957 when the informal invitation came and he was elected a Pool delegate. Unlike Gibbings, Turner had been to Pool meetings before becoming a delegate. For six years he had been on the Pool committee in his home town of Maymont. But, with a young family, it was an awkward time for Turner to take on a delegate's workload, to leave for the two-week annual meeting in November and spend time on countless other tasks. Only a sense of duty reinforced by tradition led him to accept the call. Turner's father, Thomas, had been first chairman of the Maymont Pool committee. "It was a Pool family and we just naturally gravitated to the Wheat Pool," Turner recalled.[45] Neighbor Andrew Melrose was a Pool delegate, Maymont had nothing but Pool elevators, and the area had the inspiring Jack Wesson as its district director. Ted Turner grew up with the belief that farmers needed an organization like the Pool for collective self-defence. As his father and others used to say, "a farmer is the only creature who can be skinned more than once." Turner's sense of duty was reinforced by his university agriculture studies, where he heard professor Bill Baker stress the responsibility that graduates had to become involved in bettering rural communities.

After graduation Ted Turner was at first more concerned with his noted baseball and hockey ability than with his new Pool membership. But upon taking over operation of the family farm and getting married, he found good reasons to get serious about things that would affect the future. From lobbying the Pool to build more elevator space at Maymont and asserting local producers' right to order rail cars for the elevator of their choice, Turner went on to grapple with ever-broader problems as a delegate. For three years he sat at the same District 16 table with Wesson, then was elected as the district's director as soon as Wesson retired. Turner's election as director was a significant example of the Pool's effort to bring more young people into responsible roles. He was only thirty-three, with just three years' delegate experience, and was chosen over prominent figures like

Percy Simmonds, who had been a District 16 delegate since 1929 and might have made it to the board if he had been in any district other than Jack Wesson's. District fieldman Don Sinclair, who had lobbied Turner's parents and wife for their help in persuading him to become a delegate in the first place, was suspected of having engineered Turner's election as director.[46] Sinclair, however, knew the bounds of propriety for fieldmen and had carefully avoided lobbying district delegates in connection with the director election. But the episode, and the fact that one of Turner's competitors asked for Sinclair's support, was another illustration of fieldmen's importance.

Turner, meanwhile, became one of Gibbings' most solid supporters on the Pool board. Like Gibbings, Turner had pushed for more attention to livestock in the Wesson years. With Gibbings as president, Turner became one of two or three board members on whom Gibbings relied to support management reform.[47] When he became president in 1969, Turner brought a blended style of hard-nosed, businesslike determination coupled with an unassuming, low-key personal image. The times called for someone to push Pool policies in blunt, across-the-table negotiations. Lengthy oratory and charismatic speeches could be left for political parties — one area of Saskatchewan activity that Turner avoided. A newspaper profile once summed him up as being so dedicated to the Pool and its democratically-evolved policies that his personal views and good-natured private demeanor were submerged in public:

> He's "crisp" in his dealings, say critics and fans alike, with slightly different shades of meaning. He's "blunt," they say, with the same shades of difference. Pool is a "religion" to him, others offer. He's not "warm," says another school.
>
> The overall impression seems to be that there are critics of Pool policies and practices and Turner is recognized as the spokesman for these policies, but he's not blamed personally for them.[48]

The last sentence of that 1980 assessment was to require some modification in the next three years, as Turner came in for heavy flak concerning Pool reactions to changes in Crowsnest Pass freight rates, but that is a later story.

Adding to farmers' frustrations in 1969, the year of the abortive separatism resolution, was the fact that they had been fighting a defensive battle over rail services throughout the 1950s and 1960s — and they were losing. Saskatchewan elevators had been badly congested with damp grain in 1951-52, partly because rail cars were concentrated in Alberta and Manitoba to get fast turnaround

Left: SWP secretary J. O. Wright. (SWP files)
Right: SWP President E. K. (Ted) Turner at Bulyea elevator. (SWP files)

times from the coasts and thus maximize shipment. Worse, use of the car order book had been suspended, to prevent Saskatchewan farmers from ordering their own cars to send unwanted types of grain to the terminals. That suspension ended after seven months, but new restrictions came in 1952 when the Board of Grain Commissioners required twenty-four hours notice before a farmer could place his order in the car order book at any point. Other suspensions followed, and in September 1955 farmers' generations-old right to order their own cars was severely restricted by a federal justice department ruling. The ruling stated that only the wheat board — not individual farmers — had the right to order cars for wheat delivered to the board through local elevators. In the half-century since the car order book was begun, the original problems it was designed to solve had largely disappeared. The wheat board ensured fair prices for basic grains, while government regulation and the presence of farmer-owned companies had virtually eliminated other abuses. But the car order book had acquired a new importance as a tool for Pool members to direct cars to their own elevators.

Whenever railway employees and government bureaucrats decided car allocation, Pool handling suffered. In 1954 Pool directors noted that Pool elevators handled 44 percent of the province's grain and that the percentage had been less than 50 ever since the 1949-50 railway action of allocating one car per elevator regardless of each elevator's handlings. In efforts to change the system, the prairie pools suggested first that cars be allocated according to stated producer preferences, then that cars be allocated according to 1945-49 delivery patterns, when there was no congestion denying farmers freedom of choice in where they brought their grain. Federal transport authorities, however, seemed to take the view that, for efficiency, they should encourage use of the entire elevator system. Some improvement came in 1959, after the Bracken Inquiry report on boxcar allocation, when the wheat board gave instructions for congested elevators to get two cars in addition to their normal allocation. For the crop year 1959-60, Pool elevators handled 50.5 percent of Saskatchewan grain. By 1964, however, Pool delegates were complaining about "indications of a lack of effort on the part of the Wheat Pool Management and Officials in helping eliminate discrimination against Wheat Pool facilities in the allocation of box cars, embargoes, congested orders and supply of box cars at the end of the crop year."

Looming over the whole car-allocation problem was a worri-some combination of larger issues: deteriorating rail facilities, rising freight rates, and increasing attacks on the statutory Crowsnest Pass rates for export grain. In a key 1958 move, Ottawa began paying subsidies to the railways, rolling back a nineteen-percent freight rate increase to eight percent. From then on, railway services came increasingly to depend upon a hodgepodge of federal subsidy programs. The Crow rate remained firmly in the statute books, guaranteeing farmers low-cost movement of grain to export positions, but it had to be frequently defended. In 1959 the railways tried to charge higher freight rates on the dockage and screenings that were taken out of export grain at West Coast terminals during cleaning. That effort, however, was vetoed by the board of transport commissioners. In 1960 a grain commissioners' ruling held that the Crow rate should not apply to rapeseed exports, but that ruling was overridden by new legisla-tion in 1961.

Meanwhile, all three pools were heavily engaged in 1959-61 submissions and arguments to the comprehensive MacPherson Royal Commission on rail transportation and rates. The person originally named to head the commission, Charles McTague, was thought to be sympathetic to railway arguments against the Crow rates,[49] but after ill health forced his retirement, the pools found many of their arguments endorsed by Murdo MacPherson. In a lengthy series of hearings, the pools succeeded in deflecting attention from railway losses due to Crow rates to the much heavier losses caused by passenger service and by an excessive number of small branch lines. The commission concluded that the railways lost $78 million in 1958 on passenger services, compared with $6 million on grain movement. Both figures referred only to operating costs and did not include general overhead costs. Among MacPherson's recommmendations were federal subsidies as compensation for continuing unprofitable services in the public interest, and elimination of uneconomic branch lines. Many farmers — and one member of the commission, A. R. Gobeil[50] — were still not convinced that the railways were really losing money under Crow rates, but that view was rapidly becoming unsupportable in the light of rising railway costs and general inflation. The average freight rate in Saskatchewan in 1927 was 22 cents to ship 100 pounds of wheat to the Lakehead — about 13.2 cents a bushel — and it would remain basically unchanged so long as Crow rates stayed. But 22 cents would almost buy a full-course dinner in a 1927 restaurant, at least in small-town Saskatchewan.[51] Both politically and morally, it would be increasingly difficult to justify continuing that rate.

Despite the many simmering agricultural issues in the 1950s and 1960s, Saskatchewan Wheat Pool delegates kept up at least a nominal concern with issues of general social and economic policy. Their resolutions called for: a halt to nuclear weapons tests; diplomatic recognition of the People's Republic of China; government-paid chiropractic treatment under medical care insurance plans; restrictions on public-service advertising by liquor companies; nationalizing the Canadian Pacific Railway; raising foreign aid to one percent of gross national product; and correcting alleged misuse of social aid by able-bodied recipients. Such resolutions, however, were rarely followed up with vigorous promotion or lobbying. Some were no more than idealistic but vague statements that no civil servant would know what to do with — like a 1959 resolution "that the labour, time and material spent on Canadian defence could be better employed in the development of the country on a humanitarian basis." The resolutions generally maintained a slightly-leftward tendency, including a 1965 call for limits on farm size, but with an increasing streak of conservative-style appeals for restrictions on strikes and welfare. In some ways, perhaps, Saskatchewan farmers were acquiring the viewpoint of small business.

One problem with promoting Pool policies in this 1949-69 period — and later — was the lack of a united farm movement. Creation of the Saskatchewan Farmers' Union in 1949, from the ashes of the old United Farmers of Canada, brought a radical and vigorous competitor for the role of "agricultural parliament of Saskatchewan." Increasingly, the Union portrayed the Pool as a comfortable commercial organization, too much a part of the establishment to be a policy champion for farmers. Under Joseph Lee Phelps, a former CCF cabinet minister who became Saskatchewan Farmers' Union president in 1949, Union membership grew rapidly to 72,401 by the time he left office in 1954. Battle lines were drawn early, when Phelps appealed for aid in building the Union and got $2,000 from United Grain Growers but nothing from the Pool.[52] Phelps and other Union activists "kept us on our toes" with challenging questions at Pool meetings, recalled fieldman Abel Toupin: "we didn't dare go out to a country meeting without having done our homework."[53] Other Pool figures were less philosophical. Director A. F. Sproule commented that Phelps had little substance even though his presence was painfully obvious — "like a boil on your ass."[54] With Phelps' 1954 retirement as president and subsequent internal disputes, Union membership dropped sharply, to only 13,470 in 1956. Membership recovered to 30,330 in 1960, but thereafter declined so that in the early 1980s only a few thousand Saskatchewan farmers were members of the National Farmers Union.[55]

Despite their differences, Pool delegates recognized the desirability of a united farm voice and had, in 1953, urged close Pool-Union co-operation. From the Pool viewpoint, that could be done with joint membership in the Saskatchewan Federation of Agriculture. Created in 1944, the Federation had included many representatives of co-operative businesses, leading the Union to withdraw from it in 1951. Intense negotiations in 1957-58 brought the Union back into the fold, but only at the cost of a thorough reorganization of the Federation.[56] Instead of the normal two voting representatives allowed each member organization, the Union was to have six. The Union agreed to let Federated Co-operatives Ltd. and the Saskatchewan Association of Rural Municipalities retain their memberships, but five other organizations were dropped: Canadian Co-operative Implements Ltd., Co-op Hail Insurance Co., Co-op Life Insurance Co., the Co-operative Mutual Benefit Association, and the Saskatchewan Co-operative Women's Guild. The reorganization increased the Federation's agricultural character, but in 1968 the Union withdrew again. In the interval, similar efforts had been made to bring the National Farmers' Union into the Canadian Federation of Agriculture, but those collapsed in 1962-63.[57]

Although each side wanted farmers to have a united voice, efforts at unity could probably not have succeeded without one side or the other abandoning its basic principles. The Union wanted one association with direct membership by farmers; the Pool and its allies favored a federation approach, with the board of each farm organization selecting representatives; between the two approaches there was no middle ground. A side issue, at the provincial level, was the degree of Saskatchewan Wheat Pool dominance in the Saskatchewan Federation. To Union loyalists the Federation "exists in name only because in reality the Saskatchewan Wheat Pool may be regarded as the Saskatchewan Federation of Agriculture."[58] In many ways, that assessment was valid for most of the 1949-69 period. For research and office-support services, the tiny Federation office had often to rely on the Pool. Also, Pool directors were traditionally prominent within the provincial and national federation structure — as, for example, in the 1957 negotiations for Union membership, when two of the three Federation negotiators were Pool directors, Tom Bobier and Warden Burgess. One official recalled that when the national Federation wanted to check on the fine points of the Saskatchewan Federation's grain policies, it used to telephone the Pool directly.[59] That situation was to change as more organizations joined the Federation system, including some with philosophical orientations markedly different from the Pool's.

While seeking to strengthen the Federation structure, Saskatchewan Wheat Pool was also faced with the question of whether it should expand beyond the province's boundaries. During his 1960-69 presidency, Gibbings personally promoted the idea of amalgamating the three prairie pools into one powerful organization. It was the greatest disappointment of his presidency, Gibbings said later, that the idea "didn't really get to the very serious discussion stage."[60] Gibbings would periodically mention the benefit of unification, but did not get the positive response from other pools necessary to make it "a front-burner issue". Saskatchewan Wheat Pool delegates, however, gave approval to the idea in various forms.[61] A 1961 resolution urged talks on amalgamation of the three pools and United Grain Growers; similar resolutions in 1965, 1966 and 1967 mentioned only the three pools; a 1968 motion included UGG again; and a 1971 motion was limited to the three pools. One of the few formal outside responses came in 1969, when delegates to the annual meeting of Canadian Co-operative Implements Ltd. urged merger of the three pools and UGG. In the meantime, Gibbings had also raised the possibility of a merger between Saskatchewan Wheat Pool, Federated Co-operatives and Co-op Implements, but that idea received little response.

One basic problem with Gibbings' proposals was the natural loyalty felt by Alberta and Manitoba pool members to their organizations. With smaller memberships and assets, the other two pools might easily be dominated by their central neighbor. At

Manitoba Pool Elevators in particular, former president Harold Sneath said, there was a fear of being "swallowed up in the bigness of Saskatchewan Pool." Even so, Sneath said, Manitoba members could perhaps have been sold on the concept, except it "was always kind of set aside."[62]

Rather than expanding into a truly giant organization, Saskatchewan Wheat Pool found itself cutting back in some respects. One of the first elevator-consolidation resolutions, passed in 1949, urged "that in areas served by a number of Pool elevators which consistently have a low handling, consideration be given to building a large modern elevator at a central point and the elimination of the single elevator." Similar motions came in 1950 and 1957, then a more strongly-worded one in 1961 demanding "immediate action . . . to consolidate the country elevator system." The railways were not the only ones who were feeling the costs involved in serving a large number of delivery points, many of them only minutes apart by truck. In fact, Pool studies in connection with the MacPherson Royal Commission had found that some farmers drove past their nearest elevator to get to a more modern one. Nevertheless, Pool delegates cautiously called for a comprehensive policy to ensure rail line abandonment did not get out of hand. In 1961 they said the two major railways' systems should be considered together, in co-ordinated fashion, instead of judging individual abandonment applications on a piecemeal basis. They also called for five years' notice before abandonment, and retention of sufficient lines to ensure adequate service. The Pool moved slowly at first, closing just five points permanently in 1961-62, but gradually increased the pace. In 1968-69 the Pool closed or sold elevators at 35 points and operated elevators at another 100 points on a part-time basis. It also reinforced a trend away from same-point competition by buying out the opposition at 41 points. "At today's costs of financing and reduced level of marketings, farmers cannot afford to finance wasteful competition in services to the industry," Pool directors declared bluntly in their 1969 annual report.

At the same time, the Pool was putting record sums into programs to renovate and modernize existing elevators. Increasing grainhandling volumes demonstrated that the Pool's total ability to handle grain was being improved even though the number of elevators was declining. In an effort to cut costs, the Pool also began experimenting with the laborious process of moving elevators in 1962, and within five years had moved eighteen by special trucks or tracked vehicles, to the delight of newspaper and amateur photographers. The Pool's construction department also experimented with Western Canada's first all-steel elevators, building two at Kenaston and Saskatoon in 1959-60, but found that they were less cost-effective than traditional wooden models.

The 1959-60 fiscal year also saw innovations in the livestock division, as the Pool launched a feeder-finance program. With a Pool guarantee covering twenty-five percent of any loan losses, credit unions and banks lent money to farmers to buy calves, deferring repayment until the calves had been fed to slaughter weight and sold. It was initially a small-scale program — twenty-eight loans totalling $60,961 in the first eight months — but it prompted lending institutions to adopt more flexible repayment plans on their own.[63] In 1968 the Pool introduced another feeder-finance program, under which cattle were in effect lent to competent farmers for feeding. The farmers would pay a deposit equal to about twenty percent of the animals' value, raise them to marketable weight, then in effect get the sale proceeds less the original value of the cattle and moderate interest payments on that value. Over the next fourteen years the program included 437,795 head, with a sales value of $143 million. And in 1969 the Pool persuaded the Saskatchewan government's economic development company to lend $3.5 million to finance feeder cattle. The Pool itself encouraged many local groups to set up small cattle-feeding co-operatives.

Gibbings' more activist attitude toward livestock was also evident in a program, begun in 1960-61 and continuing to the present day, of buying cattle to stabilize prices and smooth out price differences between Saskatchewan stockyards. After shipping the cattle on consignment to eastern and U.S. stockyards, the Pool lost $16,126 in 1960-61. Losses, often several times that amount, were frequent all the way into the early 1980s. Although the benefits of such stabilization measures cannot be precisely measured, the Pool was visibly trying to help and its loss was at least partly the producers' gain. Proponents of centralized marketing, however, suffered a setback in 1964 when Saskatchewan producers voted 4,179 to 4,177 against a hog marketing board, despite ninety-two meetings organized by Pool delegates and fieldmen. That episode was one occasion for more sniping at the Pool, as some Farmers' Union members accused the Pool of refraining from giving all-out support for a marketing board because such a board would undercut the Pool's livestock division.[64] Pool officials, however, organized many meetings to promote the marketing-board plan and encouraged Union spokesmen to address those meetings. Also, Pool director E. K. Turner, who represented Saskatchewan Wheat Pool on the provisional board of the hog marketing organization, found that the board's Union members greatly appreciated Pool efforts.[65] The division's strength, however, lay in cattle and calves, where it had 62 percent of 1964-65 provincial handlings compared with 53 percent in 1961-62. During the same period, hog handlings declined slightly but steadily to 24 percent, while sheep and lambs declined to 33 percent. In 1967, the division expanded to Talbotville, Ont., buying its own stockyard there so it would not have to rely on any Ontario organization to sell cattle shipped from Saskatchewan.

Meanwhile, the Saskatoon flour mill continued to be a problem. The consumer co-operative network was not large enough to take all the mill's production, so it was essential to compete in the tough domestic private markets and in export sales. After some uneven years, the mill showed respectable 1961-64 surpluses, but it was a continuing scramble to find new foreign markets to replace markets lost when developing nations built their own mills. The next six years included three more loss years as sales and income varied wildly.

Rapeseed Blooms with Pool Aid

But the vegetable oil plant was also involved in more dramatic and successful events. Although it showed even worse losses for the 1960s, the oil plant was helping build the valuable rapeseed industry. Originally built to process flax, the plant processed its first rapeseed in 1949 and by 1951 was handling all rapeseed crushing for J. Gordon Ross's pioneering rapeseed enterprise.[66] It also sponsored plots of safflower and sunflower seeds. Slowly, rapeseed oil moved from purely industrial uses to being a source of edible shortening and salad oil. The Pool plant played a part in such developments, although most pioneering work in the first half of the 1950s was done by Canada Packers and the National Research Council. After a 1956-57 setback, when the federal government temporarily banned edible uses of rapeseed oil because of health concerns, the Pool sponsored a series of experiments to see if additional industrial uses could be found for the oil. The same high erucic acid content that made rapeseed oil a possible cause of increased cholesterol in humans had made the oil a good lubricant for ship engines in World War Two — the reason prairie production started in the first place. Lengthy Pool-financed studies in 1958-65 tested rapeseed oil as an additive to crankcase oils, as the soap stock for greases, and as a lubricant for cold rolling of steel, but in each case the economics were not good enough to compete with alternative materials.

Rapeseed, however, got a major boost in 1959-60 when it began being commonly used as an ingredient in margarine and when the

Pool pioneered a direct solvent-extraction plant and developed processing techniques that came to be adopted around the world. Originally used for peanut processing, the solvent extraction method at first produced undesirable oil that would not harden properly, but an intensive effort by plant personnel and scientists from the Research Council laboratories in Saskatoon corrected that problem. The effort took more than two months, including many nights of working past 2:00 A.M., and rapeseed's future was hanging in the balance. Clare Youngs, the Research Council scientist heading the effort, said later that the large-volume and profitable rapeseed crops of following decades might never have been achieved without Saskatchewan Wheat Pool's persistence at that crucial stage. There were also problems with the rapeseed meal byproduct, which produced low growth rates in test animals. Scientists eventually traced the problem to destruction of protein components by the high temperatures and pressures used in processing. Fortunately, processing changes to improve oil quality also improved meal quality. Later, new rapeseed varieties were developed that were free of sulphur compounds involved in the early oil and meal problems.[67]

Far from being guarded or sold as trade secrets, the processing solutions found by Youngs and Pool staff were freely handed to crushing plants around the world to encourage rapeseed use. An independent, profit-oriented oil plant would have had no incentive to do that, but the Pool realized that the largest potential benefits for farmers were in growing rapeseed. Behind the rapeseed-yellow fields that were becoming more common in Saskatchewan was some red ink in the Pool plant's account books. But there were still lingering worries over health hazards from erucic acid and the Pool contracted with farmers in 1965-69 to produce low erucic acid varieties for experiments, using seed developed by federal agriculture department researchers in Saskatoon. By 1969, Saskatchewan farmers had one million acres seeded in rapeseed and production in neighboring provinces had grown to 816,000 acres in Alberta, 196,000 in Manitoba. All that could have been suddenly endangered by a 1970 Dutch study which found erucic acid caused some abnormalities in the heart tissue of rats. But low- and zero-erucic-acid varieties were by then ready for farmers to use, setting the stage for even faster expansion of the crop and a change of name to "canola" to mark elimination of erucic acid and other detrimental substances. To Canola Council of Canada director Alan Earl, the rapeseed story was a classic example of the huge rewards possible from putting money into agricultural research and development (R&D): "This is high tech R&D but because it's related to agriculture, it's not glamorous. Yet the money we've put into it has paid us back 10,000 times better than R&D into nuclear reactors."[68]

Meanwhile, development of rapeseed marketing saw Saskatchewan Wheat Pool once again become a pooling organization. Rapeseed pools in 1959-63 handled up to forty-eight percent of the Saskatchewan rapeseed crop. Rapeseed pooling, however, ended after the Pool found that it could not predict supplies — growers would sell on the open market whenever prices were good. The old idea of binding growers by contract to deliver all their production was judged unworkable for the small rapeseed crop. In 1961 legislation brought rapeseed under low Crow freight rates, giving the crop a significant economic boost. The next year the Canadian Wheat Board took control of rapeseed movement, putting deliveries under a quota system and scheduling shipments. With lower export freight rates, domestic rapeseed buyers had to pay more to farmers to match what farmers could get from export sales. Pool directors estimated in 1962 that their oil plant had to pay an extra 25 cents a bushel because of rapeseed coming under the Crow rate. Partly for that reason, the vegetable oil division lost $330,928 in 1961-62 — but farmers generally gained the extra 25 cents a bushel.

Another major Pool thrust in the 1960s was directed at the fast-growing farm supplies business. Starting in 1963, the Pool took just four years to build up a farm service department that was the largest Canadian retailer of agricultural chemicals, with annual sales of $13.6 million, seventeen central distribution depots, and 300 farm supply warehouses at country elevator points. The Pool also acquired another sideline in 1963 by absorbing the Saskatchewan Seed Grain Co-operative. And it joined Alberta Pool and Federated Co-ops in creating Western Co-operative Fertilizers Ltd., whose $22 million Calgary plant opened in 1965. The move into farm supplies, however, brought considerable internal dissension and external criticism on the grounds that community co-ops would lose business. Pool president Gibbings found some employees reluctant to get involved in a complex new operation, and a general lack of enthusiasm at every level of management.[69] One delegate resolution to limit farm service activities by having the Pool refrain from selling feeds, feed supplements and veterinary supplies was defeated in 1968, but only by a margin of 88 to 57.

But the Pool, in fact, had little choice. Competing grain companies had been moving into the business earlier and were attracting grain deliveries with their convenient, easy-credit fertilizer supplies. Both the Alberta and Manitoba pools had entered the farm supply business before Saskatchewan Wheat

Pool. Community co-ops could not in any case serve all Pool members — the members at Prairie River, for example, welcomed the Pool's move because their nearest co-op at the time was twenty-five miles away.[70] After the decision had been made to get into the business, there were still long-simmering arguments over the farm service division's operations, particularly when the bad weather and poor economy of 1969 produced a $526,586 divisional loss. Many of the arguments on pricing policies were philosophical. While some delegates felt volume discounts violated co-operative principles, others felt such discounts were essential for a competitive business. Similar differences fuelled arguments over whether to vary prices between different areas in order to meet local price-cutting competition. Even without the ideological debate, it would have been hard enough to develop balanced pricing systems in such a competitive and changeable field. Research head Bob Phillips felt the Pool could have benefitted greatly from hiring ouside experts to study such issues as pricing of farm supplies, but he found a never-explained reluctance to approve such outside studies.[71] Pool directors may well have instinctively felt that outside consultants would not appreciate the wider social and co-operative considerations involved in the Pool's unique investment policies. To Saskatchewan Wheat Pool, for example, losses on rapeseed operations would be amply justified if they meant much larger long-term gains for farmers. While such considerations would be legitimate reasons for altering or overruling a consultant's recommendations, however, they were not valid reasons for dispensing with consultants in the first place.

Saskatchewan Farmers Build Vancouver Terminal

For the Pool's terminal operations, the highlight of the 1950s and 1960s was construction of a five-million-bushel terminal in North Vancouver, the most expensive single capital project handled by Saskatchewan Wheat Pool up to that point. The need for additional facilities on the West Coast became evident in 1961 with the opening of large-scale wheat shipments to China. At a meeting called by the wheat board, representatives of all sectors of the grainhandling business agreed there should be a new terminal — and wondered who would play Santa Claus. As chairman of the wheat board's advisory committee, Gibbings was well aware of the need for a terminal, and as Pool president he was well aware that he had no authority from delegates to commit the Pool to such a venture. But, he recalled, he told the meeting it "seemed obvious" that Saskatchewan Wheat Pool should be the one to build the new facility, since Alberta Wheat Pool was already heavily committed in Vancouver and the flow of Saskatchewan

Saskatchewan Wheat Pool's Vancouver terminal, 1979. (SWP files, photo by Allen Aerial Photos Ltd.)

grain through the port was increasing. "That sort of crystallized the thing." Back in Regina, he found other Pool leaders unsure about the whole idea.[72] While a new terminal would help boost exports and bring benefits to all farmers — not just the Pool members who paid for it — the terminal did not seem to be an attractive investment in itself. Adding to uncertainties then was the Pool's lack of experts who could do precise financial forecasts for such projects.[73] Several senior management personnel were also reluctant. All in all, Gibbings said, "that was a difficult project to sell." But after two years of mulling it over, Pool delegates voted unanimously in 1963 to recommend acquisition of West Coast terminal facilities. Doubts, however, continued as the 1964 estimated cost of $13.3 million became $20.4 million in 1966 when construction tenders were opened. Pool directors delayed the project for two months, searching for ways to cut costs and unsuccessfully seeking government aid. Substantial losses were expected in the terminal's early years, but no one else was willing to undertake the project, so Pool directors went ahead basically on sheer faith, faith that was eventually justified when the terminal proved to be not only valuable to the whole grain industry, but profitable for its owners.

Pool terminals, however, did not escape trouble in this 1949-69 period. Lakehead facilities suffered another fatal explosion, with six people dying in a 24 September 1952 accident at Terminal 4A. Labor relations became a high priority as Vancouver grain-handlers staged a two-month strike in 1965 and Lakehead terminal workers struck for two months in 1968. Expansions included purchase of Terminal No. 6 at the Lakehead from the CNR, ending Manitoba Pool's lease of that terminal, and the 1956 lease of Vancouver Terminal No. 2 from the National Harbors Board.

At the *Western Producer* and the Modern Press printing operation, a different type of expansion was under way. Almost without consciously realizing it, the Pool was drifting into the book-publishing business. "Nobody started out with the idea of establishing a publishing company," one official said later,[74] but interest in the newspaper's serialized fiction and non-fiction stories led first to some reprints in booklet form, then book publication in 1958 of a biographical serial by Grant MacEwan, *Fifty Mighty Men*. The publishing sideline was to grow into Western Producer Prairie Books, a major contributor to prairie history and culture. But, as editor Tom Melville-Ness wrote in one memo to head office, the book business had very down-to-earth beginnings, related to Modern Press's Commercial Printing Division (CPD):

> the book publishing sideline was started primarily to occupy unused time on various machines in the plant . . . It is incidental that the book operation also carries out one of the objectives of The Western Producer — that of preserving western Canadian history and tradition. The main idea is to keep machines busy in CPD . . .[75]

Such practical concerns were important, for both delegates and Pool management were getting increasingly restive at seemingly-perpetual *Producer* deficits. The 1961 loss, for example, was $216,124. When it came to losing money, the *Producer* was in the same league as the flour mill and vegetable oil plant. Another source of friction was the bitter provincial controversy over medicare in 1961-62, which led to the Pool's first recorded vote on a *Western Producer* issue. The vote came when Ted Strain — later to be a Farmers' Union leader — moved a motion regretting the newspaper's coverage of the medicare controversy. Editorials on 17 May 1962 and later had generally appealed for responsibility from both sides, but had emphasized doctors' willingness to accept a reasonable form of medicare. Several letters to the editor protested the space given the doctors' position.[76] Although the motion was defeated, 66 of the 157 voting delegates endorsed it, including rising director Ted Turner. Discontent was also evident in another motion the following year, urging abandonment of the newspaper in favor of more television broadcasts, but that too was defeated. One minor problem with movements to eliminate the traditional newspaper deficits was that a devoutly anti-alcohol group usually blocked acceptance of breweries' public-service advertisements. Advocates of acceptance won a 100-49 victory in 1964, authorizing "sufficient of such advertising to test the public reaction to it." But the next year, a resolution to continue accepting such advertisements was defeated, 86-71.

8
Prosperity and Politics, 1970–82

I was a part of the first co-operative in this country.
Now I've lived to see my son worth a million and a
quarter dollars. I don't know how that happened, I've
always been a socialist.

— "Sod-buster," in the play *Paper Wheat*[1]

Saskatchewan Wheat Pool was still far from becoming a millionaires' club, but in the 1970s many of its members began operating on a financial scale undreamed of by the farmers who built the Pool a half-century earlier. They could and did spend more than $100,000 on a single piece of machinery. With average farm size approaching 1,000 acres in the early 1980s, soaring land values meant an increasing number of Saskatchewan farmers were worth over $1 million on paper. The widespread extension of electric power to farmhouses in the 1950s had seemed like the ultimate luxury; thirty years later, companies were selling satellite dishes to farmers who wanted to get dozens of television channels. But debt, driven by record interest rates, marched upward step by step with rising land values. And agricultural prices always seemed to lag behind the rising cost of farm inputs. The family farm might be worth a million dollars, but if it was to stay in the family then the generation that built it up through the Depression could never realize that value for themselves. Few young people, if any, could carry the debt load on an entire farm. Socially, there was a sense of decay as rural communities continued to fade away. Neighbors who once met daily at the village store would encounter each other less often at a distant shopping centre; where one generation of children walked to school, the next endured a sixty-mile bus ride. The political importance of farmers had also been eroded by urbanization. They were still a substantial proportion of the Saskatchewan population, and the provincial government remained fairly sensitive to their needs — 1970s legislation included restrictions on outsiders' ownership of land, plus a land bank to buy farmland from one generation and lease it to the next. In national politics, however, the prairie farm vote counted for little. It had been a long time since a prime minister followed grain-industry developments from day to day as R. B. Bennett did. Increasingly, bureaucrats and consultants guided federal agricultural policy. They may have done their best, but to farmers they were both unknown and unaccountable, a situation that produced alienation and lack of trust.

As always, Saskatchewan Wheat Pool reflected the changing countryside. The 1970s saw its greatest commercial successes, culminating in record net earnings of $72.7 million for 1980-81. Excluding the effect of inflation, that sum could have covered the disastrous 1929-30 loss five times over. The giant overpayment that crippled wheat pooling in Canada was virtually petty cash in 1981 for Saskatchewan Wheat Pool. Yet the dozen years after 1970 were politically the most frustrating that the Pool had ever endured. The two institutions that it held most sacred in the 1960s — the Canadian Wheat Board and the Crowsnest Pass freight rates — were left battered and bleeding by an alliance of the federal government, railways and the private grain trade. What may have been even more dangerous in the long run was partial erosion of Pool membership loyalty. Some farmers were attracted to a flock of small associations that sprang up to oppose such traditional Pool policies as support of Crow rates. Other farmers, perhaps even larger in numbers, went the opposite direction, turning to the Farmers' Union because they felt the Pool was not being vigorous enough in defending the Crow or the wheat board. Amid all the noise and confusion, there was a host of inter-related issues, blending together into one long, simmering controversy.

Federal Grain Takeover

The contrasting elements of corporate success and political vulnerability were both present in the Pool's most significant business venture during the 1970s — the 1972 takeover of Federal Grain Company, then the largest Canadian grain company outside the co-operative movement. The idea of purchasing Federal emerged in the late 1960s from discussions between the three prairie pools,[2] as the pools continued to increase their cooperation in joint ventures and began serious consideration about the pattern of future grainhandling. Although the three pool boards met together formally two or three times a year, their contacts had become even closer as directors were brought together for such joint responsibilities as Western Co-operative Fertilizers Ltd. Developments like Saskatchewan Wheat Pool's management reorganization and modernization in the 1960s also provided the capability to plan such an undertaking. Without its 1960s management improvements, president Ted Turner said later, Saskatchewan Wheat Pool could not have handled the Federal takeover and other 1970s expansions.[3] In arriving at their decision on Federal, the three pools were largely driven by the increasingly-obvious need for rationalization and consolidation of grainhandling facilities. With a larger system, they felt, they could better shape the hodgepodge of country elevators into an efficient, coordinated system.

Within the three pools, general manager Ira Mumford of Saskatchewan Wheat Pool played a key role in fostering the decision to bid for Federal's elevators. After discussions with his Alberta counterpart, Wally Madill, Mumford wrote a "private and confidential" letter to George Turner, president and general manager of Manitoba Pool Elevators, to see if Turner would join the other two in bringing the matter before their respective boards.[4] "This may seem initially like a real far out proposal," Mumford wrote in the 8 January 1970 letter, ". . . but it has some important favorable features". With the letter Mumford included a provocative four-page memo that he was to use in presenting the idea to the Saskatchewan board. Noting the trend to consolidation and centralization in the grainhandling system, Mumford added that chronic elevator congestion had almost eliminated serious competition between elevator companies in attracting farmers' grain deliveries: "with the decline in buying competition, reduction of profits, centralization, and the action of Government, Wheat Board and other interests, most of the reasons for the traditional abhorrence of a monopoly grain handling system have disappeared." Moreover, he said, the pools would probably have at least moral support from Ottawa if they went after the Federal system — and could be in a precarious position if they did not:

> Rumor suggests that the Government has some drastic concepts in mind in "streamlining" the entire grain industry. One senior reliable source has been actively advocating for some time that the Pools should ask to buy out the major publicly owned grain company (Federal). This source suggests that the Government may be sympathetic to diverting long term, low interest funds to the Pools for this purpose. A takeover of this magnitude would obviously give the farmer-owned organizations a virtual monopoly in the industry. . . .

There is some concern that if the Pools do not make an aggressive effort to increase their dominant position, United Grain Growers may well make a bid to do so. Much depends on the Federal Government's attitude. If the Federal Government decided that it would be in the public interest for a public utility type monopoly to take over the grain handling industry, it is conceivable that U.G.G. could put forward a persuasive case to be the basic organization. U.G.G. is a three province company and has deliberately taken a "middle of the road" approach between the Pools and the private trade. Its officers also appear to have made a conscious effort to align the organization with government policy respecting the grain industry. The Pools, with their dominant 50% of the handlings and obvious closer relationship with the producers, should still have a positive advantage in such a situation, but they should be prepared to act quickly if necessary, to retain this position.

Within two weeks Mumford's suggestion was reinforced by a memo from Pool official M. P. Bjornson, who identified 217 delivery points in Saskatchewan where acquisition of Federal

Chief negotiators for the three pools in the 1972 purchase of Federal Grain: I. K. Mumford (left), Robert Milliken, J. M. Fair. (SWP files, photo by Earl Kennedy, Winnipeg)

elevators would give the Pool a monopoly — 52 points where Federal had a local monopoly, and 165 where Federal and the Pool had the only elevators.[5] Federal, he noted, handled sixteen percent of Saskatchewan farmers' grain deliveries, and "it would appear fairly safe to estimate that their total handling could be retained." In times of congestion, elevators' receipts were determined by the number of rail cars they received to move grain out, and the car allocations would come with any Federal elevator bought by the Pool.

With the pool boards swinging in favor of the concept, preliminary discussions with Federal began at the presidential level in early 1970. They made little initial progress, because of general uncertainty about the future of the grains industry.[6] But later that year federal government intentions became clearer and it seemed that radical consolidation — perhaps far more radical than the Pool or its members wanted — was on the way. At a lunch with the three Pool presidents, Federal president George Sellers indicated he felt Federal's return on investment was inadequate and its shareholders might consider selling.[7] Not all Federal directors were ready to sell, however, and discussions following the lunch produced no result. The next stage opened during a chance encounter at Winnipeg airport in the fall of 1971, when Pool president Ted Turner asked if the sale idea was still dead and Sellers said it would be worthwhile to re-open talks. Saskatchewan Pool representatives, acting on behalf of all three pools, launched a series of confidential meetings in November, coinciding with the Pool's annual meeting. At one point, top Saskatchewan officials made an overnight trip to Calgary for inter-pool consultations on the negotiations, returning to their Regina annual meeting the next morning with no one aware of their absence.[8] The night the Pool's annual meeting ended, Turner and Mumford flew to Winnipeg for a solid day's talks the next day, ending with a handshake agreement 27 November 1971.[9] A precise purchase price had not been set, but the basic principles for the deal were established.

Now it was a race against the clock for lawyers and financial experts for each side, as they struggled to perfect a 150-page contract before word of the sale leaked out. With Federal's shares being publicly traded on stock exchanges, premature disclosure could have strongly affected share prices and brought a host of regulatory or other complications to interfere with the deal. A 20 December 1971 CBC radio report of rumors about the possible sale caused some anxious moments, but the rumors faded without confirmation. At the detailed Winnipeg negotiations, two Saskatchewan officials represented the three pools — financial expert

Milt Fair, who in a few years would be the Pool's next chief executive officer; and lawyer R. A. Milliken, son of R. H. Milliken, who helped create the Pool and was its legal representative for thirty-five years. The younger Milliken had to bow out awkwardly from a scheduled chamber of commerce speech, unable to tell his colleagues why.[10] In Winnipeg, he and Fair went through the intense, laborious process of pinning down every clause of the contract and every step of determining Federal's inventories, working each day from early morning to 10 p.m. with Federal officials in the company's directors' room. "We lived in that bloody boardroom for a month," Milliken sighed later. At least daily they reported by telephone to Mumford. Discussions with Federal lawyer J. Blair MacAulay started badly, with MacAulay complaining about a Pool document that omitted the comma in the legal title "Federal Grain, Limited". There was also the pressure of simply finding a way to travel between Winnipeg and Regina, with a strike disrupting air traffic. On one occasion the negotiators had to hire a private airplane. Even with the deal almost complete, and pool presidents waiting anxiously in Winnipeg hotel rooms to be called in to sign it, matters were tense enough that at one point Fair threatened to break off the talks, in retaliation for what he felt were time-wasting last-minute bargaining tactics.[11] But the Pool and Federal negotiators had done their work well, coming to respect each other in the process, and by February they produced a contract so complete it left no room for later disagreements over ambiguities or omissions. All that was left was a mid-March flurry of signatures, seals and cheques. Altogether, the pools were paying $90 million for Federal's grainhandling system and its current inventories.

Excluding Federal's inventories, the three pools together paid $28.2 million for 554 country elevators and five terminal elevators, plus miscellaneous structures. Saskatchewan Wheat Pool's share of that was $15.2 million. It was not the first takeover by the pools, but it was by far the largest. In 1959 the three pools had jointly bought elevators from Lake of the Woods Milling Co. and Ogilvie Flour Mills Co. Ltd. In 1948 the Saskatchewan and Manitoba pools had joined with United Grain Growers to buy Reliance Grain Co. Ltd. elevators. Saskatchewan Pool's only acquisition by itself had been the 1926 purchase of Co-op Elevators. Federal, by contrast, had taken over fourteen other companies in its history, including a 1967 merger with Searle and Alberta Pacific. One key question for Saskatchewan Wheat Pool was whether it would keep all the business that Federal had. In 1970-71, Pool elevators handled 51.3 percent of Saskatchewan grain and Federal elevators handled 16 percent; the Pool figured its share of the purchase would be profitable if it could retain 10 of Federal's 16 percentage points. For the next two years, as Bjornson predicted, it retained all Federal's share — Pool handlings were above 67 percent, declining to 63 percent at the end of the decade with rapid elevator consolidation. All in all, Pool leaders felt well justified in their actions. The timing of the deal was almost perfect, coming just before grain movement speeded up and the grainhandling business improved. Mumford for one felt that Federal would not have wanted to sell at that point if negotiations had started six months later than they did,[12] although Federal presumably would have been ready to sell in another few years, during the next downturn. Former Federal vice-president Gus Leitch complained, in a *Leader-Post* report 26 September 1981: "Saskatchewan Wheat Pool could build an elevator with cash that would have gone to Ottawa if it was a private company. That really hammered us."

The Federal takeover, however, brought both internal and external political problems for Saskatchewan Wheat Pool. Because of Federal's concern over stock markets, the deal had been negotiated in tight secrecy. It came as a surprise to delegates and committee members as well as farmers, provoking scattered complaints that the whole procedure was undemocratic. Director Gordon South faced the painful necessity, before disclosure of the takeover, of trying to squelch rumors about it: "That was probably the first time in my life I had to lie."[13] Coupled with widespread feelings that the Pool should have found some way to consult its members or their representatives was an equally-widespread concern that some farmers might suffer through lessened competition. When the takeover was just a rumor, a small group of Pool members in Pense had voted about 12 to 1 to oppose it. Later, a similar meeting in Benson voted 46 to 1 against the deal.[14] Those meetings seemed unrepresentative of the majority of Pool members, who appeared willing to accept the takeover, but they were at least signs of significant discontent. Senator Hazen Argue complained in a 9 March Senate speech that a dangerous "semi-monopoly" had been created: "It places power to close hundreds of elevators, in the hands of a few men in Regina."[15] Although Argue wondered if there should be an investigation under the Combines Act concerning possible restraint of trade, federal officials later concluded that there were no grounds for action. Farmers, meanwhile, were given an opportunity to change their authorized delivery points in response to the disappearance of competition between the pool and Federal. Although some grain companies sponsored radio advertisements urging farmers to switch to competitive points, only 531 of the 181,000 farmers with Canadian Wheat Board delivery-permit books did so — less than three-tenths of one percent.[16] The Pool responded to the general controversy with a strong educational effort, including a booklet purporting to give straightforward answers to farmers' questions about the takeover.[17] The booklet was, in fact, straightforward on some matters. For example, it expressed understanding for Pool members who were upset about not being informed in advance, adding: "The deal could not have been concluded if secrecy had not been maintained." Other sections of the booklet were less direct. "Some might say it eliminates competition," the booklet said, before trying to defuse that concern with comments about how federal agencies regulate the business. The booklet also declared: "There is nothing to prohibit other companies from going into business at any point." Nothing, that is, except the fact the whole country elevator system was shrinking. Any company that tried to reverse the consolidation process by scattering expensive new elevators among previously unserved points would go broke.

Concern over the increase in the pools' dominance of the country elevator system was predictably high among elevator companies that operated for private profit. They had, after all, lost their biggest member. But fear was also expressed by United Grain Growers. UGG president Mac Runciman said in a memo to directors of the prairie-wide co-operative that the pools now had the power to overwhelm competitors.[18] Under the latest car-allocation system, companies were given a number of cars for each shipping block and could allocate them as they pleased within that block. That, said Runciman, meant that the pool-Federal system could be miserly toward points it monopolized and practice "boxcar flooding at competitive points." The pools argued otherwise, pointing out that wheat board regulations allowed the board to send extra cars to car-starved points, as well as punishing companies guilty of "flooding" by denying them storage payments. In addition, the pools said farmers could slowly get more cars for their favorite elevator company if they kept delivering to it, since car allocations were based on average deliveries over the most recent twelve months. Farmers' Union spokesmen, meanwhile, approved the takeover, saying that farmer-owned businesses had to be huge to compete effectively with giant private corporations — but the Union spokesmen also used the occasion to note their view that large commercial organizations should not be in the farm policy field.[19] The Federal deal may also have provoked a critical reaction in some federal government circles, with fears that the pools were getting too powerful. Both Pool president Ted Turner and his predecessor — Charles Gibbings, then a wheat board commissioner — detected such resentment, although at least two well-placed government officials friendly to the pools did not notice any such feelings.[20]

The takeover, however, clearly focussed attention on Saskatchewan Wheat Pool's size at a time when many farmers were wondering if it was getting too big for genuine democratic control. It also awoke the media to the fact that Pool business was serious news — a judgment that meant more publicity for the Pool, but also for any splinter groups issuing criticism of the Pool. Instead of referring to the Pool as some type of quaint, rustic co-operative, newpaper stories would increasingly speak of a "hulking giant" with "corporate tentacles" reaching into many sectors.[21] After 1972, Turner noted, "there was no doubt then about who was the biggest kid on the block".[22] There was probably little that the Pool could have done to avoid such public relations problems, short of passing up both the opportunity to expand farmers' co-operative economic control and the responsibility to help consolidate and modernize the elevator system. But the Federal experience would make it all the more important for the Pool to strengthen its channels of democratic control and communication.

Election of Pool Delegates

Membership involvement in the committee structure, however, remained basically healthy throughout the 1970s and into the 1980s. At 31 July 1981 there were 668 committees — down by 143 over seven years with consolidation of delivery points and declining farm population, but still involving more than one of every ten active Pool members. The more serious problem was in delegate elections. With 69 to 73 subdistricts open for elections each year in the 1970s, the annual number of elections varied from four to seven. All other delegates were chosen by acclamation. Fieldmen continued to work hard to recruit new people to replace retiring delegates, but as field staff manager Ian Traquair said, "they don't encourage people to jump in and oppose a delegate."[23] More embarrassing than the lack of competition to be a Pool delegate, however, was the fact that three or four subdistricts each year found no candidate at all, necessitating a scramble to find someone in each subdistrict who would agree to be nominated for a byelection. By 1981, when 73 odd-numbered subdistricts were up for re-election, the situation had worsened: that year, there was no nomination in seven subdistricts, almost a tenth of the total. In an attempt to bring more people into Pool activities, the Pool began in 1980 an annual agricultural forum involving three couples from each subdistrict. Another sign of change came at the 1981 annual meeting, when Muriel Drysdale of Chaplin took her place, the first woman delegate in Pool history. For Pool headquarters, the arrival of a woman delegate was overdue — three years earlier, a Pool newsletter to local committees had strongly urged that Pool members consider selecting a "lady delegate." In 1982 Drysdale was joined by Lillian Fahlman, who became the first woman to be chosen delegate in an actual election. Nevertheless, member participation would remain a serious problem in the early 1980s.

In its commercial business after the Federal takeover, the Pool generally coped satisfactorily with the variable economy and strong inflation of the 1970s. Farm service division sales went through five straight years of thirty-percent-plus increases before running into a bad year in 1976-77, when the division had only a tiny surplus. An unsettled economy brought mixed results for the division in later years, including a $1.8 million loss for 1981-82 largely because of high interest rates. When retiring division director Roy McKenzie issued his last annual report in 1982, however, he was able to look back on dramatic growth and forward to prospects for additional expansion. McKenzie, who was brought in to advise on farm supply sales in 1964, the Pool's second year in that business, became manager in 1965. His first annual report as manager noted $4 million in sales, while his last one reported sales volume of $155 million. Throughout that period, he recalled, the Pool continually had to contend with excessive expectations:

> At the outset of the Pool going into the farm supply business there seemed to be an expectation that the Pool, for some reason, would be able to provide production inputs to its members at a lower price than anyone else, and at the same time provide a high level of service and maybe pay a patronage dividend besides. These expectations have not been met but still exist.

The active role of Pool delegates in supervising corporate affairs was reflected in McKenzie's farewell remarks to the annual meeting. In eighteen appearances before delegates, he noted, he had been asked about 540 questions, listened to at least as many comments or suggestions, and heard debate on more than 600 resolutions concerning farm supply sales.

The industrial division, meanwhile, continued to expand, primarily in rapeseed processing but also in barley processing and in production of various prepared flour mixes for the bakery trade. The Saskatoon vegetable oil plant's capacity was tripled in 1972. Two years later the Pool bought Agra Industries' plant at Nipawin, roughly tripling crushing capacity again, as well as adding a complete refinery for the production of margarine, shortenings and salad oils. In 1975 most industrial division operations became part of CSP Foods Ltd., a company jointly owned with Manitoba Pool Elevators. Saskatchewan Wheat Pool retained ownership of its Saskatoon flour mill, but CSP staff operated the mill. The Manitoba pool brought significant additional capacity into the new company, including a plant it took over from an Altona co-operative. The Altona plant, which concentrated on sunflower seed contracting and processing, further helped diversify CSP operations.

Moving the Bratton elevator. (photo by R. H. Macdonald)

With 1982 construction of a new crushing plant at Harrowby, Manitoba, CSP Foods became far and away the biggest oilseed crusher in the nation. Although CSP gave the Pool a $9.7 million dividend in 1980, it ran into heavy financial losses in the next few years from erratic world demand for vegetable oil and competition from a huge U.S. soybean crop. The Pool also played a part in founding the POS (Protein, Oil, Starch) pilot plant in Saskatoon for research toward such goals as additional processing of agricultural crops.

Livestock operations were trimmed in 1973, when the Saskatchewan hog marketing commission was established and the Pool as a result left the business of marketing slaughter hogs, although it continued to sell feeders. Chaotic 1973-74 beef markets gave the Pool's livestock division its first deficit, $341,686. Pool directors, however, estimated that the division's price-support measures prevented producers from losing between $8 million and $10 million in that period. Innovations and experiments continued, as the Pool opened a $2.8-million combination livestock yard and farm service centre in Regina in 1975. The new complex offered the most modern livestock facilities on the continent, including electronic displays and computer-calculated receipts. The Pool became the first to experiment with air freight shipments of live western cattle to Ontario markets, but found that the costs of air travel outweighed the gains of avoiding transit weight loss. By the time division director Charles Leask retired in 1982 after thirty-two years with the Pool's livestock operations, the division was studying the possibility of audio-visual links that would enable cattle to stay in one place but be auctioned in several distant markets. The arrival of a government marketing agency for beef, however, reduced the need for some Pool facilities. Livestock yards were active only one day a week, selling feeder cattle, whereas they had previously been busy throughout the week.

A landmark new venture came in 1970, when the three pools and United Grain Growers combined to form XCAN Grain Ltd. to market grain abroad. To some government officials and even some Pool employees, it was a puzzle why the pools had waited so long to become active internationally, as agents for the Canadian Wheat Board and as sellers of non-board products.[24] Mumford, however, recalled later that the pools deferred launching their XCAN role until it became clear that the wheat board's powers would not be expanded and that the board would continue relying on private agents for much of its sales.[25] Government officials also noted a tendency for XCAN to move cautiously in competing with the huge international food trading corporations that could juggle their profits between many different spheres of activity, from shipping to processing. Despite such qualifications, XCAN moved ahead strongly, exporting 91 million bushels of grains, oilseeds and pellet products in its second year of operations — twelve percent of total Canadian exports. Because of competition between UGG and the pools, the three pools bought UGG's share of XCAN in 1973-74 by mutual agreement. In 1975 XCAN expanded by opening its own Japanese office.

Among other innovations was the Pool's decision to join other co-operatives in 1981 in forming an oil exploration company, Co-Enerco. Involvement in the company, which was formed in response to federal incentives to Canadianize the oil industry, marked the Pool's first venture that was not directly linked to its rural base. In a more traditional investment, the Pool bought 320 acres of farmland near Watrous for research, spending $300,000 for land and machinery, and budgeting about $200,000 a year for operations. Research activities included testing new crop varieties, experimenting with farming practices and trying different fertilizers and chemicals. Saskatchewan Wheat Pool was also heavily committed financially in the thorny 1978-82 negotiations to build a major grain terminal at Prince Rupert, B.C. Before the first construction contract was awarded in 1982, the terminal's cost had soared from an estimated $60-$100 million range to a budgeted $275 million. Initial owners included the three pools, UGG, Cargill and Pioneer, with the Alberta and Saskatchewan pools holding 34 and 30 percent respectively.

A Tradition Dies: The *Producer* Becomes Profitable

Meanwhile, Saskatchewan Wheat Pool lost — at least temporarily — an old tradition. By the end of the 1970s, the familiar *Western Producer* deficit had vanished. After Bob Phillips became editor-publisher in 1973 with a mandate to curb losses, subscribers occasionally found the comics or another feature missing as he firmly enforced a new rule that editorial content could not exceed paid advertising space.[26] There was probably no danger of the *Producer* being shut down, Phillips felt in retrospect, — but continued heavy losses might have meant eventual downgrading to a membership organ. Instead, the institution entered the 1980s stronger than ever. A new plant in north-end Saskatoon brought an initial deficit, but then came surpluses, including two precedent-shattering years with net earnings of more than $1 million each. There were news-quality dividends too: "scalping" from other publications officially ended, original staff reporting increased, and full-time correspondents were stationed outside Saskatchewan. For a time, the newspaper even considered jumping into sophisticated electronic services. At the 1981 annual meeting, Phillips told delegates that *Producer* and Pool staff were studying the possibility of a computer system to deliver information to video screens in farm homes. While some observers predicted that such futuristic services could supplant newspapers, Phillips noted: "we want to be sure that the Western Producer has a viable alternative. . . . We intend very much to survive for the next 58 years."[27] The speculative project, however, was indefinitely deferred when general economic conditions turned sour.

Newspaper management also had to guard their editorial independence. Many Pool delegates' resolutions were simply helpful suggestions, like the 1973 motion "that the reasons for the extreme increase in the price of baler twine be published in The Western Producer," or the 1976 call for "on-farm interviews with farmers." But other resolutions hinted at approaches that could damage the newspaper's hard-won credibility, from which both the *Producer* and the Pool itself benefitted. Examples included a 1971 motion "that, where possible, the layout of the front page be so designed that the articles presenting views of our organization be more prominently displayed." And a 1980 resolution that

Five Western Producer *agriculture editors — seated: Adair Stuart; standing, from left: Bill Bradley (later executive editor); Grant MacEwan; Ron Toulton; Tom Melville-Ness (later editor-publisher). (photo by R. H. Macdonald)*

"when reporting on membership functions, Western Producer reporters place more emphasis on member participants." Critics of the newspaper at times included Pool president Ted Turner, who told an interviewer in 1980 that he did not want to "dictate what the paper will do," but he became "incensed if the newspaper is giving more attention to very small minority groups, or people who have not earned their credentials in the industry, than to this organization."[28] But, to the credit of *Producer* and Pool leaders alike, the full range of farm opinion continued to be reflected in news and letter columns.

The book-publishing section also expanded throughout the 1970s and into the 1980s, although its figures continued to be written in red. Under the banner of Western Producer Prairie Books, it published 13 new titles in 1983 and had 102 books in print. Gone were the days when its only offerings were amateur reminiscences. Now it also had expensive coffee-table picture books, professional histories, novels and current events books.

The mid-1970s also brought a substantial boost for Saskatchewan Wheat Pool's involvement in foreign development projects, with employees and members working in Peru, Tanzania, Zambia, Lesotho, Belize, and the Philippines. International development policies were moving away from glossy factory or hydroelectric projects, into practical agricultural development. The Pool was well suited to help in the new trend, with its expertise ranging from basic grain production to advanced processing. Volunteers had their salaries paid by the Pool, plus guarantees of continued employment when they returned to Saskatchewan, while the Canadian International Development Agency generally paid travel expenses. Among early ventures, Ken Sarsons of the industrial division helped plan a Peruvian oilseed project, while John Trew helped plan development of co-operatives within a Tanzanian economic project. Farm services division staff played a major role in projects in Lesotho and Zambia from 1974 to 1979.

The next stage, however, turned into disaster. With encouragement from United Nations agencies, Saskatchewan Wheat Pool became prime contractor for a development project in the Philippines. As project head, Trew found disheartening corruption overseas — with seven pesos to the dollar, the general rule of thumb was that every $1 million in aid made someone a peso millionaire.[29] Pool hopes for an integrated system of village co-operatives were undercut when Philippine authorities insisted that the planned feed mill be placed in an area where there was virtually no livestock and where only a few powerful people would benefit from the investment. When Trew and other project leaders tried to insist on placing the mill where it would be economically efficient, they found themselves up against a stone wall, and even subject to bureaucratic harassment over visas. Also discouraging were pressures they felt from Canada, where politically-influential manufacturers of agricultural equipment wanted everything smoothed over so the project and their sales could go ahead. Disheartened, Trew and the Pool team pulled out, prompting initial complaints from Ottawa but later winning private praise from foreign aid officials once they reported the full story.

The sour experience, however, killed tentative Pool thoughts of having the company set up its own international development division to act as prime contractors on such projects. Even before the Philippines fiasco, senior management had some concerns over loss of the services of capable staff if the organization undertook such lengthy contracts, which would take far more time and personnel than one-shot individual advisory missions. Instead, the Pool began giving modest grants to the Co-operative Development Fund for overseas work, while continuing to allow paid leaves of absence to the few Pool staff who went on approved foreign aid missions.

Thankfully, there were lighter aspects to Pool business, ranging from campaigns to keep nearly forgotten hamlets on Pool maps, to a unique institution known only as "The Club." Founded by director Gordon South, the Club's physical assets never consisted of more than a few bottles of liquor and soft drinks, bought with joint contributions and assigned to the junior director's hotel room.[30] Pool directors may have been responsible for a business with revenues approaching $2 billion, but they were also dollar-conscious farmers with no desire to waste money on cocktail-lounge prices. The Club even featured tongue-in-cheek membership cards one year, complete with paste-on pictures, courtesy of a *Western Producer* guest. For all its casualness, the Club became a highly effective means for Pool directors and visiting government officials to get to know each other. At least one serious bureaucrat sent a delighted letter of thanks after being given honorary membership.

Such informal conviviality, however, was not frequent enough in the bitter agricultural politics of the 1970s. At the centre of the Pool's darkest fears throughout this period was a cool, self-controlled rookie MP, Otto Emil Lang, who in October 1969 was appointed cabinet minister responsible for the Canadian Wheat Board. Born 14 May 1932 in Handel, Saskatchewan, Lang quickly made his mark as a bright young force in the Liberal party — with a law degree, Rhodes Scholar studies at Oxford, appointment as University of Saskatchewan law dean, and, above all, being one of only two Liberals elected in Saskatchewan in the 1968 federal election. In a year, he was supervising the wheat board, a responsibility he carried with him during the next ten years even as he went through appointments as minister of manpower, justice, and transport. As Liberal MPs became even scarcer on the prairies — so scarce that some people quipped they should be protected by game laws — Lang expanded his power to become, informally, the cabinet minister in charge of just about everything affecting the prairies, particularly Saskatchewan. At first glance he was an unlikely candidate to maintain any rural following. His public image was stiff-necked and humorless, reinforced by his practice of wearing dignified business suits even in country campaigning, and by over-use of his title, "The Honorable Otto Lang," in press releases. Not surprisingly, he became the target for continual wisecracks — ranging from an impudent Calgary agricultural columnist (who tended to mispronounce his name as "Blotto" at news conferences), to John Diefenbaker, who felt Lang had the unerring ability to walk through a pasture and step on the only cow plat in it. Such jibes, however, distracted attention from Lang's correct assessment that the West's grain handling and transportation system was in a mess. With earnest determination he set out to bring overdue reform to the system and succeeded in bringing hundreds of millions of dollars worth of new federal programs to bear on the problem. To help plan an ultra-streamlined grainhandling system, Lang established a Grains Group of analysts and planners, many of whom had no background in the grain industry. The difficulty was that the new minister's vision of an efficient new grainhandling system did not match the kind of rural society in which farmers wanted to live.

Lang also assumed his new duties in the midst of serious grain surpluses and depressed prices. Within five months he had to announce a $10.9 million deficit on the wheat board's barley pooling, marking the first time since the board got monopoly powers over wheat in 1943 that there was no money for a final payment to farmers. Before 1970 seeding, he also unveiled "Operation LIFT" (Lower Inventories For Tomorrow), a system of incentives and penalties that was one major factor in farmers' taking half Canada's wheat acreage out of production. Many farmers protested the idea of reducing production in a hungry world, and wheat board commissioners were privately opposed to the plan,[31] but Lang consulted Pool leaders in advance and won their support. Among other considerations, U.S. authorities were trying to reduce grain surpluses by taking land out of production and were placing strong pressure on Canada to co-operate. In exchange for its support the Pool also helped persuade Lang to

SWP livestock sales ring, Regina. (SWP files)

make payments for land switched to summerfallow. When markets returned to normal in a couple of years, resentful farmers remembered the lost production of 1970. The Pool continued to get criticism for its role in LIFT even a dozen years later, and President Ted Turner doubted that he could ever again support such a program.[32]

But as far as farmers were concerned, the worst was yet to come. A special "Task Force on Agriculture" report, unveiled in May 1970, shocked rural communities with a casual but well-publicized statement that only a third of Canadian farms were considered large enough for long-term economic viability. To many, that seemed to indicate plans within some government circles to drive two-thirds of existing farmers off the land. The report did recommend some measures to aid people to get out of marginal farming operations, but government spokesmen had to deny for years that they had any intention of reducing farm population by two-thirds. The Pool called a special meeting of delegates in June 1970 to discuss the report (the first time since 1931 that delegates met twice in one year) and followed that with 168 informational country meetings within ten days. The Pool's prompt action helped put things in perspective, but there were still grounds for legitimate worries and Pool directors noted that 1970 was "a year of concern, anxiety and search for direction."

Among 1970 manifestations of that anxiety was formation of the Palliser Triangle Wheat Growers' Association. The Palliser group, oriented toward open marketing and higher rail rates to encourage better rail service, quickly became a major irritation for Pool leaders. Although Palliser membership was small in comparison with the Pool, the new group showed a flair for publicity. Lang and other headline-making names spoke at their conventions, which were scheduled to coincide with the less colorful annual meetings of the Saskatchewan Federation of Agriculture.

The next major shock for Pool disciples came in 1973, when a prairie-wide plebiscite of farmers found only forty-six percent in favor of making the Canadian Wheat Board exclusive seller of the rapeseed crop. In the later assessment of the Saskatchewan agriculture department, prairie farmers paid a significant price for that decision. The department estimated that in 1977-79, farmers received $6.7 million less than they would have received if rapeseed merchants had charged no more than handling tariffs. In addition, the producers lost Vancouver cash premiums that the merchants enjoyed. Pool spokesmen felt plebiscite results were influenced by Lang's public suggestion that farmers could always have rapeseed pooling without putting rapeseed under the board. The Rapeseed Association of Canada had also been pushing for a negative vote in the plebiscite, a move that led to the Pool leaving the association for several years, until the association decided to remain neutral in farm policy whenever it lacked unanimity.

Meanwhile, major changes were brewing in feed grains policy. In 1974, the federal government ended the wheat board's monopoly over grades of wheat, oats and barley used for livestock feed in Canada. Starting 1 August, elevator companies and other merchants could buy feed grains in the West for resale to eastern livestock producers. The politically powerful eastern farm lobby had been especially vociferous in complaining about lack of direct access to western feed grain at a time of surpluses, when western livestock producers could get feed at low desperation prices. The new open market in domestic feed grains may have boosted commodity exchange business and slightly helped eastern livestock operations, but it also placed greater strain on an already-decaying rail transportation system. Predicting the most difficult year in history for trying to match export demand with farmers' deliveries, wheat board commissioner D. H. Treleaven told the 1974 Pool meeting:

> we are once again trying to operate two diverse systems in tandem. . . . It is no longer a question of moving a volume of grain to meet consumption and export requirements, it is also a matter of moving grain to meet futures market requirements, and the two objectives may not be compatible.[33]

For its part, the Pool was condemning the open-market system and demanding that Lang act on his promise to hold a plebiscite on the issue. But, a year later, Lang told Pool delegates it was still too early for a plebiscite on the open-market system because "people are still learning about it and there are measures still to be introduced." The new measures, which took effect in 1976, included a reduction in the feed freight assistance program, which paid federal subsidies on feed grain moving to eastern livestock producers. That program was replaced with a new policy of having the wheat board offer feed grains for sale in the east at prices competitive with U.S. corn. The corn-competitive formula was to cost western farmers considerable lost money and produce the bizarre situation of some Ontario farmers exporting small amounts of feed grain at prices higher than western farmers got for the grain they supplied to Ontario. Although the pools retained fundamental objections to the open-market system for feed grains, a few of their criticisms were satisfied in 1979 when the wheat board and the grain commission were given powers to set quotas on delivery and elevator storage of non-board feed grains.

Meanwhile the traditionally-close relations between Saskatchewan Wheat Pool and the University of Saskatchewan's agriculture college had become a casualty of the heated controversy over the erosion of orderly marketing. In searching for reasons why so many farmers were rejecting the idea of a monopoly marketing agency, some Pool officials came to the conclusion that agriculture professors were pushing open-market philosophy. Part of the blame lay with the Pool itself since Pool staff had drawn away from the university, said field staff head Ian Traquair.[34] To remedy matters, regular contacts were resumed with the university's governors and faculty. College dean Jacob Brown felt that the Pool was sometimes unwilling to accept the college's duty to take an independent, objective approach in describing options in grain marketing. Brown, however, also felt that the university as well as the Pool had drifted slightly away from their old close relationship. For the future he saw little or no problem, noting that ties between the university and the co-operative movement would be strengthened under plans to create a co-operative studies unit with professors from several fields.[35] Co-operative organizations as well as the university and the provincial government would fund the new unit.

Adding to Pool insecurities in 1974, the year feed grains partially returned to the open market, was the sudden arrival on the prairies of two giant international grain companies. Cargill Grain Co. jumped onto the scene with the purchase of National Grain Ltd. elevators. About the same time, Continental Grain Co.

(Canada) Ltd. started to buy feed grains and oilseeds at prairie points, handling them by truck delivery to Canadian government inland terminals. Also that year, a group of farmers announced plans to build a large inland terminal at Weyburn.[36] All these incidents seemed to be part of a pattern of mutually-supportive developments, a pattern that also included the new feed grains policy, government plans to rationalize the grainhandling system, and growing railway pressures for higher freight rates on grain. Events seemed to be moving toward a super-efficient rail system in which the thousands of prairie delivery points would be replaced by perhaps only eighty huge inland terminals — a possibility ominously mentioned in federal studies as one of several consolidation options. Such a radical change would make it easier for new companies to move into the Western Canada grain trade, since they would not have to put up chains of several hundred country elevators. It would also mean dramatically reduced costs for the railways, who could send entire trains at a time to pick up just one type of grain at one of these terminals, instead of scattering rail cars one or two at a time among many small elevators on decrepit branch lines.

To achieve all this, only one innocent-sounding change was necessary: variable rail rates. If the railways had freedom to offer substantially lower freight rates for grain delivered to a few main-line points, they could in effect force farmers to bypass their local branch-line elevators. The process could also be aided if elevator companies had the freedom to charge variable tariffs, a freedom that was granted in 1974 by the Canada Grain Commission. Variable handling charges at elevators, however, were not as crucial as variable rail rates — simply because elevator companies would have little incentive to consolidate at a very few points if they could not gain lower rail rates by doing so. By comparison with such radical consolidation possibilities, Saskatchewan Wheat Pool's own consolidation program was mild indeed. In relation to other companies' actual performance, however, the Pool had been a leader in elevator consolidation in Saskatchewan. The number of Pool elevator operating units fell from 1,224 in 1971 to 624 in 1982, a forty-nine-percent decrease. A prairie-wide system of inland terminals or extremely high-throughput elevators would have been undeniably more efficient from the viewpoint of railways and federal transportation authorities, saving many millions of dollars each year. Saskatchewan Wheat Pool naturally had an interest in protecting its extensive country elevator system, but there were more important reasons for alarm. The trouble with radical centralization was that it would simply shift massive costs onto rural society in both

Loading grain at Pool terminal No. 7. (photo by R. H. Macdonald)

human and financial terms. Without the tax base of local elevators and the shopping done by farmers while delivering grain, many villages and small towns would die. An entire way of life, the foundation of Saskatchewan's unique society, was threatened. Farmers would have to increase the time and money spent on trucking grain by several hundred percent. Provincial and municipal taxpayers — many of them farmers — would have to spend vast additional sums on road improvements and maintenance. None of these social and financial costs, however, would show up in railway account books.

There could be no variable rail rates, however, so long as the statutory Crowsnest Pass rates remained fixed by law. That was the significance behind yet another landmark event of 1974. Speaking to the Canada Grains Council in Edmonton on Tuesday, 29 October, anniversary of the 1929 "Black Tuesday" stock market crash, Otto Lang wondered publicly if it was time to open a debate on ending the Crow rates. Instead of the fixed Crow rates, he suggested, there could be some program to pay farmers the existing "Crow benefit" in another form. There could also be a comprehensive study of the rail system, consideration of variable rates to promote rationalization, and a trucking subsidy for farmers who might lose their local elevators. To the pools, that speech, coming on top of all their other concerns over federal policies, was a virtual declaration of war. At Saskatchewan Wheat Pool's annual meeting the next month, Turner declared that the Crow battle would be one of the most important that farmers would ever have to fight: "we are being asked to trade off a firmly established brick house for a cardboard house without even a decent foundation under it."[37] In an unprecedented move, Pool delegates by formal resolution asked for a new minister to be put in charge of the wheat board. With equal lack of success they also called for nationalization of the Canadian Pacific railway, and for laws to prevent foreign-controlled companies operating in the prairie grain business. In addition, they resolved that the Crow rates should stay unchanged and that Saskatchewan Wheat Pool should maintain equal tariffs among its country elevators "as long as possible." Otto Lang appeared before that meeting for a question-and-answer session that the meeting's minutes, with extreme understatement, said included "a frank exchange of opinions." The realization of farmers' vulnerability to Ottawa's decisions caused some Pool officials to reconsider the path that the organization had been following for the last few decades. Pool general manager Ira Mumford told the 1974 meeting:

> We have been quick to seek government assistance for policies which we believed would be favorable to agricultural producers, but if government interference and control is to be a by-product of such assistance, we may need to exercise restraint in seeking assistance in the future.

That realization was not confined to Pool leaders. As was often the case, some grassroots members had been quicker to state similar views. Months before Lang's 29 October speech, for example, John Whittome of Aylsham was writing in the *Western Producer* that he was a former committee chairman who started hauling grain to the Pool in 1924 but quit because directors and delegates were "turning the Pool into a political machine with their only thoughts that everything could be done better under government control."[38] As the history of the Crowsnest Pass rates testifies, however, government policies were a large and inescapable part of prairie agriculture from earliest days.

Crowsnest Pass Freight Rates

It all started when the CPR was contemplating a 300-mile rail line from Lethbridge, through the Crowsnest Pass, into coal- and mineral-rich southeast British Columbia. Both the CPR and the national government wanted to pre-empt the extension of U.S. railways into that region. Thus, Ottawa and the CPR signed the 6 September 1897 Crowsnest Pass agreement, under which Ottawa agreed to pay $11,000 for each mile of track built, up to a maximum of $3.6 million. The CPR, which actually received $3.4 million, also got 3.7 million acres in land grants from the B.C. government. Altogether, according to estimates in a 1980 Pool booklet, the cash subsidy and B.C. land grants were worth $5.2 million to the CPR, a little over half the $9.9 million construction cost of the line. In exchange the railway agreed to a permanent reduction of three cents per hundredweight in its rates for grain and flour shipments moving to Fort William, Ont., and eastward. Under the agreement, no higher rates could be charged after the reduction was put into effect. The railway also agreed to specified rate reductions of 10 to 33.3 percent for specified goods, generally settlers' needs, moving into Western Canada. The lower rates took effect in stages in 1898-99, reaching agreed levels by 1 September 1899. At that date, the rate for moving a hundred pounds of grain from Regina to the Lakehead was 20 cents; eight decades later, when a standard postage stamp cost 30 cents, the grain rate was still 20 cents, equivalent to about $4.40 for a metric tonne.

During 1903-18 the CPR actually lowered the rates to meet competition from the Canadian Northern Railway, one of the railways that were later combined to form Canadian National. For a few years after that, the Board of Railway Commissioners used the authority of the War Measures Act to allow higher rates to meet postwar costs, bringing the Regina rate at one point to 12.5 cents above Crow levels. Then, in 1922, the 1899 rates were restored and in 1925 parliamentary legislation made them part of the statutes of Canada. The 1922-25 restoration has been credited to three related factors: a minority government; vociferous western Progressives in opposition; and the demands of half the government's backbenchers.[39] Without any one of those three factors, "the Crow" might not have been reborn. Over the years, the Crow system changed, usually to the railways' disadvantage. The rate concessions for specified goods moving into the West were dropped. But the low Crow rates were extended to new agricultural products, to westward as well as eastward shipments, and to the CNR as well as the CPR. When CPR court action established that the rates should apply only to those delivery points in existence in 1897, the law was simply changed to make the rates apply everywhere. Along the way, myths grew up about the Crow rates, myths that were to play a significant part in farm opinion of the 1970s.[40] One common belief was that the imposition of Crow rates came partly in exchange for the 25 million acres of Western Canada land given to the CPR, land that the CPR used to build a rich corporate empire of hotels, real estate, industry, ships and airplanes. In fact, the Crow rates had nothing to do with those grants, which were connected with the original transcontinental railway. Only the 3.7 million acres of B.C. land grants — land that was generally sold quickly — were linked to the Crow. Even the CPR's highly-profitable Cominco mining and smelting operation in southeast B.C. was not part of the B.C. government grants, but was purchased privately. Another myth was that the CPR got monopoly rights over wide areas as part of the Crownest Pass agreement. Nor, as a prominent economic historian has noted, was the agreement originally designed as a national gift to the West: "The agreement has never been a farm subsidy; on the contrary, it was designed to stimulate settlement and the production of exports for the benefit of the commercial interest of central Canada."[41]

In subsequent years the Crow rates may well have been maintained to compensate for prairie geographic disadvantages and to make Canadian wheat exports more competitive with other nations, but that was not the original driving force behind the rates. Nor were they part of some mystical bargain when Alberta and Saskatchewan entered Confederation as provinces in 1905, although they certainly came to be regarded in the prairies as a quasi-sacred part of federal-provincial relations.

With decades of emotion behind the "holy Crow," Otto Lang was undertaking an ambitious task in trying to change it. He never did succeed before 1979 electoral defeat drove him out of politics and into the vice-presidency of Pioneer Grain. Looking back on his 1975 campaign to change the Crow, Lang identified Saskatchewan Wheat Pool as the main roadblock. He thought he had made an impression on Pool president Ted Turner: "I think Turner saw the logic of the change privately but he was fearful of the politics."[42] Turner, however, recalled the situation differently, saying that the Pool could not consider changes to such a fundamental matter without specific proposals on what would replace it. The Pool president also felt that Lang had adopted an unnecessarily public and belligerent posture with his speech before the Grains Council instead of first pursuing the idea in private with the pools. The Council, an industry-wide forum fostered by Lang, originally included the pools as members. The pools, however, resigned in protest over Council involvement in policy matters. A body in which representative farm organizations were in the minority should not be heavily involved in farm policy, the pools felt. Turner considered Lang's Council speech as "open defiance of the pools."[43] If Lang had instead chosen to sit down with the farm leaders and work out solutions to grainhandling problems, Turner felt, "it's hard to say" what might have happened. As it was, Turner in 1975 informed Pool delegates of unprecedented open conflict between their organization and the federal government, saying he would try to establish constructive relations if that could be done without compromising basic Pool beliefs.

For a few years the Crow rates seemed to become a simmering background issue while attention turned to specific rail problems. To stop the deterioration of the railways' grain boxcar fleet, Ottawa spent $257 million in 1972-79 buying 8,000 modern "hopper" cars, cylindrical cars that could carry more grain, more economically. Later the wheat board bought another 2,000 with producers' money while the Alberta and Saskatchewan governments contributed 1,000 each. The 1976 Grain Receipts Stabilization Plan brought long-overdue income-averaging facilities to prairie farmers, plus millions more federal dollars, even though the averaging formula short-changed farmers somewhat by not taking account of inflation. Rail-line abandonment issues had been partially clarified in 1974, when Ottawa announced that 12,423 miles of prairie rail line would remain to at least the year 2000 and 525 miles of unused track would go before abandonment hearings. That left over 6,200 miles of branch lines to be assessed by a commission headed by former Saskatchewan chief justice Emmett Hall. After extensive hearings in scores of prairie communities, Hall recommended abandoning 2,165 miles, keeping 1,813 miles, and referring 2,344 miles to a new western transportation authority for further review. Saskatchewan Wheat Pool played a major role in the hearings, both on its own behalf and in assisting community groups.

The Hall Commission report helped clarify the future of the prairie rail network, prompting Ottawa in 1977 to launch a two-year, $100-million branch line rehabilitation program, later expanded to $700 million over ten years. But at least equal impact came from a separate study by U.S. expert Carl Snavely into railway revenues from grain traffic. After intense investigation into the labyrinthine world of railway cost-accounting, Snavely concluded that the railways were indeed losing money hauling grain under Crow rates, even excluding railway overhead costs. For 1974, he estimated, operating costs for moving Crow grain were $231 million — of which $89.7 million was paid by farmers and grain companies, $52 million was reimbursed in federal subsidies, and $89.3 million was absorbed in losses by the railways. Both directly and through the grain companies they dealt with, farmers paid only thirty-nine percent of grain freight costs in 1974 — a proportion that would keep falling since farmers' payments were fixed under Crow but inflation was driving up railway costs. The Snavely report changed the entire tone of Western Canada's debate over Crow rates. Sceptical farmers and politicians had previously argued that there was no proof railways were really losing money under Crow rates, that modern technology allowed increasingly efficient rail movement. Such arguments were suddenly untenable, and a new question emerged: how were the railways to get revenues that would fully compensate them for grain-movement costs? The basic choice was simple: federal subsidies of some sort, or increased payments by producers, or a combination of both. Among others, some western livestock producers were arguing that grain farmers should pay more. Livestock industry spokesmen said the Crow discriminated against them because it tended to drive up the price of feed grains on the prairies except in years of great surplus. If farmers' potential earnings from export sales were cut by 50 cents a bushel because of increased rail costs, then it would take 50 cents less to persuade farmers to sell their grain to prairie livestock producers instead of exporting it. Similarly, some spokesmen for agricultural processing industries argued that the Crow rate encouraged grain exports rather than prairie-based processing of that grain into higher-value products. Still other groups contended that railway losses under Crow rates prevented railways from investing in new facilities to move more grain, potash and coal. According to such views the Holy Crow had become the Prairie Albatross.

This issue was of greatest concern to Saskatchewan, since Saskatchewan farmers faced the longest rail haul and thus the highest rail costs. One study indicated that, when efficiency gains were taken into consideration, Alberta farmers would *gain* $190 million over twenty-five years from abolition of the Crow and Manitoba farmers would lose only $33 million — but Saskatchewan farmers would lose $721 million.[44] Even though some Saskatchewan Wheat Pool delegates had said in closed 1976 sessions that some change in the Crow rate was inevitable given increasing rail costs, Pool delegates that year were still publicly

unanimous that the Crow should stay. A major break in the three
prairie pools' solid pro-Crow front, however, came in late 1978,
when president Jim Deveson of Manitoba Pool Elevators said
farmers should be willing to discuss rate changes if it would help

*SWP 50th anniversary directors and senior officials: Back row, left
to right; D. M. Lockwood, first vice-president, Regina, District 10; J.
Wm. Marshall, second vice-president, Regina, District 15; J. M.
Fair, treasurer, Regina; R. D. McKell, Regina, District 6; W.
Bernard Mundell, Leroy, District 13; Aubrey B. Wood, Ruthilda,
District 12; Ira K. Mumford, general manager, Regina. Middle
Row, left to right; J. O. Wright, secretary, Regina; Don Sinclair,
assistant secretary, Regina; James Lindsay, Limerick, District 2;
Garfield Stevenson, Whitewood, District 7; Avery K. Sahl, Moss-
bank, District 5; Walter A. Kumph, Smiley, District 11; Clifford
Murch, Lancer, District 4. Front row, left to right: William Schutz,
Saltcoats, District 8; Erling O. Johnsrude, Weyburn, District 1;
Hugh F. McLeod, Leross, District 9; E. K. Turner, president,
Regina, District 16; Gustave C. Anderson, Val Marie, District 3;
Harold Yelland, Porcupine Plain, District 4. (SWP files)*

their economic situation. The Saskatchewan NDP government stepped into the resulting controversy as agriculture minister Edgar Kaeding declared: "under no circumstances is the Crow rate negotiable."[45] And Pool delegates resolved to use their influence to persuade "sister co-operatives" not to "sell out" the Crow.

In March 1980, new Liberal transport minister Jean-Luc Pepin launched another major federal drive to change the Crow. Saskatchewan Wheat Pool was still, in public, vehemently against any such change. A Pool booklet prepared that same month forcefully argued that every other form of transportation received vast direct or indirect subsidies. The booklet also examined the effect of higher freight rates on specific Saskatchewan communities. For the 540-population town of Kyle, for example, Crow abolition would mean an extra $411,480 cost to local farmers, which in turn would mean roughly double that amount in lost economic activity in the town. But Pool directors that year were becoming increasingly worried about the need to ensure adequate railway capability to move the much larger volumes of grain exports forecast for the late 1980s. In November 1980, directors told delegates: "Grain producers can ill afford to have grain remain unsold in their bins at current high interest rates while world demand is strong." Conflicting pressures were heavy on that November 1980 meeting. The Western Agricultural Conference, consisting of representatives from the three prairie agriculture federations, had produced a compromise policy that expressed willingness to discuss how future rail cost increases might be split among government, railways and producers. The WAC policy had set several conditions for such extra payments by farmers: freight rates must continue to be statutory, changeable only by act of Parliament; there must be guarantees of good railway service; and railway rates must not be variable. The Pool meeting also featured conflicting exhortations from two federal cabinet ministers. Senator Hazen Argue, minister responsible for the Canadian Wheat Board, declared that he favored retention of the Crow rate, while transport minister Pepin said proper rail service demands Crow reform: "You are damaging your own self-interest as producers of grain by allowing this situation to continue. . . . If no change takes place, you are going to suffer for it." By a vote of 122 to 22, Pool delegates endorsed the WAC policy, including the WAC reference to discussing how future rail cost increases might be split among government, railways and producers. The Pool resolution added one qualification — "within this policy, Saskatchewan Wheat Pool press for the retention of the present statutory Crow rate for the producer."

That Pool vote, despite all its qualifications, prompted a storm of protest in the countryside. Both the National Farmers' Union and the provincial NDP government lashed the Pool for not adopting an uncompromising keep-the-Crow posture. One factor behind the torrent of abuse that descended on Pool delegates was that this was the first time such a controversial policy change had come from above — from the WAC level — instead of coming up from Saskatchewan grassroots. "Ever since we took that vote a year ago, there's been trouble back home," delegate Anthony Kambeitz told the November 1981 annual meeting.[46] A winter and summer of discontent had set the stage for a key confrontation at that November 1981 meeting as an impassioned group of delegates pressed for reconsideration of Pool support for the WAC policy. After a tough, day-long debate, the WAC policy was re-affirmed, with a 99 to 45 vote in favor of the crucial clause on discussion of farmers' share of increased rail costs.[47] The impact of membership agitation was evident in the decision of two prominent delegates to switch from 1980 support of WAC policy to 1981 rejection of it — meeting chairman Bob McKell of Regina and director Aubrey Wood of Ruthilda, the only director to cast an anti-WAC vote. Observers made much of the fact that the vote margin was narrower than the year before and that it was just barely above the two-thirds level needed to make policy under the Pool constitution. But the anti-WAC group had enjoyed several hidden advantages. Critics of the WAC policy had arranged for the 1980 policy to be restated in resolution form. If it did not get two-thirds approval, they could argue that the policy was invalid. But the 1980 resolution was Pool policy and the two-thirds requirement should have applied to those who wanted to change it, not those who wanted to keep it. In addition to that procedural perversion, there were questionable rulings against certain proposed amendments. In one case a delegate sought to make one clause more palatable by replacing it with a paragraph from a directors' statement that said essentially the same thing in more attractive language. The amendment would have subtly improved chances for retention of WAC policy, but it was ruled out of order on grounds that it was a "substitute resolution" and needed unanimous consent to be heard.[48]

Behind all the questionable procedure, however, was a profoundly sensible approach to the whole controversy. Whether consciously or instinctively, the Pool majority was giving every possible opportunity to its vociferous minority opposition. That made the final decision all the more legitimate, all the more worthy of being considered a valid consensus. Beyond the fact that many farmers were still in no mood to discuss Crow changes, there were just two problems with the policy produced by Pool delegates in November 1981 — parts were totally unrealistic and hopelessly contradictory. As finally passed, after several amendments, the resolution stated:

> That Saskatchewan Wheat Pool support a transportation policy including the following:
> 1. That the present statutory Crow rate remain.
> 2. That the federal government guarantee performance by the railroads.
> 3. That the present statutory Crow rate be extended to include all agricultural raw and processed products from the prairie region.
> 4. That the rate structure remain statutory and distance-related (non-variable).
> 5. That the compensatory rate shortfall be paid directly to the railways by the federal government.
> 6. That the federal government honor its commitment to provide necessary funding for the completion of branch line upgrading.
> 7. That the federal government ensure there is an adequate supply of railway rolling stock available to the grain industry.
> 8. If the above seven points are accepted by the federal government, future costs due to inflation shall be negotiated by producers, railroads and the federal government; and in any negotiations Saskatchewan Wheat Pool will strive to retain the present Crow rate for producers.

The contradiction between points one and eight was clear: the Pool would only negotiate changes in Crow rates if Ottawa first agreed not to change Crow rates. By a similar literal reading, point three was out of the question — as one delegate remarked, it would mean extending Crow rates to potato chips and cornflakes. NFU president Ted Strain, among others, branded the Pool resolution as a "ridiculous policy."[49] In a speech to that same meeting, he summarized the Pool position as being "committed to support the Crow rate on one hand and bargain it away with the other." But those were the directives Pool spokesmen would soon have to take into blunt negotiations over future rail rates.

In the meantime, while Pool leaders were distracted with the muddled internal situation, the Canadian Wheat Board was left to defend itself against continuing attacks. Fortunately, board spokesmen proved to be articulate and vigorous. In early 1982, at a Palliser convention in Winnipeg, one grain trade spokesman criticized board sales efforts. From 1970 to 1980, he said, the

United States tripled its grain exports while Canada stood still. The board's chief commissioner, Esmond Jarvis, effectively replied that in those ten years the United States brought 65 million acres of land back into production. Canada, he said, only had 51 million seeded acres in total — and in any case had exported a higher percentage of available wheat supplies than the United States in eight of the past eleven years.[50] Two months later, Jarvis shot down calls for a "dual marketing" system in which farmers could choose to have their wheat sold by the board or by private grain merchants:

> Now when I think of a duel, I think of two people standing in a field trying to shoot each other. In this situation, the best that can happen is that one person ends up no better than he did before, and the other person ends up a lot worse. The analogy is probably appropriate for dual marketing.
>
> The justification for dual marketing is that it would provide competition. I've always believed in competition myself. When I buy a car, or a television set, I always go to several dealers to see which one is offering the best price. There's no doubt that you can get a lower price if there are several sellers of a product instead of just one.
>
> But the proponents of dual marketing are missing a point. Farmers aren't buying grain, they're selling it. If an overseas customer had a choice of buying from several sellers of Canadian grain, he'd choose the one with the lowest price. Buyers already have enough choice among other exporting countries.[51]

In previous decades the government-appointed board had relied on the prairie pools to defend orderly marketing in such speeches but the pools had become less active in that way, being preoccupied with internal Crow policy.

The next stage in the Crow saga came in February 1982 when transport minister Pepin appointed Manitoba professor Clay Gilson as special negotiator to try to arrange a consensus among western farm groups over Crow change. Estimating that Crow rates in 1981-82 fell $612 million short of railway costs, Pepin said Ottawa would pay that $612 million Crow benefit in future years and the railways would provide guarantees of service. But there would be no extension of Crow rates to more crops or products. And, said a federal policy statement, "An increased contribution by grain farmers will be required."[52] Gilson moved quickly to bring representatives of all major western farm organizations to the negotiating table, except the NFU, which righteously refused to participate in any proceedings that envisaged abolition of Crow rates. Pepin's plan — and, by implication, Pool willingness to discuss it — was also blasted by former Pool president Charles Gibbings. Speaking in Neudorf, Saskatchewan, the wheat board commissioner said he had been invited to attend Pepin's announcement but refused: "I wouldn't go because if you voluntarily go to be raped, it's consent."[53]

Saskatchewan Wheat Pool delegates gathered in a special Saskatoon meeting in March, with press excluded and attendance strictly limited, to plan their approach to the Gilson talks. Two brief attempts to re-open discussion on the previous November's policy resolution were quickly quashed by common consent[54] — reflecting general acceptance of the legitimacy of that policy decision — and the meeting focussed on bargaining tactics. Once again, Pool representatives were burdened with an awkward directive. In a resolution that sounded like an order, but which some speakers described as non-binding, directors were told to walk out of the Gilson talks whenever any of the first seven points of Pool policy was rejected and negotiations opened on point eight, concerning farmers' share of increased costs. Taken literally, that would mean Pool representatives' walking out if the Gilson group declined to keep the Crow rates unchanged (point one) and began talking about farmers paying more. Pepin had also already ruled out the Pool's third point, extension of Crow rates to other crops and agricultural products. To confuse the situation further, some speakers at the Pool meeting suggested that the Gilson talks were merely a consultative process since decisions would be made later by cabinet — thus the Gilson meetings were not really negotiations and points one to seven could not be formally rejected in any case. Meanwhile several hundred disgruntled Pool members were meeting across the street, demanding deletion of controversial point eight. Pool delegates sent president Turner over to meet the members, but otherwise stuck to normal procedure, in effect asserting the legitimacy of the Pool's democratic structure and refusing to be swayed by possibly unrepresentative groups.

To historian John Archer, the drawn-out debate was the latest manifestation of a split that had been present in the Pool since its beginning fifty-eight years earlier.[55] In Archer's view those who thought it better to participate in policy-making sessions were continuing the tradition of the Saskatchewan Grain Growers' Association, while those who wanted all-out public confrontation were in the spirit of the old Farmers' Union of Canada. Even in 1982, it seemed, the Pool continued to be haunted by its two long-departed quarrelsome parent organizations. The controversy over the Pool's Crow policy at least had the side benefit of stirring up interest in the March 1982 delegate elections. Although the vast majority of the seventy-two subdistricts open for election were filled by acclamation, the number of actual election contests jumped to fourteen — and in nine of those elections the incumbent delegate was defeated.[56] Seven of the nine defeated delegates had voted for the WAC policy four months earlier, while two had voted against it. Considering that NFU spokesmen had urged Pool members to challenge pro-WAC delegates in the elections, the turnover was small. The Crow issue also appeared to have little impact on election of directors. The only director to vote against the WAC policy, Aubrey Wood, maintained his place on the board even though a majority of delegates in his district had voted for the WAC policy. Directors Don Lockwood and Roger Gray, the only directors to have a majority of their district's delegates opposed to the policy, retired voluntarily, with Lockwood confident that they could both have been re-elected as delegates and directors if they had run again.[57] In choosing new directors, delegates in Gray's district selected a delegate who had voted for the WAC policy, while those in Lockwood's district chose a delegate who voted anti-WAC. All told, the March 1982 elections seemed to indicate that the Pool's consensus system was still working and that the organization was avoiding the danger of being split into factions that could not work together. There were vociferous exceptions to the growing Pool consensus, however. A summer 1982 resolution by the committee at Handel called for president Turner's resignation.[58] Turner, however, was decisively vindicated at the November 1982 annual meeting, which was presented with a similar resignation resolution so that the issue could be formally addressed and there would be no appearance of member criticism being ignored. Not one delegate voted for the resolution; Turner received a standing ovation.

In May 1982 the Gilson meetings ended and prairie farm organizations waited nervously for the professor's report. Transport minister Pepin smilingly acknowledged the repercussions that could come after the historic publication of the first specific government-sponsored proposals to change the Crow rates: "Then heaven will fall, hell will open."[59] The 28 June release of Gilson's report, however, was less traumatic than that. The report did indeed call for the abolition of the old Crow rates, but in a fashion that would still shield prairie farmers from uncontrolled cost increases. Gilson proposed that farmers pay only a fraction of increasing rail costs while Ottawa paid the remainder. Farmers' basic net payments would increase no more than three percent annually in 1983-86 and 4.5 percent each year after that. Such protection, however, would apply only to annual volumes equal to the 30.4 million tonnes moved in 1981-82; cost increases on volumes above that would be wholly paid for by farmers. As for the current "Crow gap" between rate revenues and railway costs, Gilson estimated the gap at $644 million and recommended that Ottawa pay that amount annually, initially in direct payments to the railways but gradually switching to direct payments to farmers.

Reacting to the Gilson report, Saskatchewan Wheat Pool called yet another special meeting of delegates — the first time in Pool history that there had been three delegates' meetings in a twelve-month period. Not even the collapse of pooling in 1931 had provoked such an effort. But, as Pool president Turner said in an interview some months later: "there's never been a question with so much emotion attached to it, with so many traumatic possibilities, in the history of farm organizations."[60] Finally resolving the contradiction in their November 1981 policy, delegates agreed in July 1982 that the various Pool policy points would *not* have to be accepted by government and others as preconditions to Pool discussion of increased freight rates. The focus for Pool efforts became the issue of whether the Crow benefit would be paid to the railways or to farmers. Saskatchewan Wheat Pool argued that it should go to railways, to provide a more usable weapon with which to enforce performance and to avoid the appearance of a subsidy to western farmers, an appearance that might make it easier for future governments to end the payments. At the same time Pool representatives continued pushing for iron-clad assurances that variable rail rates would never be allowed.

Such issues were undeniably important, but also anti-climactic. The fundamental question of whether to change Crow rates had, in effect, been decided in 1980 and confirmed in 1981 when Pool delegates supported their directors in deciding not to go to war for the Crow. It was an historic decision, even though it was implemented amid confusion and bitterness. The embarrassing vacillations and contradictions in stated Pool policy were regrettable, but they were also signs of healthy tension between two essential elements in a strong democratic organization: the duty to provide leadership and the responsibility to stay in tune with members. Pool leaders could not march in disciplined, perfectly co-ordinated fashion into a brave new post-Crow world, because their members were not yet ready to discard that 85-year-old bird. At the same time, Pool leaders could not blindly say "no" to change, because they were painfully aware of the need to bring more revenue into the transportation system so that future generations of farmers would be able to get their grain to market. It was a tough, thankless task. It also showed the potential benefits in being both a strong commercial organization and a democratic policy-making association. If the Pool had been only a policy organization, it would have had far less incentive to take a responsible approach to modernizing the grain transportation system. If it had been only a commercial organization, it would have had less reason to fight for key safeguards for farmers and its recommendations would have been less trusted by farmers. Despite all the frustrations and trauma involved, the 1980-82 revision of freight rate policy also reconfirmed two basic facts: that Saskatchewan Wheat Pool's views on agricultural issues were still important to farmers, and that the Pool continued to reflect the hopes and fears of rural Saskatchewan.

9
Epilogue — Toward 2001

The ultimate success of the Saskatchewan Wheat Pool cannot be gauged solely by a money standard. It will continue to succeed in the highest degree only in proportion as the true spirit of co-operative effort is built up in the Province of Saskatchewan.

— Pool *Annual Report,* 1927

It has never been enough for Saskatchewan Wheat Pool to meet conventional standards for corporate success. From the beginning, Pool members had higher aims for their organization. It was supposed to be an efficient business, but it was also to provide fair treatment and service at cost to all members. On a still higher level, it was to be a democratically-controlled force working in every way possible for an improved rural society. And beyond that, it was to promote the general co-operative movement, to help people everywhere get the opportunity to work together constructively and control their own destinies. In 1927, when the infant Pool had just experienced three years of unprecedented expansion, becoming the province's largest grainhandling operation, it would have been easy for directors to do nothing but take comfortable pride in financial statistics. Instead they issued the statement quoted above, reminding themselves and their successors that the Pool had even more important purposes. Significantly, they did not talk of achieving success when co-operative assets reached some arbitrary figure — they referred to co-operative spirit, and a never-ending process where success would come only from continuing efforts to spread that spirit. The 1920s farmers who created the Pool, who built it by such means as backbreaking winters of shoveling wheat into rail cars, left a legacy that was more than an elevator system. They also handed their successors a

233

co-operative heritage, a set of duties and responsibilities, without which Saskatchewan Wheat Pool would be a soulless collection of buildings and account books.

The basic issue facing Saskatchewan Wheat Pool as it moves toward the 21st century is whether to continue that spiritual heritage or to become a mere commercial enterprise. If, by deliberate decision or apathetic drift, Pool members choose the latter route, then the history of Saskatchewan Wheat Pool is ended. A respectable business would remain, with the same name and same buildings, but it would not be the same unique entity that for six decades was more than a corporation. If, however, the Pool chooses to maintain its heritage, then it will need to cope with a series of difficult challenges.[1]

One such challenge is how to promote co-operation in an increasingly urban province and nation. In the 1930s, Pool personnel could be directly involved in helping create co-ops, providing ideas, advice and sometimes a corner of an elevator agent's office to serve as the co-op office. Today, however, there is a network of consumer co-ops and credit unions already in place. Instead of the relatively simple problem of organizing local associations, the primarily-urban co-op movement has to struggle with the frustrating task of communicating with transient members, as well as the increasingly complex task of competing with large chain stores. Even if Saskatchewan Wheat Pool could intervene with magic solutions, such an approach would be both arrogant and self-defeating. A healthy co-operative must be controlled by its own membership and must bear the responsibilities itself for member relations and management expertise.

What supportive role does that leave for Saskatchewan Wheat Pool? Pool members may not be able to have the satisfaction of directly creating new co-ops to the extent they did in the 1930s, but their organization's financial and personnel resources can still make important indirect contributions to the movement. The new co-operative oil company, Co-Enerco, is one example of a joint venture in which the Pool is continuing to try to increase co-operative control of the economy. Some dissenters have questioned Pool investment in Co-Enerco, saying it is a step outside the Pool's role of maintaining an efficient, farmer-owned grainhandling system. But it is a step that is wholly in keeping with the broader purpose of extending co-operative economic power. If that purpose is maintained, Saskatchewan Wheat Pool should be alert for opportunities to help launch similar joint ventures in future decades.[2] Increasing co-operative economic power, however, is not the same as spreading co-operative spirit. For the latter goal, there will have to be continued Pool support for such educational institutions as the Co-operative College of Canada and for joint lobbying efforts toward such aims as including more co-operative information in the school curriculum. Much could be done also with coming developments in communications technology that could some day enable co-operatives to have a two-way flow of electronic information with members' homes. With keyboards attached to their television sets, members who will not attend co-op meetings could still have a means of direct involvement. With its expertise and money the Pool could lead in developing such systems in Saskatchewan.

If it is to play such important but indirect roles, Saskatchewan Wheat Pool will more than ever need a dedicated and enlightened membership of its own. When members paid the salaries of fieldmen in the 1930s, they could see concrete, visible results as new producer and consumer co-ops sprang up. It requires greater faith and commitment to authorize spending on a host of activities where the Pool is just one of many partners and where results are less obvious. Education of co-op employees in co-operative principles and modern management techniques, for example, is an investment whose payoff cannot be measured in statistics.

Thus we come to a basic conclusion: if Saskatchewan Wheat Pool is to continue providing substantial support to the general co-operative movement, it must first ensure that its own house is in order, that its own member relations and membership participation are healthy. In interviews for this book, however, both current and retired Pool personnel expressed concern about member relations. Ominous signs included lack of candidates for delegate elections, as well as surveys showing that younger farmers tend to have less support for such traditional Pool policies as a monopoly wheat board. A 1982 communications study indicated both the extent of the problem and the type of major efforts that might be needed to deal with it.[3] One of the study's recommendations was that there should be personal contact with each of the 2,000 people who become new Pool members each year. Other suggestions included: regional offices to provide secretarial and other support services to delegates; persuading and equipping the hundreds of local committees to do more work with members; amalgamating the member relations and communications divisions; and linking delegates by telephone or computer so they could spend less time in formal meetings and more time with members. There was a blunt call for Pool officials not to "ignore issues which are aggravating to the membership," issues like the pricing of Pool farm supplies. To pretend that Pool prices are not often higher than competitors' prices, the study said, "is to insult the intelligence of the membership." A final recommendation said

Instrument panel in modern country elevator, Shaunavon. (Gibson Photos Ltd.)

emphasis should be on two-way communication and the amount of formal, impersonal material flowing from Pool headquarters should in no circumstances be increased: "There is enough printed material going out; there is none or little, coming back." In considering ways to renew and strengthen member participation, however, Pool delegates and officials must go beyond tactical improvements in communications. Even fundamental organizational and philosophical principles should be periodically reviewed to ensure they are still relevant. One occasional suggestion, for example, is that stringent delegate requirements should be eliminated. When Pool bylaws require a member to deal exclusively with the Pool for two years before becoming eligible to be a delegate, many possible candidates are thereby barred. That one simple requirement has some far-reaching effects. Not only does it make second-class members of those who deal occasionally with other elevators — perhaps just to sample the competition, perhaps in protest over the local Pool agent's actions — but by reducing the number of potential candidates, the rule increases the number of delegates chosen by acclamation. Every acclamation means that several hundred Pool members have no opportunity to vote. In some subdistricts many years could go by without members having that fundamental and clearly-visible opportunity to participate in Pool affairs. It also means that the delegate body, and thus the boards of directors, tend to be chosen from a narrower section of the rural population. The benefits of dissent, debate and constructive criticism are thereby lessened.[4] But the Pool's commitment to the co-operative movement could be weakened if it did not require 100 percent loyalty from delegates. Each generation of Pool decision-makers will have to steer its own course between the conflicting objectives of representing all Saskatchewan farmers and representing dedicated co-operators.

Similarly, there are no easy solutions to the problems of how to give local committees and farm families greater roles in Saskatchewan Wheat Pool. The family problem in particular will become increasingly significant as more women acquire equal roles in farm decision-making. A 1979 study found that the average farm wife contributed 29 hours of work each week to farm operations, in addition to 53 hours of work in the farm home.[5] An organization that depends on member participation and direct communications with members cannot forever allow half the farm population to remain uninvolved. One 1980 innovation, the first of an annual series of policy forums involving couples from every subdistrict, is an example of the kind of initiative that can be taken.

One reason that the loyalty of an informed and involved membership will be crucial in coming years is that Pool leaders may increasingly have to move ahead of the membership. As one official has noted: "Genuine leadership and popularity do not always go together."[6] The problem will be particularly acute whenever complex, far-reaching changes are decided in negotiations with government and other parties, as in the 1982 Crow rate talks. If Pool leaders are to have a timely impact on such negotiations, they will not always be able to wait for a consensus to develop slowly among Pool members. And, to have maximum bargaining power, they will have to have at least a good chance of persuading their membership to accept compromises, reached in outside negotiations.

Meanwhile there will also be a wide range of challenges on the Pool's operations side, with some possible developments that could affect member relations. Computer terminals that are currently being installed in country elevators, for example, could well have the side effect of erasing the Pool's "frumpy old lady" image, one executive has predicted.[7] Not only can the elevator computer terminals improve the Pool's internal data flow and provide more efficient service to farmers unloading grain, but they have the potential to provide consultative services covering virtually every farm operation. With proper programming, the computers could theoretically calculate the most profitable combination of crops, fertilizer, farming practices, and machinery over a period of several years for a specific farm. At the touch of a button, farmers could also get a thousand simpler services by visiting their local Pool elevator — a list of nearby people with feed or used machinery for sale, historical or up-to-the-minute data on any stock-market listing, perhaps even a version of the *Western Producer*'s classified advertisements for matrimonial partners. Such computer services are no longer just part of science-fiction speculation; they are potentially very near to becoming reality. Indeed, during 1981 and 1982 Pool officials were seriously studying a far more visionary computer initiative — a province-wide network of computer terminals in farm homes.[8] Although it would take years to build up both the physical system and a large collection of computerized services, such a network could ultimately transform the quality of rural life as much as telephones or paved all-weather roads did. A child in an isolated farmhouse could have electronic access to the best urban libraries, plus computer-education programs geared to his special needs. Parents could do banking and shopping from home, as well as the services linked to the elevator computer system.

The commercial and social possibilities connected with computers are significant not only because they show one kind of opportunity for future Pool services, but also because they demonstrate some of the problems and dangers with which Saskatchewan Wheat Pool will have to contend. Premature or ill-prepared launching of a rural computer network could involve huge monetary losses. The heavy losses incurred in 1983 by prairie co-operatives' long-established joint ventures are warnings of what might happen if the Pool became financially overextended in major enterprises. Already the capital budgets of companies like Western Co-operative Fertilizers Ltd. are, in expansionist years, several times the Pool's own capital spending. It will be a major challenge for Pool leaders merely to monitor carefully their investments in such ventures and to watch for signs of coming financial troubles that could become drains on Pool budgets.

Excessive caution, however, could mean other groups will seize opportunities first. In the computer field, that might leave no room for an economic Pool system and could perhaps result in a system that does not allow for farmers' needs. There would also be the delicate problem of how to control such a system — whether the Pool could justifiably operate a service with such powerful potential impact on rural and small-town society, or whether programming policy should be determined by an alliance of co-operatives, or even by delegates elected by the system's customers.

Yet another danger is that the glamor and expansion possibilities of such projects could draw too much managerial talent away from fundamental activities.[9] Brainpower, like money, is a limited resource that has to be carefully allocated. For many decades country and terminal elevators will remain the foundation of Pool commercial activities and they cannot be shortchanged in either talent or money if they are to remain an efficient, modern system. Radical new designs for country elevators will have to be assessed,[10] while terminals will need improved grain-cleaning equipment to remove one potential bottleneck.[11] When finances permit, there are also many more traditional areas for expansion or new ventures, ranging from a stronger role in world grain sales to purchase of ships to carry grain on the Great Lakes.

All in all, the basic principle defined by president E. K. Turner in the Pool's 50th anniversary year will probably remain desirable for at least the 60th and 70th anniversaries:

> In future, the Pool will be prepared to pursue opportunities that will improve our overall efficiency by broadening our ownership base in the agricultural industry. It is logical for grain and livestock producers to own the system they need to market and process their own product.[12]

And, as a director has written, there will have to be increasing attention to farm inputs: "Manufacturing is being concentrated in the hands of fewer and fewer companies. The members cannot be left exposed to the mercy of a few multi-nationals."[13]

Internationally, there is the possibility of re-entering the development business. Some government officials, for example, feel the pools' expertise in forage crops and livestock handling makes them well suited to be prime contractors on comprehensive development projects for livestock in the Third World.[14] Through such projects Saskatchewan Wheat Pool and its sister pools could encourage co-operative organizations elsewhere and perhaps help build a stronger global co-operative network that would be a realistic alternative to giant private trading corporations.

How well Saskatchewan Wheat Pool meets its coming challenges in both member relations and corporate services may depend on its ability to develop a sound, far-sighted policy base for such activities. Especially difficult decisions will have to be made in developing policies on the type of rural society in which future Pool members will live. How many farm families and small towns will be left when existing consolidation trends end? The answer to that will depend partly on how much farmers themselves are willing to spend to maintain farm numbers. The trend to fewer farms can be halted through government restrictions on farm size, farm ownership and farmland use, but such legislation will also restrict the range of potential buyers, thus restricting farmers in what they can obtain from selling their land. Maintenance of a dispersed country elevator system can encourage survival of more villages, but farmers will have to bear the cost of that elevator system. Yet there are major non-financial costs involved in current trends toward rural depopulation. In a 1982 speech, one wheat board official described some of these hidden costs:

The growth in farm size has a direct effect on quality of life. For one thing, it intensifies the farmer's sense of insecurity. The roots of this insecurity are varied: High levels of debt and capitalization, increasing pressure to adopt new technologies (many of them expensive), heavier demands on the farmer's ability to manage. The more the farmer worries about his ability to cope, the more his quality of life, and that of his family, is threatened. Living with insecurity is like living on a rollercoaster. And the greatest measure of insecurity falls on the younger farmer.

We can only surmise how this insecurity takes its toll; there apparently has been little research in Canada to tell us how financial strain expresses itself physically and psychologically in farmers and their families. We can assume that as financial concerns grow, there is increased likelihood of heart attack, nervous problems, psychological problems, high blood pressure, farm accidents. No doubt marriages and other personal relationships are strained. . . .

In the area of general education, the increase in farm size and the decline in rural population once again takes its toll. . . . School bus routes in Saskatchewan in 1980 averaged over 89 miles a day. How much farther can children travel to school and back before their quality of life is diminished?[15]

It is frustrating and hard enough to try to shape a grainhandling system that allocates cash costs and benefits fairly among railways, elevator companies, senior governments, municipal governments and farmers. It becomes much more complex when subjective considerations are added. But the task cannot be avoided. If Saskatchewan Wheat Pool is to remain relevant to the general social needs of farm families, it will have to focus on such issues.

Specific Pool policies to meet such developing problems cannot be unilaterally laid down by any small group — not the best outside consultants, not the brightest executives on staff, not the elected board of directors. Successful solutions — ones that are economically, socially and politically acceptable — can only emerge from a continuing policy process based on genuine grassroots participation and realistic negotiation with interests outside the Pool. As the voting power of rural residents declines, their organizations will increasingly have to work with other groups, forging and maintaining links with consumer associations, central Canadian businesses and non-agricultural government departments. In this entire process the Pool's reputation for responsibility and stablility can be valuable.

Pool members might also do well to remember that their tradition is not limited to comfortable, establishment-oriented tinkering with existing systems. Conditions and desirable objectives change with time, so coming generations of Pool members need feel no obligation to copy their forefathers' specific policies. But the new generations should keep their minds open to suggestions for fundamental change, as their predecessors did.

Saskatchewan Wheat Pool's traditional calls for nationalization of CP Rail, for example, could even now be achieved if Pool members judged it to be still desirable. Or there could be some innovative system of turning railway tracks into public facilities, like highways, with provincial governments or Saskatchewan Wheat Pool itself being among those owning and operating trains. With the pools' greater financial resources today, they could consider reviving pooling for grains that politicians refuse to place under exclusive wheat board control. Or the pools could push for a system of guaranteed prices to farmers, prices that would automatically rise in step with farmers' costs. There would be immense problems in working out proper formulas so that governments did not lose excessive amounts of money over the long run with such a parity-price system. But the other sectors of the Canadian economy have grown proportionately so they are much better able to finance such a system than they were forty years ago. It would also be a massive task to develop a consensus among farm groups on parity pricing, and to persuade the non-agricultural public of the benefits of giving farmers stable, predictable net incomes — but that is exactly the sort of ambitious effort that the Pool's founding members made.

The specific examples cited above — parity pricing, non-governmental pooling, railbed nationalization — may or may not turn out to be practical policies. The point is that they are examples of the kind of proposals that have to be periodically considered if the Pool is to be alert to opportunities for fundamental reform. At its birth Saskatchewan Wheat Pool was a radical, almost revolutionary, attempt to replace the exisiting order. Pool founders did not want to improve the Grain Exchange; they wanted to eradicate it. They did not want to become respected, influential members of the traditional free-enterprise system; they wanted to create a co-operative alternative to that system. Regardless of whether co-operation was considered as the highest form of free enterprise or as some moderate form of socialism, the ultimate goal was to see co-operation spread throughout society. One Pool official used just eight words to summarize the challenge facing present and future members of Saskatchewan Wheat Pool:

> If not us, who?
> If not now, when?[16]

Appendix A

Saskatchewan Wheat Pool — Official Corporate Names

1923-1943: Saskatchewan Co-operative Wheat Producers Ltd.
1944-1953: Saskatchewan Co-operative Producers Ltd.
1953 to date: Saskatchewan Wheat Pool

Appendix B

SWP Campaign Committee, 1923

The campaign committee that launched Saskatchewan Wheat Pool was composed of five representatives each of the SGGA, FUC and unorganized farmers, plus a few other prominent figures. Committee members were:

*John A. Maharg, SGGA president
*A. J. McPhail, SGGA central secretary
*George Edwards, SGGA vice-president
 C. C. Stoliker, SGGA member
*George Robertson, SGGA member and MLA
*Louis Brouillette, FUC member
*W. Moss Thrasher, FUC member
*Richard S. Dundas, FUC member
*J. W. Mathewson, FUC member
 Mr. Pristupa, FUC member
*A. E. Wilson, Municipal Hail president
*George Spence, MLA
*R. J. Moffat, unorganized farmers
*A. R. Reusch, unorganized farmers
 C. M. Hamilton, agriculture minister
*Thomas Moffet, Rural Municipalities president
*W. L. Noyes, elevator companies
*G. G. Wray, Retail Merchants president
 H. J. Beveridge, Retail Merchants secretary

The committee initially selected twelve persons to form the provisional board of Saskatchewan Wheat Pool, then in a few days increased that number to sixteen. Committee members marked above with asterisks became members of the provisional board, along with Michael McLachlan of Maple Creek. As presidents of the Saskatchewan Municipal Hail Insurance Association and Saskatchewan Association of Rural Municipalities respectively, Wilson and Moffet partially became directors by virtue of their offices, but both were also farmers. Wray of the Retail Merchants' Association and Noyes, a representative of private elevator companies, may seem to modern Pool members to be unusual choices for the Pool board, but the campaign committee apparently thought it important to involve such interests then. The list of committee members and affiliations appears in the *Progressive* of 27 August 1923, although with several names spelled incorrectly. The order of names suggests that the other three representatives of unorganized farmers were Wilson, Spence, and Hamilton, but Moffet may have filled that role instead of Hamilton.

Saskatchewan Wheat Pool, 1923-24 Provisional Board

Alfred Edwin Wilson, president
Alexander J. McPhail, vice-president
Louis C. Brouillette
Richard S. Dundas
George F. Edwards
John A. Maharg
J. W. Mathewson
Michael McLachlan
R. J. Moffat
Thomas H. Moffet
W. L. Noyes
A. R. Reusch
George Robertson
George Spence
W. Moss Thrasher
G. Garfield Wray

Saskatchewan Wheat Pool, 1924-25 Board

Alexander J. McPhail, president
Louis C. Brouillette, vice president
Thomas Bibby
Alfred E. Bye
Brooksbank Catton
Charles W. Coates
Richard S. Dundas
Allan Lefebvre
Harry Marsh
R. J. Moffat
Edward B. Ramsay
J. Hesketh Robson
Herbert Smyth
Avery Fenton Sproule
John H. Wesson
Alfred Edwin Wilson

Appendix C

Presidents of Saskatchewan Wheat Pool

Alfred Edwin Wilson, 1923-1924 (provisional board)
Alexander James McPhail, 1924-1931
Louis C. Brouillette, 1931-1937
John Henry Wesson, 1937-1960
Charles W. Gibbings, 1960-1969
E. K. (Ted) Turner, 1969-

Secretaries

George W. Robertson, 1924-1958
Arthur R. Stevens, 1958-1964
Ira K. Mumford, 1964-1966
James O. Wright, 1967-

Treasurers

F. A. Pragnell, 1924 (acting)
J. D. Read, 1924-1929
R. C. Findlay, 1929-1931
Wm. Riddel, 1931-1935
R. M. McIntosh, 1946-1953
E. J. Medhurst, 1954-1966
W. R. Purslow, 1967-1970
J. M. Fair, 1970-1976
C. R. Kasha, 1976-

General Manager/Chief Executive Officer

Ira K. Mumford, 1967-1979 (General Manager)
Ira K. Mumford, 1979-1981 (Chief Executive Officer)
J. M. Fair, 1981-

Appendix D

Saskatchewan Livestock Co-operative Marketing Association Ltd.

The Saskatchewan Livestock Co-operative Marketing Association Ltd. was organized in 1926, started operations in 1927 with sales offices at Moose Jaw and Prince Albert, and changed its name in 1929 to Saskatchewan Co-operative Livestock Producers Ltd. The co-operative was roughly structured along the same lines as the Pool, with a contract providing for pooling all livestock sales each year. Deductions were made from sales proceeds to build up a fund for purchase or construction of sales facilities. Unlike the Wheat Pool, however, the livestock co-op was divided into semi-autonomous local associations, which appointed their own managers, assembled livestock, and directed the livestock to various markets. At one stage there were 128 locals, later consolidated into 30 associations. With drastic drops in livestock prices in 1930, the co-op was forced to end pooling and to function as a commission agent for any members who wished to sell cattle through the co-op. A Central Livestock Co-operative, formed by the Saskatchewan co-op and its Alberta and Manitoba counterparts, marketed livestock at the St. Boniface stockyards in Manitoba. In 1928 representatives of livestock co-ops from across Canada formed Canadian Co-operative Livestock Producers Ltd. to co-ordinate sales policies, encourage livestock pools, export surplus livestock, collect information, and act as national policy spokesman. Eastern members of the national body were dropped after they refused to pay a share of a $21,000 loss the organization suffered on a 1931 export shipment to Britain when the value of the British pound fell. The Saskatchewan co-op, meanwhile, began operating a meat packing plant in Saskatoon in 1932. The plant was hampered by trade opposition, lack of working capital, and a poor general economy. It ceased operations in 1938, was leased to Intercontinental Packers two years later, and was eventually sold to that company. When the livestock co-op was amalgamated with the Pool in 1944, there were sales agencies at Regina, Saskatoon, Moose Jaw and Prince Albert. The Regina livestock yard was the only one of the four owned by the Pool. The Pool built facilities at Swift Current and Yorkton in 1948, then North Battleford in 1949. It bought the Moose Jaw yard in 1964 and built new facilities there. (SWP memo, "History and Development of Co-operative Livestock Marketing in Saskatchewan," SWP Papers)

Appendix E

Average Farm Price of Wheat in Saskatchewan, 1916-81

Year	$/tonne	Year	$/tonne
1916	47.04	1949	59.16
1917	71.66	1950	54.75
1918	73.12	1951	55.85
1919	85.25	1952	58.42
1920	56.95	1953	48.87
1921	27.93	1954	44.46
1922	31.23	1955	50.71
1923	23.88	1956	45.56
1924	44.46	1957	47.40
1925	45.92	1958	48.50
1926	39.68	1959	48.50
1927	35.64	1960	58.05
1928	28.29	1961	64.30
1929	37.85	1962	61.36
1930	17.27	1963	64.30
1931	13.96	1964	58.79
1932	12.86	1965	62.46
1933	17.27	1966	65.04
1934	22.41	1967	59.52
1935	22.05	1968	49.38
1936	33.80	1969	47.40
1937	38.58	1970	53.28
1938	21.31	1971	49.60
1939	19.84	1972	69.08
1940	21.31	1973	169.02
1941	21.68	1974	159.10
1942	28.29	1975	135.22
1943	41.89	1976	106.56
1944	45.93	1977	104.72
1945	60.26	1978	141.46
1946	59.53	1979	178.96
1947	59.89	1980	209.81
1948	59.89	1981	188.00

(Source: Saskatchewan Agriculture, *Agricultural Statistics Handbook*)

Appendix F

Saskatchewan Wheat Pool in 1984

During Saskatchewan Wheat Pool's sixty years, its basic democratic structure has not substantially changed, but the organization's growth has been phenomenal. Each year, members attending local annual meetings elect advisory committees in more than 600 communities throughout the province. These committees meet several times during the year and act as a two-way channel for the flow of information between members and Pool delegates. The delegates, who must be farmers and Pool members, are chosen in separate elections for two-year terms. Each of the 145 delegates represents a subdistrict of 450 to 750 members.

For Pool electoral purposes, Saskatchewan is divided into 16 districts, with delegates in each district choosing one of themselves annually to sit on the board of directors. The directors in turn elect the five-person executive, which includes the president and two vice-presidents, from among themselves. The Pool president and vice-presidents must thus be Pool members and farmers who win election as delegates.

Delegates meet annually to review and approve company operations, and to set policy. Special general meetings have also been held to discuss urgent policy questions. Directors meet monthly.

As a commercial enterprise, Saskatchewan Wheat Pool is one of Canada's largest corporations. At 31 July 1983, its net book value of fixed assets was $187 million. Total revenues for the preceding 12 months were $2.27 billion.

Grainhandling facilities included 595 licensed operating units at 555 country elevator delivery points. These elevators handled 11.4 million tonnes of grain, 62.9 percent of the provincial total.

Terminal elevators at Thunder Bay and Vancouver handled 11.4 million tonnes. Pool livestock yards handled 424,000 head of cattle and calves, 118,000 hogs and more than 6,000 sheep and lambs. Elevators and farm service centres sold $154.4 million in products used in farm operations. The Pool's printing and publishing activities included the *Western Producer*, with circulation of more than 140,000, plus a large commercial printing business and a book publishing venture. A flour mill in Saskatoon produced 57,000 tonnes of flour.

In addition to such wholly-owned operations, Saskatchewan Wheat Pool also was part owner of CSP Foods Ltd., Western Co-operative Fertilizers Ltd., Pool Insurance Company, XCAN Grain Ltd., Pacific Elevators Ltd., Prince Rupert Grain Ltd., and Co-Enerco.

Appendix G

The 1923 Saskatchewan Wheat Pool Contract

AGREEMENT

THIS AGREEMENT made this   day of   A.D. 1923, between Saskatchewan Co-operative Wheat Producers, Limited, a body corporate, with its head office at Regina, in the Province of Saskatchewan, hereinafter called "The Association," of the First Part and the undersigned, a person concerned in the production of wheat in the Province of Saskatchewan and in the marketing of the same, hereinafter called "The Grower," of the Second Part.

WHEREAS, the undersigned Grower desires to co-operate with others concerned in the production of wheat in the Province of Saskatchewan and in the marketing of the same, hereinafter referred to as Growers, for the purpose of promoting, fostering and encouraging the business of growing and marketing wheat co-operatively and for eliminating speculation in wheat and for stabilizing the wheat market; for co-operatively and collectively handling the problems of Growers and for improving in every legitimate way the interests of Growers in the Province of Saskatchewan, and for other pertinent purposes;

AND WHEREAS, the Association has been formed under "The Companies Act" of the Province of Saskatchewan with full power to act as agent, factor, mercantile agent and attorney, in fact, to handle wheat produced and delivered to it by its members, and with such further powers as are set forth in its Memorandum of Association;

AND WHEREAS, the Grower is desirous of becoming a member of the Association and of entering, together with other Growers, into this contract with the Association;

AND WHEREAS, this Agreement, although individual in expression, is one of a series either identical or generally similar in terms between the Association and Growers of wheat in the Province of Saskatchewan, and shall constitute one Contract between the several Growers of Wheat in the Province of Saskatchewan signing the same and this Association:

NOW THIS AGREEMENT WITNESSETH that, in consideration of the premises and in consideration of the covenants and agreements on the part of the Association as hereinafter set forth, and in consideration

250

of the execution of this Agreement, or one similar in terms, by other Growers of wheat in the Province of Saskatchewan, and in consideration of the mutual obligations herein set forth, the Parties hereto hereby agree to and with each other as follows:

1. It is expressly provided and agreed that if by the 12th day of September, 1923, signatures by Growers of Wheat and the owners, purchasers, share crop purchasers, tenants, lessors, and lessees of land whose wheat acreage taken as a whole shall be equal to fifty per cent of the acreage in wheat in the Province of Saskatchewan in the year 1923, according to the estimates of the Provincial Government of Saskatchewan, Bureau of Statistics, Department of Agriculture, shall not have been secured to this agreement or an agreement similar in terms, this agreement and all agreements similar in terms shall, except insofar as the agreements contained in clauses 17 and 18 hereof, cease and determine and be utterly null and at an end and that in case such number of signatures are not so obtained the Association shall have its affairs audited by a chartered accountant whose report shall be filed at the Head Office of the Association and shall be open to inspection at all reasonable times by any Grower who has executed this agreement and the monies received by the Association under paragraphs numbers 17 and 18 hereof shall after deducting and paying the expenses of and incidental to the formation and organization of the Association and all other proper expenses including specifically the expenses of and incidental to and of and to the formation of The Wheat Pool Organization Committee be distributed to the Growers who have executed this agreement and agreements similar in terms in such manner and at such times as the directors may decide, but so that such distribution will be on as equitable a basis as practicable.

2. The Association will give to all daily papers published in the Province of Saskatchewan, as soon as practicable after September 12th, 1923, a statement as to whether or not the signatures required by paragraph 1 hereof have been obtained.

3. It is expressly provided and agreed that, for all matters of acreage, bushelage, percentages or signatures and for all statements of fact in connection therewith and for determining whether or not by the twelfth day of September, A.D. 1923, signatures by Growers of Wheat and the owners, purchasers, share crop purchasers, tenants, lessors and lessees of land, whose wheat acreage taken as a whole equals fifty per cent (50%) of the acreage of wheat in the Province of Saskatchewan in the year 1923, have been secured to this Agreement, or an Agreement similar in terms, the Directors of the Association shall be the sole judges and a written statement signed by the chairman of the directors of the Association, or such other person as the Directors may appoint, shall be deemed to be, and shall be, conclusive evidence thereof with or without notice to the Grower.

4. The Association agrees to act as agent, factor, mercantile agent and attorney in fact for the Grower to receive, take delivery of, handle, store, transport, sell, market and otherwise dispose of the wheat produced and delivered to it by the Grower, excepting only registered seed wheat

according to its best skill and ability with a view to obtaining the best possible price therefor.

5. The Grower covenants and agrees to consign and deliver to the Association or its order at the time and place designated by the Association all of the wheat and the warehouse or storage receipts, grain tickets, bills of lading and all other documents of or evidencing title thereto covering it produced or acquired by or for him in the Province of Saskatchewan, except registered seed wheat, during the years 1923, 1924, 1925, 1926 and 1927.

6. It is agreed that the Association will, whenever and wherever possible receive and take delivery of the Grower's wheat at the Grower's most convenient delivery point and that except for good cause in the discretion of the Association, the Association will receive the Grower's wheat as soon as he is in a position to deliver same.

7. Wheat shall be deemed to be delivered to the Association within the meaning of this agreement, so as to render the Association accountable therefor only and when the storage tickets, bills of lading, warehouse receipts, shipping bills therefor or other documents of or evidencing title thereto shall have been transferred properly endorsed by the Grower to the Association.

8. The Grower hereby appoints the Association his sole and exclusive agent, factor and mercantile agent within the meaning of "The Factors Act" of the Province of Saskatchewan and also as his attorney in fact for the purposes hereinafter set forth with full power and authority in its own name, in the name of the Grower or otherwise to transact such business, and take such action as may be necessary, incidental or convenient for the accomplishment thereof, coupling such appointment with a direct financial interest as the common agent, factor and mercantile agent and attorney in fact of Growers hereunder and without power of revocation for the full term hereof:—

(a) To receive and take delivery of, handle, store, insure, transport, sell, market and otherwise dispose of the wheat produced and delivered to it by the Grower in whatsoever way and at such time and place and in such manner as the Association shall in its judgment determine to be to the best advantage of all of the Growers who have executed this Agreement, or an Agreement similar in terms.

(b) To clean, condition, mingle, blend, process, or otherwise deal with all wheat received by the Association, subject always to the laws for the time being in force and generally in every way to treat and deal therewith as if the Association were the full and absolute owners thereof.

(c) To borrow money in the name of the Association and on its own account on the wheat delivered to it or on any warehouse or storage receipt or grain receipt or on any accounts for the sale thereof or on any drafts, bills of lading, bills of exchange, notes or acceptances, orders, or on any commercial paper or on any documents of or evidencing title thereto delivered therefor and to exercise all rights of ownership without limitation and to pledge in its name and on its own account such wheat or receipts or accounts or drafts, bills of lading, notes, acceptances, orders or other commercial paper or document of or evidencing title as collateral therefor, also to sign, endorse, assign, negotiate, discharge, surrender, sell, dispose of or otherwise deal with all and every such documents or instruments and the proceeds thereof. The Association shall have the right to apply the money so received pro rata among the Growers who have executed this Agreement and delivered wheat to it or to use the said moneys for any proper association purpose deemed by the Association to be in the best interests of its members.

(d) To pay or retain and deduct from the gross returns from the sale of the wheat delivered to it by the Growers the amount necessary to cover all brokerage, advertising, taxes, tolls, freights, elevator charges, insurance interest, legal expenses, operating costs and expenses, and all other proper charges, such as salaries, fixed charges and general expenses of the Association and, in addition, the Association may deduct such percentage, not exceeding one per cent (1%) of the gross selling price of the wheat as it shall deem desirable as a commercial reserve to be used for any of the purposes or activities of the Association.

(e) To settle any and all claims for damages or otherwise which may occur in connection with the handling of the Grower's wheat during transit or otherwise or that may arise in connection with the exercise of any of the powers or authority herein grainted.

(f) To deduct from the Gross returns from the sale of all wheat handled by the Association for Growers who have executed this agreement or an agreement similar in terms a sum out of each Grower's proper proportion thereof, not exceeding two cents (2) per bushel and to invest the same for and on behalf of the Association in acquiring either by construction, purchase, lease or otherwise such facilities for handling grain as the directors of the Association may deem advisable or in the capital stock or shares of any company or association formed or to be formed for the purpose of so erecting, constructing or acquiring such facilities and to sell or otherwise dispose of any such investment and re-invest the proceeds thereof in like manner.

(g) In the event of the Grower failing to fulfil on his part the provisions of this Agreement or any of them or failing to deliver his wheat crop, as herein provided, to take exclusive possession and control of the Grower's wheat crop and to harvest and market the same according to the terms of this Agreement or at its option to take any legal action to obtain possession thereof or to have a Receiver appointed with power to take exclusive possession and control of the said wheat crop and deliver the same to this Association as hereinbefore provided or otherwise to dispose of the same as a Court having jurisdiction in that behalf and the Association may in such case take possession of, use, occupy and enjoy such of the Grower's land and property as may be necessary to carry out the powers herein contained. If possession of such wheat shall be taken by the Association by reason of such breach of contract on the part of the Grower, the Association shall be entitled to retain out of the proceeds derived from the sale thereof, in addition to the sums heretofore provided for, all additional expenses incurred in connection therewith.

(h) To enter into arrangements with and employ agents, subagents, bankers, solicitors, counsel, experts, advisers, auditors and generally to delegate its powers to others and to pay a remuneration therefor.

(i) The grower expressly agrees that all powers herein given or by law implied may be exercised by the Association whether the wheat subject to this contract shall have been actually delivered by the Grower to the Association or not and such powers may be exercised in relation to the said wheat separately or with otherwheat subject of contract similar in terms to this contract entered into by other growers.

9. Any unused balance of reserves and surpluses shall stand in the name of the Association and be owned by the members and shall, when in the opinion of the directors a distribution should be made or upon a dissolution of this Association, be divided in the same proportions in which it was contributed by the members.

10. Save as in this agreement provided the wheat of the Grower and the proceeds thereof shall not be subject to or liable for or in any way attachable for any claim of any kind whatsoever against the Association or by any creditor of the Association.

11. Notwithstanding anything hereinbefore contained, the Grower may retain wheat for his own food, seed and feed, and may, upon first receiving a permit in writing from the Association, dispose of wheat for seed or feed directly to any farmer. All other seed wheat, except registered seed wheat, shall be sold by and through the Association only.

12. The Grower expressly covenants and agrees that he will not (save as herein permitted) sell or otherwise dispose of any of the wheat produced or acquired or owned by him in the Province of Saskatchewan during the life of this Agreement to any person or persons, firm or corporation other than this Association.

13. The Grower expressly warrants that he has not heretofore mortgaged or pledged or charged or granted a lien on or contracted to sell, market, consign or deliver any of his said wheat to any person, firm or corporation except as noted at the end of this Agreement. The right of the Association to any wheat covered by such existing contracts shall be subject to such contracts and the performance of such contract by the Grower shall not be deemed to be a breach of this contract.

14. The Association shall have the right and power to deal with any wheat produced by any Grower or of which he is the beneficial owner and delivered to it, notwithstanding that there may be other claims upon the same, but this shall not derogate from the rights of such other claimants.

15. It is agreed that the Grower may, subject to the terms of this agreement and subject to any law in force for the time being, on first notifying the Association mortgage or pledge his interest in his wheat crop for the purposes set out in section 20 of The Chattel Mortgage Act or to secure an actual bona fide present advance fairly commensurate with the property mortgaged, but not exceeding fifty per cent (50%) of the value thereof, but, in such event, the Grower shall forthwith notify the Association and the Association shall, in its discretion, be at liberty to pay off or take over or assume the indebtedness under such mortgage or

pledge and to take delivery of the Grower's crop and to deduct from all moneys which become payable to the Grower by the Association a sum equal to the amount which the Association has paid out or agreed to pay with respect to such mortgage or pledge with interest at the rate therein provided.

16. The Association shall, so soon as practicable after the delivery of wheat to it by the Grower, make an advance to the Grower at such rate per bushel according to grade, quality and place of delivery as, in the discretion of the Association, it shall deem proper and the Association agrees that, subject to any laws in force for the time being, it will, in its discretion, from time to time pay over to the Grower as funds are available from the sale of the crop of each season, being his proportion of the proceeds of all wheat sold by the Association in each season for the Growers who have executed this Contract, less all deductions which the Association is entitled to make pursuant to the provisions of this Contract and less all advances made to the Grower and less all handling and other proper charges of every description whatsoever including the costs of maintaining the Association and of transporting, handling, grading, storing, selling and marketing such wheat and of other proper activities. It is agreed that all wheat received by the Association from Growers who have executed this contract or contracts similar in terms shall be treated as a pool, wheat of different grades being pooled separately, but that the Association when it deems advisable may from time to time pool one or more grades or qualities together or may pool different qualities of one or more grades separately, wheat of different seasons being pooled separately with power to the Association to make cut offs and to make one or more pools of any one or more grades or qualities for any season from time to time but so that each Grower will receive an equitable return, according to the grade delivered by him and that the Growers whole right to wheat delivered by him and the proceeds thereof shall be to receive the initial advance and his due proportionate share of the monies realized from the operation of the pool or pools in which wheat delivered by him is pooled, less the deductions herein provided for.

17. The Grower covenants and agrees to, and hereby does irrevocably apply for one (1) share out of the Ordinary Shares in the capital stock of the Association and agrees to pay to the Association the par value thereof, namely the sum of One Dollar ($1.00). The Association covenants and agrees to accept the said application and to allot to the Grower one (1) share of stock out of the Ordinary Shares in the capital stock of the Association, provided the signatures required by paragraph 1 hereof are obtained within the time therein set out. Should such signatures be not so obtained the Grower agrees that the said sum of $1.00 shall be a contribution to the association for the purposes set out in paragraph 18 hereof.

18. The Grower covenants and agrees to pay the further sum of Two Dollars ($2.00) to defray the expenses of organization, including the expenses of and of formation of the committee known as The Wheat Pool Organization Committee to carry on field service and educational work and other proper activities of the Association.

19. The Grower covenants and agrees, as and when requested by the Association or any officer, agent or servant thereof, to make application from time to time for railway cars for the shipment of his wheat pursuant to the provisions of "The Canada Grain Act" and to the laws for the time being in force and to perform such other acts and execute such documents as the Association may require in connection with the handling of the Grower's wheat.

20. The Association may sell the said wheat to such persons, firms, corporations, governments at such times, in such manner, and upon such conditions and terms as it may deem fair and advisable.

21. The Association may sell all or any part of the wheat delivered to it by its members pursuant to this Contract through any agency or by joining with any agency for the co-operative marketing of wheat of the Provinces of Alberta, Saskatchewan and Manitoba, or any of them or of other provinces or groups of provincesor of the Dominion or of other countries, under a term contract or otherwise, and under such conditions as will serve the joint interests of the Growers and the Association is hereby authorized and empowered to transfer to and confer upon any such agency (formed or to be formed) all of the powers, rights and privileges of this Association under this Contract and any proportionate or other expenses connected therewith shall be deemed marketing costs, provided always that nothing herein contained shall authorize the Association to sell through or join with any agency whereby any of the deductions authorized by this Contract of one per cent (1%) for commercial reserve and two cents (2) per bushel for facilities are increased in any amount whatsoever.

22. The Grower hereby authorizes the Association to enter into any contract for such consideration and on such terms and conditions as it may deem advisable and profitable for the inspecting, grading, receiving, handling, elevating, storing, warehousing and shipping of the wheat covered hereby, or any portion thereof, and for the use of the security thereof as collateral within the general purposes of this agreement by the Association.

23. This Agreement shall be binding upon the Grower, his personal representatives, successors and assigns, during the period hereinbefore mentioned, as long as he raises wheat directly or indirectly in Saskatchewan, or has the legal right to exercise ownership or control of any thereof, or any interest therein, or of any land on which wheat is grown during the term of this Contract.

24. From time to time each year the Grower will mail to the Association as requested a statement of his expected acreage of wheat for that year, and its condition on the forms provided for that purpose by the Association.

25. Inasmuch as the remedy at law would be inadequate and inasmuch as it is now and ever will be impracticable and extremely difficult to determine the actual damage resulting to the Association, should the Grower fail so to deliver all of his wheat, the Grower hereby agrees to pay to the Association for all wheat delivered, sold, consigned or marketed by or for him or withheld other than in accordance with the

terms hereof, the sum of Twenty-five Cents (25¢) per bushel as liquidated damages for the breach of this Contract, all parties agreeing that this Contract is one of a series dependent for its true value upon the adherence of each and all of the contracting parties to each and all of the said Contracts.

26. The Grower agrees that, in the event of a breach by him of any material provision hereof, particularly as to delivery or marketing of any wheat other than through the Association, the Association shall, upon proper action instituted by it, be entitled to an injunction to prevent further breach hereof, and other equitable relief, according to the terms of this Agreement; and the Association and the Grower expressly agree that this Agreement is not a Contract for personal services or demanding exceptional capacity or talent; and that this is a Contract of agency coupled with financial interest under special circumstances and conditions and that the Association cannot without great difficulty go into the open markets and secure wheat to replace any which the Grower may fail to deliver; and that this Contract will be the proper subject for the remedy of specific performance in the event of a breach thereof.

27. Any deduction or allowance or loss that the Association may make or suffer on account of inferior grade, quantity, quality or standard, or condition at delivery, shall be charged against the Grower and deducted from his net returns hereunder.

28. The Association may make rules and regulations and provide inspectors to standardize the quality, method and manner of handling, sacking and shipping of such wheat; and the Grower agrees to observe and perform any such rules and regulations prescribed by the Association and to accept the grading established or grading done by the Association, which shall, subject to any law in force for the time being, be conclusive.

29. The Grower appoints the Association, its directors and such of its officers, agents and servants as shall from time to time be designated by its directors and each of them, his agent and attorney in fact to make, execute and take delivery of all contracts that may be required to be entered into pursuant to the provisions of "The Canada Grain Act" or any law in force for the time being on his behalf and in his name, place and stead, which Contracts and all moneys payable in respect thereof are hereby assigned to the Association; and to receive accounts and to receive payments of all moneys payable to the Grower under such Contract in full settlement for such Contract or otherwise, all in his name, place and stead, and to account and settle for any moneys so received by crediting the same to the Grower on the Books of the Association, which moneys, less all deductions as herein provided, shall be distributed pursuant to the provisions of this Agreement. Such receipt of payment and giving of credit on the Books of the Association as aforesaid shall be deemed to be and shall be a proper accounting for and settlement in full for all such Contracts.

30. The Association may establish selling, statistical or other agencies in any place in the world and the Association may act in any of the

businesses of the Association through or by means of agents, brokers, sub-contractors or others.

31. Nothwithstanding anything hereinbefore contained, the Association will, by notice given in a newspaper in the cities and the principal towns of Saskatchewan, to be selected by the Association, fix the date at which it will commence operations and until such date the Grower or Growers may sell or otherwise dispose of his or their wheat, if accompanied by actual delivery of the same, and the Association shall not be bound to accept delivery thereof or be otherwise liable in respect thereto. This Agreement shall, subject to the provisions of paragraph 1 hereof, remain in full force, effect and virtue notwithstanding that the Association may not be able to commence operations in time to handle any of the 1923 crop.

32. The parties agree that there are no oral or other conditions, promises, covenants, representations or inducements in addition to or at variance with any of the terms hereof and that this Agreement represents the voluntary and clear understanding of both parties fully and completely.

IN WITNESS WHEREOF the Grower has hereunto set his hand and seal and the Association has hereunto affixed its seal under the hand of its proper officer in that behalf, the day and year first above written.

.... Grower.

SASKATCHEWAN CO-OPERATIVE WHEAT PRODUCERS, LIMITED

Per.. Chairman.

SEALED and DELIVERED and COUNTERSIGNED by the Chairman in the presence of ....

SIGNED, SEALED AND DELIVERED in the presence of

....

Subscribing Grower's Full Name..

(print this name)

Post Office Address...

Shipping Station ....

Description of land..................................... Section ....

Township........... Range...........

West of ....Meridian

Total Acreage in Wheat in the year 1922 ....

1923 ....

Name and nature of interest of any person other than grower in crop

....

Contracts, Mortgages, Liens or other Charges ....

....

....

....

....

....

Estimated Bushels of Wheat 1923:...

Notes

General note: To conserve space and permit inclusion of an extensive bibliography, the following footnotes list most works in abbreviated fashion. Full titles, publication information, etc., can be found in the bibliography. To avoid an excessive and distracting number of footnotes, there is also a minimum number of references to Pool annual reports, minutes of delegates' meetings, and directors' minutes. Unattributed information in the text that can logically be expected to come from those sources generally does come from there. For example, elevator grainhandling statistics are from the relevant year's *Annual Report*; descriptions of resolutions at a delegates' or directors' meeting come from that meeting's minutes.

Chapter One

1. Davisson, *Pooling Wheat*, p. 14.
2. Kirk, *Motherwell Story*, p. 5.
3. John Martin interview, 4 July 1975
4. Former SWP fieldman Bert Lee interview, 31 March 1982. Lee also recalled that farmers had a saying about such elevators: "You were lucky to get out with your wagon."
5. Motherwell, "Territorial Grain," p. 109. Motherwell himself was told that the time for organization was past — "It's bullets we want."
6. Motherwell, "Territorial Grain," p. 109.
7. Milliken, "Early History."
8. For more detail on development of government policy and farm organizations in this period, see: Wilson, *A Century*; Colquette, *First Fifty*; and Moorhouse, *Deep Furrows*. See Dryden, "Sintaluta," on the prosecution of CPR Sintaluta agent A. V. Benoit. The CPR won on appeal on five of the seven issues involved, demonstrating a need to revise legislation. The Grain Growers, however, were upheld on the issues that concerned them most.
9. Saskatchewan Co-op Elevator Co. (hereafter referred to as SCE), 1925 *Delegate's Handbook* and booklet, "A Brief Record."
10. SCE, "A Brief Record."
11. See Breckon, "The Saskatchewan Co-operative," 25.
12. Harry Marsh interview, 20 November 1975. Marsh remembered one SGGA board meeting where Musselman was dominant while Maharg "sat there like a bump on a log."
13. Edwards, "Reminiscences," pp. 16-17. Edwards, a reformer who became SGGA president, also notes (pp. 18-19) that Musselman tried to prevent the SGGA electing McPhail as Musselman's successor, although not as crudely as he tried to squelch McNaughton.

14. See Smith, *Prairie Liberalism*, pp. 131-133.
15. Quoted in Nesbitt, *Tides*, p. 11.
16. William McKenzie Ross, letter of 20 March 1982, to A. D. McLeod. (SWP Papers)
17. Wilson, *A Century*, p. 19.
18. Moorhouse, *Deep Furrows*, pp. 195-196.
19. Evidence submitted to Stamp Commission, 1931. Quoted in Wilson, *A Century*, p. 193.
20. Nesbitt, *Tides*, p. 14. Similar conclusions were reached by Working and Hobe, "Financial Results."
21. Evidence submitted to Stamp Commission, 1931. Quoted in Wilson, *A Century*, p. 193.
22. Wilfrid Eggleston, article in Toronto *Star*, 5 October 1929.
23. Gardiner recalled his experience in a 1927 speech to Alberta Wheat Pool, quoted in Nesbitt, *Tides*, p. 133.
24. See Fowke, *National Policy*, p. 191. Also Fowke, "Royal Commissions." See text of the platform in Moorhouse, *Deep Furrows*, pp. 293-298.
25. Yates, *Wheat Pool*, p. 22.
26. George Foster, minister of trade and commerce, may have best summed up the government's attitude when he wrote in his diary about setting up the wheat board: "It is a trifle paternal but seems necessary." (Quoted in Wilson, *A Century*, p. 135)
27. Bredt, "Historical Review," p. 5.
28. *Canadian Annual Review*, 1923, pp. 677-678.
29. See Dunning Papers, file M6(Q)Y 103-2, for his correspondence on possible board members. Among suggested names were T. A. Crerar of UGG and private grain merchant James Richardson.
30. McPhail, letters of 8 August 1922 and 13 June 1923, to Violet McNaughton, McNaughton Papers file D-46.
31. *Canadian Annual Review*, 1923, pp. 680-681.
32. An SGGA pamphlet, "The Contract Wheat Pool," outlining the Council plan in detail, is in Dunning Papers, file M6(Q)Y 103-6, pp. 49306-14.
33. Dunning Papers, file M6(Q)Y 103-2, 48465. Dunning, letter of 2 December 1922, to George F. Chipman of the *Grain Growers Guide*.
34. Dunning, letter of 28 May 1923, to W. M. Thrasher of the Farmer's Union, in Dunning Papers, file M6(Q)Y 103-2, pp. 48469-71.
35. Sharp, *Agrarian Revolt*, p. 161. See also the *Progressive*, 26 June 1924, for a list of SGGA accomplishments.
36. McPhail, letter of 2 May 1923, to Violet McNaughton, in McNaughton Papers file D-46.
37. Conference minutes, Innis Papers.
38. Edmonton *Journal*, 1 August 1923, reporting Wood's 28 July comments.
43. Yates, *Wheat Pool*, p. 72.

Chapter Two

1. Sapiro, speech of 7 August 1923, printed transcript in SWP Papers.
2. Yates, *Wheat Pool*, p. 10.
3. Crowell, "Nothing," p. 16. Other material on Sapiro's early years can be found in: Purich, "Lawyer becomes hero"; Stern, "Sapiro"; and *Who Was Who in America*.
4. See note 70 for details on Sapiro's fees. Organization of the Kentucky burley tobacco co-op was Sapiro's most dramatic success before he came to

Saskatchewan, and the one he stressed in his initial Saskatchewan speeches. See Jesness, *Co-operative Marketing*, and Christensen, *Co-operative Associations*.

5. Gray, *Roar of the Twenties*, p. 127. Another observer, Frank Underhill, called Sapiro "one of the greatest evangelists the west had ever seen." (June 1967 interview, quoted in MacPherson, *Each For All*, p. 73)

6. In his 20 February 1924 Regina speech (transcript in *Morning Leader*, 21 February), Sapiro noted that he received an average of twenty-two anonymous letters a month. In later life, Sapiro suffered from arthritis and died 23 November 1959 after an arthritis operation. He had no funeral since he had instructed that his body be given to a medical school. Despite his work for the tobacco co-op, he was strongly opposed to the use of tobacco as well as alcohol. (Waldron, interviews 1975-76)

7. *Co-operation*, vol. 9, no. 9, p. 146.

8. See Sapiro, 5 December 1951 Saskatoon speech.

9. A poignant account of how the judge was disillusioned with Sapiro and found his testimony untrustworthy is in *Harry Bridges*, pp. 158-163. Sapiro's papers would have formed a priceless historical collection if kept intact for his career, but he destroyed virtually all records before his death. (Son Stanley Sapiro, letter of 9 July 1982, to Garry Fairbairn)

10. In 1946, Pool distaste for Sapiro was cited as a reason for the Pool's declining to publish Yates' book, which featured Sapiro. (Frank Eliason, letter of 7 December 1946, to N. H. Schwarz, in Schwarz Papers) A proposal to have Sapiro participate in the Pool's twenty-fifth anniversary commemorations was defeated at the Pool's 1949 annual meeting. When Louis Brouillette died and Sapiro wired an effusive tribute, the editor of the Pool's subsidiary newspaper wired the newspaper from Regina: "do not play up Sapiro." (A. P. Waldron, telegram of 26 April 1937, to C. A. Lenhard, SWP Papers)

11. In an article McPhail wrote for the *Progressive*, 26 June 1924, McPhail himself gave the Farmers' Union credit for bringing Sapiro.

12. Colquette, *First Fifty*, pp. 150-151.

13. The Crerar-McPhail correspondence is in UFC Papers, file B-2 X.86(1).

14. The first Union overtures were rather uncoordinated. Union secretary N. H. Schwarz sent one invitation 23 April. President McNamee wrote another 26 May. McNamee, however, wrote the local newspapers asking if they could give him Sapiro's address. The newspaper suggested McNamee speak to Schwarz. See Yates, *Wheat Pool*, pp. 57-58, and FUC Papers, B-2 VI.8.

15. McPhail, letters to Violet McNaughton 2 May (McNaughton Papers, D-46) and to G. F. Edwards 3 May (SWP Papers). McPhail's 2 May diary entry noted that McPhail had just read Sapiro's speech to U.S. wheat growers and his testimony before an agricultural committee.

16. Yates, *Wheat Pool*, p. 60. The Saskatoon *Daily Star* was also promoting Sapiro at this time. On 12 May it printed a full-page Sapiro article taken from *World"s Work*.

17. McNamee Papers, mis-spellings in original.

18. In a 6 July letter, Brouillette tried to reassure Dunning about Sapiro's fees, saying he "makes no charge for his services as a propagandist but gets $400 per day for his services as a marketing engineer." Dunning cabled 9 July that no other organization had so far asked him to call a conference with Sapiro. Dunning Papers, file (Q) Y-103-6, pp. 49066-70.

19. Sapiro, telegram of 12 July to FUC: "Believe I can secure initial loan of ten thousand dollars from prominent American interested in co-operative marketing even in Canada." (UFC Papers, file B-2 X.86[1])

20. Conference minutes, Innis Papers.

21. For the Alberta arrangements, see: Yates, *Wheat Pool*, p. 67; Nesbitt, *Tides*, pp. 35-40; and Gray, *Boomtime*, p. 137.
22. Dunning Papers, (Q)Y-103-6, p. 49102.
23. Edmonton *Bulletin*, 10 July 1923.
24. The Union asked that Sapiro stay past the eleventh, after having first said he was not needed past the seventh. Sapiro, who had made other appointments after the seventh on the basis of that statement, said he warmly resented the Union complaining that he had initially promised to stay thirty days if needed: "Has it not occurred to you that groups of men offer five hundred to one thousand a day for services of our office and that we cannot be handled by whimsical arrangements?" (UFC Papers, B-2 X.86[1])
25. J. H. Haslam, letter of 29 July to Louis Brouillette. (UFC Papers, B-2 X.86(l)) Haslam also got into a row with Union headquarters over arrangements he made for Sapiro in Swift Current that conflicted with other Union scheduling.
26. A variety of sources provide full transcripts for Sapiro's Alberta-Saskatchewan speeches in this period: 2 August speech in Lethbridge *Herald* of 15 August; 3 August Edmonton speech in Edmonton *Journal Farm Weekly* of 8 August and Winnipeg *Farmer"s Advocate and Home Journal* of 10 August; 7 August Saskatoon speech and related comments in a printed pamphlet presumably published by the Pool organization committee. Historians have a significant debt to the unsung stenographers, typists, and other scribes who worked to preserve these and later Sapiro speeches.
27. Haslam did disclaim responsibility for the term, "Haslam-Sapiro Pool," saying that came from an "over-zealous friend." (Saskatoon *Phoenix*, 6 August) The Union meeting had all the overtones of a kangaroo court. Haslam was not invited, showed up when he heard about it from a friend, was never confronted with specific accusations, had anonymous rumors thrown at him, and received no serious reply when he demanded to know what part of the Union constitution permitted such suspension or expulsion of members. A transcript of the meeting is in FUC Papers, B-2 VI.6.
28. Saskatoon *Phoenix*, 7 August. Articles of association for the United Farmers pool had been signed 1 August by Maharg, McPhail, George Edwards, A. E. Wilson and C. M. Hamilton. (Dunning Papers (Q)Y-103-6 pp. 49287-99) Hamilton was then agriculture minister.
29. The previous day, 6 August, Sapiro spoke to a conference in Saskatoon's Empire Theatre that included Saskatchewan Agriculture Minister C. M. Hamilton, Alberta Premier Greenfield and Manitoba Premier Bracken, as well as farm organization representatives. Although somewhat hoarse from his Alberta speeches, Sapiro appears to have made a good impact. (Transcript, FUC Papers, B-2 VI.6) With that impetus and a night of private consultations, the Union and SGGA executives were able to agree on a joint campaign the next day at a Royal Hotel meeting. (Minutes, FUC Papers, B-2 IV.3) Sapiro's first public speech that evening thus confirmed the earlier decisions he had helped forge and announced them to the public.
30. Waldron, 1975-76 interviews.
31. McPhail diary, 8 August 1923; McNaughton Papers, D-46. Sapiro, meanwhile, also intervened in the Pool's selection of counsel, vetoing C. E. Gregory, K. C. Sapiro had heard erroneous reports that Gregory was in league with the Regina *Leader*. The Pool organization committee, however, did consult Gregory later. (McPhail, letter of 26 August 1923, to Violet McNaughton, McNaughton Papers D-46)
32. Saskatoon *Daily Star*, 30 August 1923. Until his death in 1959, Robert Handyside Milliken provided invaluable advice and legal counsel not only to

Saskatchewan Wheat Pool, but also to many other co-operatives, becoming a nationally recognized authority on co-operative law. His legal career included appointment as a King's Counsel in 1927 and many appearances before the Supreme Court of Canada on issues affecting co-operatives. The Manitoba native — born at Reston in 1885 — also served as a director of the Bank of Canada from 1944 to 1959. A close friend of powerful Liberal figure J. G. Gardiner, Milliken was active in the Liberal party after the Progressive movement failed. Throughout his life, Milliken was also a confirmed Christian Scientist. (See his obituary, written by a friend, in the Regina *Leader-Post*, 4 May 1959; also *Western Producer*, 7 and 14 May 1959.)

33. FUC Papers, B-2 VI.7. The T. Eaton Co. was among corporate donors. F. R. MacMillan Ltd. made its cheque out to "Farmers Club."

34. The Pool repaid the SGGA in March-June 1925, despite Co-op Elevator letters demanding that the money should come directly to the Co-op to repay the SGGA debt to it. (George Robertson, letters to George Edwards, SGGA Papers, B-2 II.39 [2])

35. McPhail, letter of 26 December 1923, to G. H. Williams, UFC Papers, B-2 X.86(2).

36. The 23-24 August meetings are described in detail in McPhail's diary and his 26 August letter to Violet McNaughton, McNaughton Papers D-46. George Edwards later quoted Maharg as complaining about the ban on directors' holding similar office with grain companies: "It has come to a pretty pass, when a man who has done all the spadework for the organization for about 15 years is kicked out, when there comes a chance of getting a job with some decent remuneration." (Edwards, "Reminiscences") For composition of the campaign committee and the 1923 provisional board, see Appendix B.

37. Many dates have been given for the birth of Saskatchewan Wheat Pool. Pool publications have generally counted it as starting 26 June 1924, when provisional directors declared the actual wheat pool in operation and farmers were thereby obliged to start delivering wheat to the pool. Some of those publications wrongly reported that the new, permanent board made that declaration on that date. The 25 August 1923 date of incorporation was confirmed by the Pool's 13th *Annual Report* as well as by the 1924 special act of the Saskatchewan legislature (Chapter 66, 1924 statutes of Saskatchewan) that provided a firmer legal basis for pooling powers. But by the time the Pool produced its 19th *Annual Report*, it gave 29 September 1923 as the date for its incorporation under Saskatchewan laws.

38. Despite several searches, the official minutes of the provisional board have not been found in Pool records. Draft minutes, prepared before some meetings to serve as an agenda, and scattered partial copies of other minutes fill some gaps, but in many cases sources like McPhail's diary are necessary. The Saskatoon *Daily Star* of 27 August states that the first shares in the Pool were allotted about 12:01 a.m., Saturday, 25 August, to three of the provisional directors: George Spence, MLA for Notukeu; R. J. Moffat of Bradwell; and Thomas H. Moffet of Viceroy. As usual, Moffet's name was spelled wrongly in the newspaper. Contemporary newspaper articles and later history books spelled his name several different ways, almost always incorrectly. Even the draft minutes of the provisional board are inaccurate in this respect. Minutes of the 1923 executive committee of the Saskatchewan Association of Rural Municipalities, however, contain his clearly-legible signature as SARM president. Robert J. Moffat's name also gave later writers trouble, but he suffered less from mis-spellings because of his later prominent roles as an elected director and managing director of the Pool. He also served as a CNR director for six years before his death in 1941.

39. George Edwards, letter of 29 August 1923, to Violet McNaughton, McNaughton Papers E-86. Edwards also noted that he and Dundas were tied after four votes for the last executive position. Edwards withdrew, presumably on the grounds that the Union should have another representative on the executive. Biographical notes on Wilson, McPhail, Robertson, and Brouillette appear in the text in chapters two and three. Richard S. Dundas, a Boer War veteran, was born in the Canary Islands in 1881 and came to Canada in 1898, settling at Pelly, Sask. He served as Pool director 1924-26 and 1928-29, in addition to being a member of the provisional board. In 1929 he left for a post on the Board of Grain Commissioners, serving there until 1943. He died in 1968. Board minutes for late 1924 show that letters were sent to him regarding his frequent absences, apparently caused by illness at that time.

40. See Saskatoon *Daily Star*, 29 August 1923, and Regina *Leader-Post*, 5 August 1937 (obituary). His $15,000 offer was recalled by Margaret Newby, George Robertson's daughter, in an interview 1 May 1982.

41. George Weese, telegram of 9 August 1923, to Louis Brouillette. (UFC Papers B2 X.86[1])

42. McPhail, memo of 16 August, in SWP Papers.

43. George Turner interview, 12 May, 1982.

44. The *Western Producer*'s history is discussed in chapter five.

45. Dunning's statements are in the Saskatoon *Daily Star*, 20 and 31 August. Perhaps as a result of the spotlight turned on him during the pool campaign, he declared to a British conference the next year: "God help a Government in Saskatchewan that was not sympathetic to co-operative enterprise!" (Plunkett, *Agricultural Co-operation*, p.181.)

46. Regina *Leader*, 31 August. Despite that comment, the same editorial still maintained that the *Leader* view was that farmers must decide by themselves.

47. Edmonton *Morning Bulletin*, 22 and 27 August 1923.

48. Edmonton *Journal*, 28 August, 1923.

49. Meetings that went the other way apparently attracted little publicity. Frank Schweitzer, later a Pool delegate, recalled in a 30 July 1982 interview that he was the only one of twelve farmers at a Kandahar meeting to sign up in 1923. The other eleven had fun razzing the 23-year-old for his alleged recklessness.

50. The Saskatoon *Daily Star* reported such offers by western manager D. Kane of the Canada West Grain Co., which had twenty-five Saskatchewan-Manitoba elevators, and by L. Leadbetter, owner of five northern Saskatchewan elevators, in editions of 23 and 28 August.

51. Manitoba organizers decided 30 August they should not organize a pool for the 1923 crop. They feared that high organization expenses would be a heavy load on the small amount of wheat they could expect in 1923 after their disappointing initial drive. See Hamilton, *Service at Cost*.

52. Four constituencies managed sign-ups over the two-thirds mark: Last Mountain 94.7%, Shellbrook 84.3%, Kerrobert 79.2%, the Battlefords 66.9%. Also over the 50% level were Hanley, North Qu'Appelle, Rosetown, Saskatoon, Tisdale and Turtleford. Yorkton had least success, at 1.7%. (SGGA Papers, B-2 II.39)

53. Early Pool director Harry Marsh recalled that Premier Dunning insisted on repayment of the loan even before the Pool had income from selling wheat. By that time, banks had more faith in the Pool than Dunning seemed to have and the money was borrowed to repay the government. (Marsh interview, 20 November 1975)

54. Yates, *Wheat Pool*, p. 87, and *Progressive*, 29 November 1923. Sapiro had presumably changed his mind since a July 1920 Chicago speech in which he declared: "I would never try to form a co-operative association two months before delivery time. It would be hopeless." (Sapiro, "Co-operative Marketing")
55. Nesbitt, *Tides*, p. 63.
56. *Progressive*, 22 November 1923.
57. McPhail, letter of 26 August 1923, to Violet McNaughton. (McNaughton Papers D-46)
58. Waldron, interview.
59. Edwards, "Some Reflections," p. 9. In "Reminiscences," p. 26, Edwards says McNamee sent back not even one contract. FUC Papers, VI.8, contain telegrams showing that McNamee was sent $268 in expenses for 19 September–4 October 1923.
60. Executive minutes, FUC Papers, B-2 IV.3.
61. Quoted in Wright, *Prairie Progress*, p. 21.
62. McPhail, letter of 24 April 1924, to Violet McNaughton. (McNaughton Papers D-46)
63. See Spafford, "Left Wing," and Smith, *Prairie Liberalism*, pp. 131-133. Also Spafford, "The Origin of the Farmers' Union of Canada." The Union's power, however, was limited. Its executive resolved 4 November 1923 to instruct lodges to suspend members who refused to join the Pool where the majority of other lodge members did. But the lodges were to vote on this order before it became effective. The executive had to rescind the resolution 11 December and it was not restored until 15 January, in conjunction with the Union convention. (Executive minutes, FUC Papers, B-2 IV.3)
64. FUC Papers, B-2 VI.8.
65. Regina *Leader*, 15 December 1923.
66. See *Progressive*, 23 and 31 January, and McPhail's diary for SGGA convention details.
67. Waldron, interview.
68. Regina *Leader*, 16 February 1924.
69. Regina *Leader*, 21 February 1924.
70. See UFC Papers, B2 X.86(2); Pool directors minutes, 12 November 1924, SWP Papers; Manitoba *Free Press*, 15 February. For Robertson letter, see Gilbert Johnson Papers. Some of those amounts would have included expenses, but there would also presumably have been Farmers' Union and United Farmers payments in addition. Robertson said he was "reasonably sure" Sapiro received no other consultation fees from the Manitoba and Alberta pools. Sapiro's income was a source of controversy from early in his career. Col. Harris Weinstock, California market director, had helped steer Sapiro into co-operative legal work but broke with him in 1919, alleging that Sapiro had inflicted excessive charges on a firm in which Weinstock was a shareholder, as well as on various co-operatives. (Larsen, "Genius," pp. 250-251) During the lawsuit against Henry Ford, when Sapiro was seeking to show that Ford's newspaper had damaged his income, Sapiro testified that he earned $10,000 from co-operative-related work in 1916, rising to $17,200 in 1919 and then jumping sharply to $30,000 in 1920, $46,000 in 1921, and $61,000 in 1922. From there it declined to $42,900 in 1926. (New York *Times*, 30 March 1927) In an interview earlier, Sapiro said he and his associates received more than $1 million from their co-operative work. But those fees were divided among many lawyers — at one time Sapiro had twelve other lawyers working with him — and the costs of running various offices. (New York *Times*, 20 March 1927) The net result of Sapiro's meteoric co-operative

career and his battle against Ford's newspaper was far from profitable. Decades later, he wrote about the Ford lawsuit: "When the case started I had approximately $88,000.00 on hand and my wife pawned her jewels to help in the fight. When we finished, I owed over $80,000.00, part of which I have never yet been able to repay." (Sapiro, letter of 1 March 1959, to Harry Simonhoff, copy courtesy Stanley Sapiro.)

71. See Yates, *Wheat Pool*, p. 99; Pool annual meeting minutes, 23 October 1925.

72. Transcripts were printed in a *Progressive* supplement 28 February. The same supplement also printed a transcript of the Kindersley speech. The earlier Regina speech was printed in full in the Regina *Leader* 21 February 21, an example of the newspaper giving full coverage to its critics.

73. Transcript, Regina *Leader*, 23 February. The *Leader*, which had portrayed Howard's speech in advance as a landmark refutation of Sapiro's views, also noted that its associated radio station broadcast the speech live "all over" North America.

74. Transcript, *Progressive*, 28 February.

75. A 16 April Pool memo to the government asking for more money gave the payments in detail. (Dunning Papers (Q) Y-103-6, p. 49263) A McPhail memo of 14 September 1923 to constituency chairmen explained their expenses at that time. (SGGA Papers, B-2 II.39)

76. Acreage figures were given almost weekly in the *Progressive*.

77. Saskatoon *Star*, 6 May 1924.

78. *Progressive*, 1 May 1924, and Yates, *Wheat Pool*, pp. 97-98.

79. *Progressive*, 8 May 1924.

80. McPhail diary, 31 May 1924.

81. All ads were in the *Progressive* of 5 June.

82. McPhail, "Farmers." The *Progressive* of 3 July 1924 used different figures, reporting 46,632 contracts on hand covering 6,445,897 acres when the board formally authorized the start of Pool operations. Those, however, were probably preliminary figures and could well have included cases where farmers may have signed the contract more than once. The 45,725 figure was also used in Boyd's *New Breaking*, a book that Pool officials of the 1930s checked before publication.

83. Directors' minutes and McPhail diary, 25 July 1924; *Progressive*, 24 July 1924, and Ivan McDonald interview, 8 February 1982. Two other provisional directors, Michael McLachlan of Maple Creek and A. R. Reusch of Yorkton, were also defeated in delegate elections. Neither made it to the board as Wilson and Marsh did.

84. For many Saskatchewan residents, however, there would be equal or greater interest in another type of voting in this period — the 16 July 1924 referendum that went 119,337 to 80,381 against prohibition.

85. See Regina *Leader*, 5 July; *Progressive*, 10 July.

86. The letter was dated 15 July, read in convention 21 July, and published in the *Progressive* 31 July. Thus it missed the delegate and director elections.

87. McPhail, letter of 5 July 1924, to Violet McNaughton. (McNaughton Papers D-46); McPhail diary, 3 July.

88. Milliken, "Early History."

89. Directors' minutes, 30-31 July.

90. Waldron, interview.

91. Milliken, "Early History."

Chapter Three

1. McPhail, speech of 3 July 1929, text in *Western Producer* of 29 October 1931.
2. Burgess interview, 27 June 1975.
3. SWP Papers.
4. Waldron, "Three Presidents."
5. Hornford interview, 10 July 1975.
6. W. A. MacLeod, letter of 1 March 1937, to Violet McNaughton, in McNaughton Papers, file D-44.
7. See Innis, *The Diary*, pp. 1-5.
8. The Innis Papers contain letters from the department of national defence in 1936 saying departmental records show no clear reason why McPhail was transferred to the militia and kept in Canada. Perhaps even at this early stage McPhail was already beginning to suffer from stomach upsets.
9. Hugh McPhail interview, 14 July 1982.
10. Robertson interview, 14 May 1982.
11. George Robertson, letter of 17 January 1936, to W. C. Murray, in SWP Papers.
12. McPhail, speech of 3 July 1929.
13. Hugh McPhail interview, 14 July 1982.
14. Marsh interview, 20 November 1975.
15. Findlay, "Notes," pp. 3-4.
16. McPhail, letter of 20 March 1922, to Violet McNaughton, in McNaughton Papers, file D-46.
17. McPhail, letter of 8 August 1922, to Violet McNaughton, in McNaughton Papers D-46. The next quotation is also from that letter.
18. Those tax assessments are in SWP Papers.
19. List of tributes after McPhail's death, SWP Papers.
20. McPhail, letter of 28 September 1922, to Violet McNaughton, McNaughton Papers file D-46.
21. McPhail, letter of 14 April, 1923, to Violet McNaughton, McNaughton Papers D-46. Also following quotation.
22. McPhail, letter of 22 September 1924, to Violet McNaughton, McNaughton Papers D-46. Also following quotation.
23. McPhail, speech of 3 July 1929.
24. McPhail, letter of 3 April 1926, to Violet McNaughton, McNaughton Papers D-46.
25. McPhail, letter of 18 April 1926, to Violet McNaughton, in McNaughton Papers D-46.
26. Marsh interview, 20 November 1975.
27. McPhail described events in this stressful period in a series of letters to Violet McNaughton. (McNaughton Papers D-46)
28. Waldron, "Three Presidents."
29. Innis, *The Dairy*, p. 265. See chapter four, note 60, for details on McPhail's death.
30. Waldron, "Three Presidents."
31. Mary Lou Bost, (Brouillette's daughter) letter of 21 May 1982, to Garry Fairbairn.
32. Brouillette, letter of 12 March 1923, to N. H. Schwarz, UFC Papers file B2 X.86(1).
33. *Western Producer*, 29 April 1937.
34. *Producer* editor Pat Waldron instructed his staff not to "play up" Sapiro's comment in the list of tributes published after Brouillette's death. (SWP Papers)

35. Brouillette, 4 December 1935 Chicago speech to Farmers National Grain Corp., text in *Co-op Reporter*, 20 December 1935.
36. Waldron, "Three Presidents."
37. Robertson interview, 14 May 1982.
38. Barbara Burr-Hubbs, Jackson County Historical Society, letter of 7 June 1982, to Garry Fairbairn. Also, Abel Toupin interview, 16 February 1982. The Illinois Brouillettes trace their ancestry to a 1664 immigrant to Quebec.
39. Mary Lou Bost, letter of 21 May 1982, to Garry Fairbairn.
40. McPhail, diary entry of 23 November 1928. The typed version of the diary and the published version both omit the names of Sproule and Marsh, but professor Innis had access to the original diary and filled in the blanks in his copy of the typed diary. (Innis Papers) See the Bibliographical Notes for discussion of the various versions of McPhail's diary.
41. Gordon South, interview of 1 August 1982.
42. Don Sinclair interview, 19 April 1982.
43. Metz, *The Pioneers*, p. 43.
44. McPhail, letter of 21 June 1930, to A. F. Sproule, in SWP Papers.
45. Nyhus interview, 19 February 1982.
46. Marsh interview, 20 November 1975.
47. Marsh interview, 20 November 1975. The SWP Papers have lengthy correspondence and memoes on the complex incident.
48. R. H. Milliken, remarks to Robertson's retirement dinner, 15 December 1958. A tape of the various speeches was made available by Robertson's daughter, Margaret Newby. Wesson's speech recalled how he first met Robertson in 1920, when Robertson was leading a Wynyard group at the SGGA annual meeting, demanding all-out efforts to bring back the wartime wheat board. Government figures at the conference were struck by Robertson's ability, and asked Wesson who the man with the "little whimsical smile" was. Robertson's retirement dinner was a high-powered affair, with the presence of cabinet ministers and bank executives testifying to his influence. W. C. McNamara, then commissioner of the Canadian Wheat Board, described how Robertson was responsible for McNamara's entry into the grain business. McNamara was a junior bank clerk who decided he would rather try another line of work, rather than take a mandatory transfer to another city. Reading about Robertson's appointment as secretary of the new Saskatchewan Wheat Pool, McNamara assumed that Robertson was the same person he had known when McNamara was a legislature page boy. He called on Robertson, who turned out to be a stranger but who hired McNamara anyway, at sixty cents an hour. Other speakers twitted Robertson for managing a co-op store in Wynyard that went broke and recalled such hobbies as his umpiring the Pool cricket club. What McNamara apparently did not know was that his mother had prepared the way for him by telephoning Robertson to say she was recently widowed and did not want her son to have to leave town to work. She asked Robertson to consider the youth for a job and to keep a fatherly eye on him if hired. (Margaret Newby, letter of December 1982 to Garry Fairbairn)
49. Margaret Newby, letter of 14 April 1982, to Garry Fairbairn.
50. Newby interview, 1 May 1982.
51. Sharp interview, 11 May 1982.
52. McPhail interview, 14 July 1982.
53. Newby interview, 1 May 1982.
54. Wilson, *A Century*, p. 726.
55. Waldron interviews, 1975-76.

56. Robertson interview, 14 May 1982.
57. Newby interview, 1 May 1982.
58. Milliken, "Early History."
59. McPhail diary, 4-10 September 1924; and McPhail, letter of 11 September 1924, to Violet McNaughton, McNaughton Papers file D-46.
60. SWP directors' minutes, 9 October 1924.
61. Yates, *Wheat Pool*, p. 119.
62. Saskatchewan Co-operative Elevator Co., 1925 *Delegate Handbook*, p. 24.
63. McPhail, diary entry of 2 February 1925.
64. Saskatchewan Co-operative Elevator Co., 1925 *Delegate Handbook*, p. 31
65. McPhail, letter of 2 March 1925, to Violet McNaughton, McNaughton Papers file D-46.
66. McPhail, letter of 26 March 1925, to John McNaughton, McNaughton Papers D-46.
67. Innis, *The Diary*, p. 114.
68. Innis, *The Diary*, p. 115.
69. McPhail, diary entry of 31 January 1925.
70. McPhail, diary entry of 7 March 1925.
71. McPhail, diary entry of 31 March 1925. See also 2 April.
72. McPhail, diary entry of 3 April 1925.
73. McPhail, diary entry of 6 April 1925.
74. R. C. Findlay (CSA treasurer), letter of 18 February 1931, to McPhail, SWP Papers. The letter was a detailed report on all CSA futures-market interventions from 1924 to 1931.
75. McPhail diary, 13 March 1925.
76. McPhail diary, 8 April 1925.
77. McPhail diary, 9 April 1925.
78. McPhail, letter of 27 May 1925, to Violet McNaughton, McNaughton Papers D-46.
79. SWP directors minutes and McPhail diary, 26 May 1925. The diary entry said directors Louis Brouillette, Herbert Smyth, A. F. Sproule, and J. H. Robson would never agree to working with Co-op Elevators because they so intensely disliked the Co-op's leaders.
80. Brochure on Bulyea opening, SWP Papers.
81. W. M. Ross, letter of 20 March 1982, to A. D. McLeod.
82. Saskatchewan Co-operative Elevator Co., transcript of annual meeting, in SWP Papers.
83. McPhail diary, 20 December 1925. McPhail's allies were Bill Robinson and B. McKenzie.
84. McPhail diary, 21 December 1925.
85. Innis, *The Diary*, p. 90.
86. A transcript of McPhail's speech is in SWP Papers.
87. McPhail, letter of 3 April 1926, to Violet McNaughton, McNaughton Papers D-46. Emphasis in original.
88. Brouillette, letter of 20 February 1926, to his mother. Letter courtesy of Mary Lou Bost.
89. At the meeting, Pool directors disclosed their personal shareholdings in Co-op Elevators. Herbert Smyth had none, while McPhail, Brouillette, Jack Wesson and Harry Marsh held only the one share needed to qualify them as Co-op members. Brooks Catton and R. J. Moffat owned twenty shares each, with the remainder of Pool directors owning two to seven.
90. SWP, third *Annual Report*, p. 8.
91. Colquette, *First Fifty*, p. 200. See MacPherson, "Co-operative Union," p. 69.

92. McPhail, letter of 11 October 1926, to E. A. W. R. McKenzie, SWP Papers.
93. Regina *Leader*, 21 and 22 June 1926; Yates, *Wheat Pool*, pp. 129-30; John Cook interview, 28 July 1976.
94. SWP directors minutes; George Robertson December 1925 memo in SGGA Papers, file B-2 II.39(2).
95. Windsor *Border Cities Star*, 9 April 1928, interview with Milliken. See also: Milliken radio speech transcript of 2 May 1929; unsigned memo of 27 October 1927 on lawsuits under way; and files of Milliken correspondence on various cases. (All in SWP Papers)
96. SWP, second *Annual Report*, p. 13.
97. Tom Bentley interview, 2 November 1979, quoted in Robinson, *Changing Role*, p. 32.
98. Philip Durham interview, 15 July 1975; John Stratychuk interview, 1975. Stratychuk worked as a fieldman and later division director in his forty-year career with Saskatchewan Wheat Pool. He was invaluable in Ukrainian-speaking areas, as well as being an excellent communicator in English.
99. Saskatoon *Star*, 9 November 1926.
100. *Sweet Pea*, November 1960, p. 4.
101. SWP, fourth *Annual Report*, p. 8.
102. McPhail diary, 13 August 1926: "The greatest mistake we ever made was to have a Board of 16 members. The best and most valuable members are without exception the ones who have least to say."
103. Innis, *The Diary*, pp. 266, 269-270.
104. McPhail diary, 9 December 1926. See also the 12 November 1926 entry.
105. Nesbitt, *Tides*, p. 125.
106. Presidents George Edwards of the SGGA and J. A. Stoneman of the Union conferred with McPhail and Pool secretary George Robertson. (McPhail diary, 6 October 1925) The awkward UFC(SS) name was the result of conflicting desires: the Farmer's Union of Canada wanted a name, like its own, that had a national perspective; the SGGA wanted a name, like its own, that would stress the organization's Saskatchewan identity. No one seemed enthusiastic over "United Farmers of Canada (Saskatchewan Section) Ltd.," but that compromise at least enabled the two organizations to proceed with their merger.
107. Saskatoon council minutes, 1925, 1026-1027. Some articles have erroneously reported that the presentation was made in 1923.
108. McPhail diary, 14 July 1926.
109. McPhail, letter of 14 August 1926, to Violet McNaughton, McNaughton Papers file D-46.
110. McPhail diary, 13 December 1927.
111. Third International Wheat Pool Conference, *Proceedings*, p. 41.
112. McPhail diary, 28 November 1928.
113. McPhail diary, 21 June 1929. There was no recorded vote on the basic motion. A Wesson motion to add explanatory "whereas" clauses to the basic motion was defeated, 56-93. (SWP delegates' minutes)
114. McPhail diary, 15 and 25 June 1929.
115. Sapiro-UFC telegram, UFC Papers file B-2 X.59; also Sapiro speech of 26 June 1929, transcript in UFC Papers B-2 X.60.
116. Sapiro Regina speech, 20 September 1929.
117. Transcript of question-and-answer session with Sapiro at Humboldt 24 September 1929, in UFC Papers file B-2 IX.259.
118. Lloyd, *Memories*, p. 60.

119. McPhail diary, 7 September 1929.
120. McPhail, letter of 2 January 1930, to Hector L. Roberge, SWP Papers. Noting Roberge's assertion that 96 percent of members in his North Battleford-area subdistrict favored compulsion, McPhail said if that figure was correct, then Roberge would be luckier than any other delegate since his constituents would be united behind him.
121. International Wheat Pool Conference, *Proceedings*, p. 83.
122. International Wheat Pool Conference, *Proceedings*, pp. 69-70.
123. Second International Wheat Pool Conference, *Proceedings*, pp. 34-35.
124. Third International Wheat Pool Conference, *Proceedings*, p. 33. The conference was also called the "First International Pool Conference."
125. Nesbitt, *Tides*, p. 85.
126. Taylor, "National Wheat Growers," p. 148.
127. Birmingham *Gazette*, 5 December 1927.
128. Untitled memo, Keen Papers, vol. 5, file labeled "Memoranda, Drafts etc." Keen, who later helped persuade British and American co-operators to let the Canadian Wheat Pool into the International Co-operative Alliance, was surprised to get a $500 unsolicited cheque from the pools for his work on their behalf. He donated it to the Co-operative Union of Canada.
129. A. H. Hobley speech, 19 January 1928, text in *Scoop Shovel*, April 1928.
130. SWP fourth *Annual Report*, p. 25. The Pool annual reports included CSA annual reports.
131. "Wheat," *Round Table*, vol. 21, 1930-31, pp. 420-421.
132. "Report of D. W. McIntyre on European Trip," SWP Papers.
133. McPhail diary, 11 December 1926, and 22 September 1927; see also Innis, *The Diary*, p. 158.
134. Regina *Daily Star*, 5 April 5, 1930.
135. Irwin, "The Canadian."
136. James E. Boyle, *Marketing of Agricultural Products* (New York, 1925), cited in Fowke, *National Policy*, p. 222.
137. See the Manitoba *Free Press*, 8 October 1925, for the original Exchange charges and a Pool rebuttal; the 17 October issue carried still more Exchange charges.
138. Fowke, *National Policy*, p. 235. Patton, "The Market Influence," and *Grain Growers*, also defended the pools.
139. The anonymous director was quoted in an article by Manitoba Pool general manager R. M. Mahoney, "In the Grain Bin," *Scoop Shovel*, March 1930, p. 7.
140. CSA report, in SWP fourth *Annual Report*, p. 17.

Chapter Four

1. *The Canadian Wheat Pool*, 1929.
2. CSA general sales manager's report to board for January 1929, in SWP Papers. McIvor's subsequent statements are from later monthly reports.
3. *Western Producer*, 16 May 1929.
4. CSA treasurer R. C. Findlay, letter of 18 February 1931, to A. J. McPhail, SWP Papers.
5. London *The People*, 2 June 1929.
6. Gampell, *Canada and Her Wheat Pool*, pp. 30-31.
7. CSA general sales manager's report for June 1929, SWP Papers.
8. Letter of 10 November 1930, to Violet McNaughton, quoted in Innis, *The Diary*, p. 199.
9. McPhail diary, 23 September 1929.

10. CSA monthly reports, SWP Papers; and McPhail diary, 15 August 1929.
11. Regina *Leader*, 20 August 1929.
12. CSA report in SWP sixth annual report, p. 20.
13. Bredt, "Historical Review," p. 18. See also Bredt's letter in the Manitoba *Free Press*, 15 August 1935.
14. Andrew Cairns, evidence to Stamp Commission, 22 April 1931, quoted in Innis, *The Diary*, p. 243n.
15. Sapiro speech text, UFC Papers file B-2 IX.259.
16. Findlay, "Notes," pp. 5-6.
17. Edmonton *Journal*, 18 December 1929.
18. Regina *Star*, 11 January 1930; and *Western Producer*, 16 January.
19. *Barron"'s*, 27 January 1930.
20. Regina *Leader*, 30 January 1930.
21. George McIvor, letter of 14 February 1930, to Beaudry Leman, Innis Papers.
22. Winnipeg *Tribune*, 7 February 1930.
23. McPhail speech of 5 February 1930, printed transcript in SWP Papers.
24. McPhail diary, 12 and 13 February 1930.
25. Findlay, memo of 6 February 1930, to R. J. Moffat, Innis Papers.
26. McPhail diary, 18 February 1930; also CSA report in SWP sixth *Annual Report*, p. 20.
27. McPhail diary, 28 February 1930.
28. McPhail diary, 15 March 1930.
29. Sapiro, speech of 1 April 1930, transcript in SWP Papers; see also *Manitoba Free Press*, 2 April.
30. For several months, McPhail had virtually been acting as CSA general manager, since E. B. Ramsay left that post to become chairman of the Board of Grain Commissioners.
31. McPhail diary, 8 May 1930. Emphasis in original.
32. Wilson Parker interview.
33. Findlay, "Notes," p. 9.
34. McPhail diary, 31 July 1930; Findlay, "Notes," p. 8.
35. Brownlee interview, March-May 1961, p. 102.
36. McPhail diary, 23 August 1930.
37. McPhail diary, 24 November 1930 and CSA report in SWP seventh *Annual Report*, p. 31. The previous day's diary entry paid tribute to the three prairie premiers: "Brownlee, Bracken and Anderson are standing up to this situation like men. Their attitude is as fine as the most radical farmer could wish."
38. McPhail diary, 15 November 1930.
39. McPhail diary, 19 November 1930.
40. McPhail diary, 19 November 1930.
41. McPhail diary, 22 November 1930.
42. McPhail diary, 21 November 1930.
43. Even with the federal guarantees, the pools found some banks reluctant to continue already-existing loans. Over a decade later, Jack Wesson was still mad at the Bank of Nova Scotia. A Pool livestock division official innocently suggested that he should open an account with a convenient BNS branch — Wesson, then Pool president, said that would happen "over my dead body." Secretary George Robertson declared that he would drive to the next town rather than cash a cheque at a BNS branch. (Burgess interview, 27 June 1975)
44. Nesbitt, *Tides*, p. 214.
45. Sir Arthur Balfour, quoted in Bristol *Western Daily Press*, 23 May 1931.

46. Although the Alberta and Saskatchewan organizations avoided formal bankruptcy, Manitoba Wheat Pool was in a weaker position since it technically did not own its elevator system — that was the property of 153 local elevator associations. A complex 1931 reorganization made Manitoba Pool Elevators the parent company and virtually erased the former main company. When the Gillespie Terminal Grain Company filed suit to recover damages for early termination of a lease on one of its terminals, sheriffs reported that they "could find no goods whereon to levy or to seize or to take" in December 1931. The next year, Manitoba Wheat Pool was declared formally bankrupt. Manitoba Pool Elevators, however, continued operating and making repayments on the debt for 1929-30 overpayments. (Hamilton, *Service*, pp. 128-131)

47. McPhail diary, 21 March 1930.

48. McPhail diary, 25 March 1930.

49. Anonymous leaflet in SWP Papers, appealing for subscriptions to the "Western Tribune," care of grain buyer C. R. Muirhead of Khedive, to oppose compulsion.

50. H. W. Wood, letter of 25 March 1931, to McPhail, SWP Papers.

51. Circular W-200-A, Innis Papers; also Saskatoon *Star-Phoenix*, 6 April 1931. Letter in SWP Papers.

52. *Western Producer*, 23 April 1931.

53. Sapiro, letter of 21 April 1930, to "G. Johnson, Regina Leader." Since the original letter wound up in SWP Papers, the recipient presumably rejected the invitation and passed the letter to the Pool.

54. Sapiro, letter of 18 April 1931. (SWP Papers)

55. An Alberta Wheat Pool vote on compulsory pooling resulted in 4,238 votes against the idea and 3,191 for. (Edmonton *Journal*, 11 September 1931)

56. Meeting minutes, SWP Papers, and McPhail diary, 4 May 1931.

57. McPhail, broadcast text, SWP Papers.

58. McPhail diary, 24 July 1931.

59. McPhail diary, 17 September 1931.

60. He had been in hospital to have his appendix removed and developed complications after the operation. (Marion McPhail, letter of 15 October 1931, to Violet McNaughton, McNaughton Papers file D-47) *The Link*, publication of the C.W.S. Press Agency, Manchester, reported 10 November 1931 that McPhail died from a blood clot that reached his heart. He had seemed to be recovered from the appendectomy, was in good spirits, and had been scheduled to leave the hospital on the day he died.

61. A confidential 1934 Pool memo to delegates explained that McPhail's insurance and land holdings totalled less than $7,000 and the land was tied up for ten years so that it could not be sold. McPhail's wife and son had only $2,000 insurance and $400 annual land revenues. Mrs. McPhail also had to go to a sanitarium for several months in 1933. Pool directors thus set up a fund to provide McPhail's family with another $80 a month.

62. News story carbon, SWP Papers.

63. Working, "Pool and Prices," p. 140.

64. Brownlee memo, SWP Papers.

65. D. R. McIntyre speech, 17 February 1926. (International Wheat Pool Conference, *Proceedings*, p. 72) George McIvor speech, 6 June 1928. (Third International Wheat Pool Conference, *Proceedings*, p. 47)

66. Jack Wesson speech, April 1931. (*Western Producer*, 23 April 1931) R. C. Findlay, letter of 1 March 1932, to R. J. Moffat. (Innis Papers.)

67. Cartwright, "Wheat Pool's Policies."

68. D. R. McIntyre, report to Pool directors 22 May 1930, SWP Papers.

69. Article by Sir Malcolm Robertson, former British ambassador to Argentina, London *Times*, 31 July 1930.

Chapter Five

1. Ross, letter of 20 March 1982, to A. D. McLeod, SWP Papers.
2. Robertson, radio debate 29 January 1951, transcript in SWP Papers.
3. CSA report, in SWP seventh *Annual Report*, p. 36. The same report noted that farmers' return per acre of wheat went from $18.60 in 1927 to $5.83 in 1930. In this and subsequent years, Pool annual reports contained extensive statistics on general farm incomes and grain handling, as well as political and governmental developments.
4. See Gray, *Men Against*, p. 22.
5. Gray, *Winter Years*, p. 115.
6. McGinnis, "Wheat Production," p. 299.
7. Manifestations of separatist feelings included a pro-secession resolution passed by the Last Mountain constituency Progressive convention (*Western Producer*, 27 November 1930). At its November 1930 annual meeting, Alberta Wheat Pool passed a resolution urging that the three prairie provinces obtain the constitutional power to practice free trade. That resolution was interpreted by some "as virtually endorsing secession," according to the *Producer* of 4 December 1930. The idea of western independence had been vigorously pushed by farm leader Ed Partridge in his 1926 book, *A War on Poverty* (pp. 197-202) and was also debated at the 1931 convention of the United Farmers of Alberta. (Saskatoon *Star-Phoenix*, 21 and 22 January 1931) The Regina *Leader-Post* of 12 November 1938 published the results of its unscientific mail-in ballot on secession: 1,647 approved the idea, 1,644 opposed it, and 398 said they would consider it. Jack Wesson, during his term as Pool vice-president, on at least one occasion privately expressed agreement with separatist views. (Jack Wesson, letter of 30 March 1931, to A. J. MacAuley, UFC Papers file B2 X.77[2]) There is no indication, however, that he had such views while Pool president.
8. J.D. Read memo, 13 November 1930, SWP Papers.
9. In the Lac Vert area, for example, many members were badly disillusioned at the collapse of pooling and quit patronizing the Pool when overpayments were related to individuals. But nearly all returned when the debt became a company liability. (Ross interview, 31 July 1982)
10. William Riddel, 9 November 1938 memo to delegates, SWP Papers.
11. Moffet, "The Commercial Reserves."
12. Minutes of 18 September 1932 conference, UFC Papers file B-2 X.77(2). See also H. G. L. Strange, letter of 21 October 1923, to Frank Eliason, same file. Strange, president of Searle Grain Co. Ltd., sent the documents to UFC secretary Eliason to demonstrate that the private grain trade was not operating alone in grading policy.
13. The requirement for delegates and directors to deliver to Pool elevators was a controversial one. The 1934 annual meeting passed a resolution favoring that requirement and giving notice of intention to add it to official bylaws in 1935. But then the 1935 meeting rejected the idea. When the requirement was passed as a bylaw in 1937, it was in even more stringent form: a Pool member had to have delivered all his grain to Pool facilities, if available, for three years prior to election as delegate.
14. Oliver Olson, quoted in Robinson, "Changing Role," p. 119.
15. Everett Baker interview, 1975.
16. Stratychuk's activities were described in Robinson, "Changing Role," p. 78. Bentley was mentioned in Lloyd, *Memories*, pp. 56-58.

17. Stratychuk interview, 1975. Stratychuk also noted that at one point in the late 1930s or early 1940s, more than forty Pool elevator agents were credit union secretary-treasurers, serving without pay.
18. Wilson Parker interview.
19. Abel Toupin interview, 16 February 1982.
20. Country organization report for June 1941, SWP Papers.
21. R. B. Evans memo, 31 March 1944, SWP Papers,
22. Don Sinclair interview, 19 April 1982.
23. Lipset, *Agrarian Socialism*, p. 222. The following Pool survey is from page 225.
24. Frank Eliason, letter of 25 September 1931, to R. J. Moffat. UFC Papers file B-2 X.77(2).
25. George Robertson, letter of 17 January 1935, to Frank Eliason. UFC Papers file B-2 X.77(3).
26. Schulz, *Rise and Fall*, p. 87.
27. For the *Western Producer*'s general history, see the Waldron interview and also Dryden, "Half Century."
28. McPhail, memo of 23 May 1923, to SGGA directors, SWP Papers. Turner and his partners were joined about this time by advertising specialist E. M. Holiday. Like Turner and Waldron, Holiday had been seriously wounded in World War One, where he was awarded the Military Cross. Although a cavalry major in wartime, Holiday later became Saskatchewan president of the Navy League of Canada.
29. Meeting minutes, McNaughton Papers file E-86. The *Progressive* would even have freedom to accept advertising from anti-Prohibition groups, although its editorials would support the SGGA's policy in favor of banning alcohol.
30. Memorandum of agreement, SWP Papers. Although Pool director Harry Marsh is generally credited with suggesting the newspaper's new name, minutes of the 15 August editorial board meeting show that the motion for the *Western Producer* name came from A. Baynton and Violet McNaughton. (McNaughton Papers file E-86) But Marsh was not a member of the editorial board and they may have been following an earlier suggestion of his. See Dryden, "Half Century."
31. McPhail, letter of 21 November 1924, to Violet McNaughton. McNaughton Papers file D-46. In 1934, George Robertson was concerned over Saskatchewan Liberal complaints that *Western Producer* management showed pro-CCF attitudes. (Nesbitt, "Survey," p. 6)
32. McPhail's letters are in McNaughton Papers, file D-46. For McNaughton's biographical information, see: her typed recollections in McNaughton Papers file C-1; Waldron interview; Wright, "Mothering the Prairies"; Dryden, "Mrs. Mac."
33. McDonald interview, 8 February 1982.
34. The 25 February 1928 contract is in UFC Papers, file B-2 X.73.
35. R. H. Milliken, "Memo re: Western Producer," 22 December 1932, SWP Papers. See also Nesbitt, "Survey."
36. Waldron interview.
37. In his 20 November 1975, interview, Harry Marsh said: "I recall the rottenest job I had to do when I had to go and tell Harry that we were going to take over the Producer from him. . . . we decided the best thing to do was to take the damn thing over and that was a shock to Harry." Marsh, however, was showing signs of imperfect memory in that interview — he erroneously said the takeover came before the newspaper was called the *Producer* — and probably exaggerated the Pool's initiatives. Also, McPhail wrote in his diary

21 May 1931, that he — not Marsh — personally informed Turner and Holiday the same day that the Pool board decided to take over the newpaper: "They are very disappointed at not getting any cash. They are pretty well done physically, both, and wonderfully fine fellows. We must try and do what we can for them." Other than Marsh's interview, there is no evidence that Turner saw any way to keep the newspaper operating under his ownership. All other evidence is to the contrary, that he saw the need for someone else to step in to save the newspaper.

38. McPhail diary, 21 May 1931. Milliken's memo in note 35 was drafted for the government's information.

39. Wilson Parker interview.

40. McPhail diary, 22 August 1931. McPhail wanted elevator agents to sell 25,000 *Producer* subscriptions: "It is a hell of a condition where a Board have certain ideas and ideals and their managment can thwart them simply because they are not in sympathy."

41. Minutes of 11 September 1931, meeting between *Producer*, Pool, UFC and other farm organizations officials, SWP Papers.

42. Newby interview, 1 May 1982.

43. Nesbitt, "Survey."

44. Waldron interview.

45. For the Producer-Pool-UFC bickering, see UFC Papers file B-2 X.77(3). Eliason, "Biography," pp. 81-82, recounted how the *Producer* ceased providing space to the UFC. The *Producer* complained that UFC statements were editorials, not news. Eliason noted, however, that the Saskatoon *Daily Star* and the Canadian Press news agency used the same statements that the *Producer* rejected.

46. Minutes of 27 April 1936 meeting of Interprovincial Publicity Committee, Alberta Wheat Pool Papers, box 45 file 503.

47. W. L. McQuarrie, secretary of Saskatchewan retail merchants' association, speech to SWP annual meeting, 3 November 1932, text in SWP Papers.

48. SWP Papers.

49. Provincial Treasurer M. A. MacPherson, speech to SWP annual meeting 10 November 1933, meeting minutes.

50. CCWP report, in SWP 11th *Annual Report*, p. 67.

51. McFarland, letter of 14 April 1931, to Bennett, Bennett Papers, quoted in Wilson, *A Century*, p. 313. McFarland had entered the grain business at the age of twenty-five, in Calgary in 1898, becoming involved with the Alberta Pacific Grain Company about the same time R. B. Bennett and publisher Max Aitken were investing in the company. Bennett and Aitken made large profits when the company was sold (Beaverbrook, *Friends*, p. 45) and McFarland presumably also did well with his investment. He stayed as president of the company after the sale, from 1922 to 1926 before moving into non-grain business. In 1923, he started to help organize Alberta Wheat Pool, but resigned from the organizing committee because it was not arranging for elevator facilities. Under McFarland, Alberta Pacific co-operated with the new pool and even offered to sell its facilities to Alberta Pool with no charge for goodwill. (Nesbitt, *Tides*, pp. 46-48) When McFarland took over management of the Central Selling Agency, he insisted on serving without pay.

52. Jack Wesson, letter of 30 March 1931, to A. J. MacAuley: "Personally I am sure of this after reading the speech from the throne, that if we do not get this one hundred per cent pool controlled by ourselves as producers, there is no doubt in my mind that the federal government will reinstate the Canada

Wheat Board to save the farmers of Western Canada from them-selves."(UFC Papers, file B-2 X.77[2])

53. Wilson, *A Century*, pp. 381-382.
54. McFarland report to CSA, in SWP 10th *Annual Report*, p. 63.
55. McFarland, letter of 14 July 1932, to Bennett, Bennett Papers, quoted in Hamilton, *Service*, p. 159.
56. McFarland report to CSA, in SWP 9th *Annual Report*, p. 68. He also noted that the United States had more than fifty percent of the world wheat carryover for the previous three years: "Had it not been for this, our operations would have been futile and would have been unwarranted."
57. McFarland and Bennett letters, Bennett Papers, quoted in Hamilton, *Service*, pp. 161-163.
58. Bennett Papers, quoted in Wilson, *A Century*, p. 443.
59. Finlayson, *Life With*, p. 204.
60. Bennett Papers, quoted in Wilson, *A Century*, p. 460.
61. McFarland, testimony to Royal Grain Inquiry Commission 1936, quoted in Hamilton, *Service*, p. 175.
62. R. H. Milliken, letter of 19 April 1934, to George Robertson, copy courtesy R. A. Milliken. Weir became a Saskatchewan Wheat Pool delegate after the Conservative government was defeated.
63. The first advisors were: Robert McKee of the Canadian Grain Export Company; Alberta Pool director Lew Hutchinson; Saskatchewan Pool president Louis Brouillette; Saskatchewan Pool director Brooks Catton; former president Sydney T. Smith of the Winnipeg Grain Exchange; president Paul F. Bredt of Manitoba Pool Elevators; and C. G. C. Short of the Lake of the Woods Milling Company.
64. The second board consisted of: J.R. Murray, former manager of the Alberta Pacific Grain Company; George H. McIvor, former CSA sales manager; and Dean A. M. Shaw of the University of Saskatchewan's agriculture faculty. After Murray resigned in 1937, McIvor became chairman. Former CSA treasurer R. C. Findlay, who had been working as wheat board treasurer, became a commissioner in 1937. Veterans of the Central Selling Agency thus held two of the three positions on the board.
65. Winnipeg *Free Press*, 20 December 1935.
68. Wilson, *A Century*, p. 584.

Chapter Six

1. Quoted in Nesbitt, *Tides*, p. 368.
2. Winifred Pike interview, 14 July 1982.
3. Kathleen Parker interview, 24 February 1982.
4. Baker, "In Memory," Don Sinclair interview 19 April 1982, and Christine Pike, letter of 14 December 1982, to A. D. McLeod, SWP Papers.
5. Mitchell Sharp interview, 11 May 1982.
6. Kathleen Parker interview, 24 February 1982.
7. McPhail, letter of 2 December 1925, to Violet McNaughton, McNaughton Papers file D-46.
8. Kathleen Parker interview, 24 February 1982.
9. C. F. Wilson interview, 17 May 1982.
10. Parker interview, 24 February 1982. (Also source of stories about the radio debaters and Swiss maids)
11. Sinclair interview, 19 April 1982. (Source for rest of paragraph also)
12. Myron Feeley interview, 20 June 1975.
13. Country organization monthly report for November 1940, quoted in

Lonergan, "Agricultural Organizations," p. 189. That monthly report is among many that have been lost from the SWP Papers in the past twenty-five years.

14. Everett Baker Papers, file 31C (R-561).
15. Doug Kirk interview, quoted in Robinson, "Changing Role," p. 131.
16. Country organization report for March 1942, SWP Papers.
17. Wilf MacLeod interview, 31 March 1982.
18. Information division release, 29 January 1980, SWP Papers.
19. Cliff Leach interview 22 February 1982, and Harry Smith interview, 25 February 1982.
20. Effective 1 April 1943, a pension plan began with the Pool paying fifty percent of contributions. The plan was designed to provide a pension of $1.50 monthly for each year of service — for example, $15 a month would be paid to someone with ten years' contributions. Male employees could retire at 65, women at 60, or they could continue working another five years if they and the company agreed. (SWP, 19th *Annual Report*, p. 30) Although the pension plan terms were decent for 1943, inflation over the next twenty-five years made pensions meagre for some employees who retired before the plan was improved. The Pool eventually made voluntary extra payments to those pensioners.
21. The development of farm policy and government regulations throughout this period was recorded in considerable detail in Pool annual reports, which amount to a running history of agricultural policy.
22. Country organization report for March 1941, SWP Papers.
23. Country organization report for September 1941, SWP Papers.
24. Country organization report for October 1941, SWP Papers.
25. SWP 18th *Annual Report*, p. 27; Thies interview, 4 June 1975.
26. George Robertson memo, "Summary of Proceedings of the Ottawa Delegation," undated, SWP Papers. Includes lengthy quotations.
27. George Robertson memo, "Summary of Proceedings."
28. R. B. Evans, memo to committees, 16 April 1942, SWP Papers. The plebiscite was held 27 April, with a pro-conscription result.
29. CCWP report, in SWP 19th *Annual Report*, p. 63.
30. Wilson, *A Century*, p. 1047.
31. Wilson, *A Century*, p. 1047.
32. C. D. Howe was the nominee of the Saskatchewan Co-operative Elevator Company on the arbitration committtee that fixed the price for the Pool's purchase of the company. He also helped invent the Dominion-Howe unloader that tilted boxcars to unload grain. (Bothwell, *Howe*, p. 43) His work for Co-op Elevators and the pools in designing terminals seems to have put him in disfavor with the private grain trade, since he got no contracts from them in 1917-31. (Bothwell, *Howe*, p. 42) His first venture for the Co-op Elevator Company almost ended in personal financial disaster, when a winter storm in 1916 wrecked the partly-built Port Arthur terminal. Howe would have lost about $400,000 on the project, but the Co-op was so pleased with his speed in getting the terminal built despite the storm damage that the company gave him an extra payment to cover the loss. (Wilson, *Howe*, pp. 11, 35-40) Several interview subjects, including retired Pool delegates, erroneously recalled that the Pool was involved in that episode, but the record clearly shows that it happened before the Pool was formed.
33. Treleaven interview, 2 May 1982.
34. CCWP report in SWP 26th *Annual Report*, pp. 82-83.
35. Ross interview, 31 July 1982.
36. Country organization report for August 1947, SWP Papers.

37. North-West Line Elevator Association, "A Statement."
38. North-West Line Elevator Association, "A Statement."
39. Frank Eliason, circular of 24 January 1944, and letter of 4 March 1944, in UFC Papers file B-2 X.77(4).
40. Transcript, SWP Papers; and UFC Papers File B-2 X.42.
41. L. P. McNamee, draft letter of 21 September 1950, to the *Western Producer* Open Forum, in McNamee Papers.
42. CCWP report, in SWP 43rd *Annual Report*, p. 39. Taking the 1949 purchasing power of a bushel of wheat as 100, the CCWP calculated comparable values for other years. For example: 1919 = 185; 1923 = 61; 1925 = 120; 1930 = 50; 1941 = 66; 1945 = 137; 1955 = 74; 1959 = 61; 1965 = 72.
43. See Appendix.
44. Robertson's statement was quoted in "History and Development of Co-operative Livestock Marketing in Saskatchewan," SWP Papers.
45. Wright, *Prairie Progress*, pp. 118-119.
46. Ball interview, 26 June 1975.
47. SWP 24th *Annual Report*, p. 15.
48. Hugh McPhail interview, 14 July 1982.
49. MacPherson, *CIS*, p. 5.
50. Wilf MacLeod interview, 31 March 1982; and MacPherson, *CIS*, p. 8.
51. MacPherson, *CIS*, p. 8, says the informal urine-test system worked well — even ten years later there had been no sickness-related loss on the initial batch of policies.
52. Alberta Wheat Pool cleared its debt with a final payment two years earlier, on 1 June 1947. Manitoba Pool Elevators made its final payment in October 1949. Various figures have been given over the years for Saskatchewan Wheat Pool's share of the 1929-30 overpayments. The 1949 *Annual Report* listed that share as $13.75 million. That figure, however, apparently included interest and other charges that accumulated between the overpayments and the start of the government-backed repayment plan. The 1931 *Annual Report* reported final settlement of Saskatchewan Pool's share of the 1929-30 pooling as: gross overpayment $14.8 million; plus operating expenses; minus various amounts due on current account; net $15 million loss on 1929-30 pooling operations. That, however, was offset by an undistributed surplus on 1928-29 pooling, leaving net overpayments to farmers of $13.3 million.

Chapter Seven

1. Wesson retired voluntarily, although two or three directors did advise him that he should consider that action. (Bickle interview, 14 October 1982)
2. A. D. McLeod interview, 15 November 1982.
3. Report of country organization department for August 1959, SWP Papers.
4. R. H. Milliken, letter of 10 January 1947, to George Robertson, SWP Papers.
5. The Fisher, Northcott, and Melville-Ness letters were written 25-26 June 1952, in response to a George Robertson memo.
6. "Two Lives."
7. Gibbings, radio speech of 3 January 1961, transcript, SWP Papers.
8. Gibbings interview, 23 February 1982.
9. Jim Wright interview, 15 January 1982. Wright was next in line to speak but had to pass after hearing Gibbings forcefully voice all Wright's planned arguments. Wright, who went on to become Pool secretary, was left wondering in later years whether a reversed speaking order might have

meant switched careers for the two men. Wright's knowledge of the Pool told him there would probably have been no difference, since Pool delegates take their time in judging one another — but there would always be that "what if?" feeling.

10. Traquair interview, 15 October 1982.
11. Ross interview, 31 July 1982.
12. Gibbings interview, 23 February 1982.
13. "Two Lives."
14. A. D. McLeod interview, 13 October 1982.
15. "Two Lives."
16. Gibbings, speech to SWP annual meeting, 16 November 1973, transcript in SWP Papers.
17. Phillips interview, 5 April 1982; McLeod interview, 13 October 1982.
18. Turner interview, 15 January 1982.
19. Lee interview, 31 March 1982.
20. Mumford interview, 14 January 1982.
21. SWP, annual meeting minutes.
22. Traquair interview, 26 April 1982. Traquair saw the fuss over corporate donations as the first concerted effort by delegates to protest "big management."
23. Craig, "Co-operative Democracy," pp. 81-87.
24. Lonergan, "Agricultural Organizations," table VI.
25. Another tradition was also changed shortly afterward. Until the 1960s, delegates were elected just before the annual meeting, but their terms started *after* the meeting. A new delegate thus had a year to gain experience before participating in his first annual meeting, but it was an odd situation where a retiring delegate would still be voting on major issues when Pool members had already chosen his successor. The November 1969 annual meeting was the first where newly-elected delegates could vote. That meeting resolved, however, to simplify matters by having elections held within a few months after the annual meeting. The new system gave new delegates about nine months to gain experience, while avoiding the problem of retiring delegates voting while their successors watched.
26. Craig, "Co-operative Democracy," p. 63.
27. Kristjanson, *Evaluation*, p. 108.
28. Schweitzer, "My Experiences."
29. Gordon South interview, 1 August 1982. South had a particularly heavy load of co-operative activities. One year, he was away from home 220 days, 120 of those on Pool business.
30. Ivan McDonald interview, 8 February 1982.
31. Sinclair interview, 19 April 1982.
32. The 1952 international wheat conference was the only one that Pool secretary George Robertson missed in his 34-year Pool career. Robertson had to have an emergency operation on board the *Queen Elizabeth* on his way to London. (Regina *Leader-Post* obituary, 29 May 1963; Newby interview, 1 May 1982)
33. William Miner interview, 17 May 1982; Gibbings interview, 23 February 1982.
34. SWP, 29th *Annual Report*, p. 48.
35. Regina *Leader-Post*, 1 February 1982.
36. Country organization report for January 1959, SWP Papers.
37. Nyhus interview, 19 February 1982. Many members of the expedition would have had useful personal contacts in the capital. Saskatchewan Pool delegate Ennis Sproat, for example, had served in the same wartime air unit as

cabinet minister Alvin Hamilton and was invited to Hamilton's Ottawa home for informal talks during the group's stay in Ottawa. (Cunningham, "Biography," p. 322)

38. Treleaven, letter of 23 October 1982, to Garry Fairbairn. See also Treleaven interview of 2 May 1982.
39. See the Hamilton and Churchill remarks in Stursberg, *Leadership Gained*, pp. 134-138.
40. Morgan, *Merchants*, p. 161.
41. Anderson, *Canadian Wheat*.
42. Forrest, quoted in Robinson, "Changing Role," p. 155; and SWP, 45th *Annual Report*, p. 22.
43. Smith, *Regional Decline*, p. 96.
44. Jim Wright, memo of 27 November 1969 to delegates, quoting a transcript of Turner's remarks to the news media. The memo was sent to "assist you in interpreting this item in dealing with questions in your sub-district."
45. Turner interview, 15 January 1982.
46. Sinclair interview, 19 April 1982.
47. Turner interview, 15 January 1982.
48. Fairbairn, "Turner Tough."
49. Phillips interview, 5 April 1982.
50. CCWP report, in SWP 37th *Annual Report*, pp. 93-95.
51. For example, Earl and Kathleen Bratvold ran restaurants in Scotsguard and Simmie during the 1930s, charging twenty-five cents for chicken, potatoes, vegetables, apple pie and coffee. See *Simmie Saga* (Simmie, Sask.: Simmie and District History Book Club, 1981), p. 573.
52. McCrorie, *In Union*, p. 53.
53. Toupin interview, 16 February 1982.
54. Quoted by Toupin, interview 16 February 1982.
55. McCrorie, *In Union*, p. 51.
56. Minutes of 3 January 1958 SFA-SFU meeting, SWP Papers.
57. Minutes of 2-3 October 1962 and subsequent meetings, Canadian Federation of Agriculture files, Ottawa.
58. Schulz, *Rise and Fall*, p. 94.
59. Private interview by author.
60. Gibbings interview, 23 February 1982. The amalgamation discussions were not unprecedented — on 9 October 1937 the three pools, UGG, and Manitoba premier John Bracken met in Winnipeg to discuss amalgamation. A UGG spokesman said all parties were facing either unity or ruin with the 1937 crop failure and generally poor economy. But president Paul Bredt of Manitoba Pool Elevators said his members had not shown any sign of wanting such amalgamation for five years. Jack Wesson of Saskatchewan Wheat Pool noted that UGG was proportionately weaker in Saskatchewan than other provinces, having only 109 Saskatchewan elevators to Saskatchewan Pool's 1,090. But Wesson added that Saskatchewan Pool would try to adapt to any amalgamation plan suitable to others. Bracken noted that the pools and UGG would have more political power if they spoke with a united voice. The meeting unanimously agreed to continue studying the amalgamation possibility, but the idea later faded as prosperity returned and it became clear that all parties could survive on their own. (Meeting minutes, SWP Papers)
61. Don Lockwood, who represented the Pool in many co-operative organizations during his twenty years as a Pool director, moved a successful 1961 resolution urging amalgamation of the three pools with UGG. Lockwood, however, said in retrospect that he did not know if amalgamation would

have brought any real advantages in view of the way the three pools showed themselves capable of co-operating closely in joint ventures. (Lockwood interview, 19 April 1982)

62. Sneath interview, 24 February 1982.
63. SWP 36th *Annual Report*, p. 27; Phillips interview, 5 April 1982.
64. McCrorie, *In Union*, p. 44. Pool newsletters to committees, however, strongly urged approval of a hog marketing board. (SWP Papers)
65. E. K. Turner, memo to A. D. McLeod, 31 December 1982, SWP Papers. Grassroots co-operation with the Farmers' Union was also recalled by Ian Traquair in an interview, 18 November 1982. Traquair remembered organizing meetings to promote an egg marketing board in the late 1950s, when he was a fieldman. Farmers' Union spokesmen would be given rides to the meetings, but occasionally Traquair felt the spokesmen were primarily interested in promoting sales of Union memberships.
66. For details of rapeseed development, see: McLeod, *Rapeseed*; Gray, "The Seed"; and SWP annual reports. The Pool's first plant manager was Alec D. Miller. He and his successors — C. A. Warren, C. S. Fisher, K. D. Sarsons — were all active in promoting rapeseed and its products. Technical problems were frequent in the early days, creating much work for chief chemist J. R. Reynolds and production manager Bruce Cameron.
67. Youngs interview, 12 February 1982. Scientists from the University of Saskatchewan, University of Alberta, federal agricultural research stations, and the Saskatoon laboratory of the National Research Council were all involved in studying the meal problem. The Pool's vegetable oil plant became a testing ground for work done by a wide variety of university and federal government scientists. Meanwhile, good progress was made in international marketing activities. The Pool helped sponsor a six-week technical mission to Europe, during which Pool officials and National Research Council scientists exchanged information with processors in nine countries. That launched a continuing series of such missions, including visits to Canada by foreign experts. Pool officials were almost always part of the outgoing missions and Pool facilities were usually on the agenda for foreign visitors to Canada. (Youngs interview, 30 December 1982)
68. Quoted in Steed, "High Tech."
69. Gibbings interview, 23 February 1982.
70. Merle Turnquist interview, 31 July 1982.
71. Phillips interview, 5 April 1982.
72. Gibbings interview, 23 February 1982. Delegate Delmar Burke was one of those opposed to building the Vancouver terminal, believing the project to be one that the government should undertake since the new terminal would probably not pay for itself. Later, however, he agreed that the Pool's initiative "turned out to be the right move." (Burke interview, 22 July 1975)
73. Turner interview, 15 January 1982.
74. Rob Sanders, quoted in Saskatoon *Star-Phoenix*, 21 August 1982.
75. T. R. Melville-Ness, letter of 12 November 1971, to J. M. Fair, SWP Papers. Melville-Ness also frequently mentioned the possibility of expansion by merging the *Producer* and the *Co-op Consumer*, publication of Federated Co-operatives Ltd. The idea, however, received little support — in his successor's view, because the Pool was reluctant to see a consumerism element injected into *Producer* editorials. (Phillips interview, 5 April 1982)
76. SWP annual meeting minutes, 10 November 1962.
77. Everett Baker, letter of 9 November 1965, to Ira Mumford, SWP Papers.
78. In 1967-68, the *Producer* tried a subsidiary publication, the monthly *Alberta*

Producer, distributed free to all Alberta farmers as an advertising vehicle and a means of promoting the *Western Producer.* But the deficit soared to $326,541 that year. In 1969, when a jump in postal rates added $2,000 to the cost of each issue of the *Western Producer,* Pool directors noted an overall loss of $290,785 on the newspaper plus growing problems with obsolescent machinery. The directors added ominously: "Your Board continues to evaluate the cost of maintaining the Western Producer against its informational value to the membership and the public."

Chapter Eight

1. Twenty-Fifth Street Theatre, *Paper Wheat,* p. 75.
2. Mumford interview, 14 January 1982.
3. Turner interview, 15 January 1982.
4. Letter and memo, SWP Papers. In a telephone interview 9 November 1982, Mumford said he could not with certainty recall the name of the "senior reliable source" mentioned in the 1970 letter.
5. M. P. Bjornson, memo of 19 January 1970, to I. K. Mumford, SWP Papers.
6. SWP, *Questions.*
7. Turner interview, 15 January 1982. (Also source for airport encounter) The first serious negotiating meeting was 1 November 1971 in the Manitoba Pool Elevators boardroom. (E. K. Turner, letter of 12 March 1973, to G. H. Sellers, SWP Papers)
8. Fair interview, 13 October 1982.
9. Turner interview, 15 January 1982.
10. Milliken interview, 17 February 1982.
11. Fair interview, 13 October 1982.
12. Mumford interview, 14 January 1982.
13. South interview, 1 August 1982.
14. Regina *Leader-Post,* 24 February 1972.
15. Argue press release, SWP Papers.
16. Manitoba *Co-operator,* 4 May 1972.
17. SWP, *Questions.*
18. SWP Papers; and Regina *Leader-Post,* 23 February 1972. An 18 February 1972 UGG memo to UGG local boards said that UGG had a chance to buy Federal some years earlier but decided to do its own renovation and new building rather than to buy "a large, but very old, elevator system." (SWP Papers) In a telephone interview 9 November 1982, Mumford said that, at the time of the negotiations with Federal, Pool officials were unaware of any such offer, but Pool officials did wonder if any other suitor was waiting in the wings, ready to step in if the Pool-Federal talks broke down.
19. Mumford interview, 14 January 1982.
20. Turner interview, 15 January 1982; Gibbings interview 23 February 1982; W. M. Miner interview 17 May 1982; W. J. O'Connor interview 22 February 1982. Gibbings personally approved strongly of the purchase, saying that "farmers had already paid for Federal Grain two or three times" in the company's profits over the years.
21. The quoted phrases are from the Regina *Leader-Post,* 26 September 1981, and the *Financial Post,* 3 October 1981, but similar terminology could be found in many news stories over the years.
22. Turner interview, 15 January 1982. By 1976, Saskatchewan Wheat Pool was 15th on *Canadian Business*'s list of corporations. (Annual meeting minutes, 16 November 1976)

23. Traquair interview, 26 April 1982.
24. W. M. Miner interview, 17 May 1982. Some Pool officials had the same sentiments. (A. D. McLeod interview, 13 October 1982) The pools in the 1950s did have a flour sales agent in Hong Kong and a London agent for sales of seeds.
25. Telephone interview, 9 November 1982.
26. Phillips interview, 5 April 1982. In other moves, an understaffed travel-agency service was chopped, and departments were held to firm budgets. Aided by a decline in other farm publications and by improved commercial printing business, the Pool's printing and publishing division recorded in 1974-75 its first positive showing in 17 years. Within the divisional total, the *Producer* itself still had a loss, but people were beginning to believe that every part of the operation could be made profitable.
27. Author's notes on annual meeting. The only delegate response to Phillips' suggestion came from one delegate who said not to be too cautious,.
28. Fairbairn, "Turner Tough."
29. Trew interview, 20 April 1982.
30. South interview, 1 August 1982.
31. Treleaven interview, 2 May 1982.
32. Turner interview, 15 January 1982.
33. Annual meeting minutes, 15 November 1974.
34. Traquair interview, 26 April 1982.
35. Jacob A. Brown, telephone interview, 2 February 1983.
36. The Pool's opposition to the Weyburn terminal did not stop Federated Co-operatives Ltd. from buying grain screenings from the terminal. Federated president G. M. Sinclair told the Pool's 1976 annual meeting, however, that Federated took all the screenings it could get from the Pool and CPS Foods Ltd.
37. Annual meeting minutes, 22 November 1974.
38. *Western Producer*, 4 April 1974.
39. Morton, *Progressive*, pp. 156-7. The Crow rate for shipping 100 pounds of grain from Regina to the Lakehead was 20 cents, but the rate charged in 1918-20 was 24 cents, rising to 32.5 cents for part of 1920, then 31 cents throughout most of 1921 and 29 cents from December 1921 to 6 July 1922. On that last date, the Crow rate was restored, to remain unchanged for more than six decades. (See Turgeon, *Report*)
40. The 1980 SWP booklet, "Keep the Crow," took pains to correct such myths even though the myths tended to support the Pool's policy of keeping the Crow rates unchanged.
41. Fowke, "Political Economy," p. 216.
42. Quoted in Wilson, *Beyond*, pp. 179, 189.
43. Turner interview, 15 January 1982.
44. Report to Alberta government in 1978 by economists M. S. Anderson and W. H. C. Hendriks, quoted in Wilson, *Beyond*, p. 183. Another study found that through higher export prices foreign consumers would pay part of the cost if rail rates were raised above Crow levels. See Nagy, "Canadian," p.30
45. Annual meeting minutes, 14 November 1978.
46. *Western Producer*, 23 November 1981.
47. The same month, Manitoba Pool Elevators delegates arrived at a much clearer and more united policy, voting 95 percent in favor of the proposition that "grain producers in Western Canada be prepared to accept some financial responsibility for the future increases in the cost of moving grain as negotiated by railroads, producers and government." (*Western Producer*, 12 November 1981)

48. Author's notes.
49. *Western Producer*, 3 December 1981.
50. *Western Producer*, 21 January 1982.
51. Jarvis, 9 March 1982 speech to the Pool's "Forum '82" in Saskatoon, text distributed at conference.
52. *Western Producer*, 11 February 1982.
53. Regina *Leader-Post*, 16 February 1982.
54. Author's notes.
55. Archer interview, 26 April 1982. Archer had considerable personal exposure to Pool matters after he married into the family of Leonard Widdup, who was an original Pool delegate as well as Pool vice-president from 1938 to 1941. Archer also played a profitable role in building up *Western Producer* circulation in the 1930s. As a schoolteacher, he entered a *Producer* puzzle contest, then found he was tied with several other contestants who would all compete in selling subscriptions for the big prize. In 10 days, he sold 434 subscriptions, travelling by horse and snowshoe, to win $1,100. (Phillips, *Out West*, pp. 20-21)
56. *Western Producer*, 6 April 1982.
57. Lockwood interview, 19 April 1982.
58. See Saskatoon *Star-Phoenix*, 3 June 1982.
59. Saskatoon *Star-Phoenix*, 3 June 1982.
60. Turner interview, 13 October 1982.

Chapter Nine

1. The thoughts and questions expressed in this chapter are the product of many interviews and informal conversations with a wide range of Pool staff and elected officials, both past and present, as well as selected outside observers. The resulting blend of ideas, however, does not necessarily match the views of any single person interviewed and is not official Pool policy.
2. Participation in such joint ventures, however, may contribute little to the Pool's image among farmers. In a January 1983 memo to Pool official A. D. McLeod, director George A. Siemens warned: "Consortiums are the 'in' thing presently, however in order to maintain our identity we will have to go more ventures alone so farmers can more readily feel a part of S.W.P."
3. J. O. Wright, memo of 6 October 1982 to SWP directors, summarizing results of a study by consultant Bonnie Laing.
4. One former Pool official believed that as early as the 1950s, Pool directors were showing signs of thinking too much alike, with not enough healthy questioning of conventional views. He felt one reason for this was simply that directors spent so much time together, meeting for at least a week every month. The official, however, also noted that unity brought certain advantages. (Private interview)
5. Council on Rural Development. *Rural Women: Their Work, Their Needs and Their Role in Rural Development* (January 1979 report), p. vii. Quoted in speech by Maureen Hunter, 9 March 1982, to the Saskatchewan Wheat Pool's Forum '82 in Saskatoon.
6. A. D. McLeod, "Comments Re: Saskatchewan Wheat Pool Future," September 1982 memo to Garry Fairbairn. Emphasizing the need for the Pool to remain innovative, McLeod also wrote: "I feel the most important challenge for Saskatchewan Wheat Pool in the decades ahead will be to predict change and adapt to it. . . . In a number of fields, the Pool has now become 'the establishment.' It has achieved the status of the largest grain handler, merchandiser of farm supplies, terminal operator, farm organiza-

tion. It is closing old elevators faster than building new ones. In many cases it is seen to be defending the status quo."

7. Glenn Peardon interview, 6 October 1982. Peardon, who then supervised the Pool's corporate planning, also said that the Pool could benefit from some form of reorganization that would distinguish between its commercial and policy roles. While recognizing the need to keep commercial operations in tune with social policy, he noted that some farmers dislike the idea that their patronage of Pool facilities indicates approval of all Pool policies. The Pool, he suggested, could partly avoid such feelings and possible loss of patronage by publicly recognizing differences of opinion within its membership and by not implying that Pool policies have the total support of all 70,000 active members. In addition, he said, the Pool could consider forming a separate board of directors to handle operational decisions. The operational board could include both elected Pool directors and several outside directors who would bring fresh viewpoints and expertise to Pool operations. Such a structure would distinguish between operations and policy, perhaps lessening criticism from those farmers who feel there is a conflict of interest in any board that combines both functions. The workload for the existing board would be eased, allowing elected directors to concentrate more on policy issues and member relations, but the elected board, would retain supreme authority. (Peardon left the Pool in late 1982 without having won any widespread support within the Pool for his proposals, which are noted here as an example of the kind of fundamental questioning that can help an organization maintain an effective internal structure.)

8. The study involved both Pool and *Western Producer* personnel, since the Producer would presumably play a large role in news and information input into any such system. Despite a favorable verdict from the study, top Pool officials decided in 1982 to set the plan aside indefinitely, since they felt not enough money was available that year. Pool planner Glenn Peardon predicted that the proposal could one day be revived when conditions change, adding that if some other organization launches such a system in the meantime, the Pool could still provide news and information over the other organization's system. (Peardon interview, 6 October 1982; and various conversations with *Producer* managing editor C. B. Fairbairn, another participant in the study)

9. R. H. D. Phillips interview, 5 April 1982. Phillips emphasized the amount of executive energy that has to be spent monitoring joint ventures in which the Pool is a minority partner.

10. Saskatchewan Wheat Pool, of course, will have the benefit of other organizations' work. Alberta Wheat Pool, for example, has put extensive work into testing the unconventional Buffalo Sloped Bin Elevator. Techological change could produce much more exotic developments in coming decades — in a 16 January 1983 letter to E. K. Turner, former director Merle Sproule noted the theoretical possibility of moving grain in capsules through pipelines or by modern dirigibles. For the nearer-term future, Sproule suggested consideration of mobile grain-handling facilities. He also forecast a continuing trend to larger farms with more specialized machinery, opening the way for a possible new role for the pools and Co-op Implements in renting such machinery to farmers.

11. J. K. MacDonald, letter of 28 September 1982, to Garry Fairbairn. MacDonald, general manager of the Pool's terminal elevator division, noted that the receiving and shipping capabilities of modern terminals exceed their grain-cleaning capability. He also identified a need to continue improving efficiency and throughput by automation.

12. Foreword by E. K. Turner to 50th anniversary booklet, 1974.
13. Pool director Raymond W. Luterbach, January 1983 memo to A. D. McLeod. In a similar memo, director Clifford E. Murch expressed hope that Saskatchewan Wheat Pool would be much more heavily involved, in co-operation with federal agriculture research stations, in extension work to train farmers in better production and soil conservation practices.
14. W. J. O'Connor interview, 22 February 1982.
15. Maureen Hunter, speech of 9 March 1982 to Forum '82 in Saskatoon, text distributed at conference. The Pool board, however, turned down a staff suggestion that the organization should be developing new land-tenure policies and looking at the possibility that lease arrangements would enable more young farmers to get into the business. (Private interview)
16. J. O. Wright, speech of 10 March 1982 to Forum '82 in Saskatoon, text distributed at conference. Wright's questions were general, not related to the specific examples mentioned in this chapter.

List of Abbreviations

CCWP — Canadian Co-operative Wheat Producers Ltd., the company jointly owned by the three prairie pools.

CFA — Canadian Federation of Agriculture.

CSA — Central Selling Agency, informal name for CCWP from 1924 to 1931.

FUC — Farmers' Union of Canada; amalgamated with SGGA to form UFC.

NFU — National Farmers' Union.

SAB — Saskatchewan Archives Board, offices Regina and Saskatoon.

SFA — Saskatchewan Federation of Agriculture, one of the provincial bodies that make up the CFA.

SFU — Saskatchewan Farmers' Union; became part of the NFU.

SGGA — Saskatchewan Grain Growers' Association; amalgamated with FUC to form UFC.

SWP — Saskatchewan Wheat Pool, including periods when the Pool was formally called Saskatchewan Co-operative Wheat Producers Ltd. and Saskatchewan Co-operative Producers Ltd.

UFC — United Farmers of Canada (Saskatchewan Section) Ltd.; became SFU.

UGG — United Grain Growers Ltd., a prairie-wide co-operative.

WAC — Western Agricultural Conference, an annual joint meeting of representatives from the three prairie federations of agriculture; UGG had direct membership in WAC.

Bibliography

General Note: The following bibliography of works consulted in the preparation of this book is presented in the hope that it will not only be of some use to students of farm organizations, but also serve to guide general readers into some of the many topics that overlap Pool history. Unfortunately, a list of works focussing specifically on Saskatchewan Wheat Pool would be short. Among books there is only Samuel Yates' *The Saskatchewan Wheat Pool*, a good account of the early years, but one that is out of print and increasingly obsolete. Among theses there are: John Craig's "Co-operative Democracy"; Roger Gray's look at Pool committees; and Sylvia Robinson's perceptive study of "The Changing Role of the Field Man." Despite the Pool's six decades of being an important force in Saskatchewan society, it seems in some senses as though the historical community rates the Pool as a topic only slightly more worth of interest than the brief Saskatchewan flowering of the Ku Klux Klan. The gap is partially filled, however, by some general works that include substantial references to Saskatchewan Wheat Pool, including Hugh Boyd's *New Breaking* and Walter Davisson's *Pooling Wheat in Canada*. Leonard Nesbitt's history of Alberta Wheat Pool and F. W. Hamilton's history of Manitoba Pool Elevators provide comprehensive views of neighboring pools.

One major exception to the comparative lack of material on Saskatchewan Wheat Pool is *The Diary of Alexander James McPhail*, edited by Professor Harold Innis and published in 1940. Its wealth of detail does much for the historian, while the Pool president's frank — sometimes brutal — characterizations of his colleagues bring the era to life for general readers. But, even with all that material available on McPhail, Innis still wrote in his conclusion: "It will not be possible to appraise the work of McPhail until we have had biographies of such men as Brouillette and Robertson in the Saskatchewan organization, of Wood, Brownlee and McFarland in Alberta, and of Burnell and Bredt in Manitoba." After more than forty years, students of the pools' history are still waiting for those biographies. Henry Wise Wood has been the subject of a biography, but most of the others are becoming forgotten names, their papers lost and their associates dead.

Thankfully, many primary historical sources still survive. (See below for notes on Saskatchewan Wheat Pool files.) Papers of the Farmers' Union of Canada, Saskatchewan Grain Growers' Association, United Farmers of Canada (Saskatchewan Section) and certain individuals have been preserved by the Saskatchewan Archives Board. The Board has also collected taped interviews with farm activists, including a notable 1975-76 oral history project conducted by John Turner and dealing specifically with Pool development. One primary source that may not have survived is the set of McPhail's original handwritten diaries. After his 1931 death, they were used by his widow in preparing a typed, edited version of the diaries, with some entries deleted and some names replaced by blanks. After Mrs. McPhail died in 1936, the diaries apparently went with their only son to his new foster home with McPhail's sister in Winnipeg, and were lent for a time to professor Innis. The original diaries, however, are not with Innis's "McPhail Papers" in Toronto and their current location is unknown to either McPhail's son or McPhail's Saskatchewan relatives. Officials of the Saskatchewan and Manitoba pools have not found them in their files.

I. Saskatchewan Wheat Pool Papers

Throughout the footnotes of this book, there occurs an innocent-sounding phrase — "SWP Papers" — that conceals one of the most chaotic masses of historical documents in Saskatchewan. In the case of Alberta Wheat Pool papers, for example, footnotes can direct future researchers to such specific places as "box 45, file 503" among the neat files of Calgary's Glenbow-Alberta Institute, which has organized the papers. If similar precise footnotes were attempted in this book, they would at times read something like: "loose papers, about halfway down the second-from-the-left heap on the third-from-the-bottom shelf beside the green filing cabinet in the library's basement storage room." The footnote, of course, would be obsolete as soon as the heap was moved to make room for more documents. The lack of elaborate organization and indexing is, of course, no reflection on Pool personnel. They have full-time duties connected with current business, and it would take a team of trained archivists considerable time to organize the old records. Historians can only wait for the records to be transferred to the Saskatchewan Archives Board, and speculate on what documents remain to be discovered — perhaps even the McPhail diaries may turn up at the bottom of a box of yellowing grain tickets.

A more serious problem is the loss, or at least misplacement, of key documents over the years. With the awesome masses of paper that have flowed into and out of Pool headquarters over the decades — millions of pieces of paper annually — it is perhaps surprising that losses have not been more serious as a result of inevitable housecleaning. But there are some significant missing items. Searches have failed to turn up official copies of the 1923-24 provisional board's minutes. A set of 1939-40 monthly reports of the country organization department was available for a researcher to consult in the mid-1950s, but is no longer. Exchanges of correspondence in old files often start and end abruptly in the middle of a continuing subject, leaving the beginning and ending unclear. Perhaps the greatest tragedy is the loss of the voluminous records of George Robertson, Pool secretary from 1924 to 1958, a perceptive and knowledgeable participant in every aspect of farm policy during that period. Before retiring, Robertson disposed of virtually all his files, leaving comparatively few file drawers of selected clippings and other material. Presumed gone in that cleanout were his personal diaries, documents that could have far overshadowed McPhail's diaries in historical value.

Even with such losses, the Saskatchewan Wheat Pool records remain rich in historical material, containing enough to support a multi-volume academic study. Because of the Pool's broad policy role, its concern with social issues and its duty to inform members, such basic documents as the annual reports have more historical substance than usual. In addition to detailed descriptions of Pool activities, they provide contemporary accounts of the state of agriculture, the evolution of government programs and the goals of farm organizations. Minutes of delegate meetings contain the results of debate on social issues, and the official set of minutes frequently includes transcripts and texts of remarks by visiting dignitaries. The monthly reports of the country organization department — now called member relations — feature extensive quotations from the day-to-day reports of fieldmen, describing rural activities and opinions. Among the remnants of the Pool's mail-service library are scores of rare booklets and pamphlets. For new Pool personalities and occasional internal debates, there are back copies of staff publications, the *Co-optimist* and its successor, *Sweet Pea.* (Named after the SWP Employees' Association, SWPEA) At the time of writing, Saskatchewan Wheat Pool was also sponsoring verbatim transcripts of all the interviews conducted by the author for this book. The transcripts were intended for deposit in the Saskatchewan Archives, Regina office. And, in addition to all the memoes and letters to or from headquarters personnel, there are varied batches of material sent in from country committees and individual members — everything from a local committee's minutes to souvenir examples of anti-pool propaganda. When organized in public archives, the SWP Papers will undoubtedly make substantial contributions to a wide range of Saskatchewan histories, in the same way the Pool itself had an impact on so many aspects of Saskatchewan society.

II. Document Collections

Alberta Wheat Pool. Papers. Glenbow-Alberta Institute, Calgary.

Baker, Everett. Papers. Saskatchewan Archives Board (SAB) Regina. Rich material on Baker's long service in the Pool field staff and co-op organizations.

Canadian Federation of Agriculture. Papers. Public Archives of Canada, Ottawa; and CFA library, Ottawa.

Dunning, Charles Avery. Papers. SAB Saskatoon. Saskatchewan premier when the Pool was created.

Edwards, George F. Papers. SAB Saskatoon. UFC leader.

Eliason, Frank. Papers. SAB Saskatoon. UFC official.

Farmers' Union of Canada. Papers. SAB Saskatoon.

Innis, Harold A. Papers. Thomas Fisher Rare Book Library, University of Toronto. Filed under the title "McPhail Papers." Includes correspondence and source material for Innis' edition of the McPhail diaries.

Johnson, Gilbert. Papers. SAB Saskatoon. An early Farmers' Union member and Pool elevator agent.

Keen, George. Papers. Public Archives of Canada, Ottawa. Long-time secretary of the Co-operative Union of Canada.

McNamee, Louis P. Papers. SAB Saskatoon. Farmers' Union leader.

McNaughton, Violet Clara. Papers. SAB Saskatoon. An extremely rich collection of correspondence and farm movement documents, 1900 to 1964. Includes typed versions of McPhail's diary (see bibliography, section IV) and many of McPhail's letters.

Ralston, James Layton. Papers. Public Archives of Canada, Ottawa. Volume 103 includes correspondence with Saskatchewan Wheat Pool on the 1936-37 royal grain commission.

Saskatchewan Grain Growers' Association. Papers. SAB Saskatoon.

Schwarz, N. H. Papers. SAB Saskatoon. An early Farmers' Union official.

United Farmers of Canada. (Saskatchewan Section) Ltd. Papers. SAB Saskatoon.

Williams, George Hara. Papers. SAB Saskatoon. An early UFC leader.

III. Interviews

Alexander, Hugh Thomas James. (SWP-CCF activist) Interview with John Turner, 22 July 1975, transcript A-980, SAB Regina.

Anderson, George. (SWP committeeman) Interview with John Turner, 18 July 1975, tape A-1237, SAB Regina.

Archer, John. (historian) Interview with Garry Fairbairn, Regina, 26 April 1982.

Arnason, Rosmundur. (farmer) Interview with John Turner, 11 July 1975 transcript A-981, SAB Regina.

Baker, Everett. (SWP fieldman) Interview with Ivan McDonald, undated transcript courtesy Ivan McDonald. And interview with Lorna Moen and Connie Stus, 1975, Saskatchewan Co-operative Youth Program, Co-op Pioneer Tape Library, Co-operative College of Canada.

Ball, Wes J. (SWP management and director) Interview with John Turner, 16 June 16 1975, tape A-910, SAB Regina.

Bickle, Ian. (SWP management) Interview with Garry Fairbairn, Regina, 14 October 1982.

Bobier, T. G. (SWP director) Interview with Garry Fairbairn, Moose Jaw, 19 February 1982.

Brownlee, John E. (premier) Interview with Una MacLean, 28 March to 12 May 1961, transcripts D-920.Ml63G, Glenbow-Alberta Institute, Calgary.

Burke, Delmar. (SWP delegate) Interview with Connie Stus and Barry Hanson, 22 July 1975, Saskatchewan Co-operative Youth Program, Co-op Pioneer Tape Library, Co-operative College of Canada.

Burgess, Warden. (SWP director, MLA) Interviews with John Turner, 27 and 30 June 1975, tapes A-982 and A-983, SAB Regina.

Carlson, Gary. (SFA offical) Interview with Garry Fairbairn, Regina, 26 April 1982.

Cook, John T. (SWP delegate) Interview with John Turner, 28 July 1976, tapes A-1012 and A-1013, SAB Regina.

Durham, Phillip E. (SWP committeeman) Interview with John Turner, 15 July 1975, tape A-1232, SAB Regina.

Fair, J. Milton. (SWP management) Interview with Garry Fairbairn, Regina, 13 October 1982.

Feeley, Myron H. (SWP delegate, MLA) Interview with John Turner, 20 June 1975, tapes A-1220 and 1221, SAB Regina.

Ferraton, Reg. (SWP delegate) Interview with Connie Stus and James Sarauer, 12 August 1975, Saskatchewan Co-operative Youth Program, Co-op Pioneer Tape Library, Co-operative College of Canada.

Ford, Harry. (SWP delegate) Interview with A. N. Nicholson, 4 August 1974, transcript C-100, SAB Saskatoon.

Ford, Harry. (SWP delegate) Interview with Connie Stus and James Sarauer, 1975, Saskatchewan Co-operative Youth Program, Co-op Pioneer Tape Library, Co-operative College of Canada.

Fox, John. (SWP director) Interview with John Turner, 17 September 1976, tape A-1216, SAB Regina.

Gibbings, Charles W. (SWP president) Interview with Garry Fairbairn, Winnipeg, 23 February 1982.

Gibson, Allan. (AWP official) Interview with Garry Fairbairn, Calgary, 30 April 1982.

Gilliland, Alexander. (SWP fieldman) Interview, 1975, Saskatchewan Co-operative Youth Program, Co-op Pioneer Tape Library, Co-operative College of Canada.

Gleave, Alf. (SFU leader, MP) Interview with Garry Fairbairn, Ottawa, 13 May 1982.

Hall, Emmett. (Royal commission head) Interview with Garry Fairbairn, Saskatoon, 16 April 1982.

Hamilton, Fred. (MPE official) Interview with Garry Fairbairn, Winnipeg, 23 February 1982.

Hart, Elsie. (farm leader, Brouillette neighbor) Interview with Garry Fairbairn, Saskatoon, 8 November 1982.

Horner, W. H. (Sask. deputy minister) Interview with Garry Fairbairn, Regina, 16 February 1982.

Hornford, Helgi. (SWP committeeman) Interview with John Turner, 10 July 1975, tape A-985, SAB Regina

Howe, Peter Anton. (SWP delegate, MLA) Interview with A. M. Nicholson, 7 July 1971, transcript C-74, SAB Saskatoon. Interview with John Turner, 14 July 1975, tape A-986, SAB Regina.

Irwin, George. (Federated Co-ops president) Interview with A. M. Nicholson, January 8-10, 1966; and D. H. Bocking, 12 January 1966, transcript C-26, SAB Saskatoon.

Jefferson, Tom. (SWP staff) Interview with Garry Fairbairn, Winnipeg, 25 February 1982.

Johnson, Gilbert. (SWP agent) Interview with D'Arcy Houde, 13 March 1976, transcipt C-105, SAB Saskatoon.

Kendel, Adolf. (SWP committeeman) Interview with John Turner, 5 June 1975, transcript A-922, SAB Regina.

Kirk, David. (CFA-SWP staff) Interviews with Garry Fairbairn, Ottawa, 12 and 15 May 1982; 12 January 1983.

Leach, Cliff. (SWP staff) Interview by Garry Fairbairn, Winnipeg, 22 February 1982.

Leask, Charles. (SWP management) Interview by Garry Fairbairn, Regina, 3 December 1982.

Leask. John. (federal livestock director) Interview with Garry Fairbairn, Saskatoon, 27 July 1982.

Lee, Bert. (SWP fieldman) Interview with Garry Fairbairn, Saskatoon, 31 March 1982.

Lockwood, Don. (SWP director) Interview with Garry Fairbairn, Regina, 19 April 1982.

McCallum, James. (SWP director) Interview with Garry Fairbairn, Swift Current, 11 April 1982. Interview with John Turner, 18 July 1975, tape and partial transcript A-1014 and 1015, SAB Regina.

McDonald, Ivan. (SWP fieldman) Interview with Garry Fairbairn, Saskatoon, 8 February 1982.

McLeod, Allan D. (SWP management) Interviews with Garry Fairbairn, Regina, 13 October and 19 November 1982; and numerous informal consultations.

MacLeod, Wilf. (SWP fieldman) Interview with Garry Fairbairn, Saskatoon, 31 March 1982.

McPhail, Hugh D. (SWP fieldman, McPhail nephew) Interview with Garry Fairbairn, North Battleford, 14 July 1982.

Macpherson, A. J. (AWP president) Interview with Garry Fairbairn, Calgary, 30 April 1982.

Malm, Nels. (AWP director) Interview with Garry Fairbairn, Calgary, 30 April 1982.

Marsh, Harry. (SWP director) Interview with Arthur Ross and Douglas Bocking, 20 November 1975, transcript C-101, SAB Saskatoon.

Martin, John. (SWP committeeman) Interview with John Turner, 4 July 1975 tape A-987, SAB Regina.

Melvin, Breen (Co-op Union official) Interview with Garry Fairbairn, Regina, 18 February 1982.

Milliken, R. A. (SWP lawyer) Interview with Garry Fairbairn, Regina, 17 February 1982.

Miner, William M. (federal grains official) Interview with Garry Fairbairn, Ottawa, 17 May 1982.

Mumford, Ira K. (SWP managment) Interview with Garry Fairbairn, Regina, 14 January 1982; and by telephone 9 November 1982.

Newby, Margaret R. (daughter of George Robertson) Interview with Garry Fairbairn, Calgary, 1 May 1982.

Nyhus, Ted. (SWP fieldman) Interview with Garry Fairbairn, Moose Jaw, 19 February 1982.

O'Connor, W. John. (Grain Commission director) Interview with Garry Fairbairn, Winnipeg, 22 February 1982.

Olson, Oliver. (SWP fieldman) Interview with Ivan McDonald, undated transcript courtesy Ivan McDonald.

Parker, Kathleen. (daughter of Jack Wesson) Interview with Garry Fairbairn, Winnipeg, 24 February 1982.

Parker, Wilson. (SWP fieldman) Interview with Ivan McDonald, undated transcript courtesy Ivan McDonald.

Peardon, Glenn. (SWP executive) Interview with Garry Fairbairn, Regina, 6 October 1982.

Phelps, Joseph L. (SFU leader, MLA) Interview with L. W. Rodwell, 1 December 1970, transcript C-57, SAB Saskatoon.

Phillips, Robert H.D. (*Producer* editor) Interview with Garry Fairbairn, Saskatoon, 5 April 1982.

Pike, Christine. (niece of Jack Wesson) Interview with Garry Fairbairn, Waseca, 14 July 1982.

Pike, Winifred. (sister of Jack Wesson) Interview with Garry Fairbairn, Waseca, 14 July 1982.

Pollon, Albert E. "Dick" (SWP committeeman) Interview with John Turner, 3 September 1976, transcript A-1016, SAB Regina.

Prince, Leo. (farmer) Interview with John Turner, 5 June 1975, transcript A-924, SAB Regina.

Richardson, Jack T. (SWP delegate) Interview with Garry Fairbairn, Lloydminster, 14 July 1982.

Robertson, R. W. W. (brother of George Robertson) Interview with Garry Fairbairn, Richmond Hill, 14 May 1982.

Ross, William McKenzie. (SWP director) Interview with Garry Fairbairn, Lac Vert, 31 July 1982.

Schweitzer, Frank. (SWP delegate) Interview with Garry Fairbairn, Regina, 30 July 1982.

Sharp, Mitchell. (trade minister) Interview with Garry Fairbairn, Ottawa, 11 May 1982.

Sinclair, Don. (SWP fieldman, management) Interview with Garry Fairbairn, Regina, 19 April 1982.

Smith, Harry. (SWP staff) Interview with Garry Fairbairn, Winnipeg, 25 February 1982.

Sneath, Harold. (MPE president) Interview with Garry Fairbairn, Winnipeg, 24 February 1982.

South, Gordon. (SWP director) Interview with Garry Fairbairn, Melfort, 1 August 1982.

Sproule, Ron. (SWP management, son of A. F. Sproule) Interview with Garry Fairbairn, Winnipeg, 22 February 1982.

Steele, Kenneth. (son of McPhail) Interview with Garry Fairbairn, Ottawa, 12 May 1982.

Stratychuk, John. (SWP fieldman) Interview, 1975, Saskatchewan Co-operative Youth Program, Co-op Pioneer Tape Library, Co-operative College of Canada.

Thies, Paul E. and Helen J. (farmers) Interview with John Turner, 4 June 1975, transcript A-785, SAB Regina.

Toupin, J. Abel. (SWP fieldman) Interview with Garry Fairbairn, Regina, 16 February 1982. Interview with Ivan McDonald, undated transcript courtesy Ivan McDonald.

Traquair, Ian. (SWP fieldman, management) Interviews with Garry Fairbairn, Regina, 26 April and 15 October 1982.

Treleaven, D. H. (wheat board) Interview with Garry Fairbairn, Edmonton, 2 May 1982.

Trew, John. (SWP management) Interview with Garry Fairbairn, Regina, 20 April 1982.

Turner, Edward K. (SWP president) Interviews with Garry Fairbairn, Regina, 15 January and 13 October 1982.

Turner, George S. (MPE management) Telephone interview with Garry Fairbairn, Ottawa, 12 May 1982.

Turnquist, Merle. (SWP committeeman) Interview with Garry Fairbairn, Tisdale, 31 July 1982.

Turnquist, Milton. (SWP delegate) Interview with Garry Fairbairn, Tisdale, 31 July 1982.

Waldron, A. Patrick. (*Producer* editor) Interviews with Keith Dryden, 1975-76, transcripts courtesy Keith Dryden.

Wilson, Charles F. (federal grains official, historian) Interview with Garry Fairbairn, Ottawa, 17 May 1982.

Wotherspoon, David L. (SWP delegate) Interview with John Turner, 30 May 1975, tape A-926, SAB Regina.

Wright, James O. (SWP delegate, management) Interview with Garry Fairbairn, Regina, 15 January 1982.

Youngs, Clare. (scientist) Interviews with Garry Fairbairn, Saskatoon, 12 February and 30 December 1982.

IV. Other Sources

"Aaron Sapiro and the Farmers." *Co-operation*, vol. 9, no. 9, September 1923, p. 146.

Aikin, J. Alexander. "The Western Provinces in 1923." *Canadian Annual Review 1923*, pp. 676-750.

Anderson, Duncan Tracy. "The Cultivation of Wheat." In Kenneth F. Nielsen (ed.), *Proceedings of the Canadian Centennial Wheat Symposium.* Saskatoon: Modern Press, 1967, pp. 338-355.

Anderson, Frederick Woodley. "Farmers in Politics 1915-1935: Some Political Aspects of the Grain Growers' Movement, 1915-1935, with Particular Reference to Saskatchewan." Master's thesis, University of Saskatchewan, 1949.

Anderson, Walton J. *Canadian Wheat in Relation to the World's Food Production and Distribution.* Saskatoon: Modern Press, 1964. Sponsored by the three pools.

Archer, John H. "An Early Co-operative: The Saskatchewan Purchasing Company." *Saskatchewan History*, vol. 5, Spring 1953, pp. 55-56.

Archer, John H. *Saskatchewan, a history.* Saskatoon: Western Producer Prairie Books, 1980.

Bailey, Mrs. A. W. "The Year We Moved." in D. H. Bocking (ed.), *Pages from the Past* Saskatoon: Western Producer Prairie Books, 1979, pp. 225-238. Reprinted from *Saskatchewan History*, vol. 20, Winter 1967, pp. 19-31. Depression experiences.

Baker, Everett. "In Memory of J. H. Wesson." *Sweet Pea*, December 1965, pp. 2-3.

Beamish, Dick. "Divided We Stand." *Family Herald*, 15 March 1962, pp. 6-7. On CFA-NFU disagreements.

Beaverbrook, William Maxwell Aitken, baron. *Friends: sixty years of intimate personal relations with Richard Bedford Bennett.* Toronto: Heineman, 1959.

Bocking, D. H. (ed.) *Saskatchewan: a Pictorial History.* Saskatoon: Saskatchewan Archives Board and Western Producer Prairie Books, 1979.

Booth, J. F. *Cooperative Marketing of Grain in Western Canada.* United States Department of Agriculture technical bulletin no. 63, 1928.

Bost, Mary Lou. "A Resume of the Louis Brouillette Family." eight pages, courtesy Mrs. Bost (daughter of Brouillette.

Bothwell, Robert; and Kilbourn, William. *C. D. Howe: A Biography.* Toronto: McClelland and Stewart, 1979.

Boyd, Hugh. *New Breaking: An Outline of Co-operation Among the Farmers of Western Canada.* Toronto: J. M. Dent and Sons (Canada) Ltd., 1938. Sponsored by Saskatchewan Wheat Pool.

Boyle, James Ernest. *Marketing Canada's Wheat.* Winnipeg: Winnipeg Grain Exchange, 1929.

Bracken, John. *Report of the Commission of Inquiry into the Distribution of Railway Box Cars.* Ottawa: Queen's Printer, 1958.

Breckon, S. S. "The Saskatchewan Co-operative Elevator Co. Ltd ... " Fourth Year thesis, Ontario Agricultural College, 1923.

Bredt, Paul F. "The Canadian Wheat Pools: Historical Review." In *Submissions by Wheat Pool Organizations of Western Canada to Royal Grain Inquiry Commission at Calgary and Regina April-May 1937.* Winnipeg(?): Canadian Co-operative Wheat Producers(?), 1937(?), pp. 5-30. Thorough, detailed review with many statistics as well as explanations of Central Selling Agency policies.

Brennan, James William George. "C. A. Dunning and the Challenge of the Progressives, 1922-1925.". In D. H. Bocking (ed.) *Pages from the Past* Saskatoon: Western Producer Prairie Books, 1979, pp. 197-209. Reprinted from *Saskatchewan History*, vol. 22, Winter 1969.

Brennan, James William George. "A Political History of Saskatchewan 1905-1929." Ph.D. thesis, University of Alberta, 1976.

Brennan, James William George. "Public Career of Charles A. Dunning in Saskatchewan." Master's thesis, University of Saskatchewan, Regina 1968.

Britnell, George E.; and Fowke, Vernon C. *Canadian Agriculture in War and Peace.* Stanford: Stanford University Press, 1962.

Britnell, George E.; and Fowke, Vernon C. "Development of Wheat Marketing Policy of Canada." *Journal of Farm Economics*, vol. 31, no. 4, November 1949, pp. 627-642.

Britnell, George E. *The Wheat Economy.* Toronto: University of Toronto Press, 1939.

Broadfoot, Barry. *Ten Lost Years: 1929-1937.* Toronto: Doubleday Canada Ltd., 1973.

Bromberger, Norman. *Conflict and Co-operation.* Regina?: Saskatchewan Co-operative Credit Society, 1973?.

Brown, Lorne A. "Unemployment Relief Camps in Saskatchewan, 1933-36." *Saskatchewan History*, vol. 23, Autumn 1970, pp. 81-104.

Cadbury, George. "Planning in Saskatchewan." In Laurier LaPierre (ed.) *Essays on the Left: Essays in Honour of T.C. Douglas* (Toronto: McClelland and Stewart, 1971), pp. 51-64.

Calderwood, William. "The Decline of the Progressive Party in Saskatchewan, 1925-1930." *Saskatchewan History*, vol. 21, Autumn 1968, pp. 81-99.

Calderwood, William. "Pulpit, Press and Political Reactions to the Ku Klux Klan in Saskatchewan." In S. M. Trofimenkoff (ed.) *The Twenties in Western Canada: Papers of the Western Canada Studies Conference* Ottawa: National Museum of Man, 1972, pp. 191-219.

Cameron, Alexander Russell. *Crises in Wheat 1926-1954*. Regina: Saskatchewan Wheat Pool, 1954. Booklet reprinting series of *Western Producer* articles, March-April 1954.

Canadian Co-operative Wheat Producers. *The Canadian Wheat Pools on the Air: A Series of Radio Messages*. Booklet, January 1935.

Canadian Co-operative Wheat Producers. *The Canadian Wheat Pool Year Book 1930*. (No publication information)

Canadian Co-operative Wheat Producers. *The Wheat Pools in Relation to Rural Community Life in Western Canada*. Winnipeg: The Canadian Wheat Pools, 1935.

Canadian Co-operative Wheat Producers. *Wheat Prices 1927-28: The Pool and the Grain Trade*. Booklet, October 1928.

Carlson, Gary C. *Farm Voices: A Brief History and Reference Guide of Prairie Farm Organizations and their Leaders 1870 to 1980*. Regina: Saskatchewan Federation of Agriculture, 1981. Booklet.

Cartwright, G. S. "Wheat Pool's Policies and the Depression." *Farmer's Sun*, 27 October 1932.

Christensen, Chris L. *Farmers' Cooperative Associations in the United States, 1929*. U.S. Department of Agriculture circular no. 94, August 1929.

Church, G. C. "Farm Organizations on the Prairies: Co-operatives." In University of Regina, *Development of Agriculture on the Prairies: Proceedings of Seminar* Regina: University of Regina, 1975, pp. 43-49.

Clancey, Brian. "The Awesome Clout of the Co-ops." *Canadian Business*, January 1979, pp. 27-31, 61-63.

Clements, Muriel. *By Their Bootstraps: A History of the Credit Union Movement in Saskatchewan*. Toronto: Clarke, Irwin & Co. Ltd., 1965.

Colquette, R. D. *The First Fifty Years: A History of United Grain Growers Ltd.* Winnipeg: The Public Press Ltd., 1957.

Courville, L. D. "The Saskatchewan Progressives." Master's Thesis, University of Saskatchewan, Regina 1971.

Craig, John G. "Co-operative Democracy: a Case Study of the Saskatchewan Wheat Pool." Master's thesis, University of Washington, 1969.

Craig, J. G. *Multinational Co-operatives: An Alternative for World Development*. Saskatoon: Western Producer Prairie Books, 1976.

Crowell, Merle. "Nothing Could Keep This Boy Down." *American Magazine*, vol. 95, no. 4, April 1923. Excellent insights into Sapiro's early life.

Cunningham, David Alexander. "The Biography of the Cunningham Family 1825 to 1972." Manuscript, SAB Saskatoon, file A-169.

Darling, Howard. *The Politics of Freight Rates: The Railway Freight Rate Issue in Canada*. Toronto: McClelland and Stewart, for Canadian Institute of Guided Ground Transport, 1980.

Davidson, C. B.; and Grindley, T. W. "The Canadian Wheat Board, 1939-46." In *The Canada Year Book 1947* Ottawa: King's Printer, 1947.

Davisson, Walter P. *Pooling Wheat In Canada*. Ottawa: The Graphic Publishers Ltd., 1927.

Dawson, Helen Jones. "An Interest Group: the Canadian Federation of Agriculture." *Canadian Public Administration*, vol. 3, no. 2, June 1960, pp. 134-149.

Day, Bill. "Fifty Years Ago." *Western Producer*, 13 December 1973, p.30. An Open Forum poem.

Digby, Margaret. *Agricultural Co-operation in the Commonwealth*. Oxford: Basil Blackwell, 1951.

Downey, R. K.; and Klassen, A. J.; and McAnsh, J. *Rapeseed: Canada's 'Cinderella' Crop*. Rapeseed Association of Canada, third edition, 1974. Booklet.

"Dr. G. W. Robertson." *Sweet Pea*, vol. 32, no. 1, January 1959, pp. 6-7. (Magazine of SWP Employees' Association, 1959 editor G. A. Mills)

Dryden, Keith. "Mrs. Mac." *Western Producer* magazine, 22 October 1981.

Dryden, Keith. "The Sintaluta Trial." *Western Producer* magazine, 8-15-22 June 1961.

Dryden, Keith. *The Western Producer's First Half Century*. Saskatoon: Modern Press, 1973. Reprinted from 50th Anniversary edition, 23 August 1973.

Duke, Dorothy Mary. "Agricultural periodicals Published in Canada, 1836-1960." M.L.A. thesis, McGill University, 1961.

Eager, Evelyn Lucille. "The Conservatism of the Saskatchewan Electorate." In Norman Ward and Duff Spafford (eds.) *Politics in Saskatchewan* Don Mills, Ont.: Longmans Canada Ltd., 1968, pp. 1-19.

Eager, Evelyn. *Saskatchewan Government: Politics and Pragmatism*. Saskatoon: Western Producer Prairie Books, 1980.

Eagle, Jeanne. "Saskatchewan Wheat Pool." Harvard Business School case study 4-582-050, 1981, revised June 1982.

Edwards, George F. "The Progressive Party — Its Origin in Saskatchewan." Typed recollections, Edwards Papers file 35.

Edwards, George F. "Reminiscences." Transcript of dictated tape, Edwards Papers file 35.

Edwards, George F. "Some Recollections of Mrs. Violet McNaughton and Myself." Typed recollections, Edwards Papers file 35.

Edwards, George F. "Some Reflections on the Saskatchewan Grain Growers' Association & the Farmers' Union prior to and following Amalgamation." Recollections, Edward Papers File 35.

Eliason, Frank. "Biography of a Swedish Emmigrant." Manuscript, SAB Saskatoon file A-90.3(2.

Eliason, Frank. "Memorandum explaining relationship as between the Western Producer and the United Farmers of Canada." Handwritten, UFC Papers file B-2 IX.252.

Equitable Income Tax Foundation. *A Pictorial Study of Canada's Three Billion Dollar Co-operative — Income Tax-Favored — Colossus*. Toronto: Foundation(?), 1964.

Evans, W. Sanford. "Canadian Wheat Stabilization Operations, 1929-1935." *Wheat Studies*, vol. 12, no. 7, March 1936, pp. 249-271.

Fairbairn, Clarence B. "Turner Tough Behind Facade." *Western Producer* magazine, 20 November 1980.

Fay. C. R. "Agricultural Cooperation in the Canadian West." *Annals of the American Academy of Political and Social Science*, May 1923.

Fetherling, Doug. *Gold Diggers of 1929: Canada and the Great Stock Market Crash*. Toronto: Macmillan of Canada, 1979.

Filley, H. Clyde. *Cooperation in Agriculture*. New York: John Wiley and Sons Inc., 1929.

Findlay, R. C. "Notes Re: Late Mr. A. J. McPhail." Memo prepared for H.A. Innis, 1936. Innis Papers.

Finlayson, Roderick. *Life With R.B.: That Man Bennett.* Unpublished manuscript, edited by J. R. K. Wilbur. Public Archives of Canada file MG3OE143.

Fowke, Vernon C. *The National Policy and the Wheat Economy.* Toronto: University of Toronto Press, 1957.

Fowke, Vernon C. "Political Economy and the Canadian Wheat Grower." In Norman Ward and Duff Spafford (eds.) *Politics in Saskatchewan* (Don Mills, Ont.: Longmans Canada Ltd., 1968), pp. 207-220.

Francis, W. B. *Canadian Co-operative Law.* Toronto: The Carswell Co. Ltd., 1959.

Gagan, David P. (ed.) *Prairie Perspectives: Papers of the Western Canadian Studies Conference.* Toronto: Holt, Rinehart & Winston of Canada Ltd., 1970.

Galbraith, John Kenneth. *American Capitalism: the Concept of Countervailing Power.* Cambridge: the Riverside Press, 1952. See pages 166-7 (160-1 of 1956 edition) for a judgment on Sapiro.

Gampell, Sydney S. *Canada and Her Wheat Pool.* Winnipeg: Dawson Richardson Publications, 1930)Text of lengthy lecture at City of London College, 22 October 1930, also reprinted in *Grain Trade News.* Perhaps the most comprehensive and credible of the attacks on pooling.

Gardiner, J. G. "A History of the Wheat Position." Cabinet Document 44-51, 11 October 1950, reproduced in C. F. Wilson, *A Century of Canadian Grain: Government Policy to 1951* Saskatoon: Western Producer Prairie Books, 1978), appendix 6. A useful summary of the British wheat agreement and its shorcomings.

Gardiner, J. W. Letter, *Saskatchewan History*, vol. 22, 1969, pp. 38-40. Comments on R. H. Milliken.

Garoian, Leon; and Haseley, Arnold F. *The Board of Directors in Agricultural Marketing Businesses.* Cooperative Extension Service, Oregon State University, 1963.

Gibbins, Roger. *Prairie Politics and Society: Regionalism in Decline.* Toronto: Butterworth and Co. (Canada) Ltd., 1980.

Gibbings, Charles W. "Wheat, Canada and the World." In Kenneth F. Nielsen (ed.) *Proceedings of the Canadian Centennial Wheat Symposium.* Saskatoon: Modern Press, 1967, pp. 5-23.

Gray, Grattan. "The Seed that Grew a Prairie Industry." *Canadian Business,* October 1979. The dramatic rapeseed story.

Gray, James H. *Boomtime: Peopling the Canadian Prairies.* Saskatoon: Western Producer Prairie Books, 1979.

Gray, James H. *The Boy from Winnipeg.* Toronto: Macmillan of Canada, 1970. Includes inside account of 1920s Grain Exchange.

Gray, James H. *Men Against the Desert.* Saskatoon: Western Producer Prairie Books, 1978. Reclamation of the Alberta-Saskatchewan dust bowl, first published 1967.

Gray, James H. *The Roar of the Twenties.* Toronto: Macmillan of Canada, 1975. Strong chapter on Sapiro and the pools, despite some inaccurate dates.

Gray, James H. *The Winter Years: The Depression on the Prairies.* Toronto: Macmillan of Canada, 1966.

Gray, Roger Thomas. "A Study on the Effectiveness of Local Committees of the Saskatchewan Wheat Pool." M.C.E. thesis, University of Saskatchewan, 1971.

Greenspon, Edward. "The Saskatchewan Wheat Pool is one of the big boys." Regina *Leader-Post*, 26 September 1981.

Griezic, Foster J. K. "The Honourable Thomas Alexander Crerar." In S. M. Trofimenkoff (ed.) *The Twenties in Western Canada: Papers of the Western Canada Studies Conference* Ottawa: National Museum of Man, 1972, pp. 107-131.

Grindley, T. W. "The Canadian Wheat Board." In *The Canada Year Book 1939* Ottawa: King's Printer, 1939.

Hamilton, F. W. *Service at Cost: A History of Manitoba Pool Elevators 1925-1975*. Saskatoon: Modern Press, 1976?.

Hannam, H. H. *Co-operation: The Plan for Tomorrow Which Works Today*. Ottawa: H. H. Hannam, ninth edition, 1945.

Harbron, John D. *C. D. Howe*. Don Mills: Fitzhenry and Whiteside Ltd., 1980.

Hawkes, David Craig. "Democracy, Ideology and Interest Groups: A Case Study of Saskatchewan Credit Unions as a Political Interest Group." Master's thesis, Queen's University, 1972.

Hedlin, Ralph Olaf. "The Growth of Grain Growers Co-operation in Western Canada with Special Emphasis on the Influence of Aaron Sapiro." M.Sc. thesis, University of Saskatchewan, 1949.

Hewlett, A. E. M. *A Too Short Yesterday*. Saskatoon: Western Producer, 1970. Pioneer reminiscences.

Higginbotham, C. H. *Off the Record: The CCF in Saskatchewan*. Toronto: McClelland and Stewart, 1968.

Hlushko, William. "The Program Planning Process in the Extension Department of the Saskatchewan Wheat Pool." Paper for continuing education 882, University of Saskatchewan, April 1967. By a member of the extension department of the Pool.

Hoffman, George. "The Entry of the United Farmers of Canada, Saskatchewan Section into Politics: A Reassessment." *Saskatchewan History*, vol. 30, no. 3, Autumn 1977, pp. 99-109.

Hoffman, George. "The Saskatchewan Farmer-Labor Party, 1932-1934: How Radical Was It at Its Origins?" In D. H. Bocking (ed.) *Pages from the Past* Saskatoon: Western Producer Prairie Books, 1979), pp. 210-224. Reprinted from *Saskatchewan History*, Spring 1975.

Hope, E. C. "Agriculture's Share of the National Income." *Canadian Journal of Economics and Political Science*, vol. 9, no. 3, August 1943, pp. 384-393.

Horn, Michiel. *The Dirty Thirties: Canadians in the Great Depression*. Toronto?: Copp Clark Publishing Co., 1972.

Horner, Jack. *My Own Brand*. Edmonton: Hurtig Publishers Ltd., 1980.

Innis, Harold Adams (ed.) *The Diary of Alexander James McPhail*. Toronto: University of Toronto Press, 1940.

International Wheat Pool Conference. *Proceedings of the International Wheat Pool Conference at St. Paul, Minn., February 16th, 17th, 18th, 1926*. Winnipeg: Canadian Co-operative Wheat Producers, 1926?.

International Wheat Pool Conference, Second. *Proceedings of the Second International Co-operative Wheat Pool Conference, held at Kansas City, Missouri, May 5th, 6th and 7th, 1927*. (No publication data.)

International Wheat Pool Conference, Third. *Proceedings of the First International Pool Conference which includes the Third International Wheat Pool Conference held at Regina, Saskatchewan June 5th, 6th and 7th, 1928*. (No publication data.)

Irvine, G. N. "Wheat and its Quality." In Kenneth F. Nielsen (ed.) *Proceedings of the Canadian Wheat Symposium* Saskatoon: Modern Press, 1967, pp. 233-247.

Irvine, G. N., and Anderson, J. A. "Some Technical Factors in the Production and Marketing of Canadian Wheat." *Canadian Journal of Economics and Political Science*, vol. 25, no.4, November 1959, pp. 439-449.

Irvine, William. *The Farmers in Politics.* Toronto: McClelland and Stewart, 1976, Carleton Library Edition. Originally published 1920.

Irwin, W. A. *The Canadian Wheat Pool.* Winnipeg: Canadian Wheat Pool Publicity Dept., 1929. Booklet reprinting MacLean's Magazine articles of 1 June, 15 June, and 1 July 1929.

Jaques, Edna. *Uphill All the Way.* Saskatoon: Western Producer Prairie Books, 1977. Depression homesteading.

Jesness, O. B. *The Cooperative Marketing of Farm Products.* Philadelphia: J. B. Lippincott Co., 1923.

Jesness, O. B. *The Cooperative Marketing of Tobacco.* Kentucky Agricultural Experiment Station, Bulletin No. 288. Lexington: University of Kentucky, 1928.

Jones, Helen Ingrid. "The Canadian Federation of Agriculture." Master's thesis, Queen's University, 1954.

Kelsey, Lincoln David, and Hearne, Cannon Chiles. *Cooperative Extension Work.* Ithaca: Comstock publishing Associates, third edition, 1963.

Kerr, Don, and Hanson, Stan. *Saskatoon: The First Half-Century.* Edmonton: NeWest Press, 1982. Mentions business involvement in the Pool sign-up campaign.

Khan, Dilawar Ali. "A Critique of Mr. Aaron Sapiro's Cooperative Philosophy." Ph.D. thesis, University of Wisconsin-Madison, 1970.

Kindleberger, Charles P. *The World in Depression 1929-1939.* Berkeley: University of California Press, 1973. Critical of Pool selling policy.

Kirk, Douglas. "Saskatchewan Wheat Pool." *Canadian Co-operative Digest*, vol. 13, winter 1970-71, pp. 19-27.

Kirk, D. W. *The Motherwell Story.* Regina: Canada Department of Agriculture, 1956. Booklet.

Knapp, Joseph Grant. *Farmers in Business: Studies in Cooperative Enterprise.* Washington: American Institute of Cooperation, 1963.

Kristjanson, L. F.; Baker, W. B.; Everson, F. C. *An Evaluation of the Educational Activities of Co-operatives in Saskatchewan.* Saskatoon: Center for Community Studies, 1964.

Kulshreshtha, Surendra N. *A Current Perspective on the Prairie Grain Handling and Transportation System.* Saskatoon: University of Saskatchewan, transportation centre, extension division publication no. 269, 1975.

Laidlaw, A. F. "Co-operatives in the Year 2000." Paper prepared for the 27th Congress of the International Co-operative Alliance, Moscow 1980. Ottawa: Co-operative Union of Canada.

Lamont. Cecil. *Prairie Sentinels.* Winnipeg: North-West Line Elevators Association, 1939?.

Larrowe, Charles P. *Harry Bridges: the Rise and Fall of Radical Labor in the United States.* New York: Lawrence Hill and Co., 1972. Section on Sapiro in decline.

Larsen, Grace E.; and Erdman, Henry E. "Aaron Sapiro: Genius of Farm Cooperative Promotion." *The Mississippi Valley Review*, vol. 49, no. 2, September 1962, 242-268.

Larsen, Grace H. "Cooperative Evangelist: Aaron Sapiro." In Joseph G. Knapp and Associates, *Great American Cooperators* Washington: American Institute of Cooperation, 1967, pp. 446-454. Condensed from the above work.

Lawton, Alma. "Relief Administration in Saskatchewan During the Depression." *Saskatchewan History*, vol. 22, 1969.

Lipset, Seymour Martin. *Agrarian Socialism: The Co-operative Commonwealth Federation in Saskatchewan*. Berkeley: University of California Press, 1971. Originally published 1950, revised 1968.

Lloyd, Lewis L. "Memories of a Co-operative Statesman." Saskatoon: Federated Co-operatives Ltd., typescript, no date. Lloyd was at one time a Pool delegate and attended meetings in 368 different Saskatchewan communities.

Lonergan, Sheila Gailene. "Agricultural Organization and Canadian Grain Marketing Policy 1935-55." Master's thesis, University of Saskatchewan, 1957.

Lonergan, Sheila Gailene. "The Influence of the Saskatchewan Wheat Pool on the Formulation of Federal Agricultural Policy." Economics essay, University of Saskatchewan, 1954.

MacCormick, Rev. Dr. Daniel. *The Antigonish Way*. Regina: Co-operative Union of Saskatchewan, 1947. Booklet on the co-operative movement inspired by St. Francis Xavier University.

McCourt, Edward. *Saskatchewan*. Toronto: Macmillan of Canada, 1968.

McCrorie, James Napier. *In Union is Strength*. Saskatoon: University of Saskatchewan, Centre for Community Studies, 1964. On the Farmers' Union movement.

MacEwan, John W. Grant. *Between the Red and the Rockies*. Saskatoon: Western Producer Prairie Books, 1979. First published 1952.

MacEwan, John W. Grant. *Fifty Mighty Men*. Saskatoon: Western Producer, 1958. Profile of McPhail.

MacEwan, John W. Grant. *Grant MacEwan's Illustrated History of Western Canadian Agriculture*. Saskatoon: Western Producer Prairie Books, 1980.

MacEwan, John W. Grant. *Power for Prairie Plows*. Saskatoon: Western Producer Prairie Books, 1971.

MacGibbon, Duncan Alexander. *The Canadian Grain Trade*. Toronto: The MacMillan Co. of Canada Ltd., 1932. Comprehensive overview by a member of the Board of Grain Commissioners.

MacGibbon, Duncan Alexander. *The Canadian Grain Trade 1931-1951*. Toronto: University of Toronto Press, 1952.

McGinnis, A J.; and Kasting, Robert. "Wheat Production and Insects." In Kenneth F. Nielsen (ed.) *Proceedings of the Canadian Centennial Wheat Symposium*. Saskatoon: Modern Press, 1967.

MacKintosh, W. A. "The Canadian Wheat Pools." *Bulletin of the departments of history and political and economic science in Queen's University*, no. 51, November 1925.

McLeod, Allan D. (ed.) *The Story of Rapeseed in Western Canada*. Saskatchewan Wheat Pool, 1974. Booklet.

McPhail, Alexander James. *Diaries*, 1919-31. The McNaughton Papers have two versions, typed by Mrs. McPhail, with certain names replaced by dashes. File E-35(1) has the first draft. File E-35(2) has a carbon copy of a reduced and slightly edited version. The original of the second version is in the Innis Papers, with handwritten notes by Professor Innis.

McPhail, Alexander James. "Farmers of Western Canada Encouraged by Success of Pool." Saskatoon *Daily Star*, 15 July 1926.

McPhail, Alexander James. Speech of 3 July 1929, Carlyle Lake. Reprinted in *Western Producer*, 29 October 1931, after McPhail's death.

MacPherson, Ian. "The Co-operative Union of Canada and the Prairies 1919-1929." In S. M. Trofimenkoff (ed.), *The Twenties in Western Canada:*

Papers of the Western Canada Studies Conference Ottawa: National Museum of Man, 1972, pp. 50-71.

MacPherson, Ian. *Each For All: A History of the Co-operative Movement in English Canada, 1900-1945.* Carleton Library series, no. 116. Toronto: The Macmillan Co. of Canada Ltd., 1979.

MacPherson, Ian. *The Story of CIS Ltd.: Co-operative Insurance Services.* CIS Ltd., 1974.

McPherson, W. J. "The Canadian Wheat Pool: An Analysis of Aims, Policies and Results." M.Sc. Thesis, University of Saskatchewan, 1937.

Malach, Vernon W. *International Cycles and Canada's Balance of Payments 1921-33.* Toronto: University of Toronto Press, 1954. Discusses wheat sales policy.

Marcus, Edward. *Canada and the International Business Cycle 1927-39.* New York: Bookman Associates, 1954. Discusses 1929-30 wheat sales.

Melville-Ness, Thomas R. "Impressions of Aaron Sapiro On the Occasion of His Appearance in Saskatoon." Undated recollections of Sapiro's 1951 Saskatoon speech and conversations. SWP Papers.

Menzies, Merril Warren. "The Canadian Wheat Board and the International Wheat Trade." Ph.D. thesis, University of London, 1956.

Metz, Sharon. *The Pioneers.* Regina: Crown Investments Corp. of Saskatchewan, 1981. Anecdotes from radio series, edited by Murray Long.

Milliken, Robert H. "The Early History and Development of the Wheat Pool Organization." Undated speech text, SWP Papers.

Milliken, Robert H. "Memo re Western Producer." 22 December 1932 memo to W. A. MacPherson, SWP Papers.

Milnor, A. J. "Agrarian Protest in Saskatchewan, 1929-1948: A Study in Ethnic Politics." Ph.D. Thesis, Duke University, 1962.

Milnor, Andrew. "The New Politics and Ethnic Revolt: 1929-1938." In Norman Ward and Duff Spafford (eds.) *Politics in Saskatchewan* Don Mills: Longmans Canada Ltd., 1968, pp. 151-177.

Moffet, Thomas H. "The Commercial Reserves and Elevator Deductions of the Saskatchewan Co-operative Wheat Producers Ltd ... " 1937-38 internal study, SWP Papers.

Moore, Gary. "Pool Personalities: Intimate Pen Pictures of Those at the Helm of the World's Greatest Co-operative Marketing Organization." *Saturday Night,* 11 April 1931.

Moorhouse, Herbert Joseph (Hopkins). *Deep Furrows.* Toronto and Winnipeg: George J. McLeod Ltd., 1918. The classic, inspirational book about the early farm movement on the prairies.

Morgan, Dan. *Merchants of Grain.* New York: Penguin Books, 1980. First published 1979. On the giant multinational firms.

Morrison, Ralph. "History of Robsart Wheat Pool Local." Handwritten recollections, April 1982, SWP Papers.

Morton, William Lewis. "The Bias of Prairie Politics." In Donald Swainson (eds.) *Historical Essays on the Prairie Provinces* Toronto: The Macmillan Co. of Canada Ltd., 1978, first published 1970. Reprinted from *Transactions of the Royal Society of Canada,* vol. 49, series 3, section 2, June 1955.

Morton, William Lewis. *The Progressive Party in Canada.* Toronto: University of Toronto Press, 1950.

Motherwell, W. R. "The Territorial Grain Growers' Association." As told to Hopkins Moorhouse, *Saskatchewan History,* vol.8, 1955, pp. 108-112.

Nagy, J. G., and Furtan, W. Hartley; and Kulshreshtha, Surendra N. *The Canadian Wheat Economy: Economic Implications of Changes in the Crowsnest*

Pass Freight Rates. University of Saskatchewan technical bulletin no. 79-1, 1979.

Nagy, J. G.; and Furtan, W. H. "The Socio-Economic Costs and Returns from Rapeseed Breeding in Canada." University of Saskatchewan technical bulletin no. 77-1, May 1977.

Neatby, Blair. "The Saskatchewan Relief Commission 1931-34." *Saskatchewan History,* vol. 3, Spring 1950, pp. 41-56.

Nesbitt, Leonard D. "Survey of the Western Producer." 7 July 1934 study, Alberta Wheat Pool Papers, box 45 file 503.

Nesbitt, Leonard D. *Tides in the West.* Saskatoon: Modern Press, about 1962(?). A valuable history of Alberta Wheat Pool by one of its former senior officials — but flawed by incorrect dates in many places.

Nesbitt, Leonard D. *The Story of Wheat.* Calgary: Alberta Wheat Pool, 1946. Booklet.

North-West Line Elevators Association. "A Statement, in Chronological Order, of the Facts Pertaining to the Tax Liability of the Wheat Pools." Brief dated 1 June 1946.

Oddie, Emma. "Western Women in Agriculture." In University of Regina, *Development of Agriculture on the Prairies: Proceedings of Seminar.* University of Regina, 1975, pp. 30-34.

Parsons, Nell Wilson. *Upon a Sagebrush Harp.* Saskatoon: Western Producer Prairie Books, 1969. About one of the many farm families that could not overcome Depression and drought to keep farming.

Partridge, E. A. *A War on Poverty: the One War That Can End War.* Winnipeg: Wallingford Press Ltd., 1926.

Patton, Harald S. "The Canadian Wheat Pool in Prosperity and Depression." Central Selling Agency booklet reprinting article from N. E. Himes (ed.) *Economics, Sociology and the Modern World: Essays in Honor of T. N. Carver* Cambridge: Harvard University Press, 1935.

Patton, Harald S. *Grain Growers' Co-operation in Western Canada.* Cambridge: Harvard University Press, 1928.

Patton, Harald S. "The Market Influence of the Canadian Wheat Pool." Reprint from *Proceedings of the American Statistical Association,* March 1929.

Peacock, J. W. *From Lumberjack to Wheat Farmer.* Regina: Banting Publishers, about 1974. Typescript recollections.

Pearson, Lester Bowles. *Mike: The Memoirs of the Right Honourable Lester B. Pearson.* Toronto: University of Toronto Press, 1972. Describes argument with R. B. Bennett over anti-pool propaganda in a royal commission report.

Peterson, Charles W. *Wheat — the Riddle of Markets.* Calgary: Farm and Ranch Review Ltd., 1930.

Phillips, Robert H. D. "The Dean of Wheat Pool Fieldmen." *Western Producer,* 11 December 1975. On Howard Tyler.

Phillips, Robert H. D. "Farmers, Government and Public Policy for Agriculture." In University of Regina, *Development of Agriculture on the Prairies: Proceedings of Seminar* University of Regina, 1975, pp. 64-81.

Phillips, Robert H. D. *Out West.* Saskatoon: Western Producer Prairie Books, 1977. Columns from *Western Producer.*

Plunkett, Sir Horace. *Agricultural Co-operation in its Application to the Industry, the Business, and the Life of the Farmer in the British Empire.* London: George Routledge and Sons Inc., 1925. Includes transcript of 28-31 July 1924 Wembley conference on Empire agriculture, speech by Premier Dunning.

Powell, Oscar Reginald. *So Soon Forgotten.* Saskatoon: Modern Press, 1955. Prairie stories, 1904-1919, under pseudonym of Dick Fairfax.

Priestley, Norman F., and Swindlehurst, Edward B. *Furrows, Faith and Fellowship.* Edmonton: Co-op Press Ltd., 1967. On Alberta United Farmers movement.

Purden, Christine. *Agents for Change, Credit Unions in Saskatchewan.* Saskatoon: Credit Union Central of Saskatchewan, 1980.

Purich, Donald John. "Lawyer becomes hero to farmers." *Western Producer*, magazine, 16 October 1980. A good profile, despite wrong date for Saskatoon's award to Sapiro.

Regehr, Ted. *Remembering Saskatchewan: A History of Rural Saskatchewan.* Saskatoon: University of Saskatchewan, 1979. Booklet.

Reid, Escott. "The Saskatchewan Liberal Machine Before 1929." In Norman Ward and Duff Spafford (eds.), *Politics in Saskatchewan* Don Mills: Longmans Canada Ltd., 1968, pp. 93-104. Reprinted from *Canadian Journal of Economics and Political Science*, 1936.

Richards, John; and Pratt, Larry. *Prairie Capitalism: Power and Influence in the New West.* Toronto: McClelland and Stewart Ltd., 1979.

Robertson, George Wilson. "Au Revoir." *The Co-optimist*, vol. 20. no. 6, June 1947, p. 2. On Gertrude Willcott, the Pool's first stenographer.

Robertson, George Wilson. "Co-operative Movement in this Province Challenges Attention of Whole World." Saskatoon *Daily Star*, 15 July 1926.

Robertson, George Wilson. "Summary of Proceedings of the Ottawa Delegations." Undated memo (1942), SWP Papers.

Robinson, Sylvia Ann. "The Changing Role of the Field Man." M.C.E. thesis, University of Saskatchewan, 1981.

Rolph, William Kirby. *Henry Wise Wood of Alberta.* Toronto: University of Toronto Press, 1950.

Rolph, William Kirby. "Turner's Weekly: An Episode in Prairie Journalism." *Saskatchewan History*, vol. 4, Autumn 1951, pp. 81-92.

Roy, Wendy. "Jake Schulz." *Western Producer*, magazine, 4 February 1982.

Roy, Wendy. "Joe Phelps rebuilt SFU, 1949-54." *Western Producer*, magazine, 29 April 1982.

Sapiro, Aaron. "Organise to Sell Products, Them Sell Them." Saskatoon *Daily Star*, 12 May 1923, article reprinted from *World's Work*.

Sapiro, Aaron. Speech of July 1920, Chicago; text in American Farm Bureau booklet, "Co-operative Marketing."

Sapiro, Aaron. Speech of 2 August 1923, Calgary; text in Lethbridge *Herald*, 15 August 1923.

Sapiro, Aaron. Speech of 3 August 1923, Edmonton; text in Winnipeg *Farmer's Advocate and Home Journal* of 10 August Edmonton *Journal farm weekly* of 8 August.

Sapiro, Aaron. Speech of 6 August 1923, to Saskatoon conference of farm leaders; text in Farmers' Union of Canada Papers, file B-2 VI.6.

Sapiro, Aaron. Speech of 7 August 1923, to Saskatoon public rally; transcript in booklet "Report of Mass Meeting Addressed by Mr. Aaron Sapiro."

Sapiro, Aaron. Speech of 11 December 1923, Chicago; text in American Farm Bureau Federation booklet "An Analysis of Marketing."

Sapiro, Aaron. Speech of 20 February 1924, Regina; transcript in Regina *Morning Leader*, 21 February 1924.

Sapiro, Aaron. Speeches of 14-15 July 1926, Saskatoon; transcripts in proceedings of FUC-SGGA amalgamation convention, Farmers' Union of Canada Papers, file B-2 V.3.

Sapiro, Aaron. Speech of 30 October 1927, to the Free Synagogue, Carnegie Hall, New York; text in booklet "An Experience With American Justice." Gives details of lawsuit against Henry Ford.

Sapiro, Aaron. Speech of 14 July 1926, Saskatoon; transcript in UFC Papers file B-2 X.60.

Sapiro, Aaron. Speech of 26 June 1929, Saskatoon; transcript in UFC Papers file B-2 X.60.

Sapiro, Aaron. Speech of 20 September 1929, Regina; transcript in UFC Papers file B-2 IX.259.

Sapiro, Aaron, speech of about 20 September 1929, Kerrobert; text in UFC Papers file B-2 IX.259. Sapiro's voice had failed and this speech was read for him.

Sapiro, Aaron. Speech of 5 December 1951, Saskatoon; transcript C-120, Saskatchewan Archives Board, Saskatoon; slightly-different transcript in SWP Papers.

Saskatchewan Co-operative Elevator Company. *A Brief Record of the History and Development of the Saskatchewan Co-operative Elevator Company, Limited.* 1924 booklet.

Saskatchewan Co-operative Elevator Company. *Delegate's Handbook.* 1925.

Saskatchewan Co-operative Elevator Company. Transcript of annual meeting, 16-18 December 1925, SWP Papers.

Saskatchewan Wheat Pool. *Beyond the Farm Gate: Story of Saskatchewan Wheat Pool.* SWP extension division booklet, no date, post-1969.

Saskatchewan Wheat Pool. *Field to Market.* SWP information division, August 1980. Booklet on grainhandling stages.

Saskatchewan Wheat Pool. *50: Saskatchewan Wheat Pool 1924-1974.* Regina: Saskatchewan Wheat Pool, 1974. Booklet, historical perspectives.

Saskatchewan Wheat Pool. *50 Years Saskatchewan: Highlights of Saskatchewan Wheat Pool's 50-Year History.* SWP publicity and advertising division, 1974. Booklet reprinting *Western Producer* articles.

Saskatchewan Wheat Pool. *Lest We Forget.* Regina: Saskatchewan Wheat Pool, 1931. Booklet, quotations on pooling achievements

Saskatchewan Wheat Pool. *Pool.* Regina: information division, 1979. Booklet, overview of SWP functions.

Saskatchewan Wheat Pool. *Pool: Saskatchewan Wheat Pool.* Communications division, 1981. Booklet, some history.

Saskatchewan Wheat Pool. *Questions and Answers about Pool Purchase of Federal.* Saskatchewan Wheat Pool, 1972.

Saskatchewan Wheat Pool. *Twenty One Years of Progress.* Saskatchewan Co-operative Producers Ltd., 1945. Booklet.

Saskatchewan Wheat Pool. *25 Years with the Saskatchewan Wheat Pool.* Saskatchewan Co-operative Producers Ltd., 1949. Booklet.

Saskatchewan Wheat Pool. *Your Wheat 1929.* Saskatchewan Co-operative Wheat Producers Ltd., Pamphlet No. 2, revised, 1929.

Scharf, E. Forrest. *Co-operatives in Saskatchewan.* Regina: Co-operative Union of Saskatchewan, about 1960.

Schulz, Jacob. *Rise and Fall of Canadian Farm Organizations.* (Winnipeg: J. Schulz, 1955. Farmers' Union viewpoint.

Schwarz, N. H. "Why I have the full and only right to claim that I am the one and only man who started the Farmers' Union of Canada and laid the foundation for the Canadian Wheat Pool." Typed reminiscences, Schwarz Papers.

Schweitzer, Frank. "My Experiences in the Consumer and Producer Co-operatives 1938-1951." Typed recollections, 1980. Interesting detail on a Pool delegate's activities.

Shackleton, Doris French. *Tommy Douglas.* Toronto: McClelland and Stewart, 1975.

Sharp, Paul F. *The Agrarian Revolt in Western Canada: A Survey Showing American Parallels.* Minneapolis: University of Minnesota Press, 1948.

Shebeski, L. H. "Wheat and Breeding." In Kenneth F. Nielsen (ed.) *Proceedings of the Canadian Centennial Wheat Symposium* Saskatoon: Modern Press, 1967, pp. 253-271.

Sherriff, Annie Bell. "Agricultural Co-operation in Saskatchewan." Master's thesis, University of Saskatchewan, 1923.

Smith, David E. *Prairie Liberalism: The Liberal Party in Saskatchewan 1905-71.* Toronto: University of Toronto Press, 1975.

Smith, David E. *The Regional Decline of a National Party: Liberals on the Prairies.* Toronto: University of Toronto Press, 1981.

Smith, D. L. "Did the Pool's London Office Antagonize Buyers?" 1934 memo, SWP Papers.

Snodgrass, Katharine. "Price Spreads and Shipment Costs in the Wheat Export Trade of Canada." *Wheat Studies,* vol. 2, no. 5, March 1926, pp. 177-194.

Spafford, Duff S. "The Elevator Issue, the Organized Farmers, and the Government 1908-1911." In D. H. Bocking (ed.) *Pages from the Past* Saskatoon: Western Producer Prairie Books, 1979), pp. 170-180. Reprinted from *Saskatchewan History,* vol. 15, Autumn 1962.

Spafford, Duff S. "The "Left Wing" 1921-1931." In Norman Ward and Duff Spafford (eds.) *Politics in Saskatchewan* Don Mills: Longmans Canada Ltd., 1968, pp. 44-58.

Spafford, Duff S. "The Origin of the Farmers' Union of Canada." *Saskatchewan History,* vol. 18, Autumn 1965, pp. 89-98.

Spector, David. *Field Agriculture in the Canadian Prairie West, 1870 to 1940, With Emphasis on the Period 1870-1920.* Ottawa: Parks Canada, 1977. Manuscript report no. 205, National Historic Parks and Sites Branch.

Stapleford, E. W. *Report on Rural Relief Due to Drought Conditions and Crop Failures in Western Canada 1930-37.* Ottawa: Canada Department of Agriculture, 1939.

Steed, Judy. "High Tech Enters the Farm Gate." Toronto *Globe and Mail,* 6 March 1982.

Steen, Herman. *Cooperative Marketing: The Golden Rule in Agriculture.* New York: Doubleday, Page & Co., 1923. Pre-publication consultation with Sapiro, lists Sapiro involvements.

Stern, Norton B. "Aaron L. Sapiro: the Man Who Sued Henry Ford." *Western States Jewish Historical Quarterly,* vol. 13, no. 4, July 1981, pp. 303-312.

Strange, H. G. L. *A Short History of Prairie Agriculture.* Winnipeg: Searle Grain Co. Ltd., 1954.

Stursberg, Peter. *Diefenbaker: Leadership Gained 1956-62.* Toronto: University of Toronto Press, 1975-76. Oral history transcripts.

Stutt, R. L. "Prairie Project." *Food for Thought,* vol. 8, no. 7, April 1948, pp. 17-18. A Pool field staff supervisor's account of the delegate system.

Taylor, Alonzo E. "A National Wheat-Growers' Co-operative: its Problems, Opportunities and Limitations." *Wheat Studies,* vol. 2, January 1926, pp. 101-162. Frequent references to Canadian pools.

Trevena, Jack. *Prairie Co-operation — A Diary.* Saskatoon: Co-operative College of Canada, 1976.

Turgeon, W. F. A. *Report of the Royal Commission on Transportation.* Ottawa: King's Printer, 1951.

Turner, Allan R. "W. R. Motherwell: the Emergence of a Farm Leader." *Saskatchewan History,* vol. 9, Autumn 1958, pp. 94-103.

Twenty-Fifth Street House Theatre. *Paper Wheat: the Book.* Saskatoon: Western

Producer Prairie Books, 1982. Text and music to the sensitive play, with historical introduction by John Archer.

"The Two Lives of Charlie Gibbings." *Family Herald*, 22 June 1967.

Unger, Gordon. "James G. Gardiner and the Constitutional Crisis of 1929." *Saskatchewan History*, vol. 23, Spring 1970, pp. 41-49.

United Grain Growers Lld. *The Grain Growers Record 1906 to 1943*. Winnipeg: United Grain Growers Ltd., 1944.

United Nations. Food and Agriculture Organization. *The Stabilization of International Trade in Grains*. Italy: FAC Commodity Policy Studies 20, 1970.

United States Senate. Committee on Agriculture and Forestry. *Hearings*. 71st Congress, first session. McPhail testimony 4 April 1929, pp. 555-588.

Waldron, A. Patrick. "Three Presidents." *Western Producer*, 12 January 1961. Short but extremely perceptive essay on McPhail, Brouillette and Wesson.

Warbasse, James Peter. *Co-operative Democracy*. New York: Harper and Brothers Publishers, fifth edition, 1947. A onetime president of the Co-operative League of the U.S.A. who viewed producer co-operatives as flawed junior partners of the consumer co-op movement.

Ward, John W. *The Canadian Council of Agriculture: a Review of the History and work of the National Farm Organization of Canada*. Winnipeg: Canadian Council of Agriculture, 1925. Booklet.

Ward, Norman. "The Contemporary Scene." In Norman Ward and Duff Spafford, *Politics in Saskatchewan* Don Mills: Longmans Canada Ltd., 1968, pp. 280-303.

Watkins, Ernest. *R. B. Bennett*. Toronto: Kingswood House, 1963.

"Wheat." *Round Table*, vol. 21, 1930-31, pp. 415-423.

"The Wheat Pool Marketing Experiment 1921-1932." (No source listed, marked "compiled in 1933") A mimeographed, 608-page collection of anti-pool news excerpts and commentary, perhaps intended for use in lobbying against the pools. One copy is in the Rare Books Room, National Library, Ottawa.

"The Wheat Pools of Western Canada." *Round Table*, vol. 18, 1927-28, pp. 154-63.

Wheeler, Elizabeth (ed.) *Glistening in the Sun: An Anthology of YC Verse*. Saskatoon: Western Producer Prairie Books, 1977. From the Young Co-operators pages of the *Western Producer*.

Wilkes, Fred A. *They Rose From the Dust*. Saskatoon: Modern Press, 1958. Moose Jaw area history.

Williams, Blair. "The Canadian Federation of Agriculture: the Problems of a General Political Interest Group." Ph. D. thesis, Carleton University, 1974.

Williams, E. K. *Report of the Royal Commission to Inquire into Charges Against Manitoba Pool Elevators Limited*. Winnipeg: King's Printers, 1931.

Willmott, Donald E. "The Formal Organizations of Saskatchewan Farmers, 1900-65." In Anthony W. Rasporich (ed.), *Western Canada Past and Present*; Calgary: University of Calgary and McClelland and Stewart West Ltd., 1975, pp. 28-41.

Wilson, Barry. *Beyond the Harvest: Canadian Grain at the Crossroads*. Saskatoon: Western Producer Prairie Books, 1981.

Wilson, Barry. *Politics of Defeat: The Decline of the Liberal Party in Saskatchewan*. Saskatoon: Western Producer Prairie Books, 1980.

Wilson, Charles F. *A Century of Canadian Grain: Government Policy to 1951*. Saskatoon: Western Producer Prairie Books, 1978. An invaluable and comprehensive account, by a senior grain policy official. Features lengthy quotations from official documents.

Wilson, Charles F. *C. D. Howe: An Optimist's Response to a Surfeit of Grain.* Ottawa: Grains Group, 1980.

Wilson, Charles F. *Grain Marketing in Canada.* Winnipeg: Canadian International Grains Institute, 1979.

Working, Holbrook. "The Canadian Wheat Pool and Prices." *Wheat Studies,* vol. 7, December 1930, pp. 140-144.

Working, Holbrook; and Hobe, Adelaide M. "Financial Results of Speculative Holding of Wheat." *Wheat Studies,* vol. 7, July 1931, pp. 405-435.

Working, Holbrook; and Hobe, Adelaide M. "The Post-Harvest Depression of Wheat Prices." *Wheat Studies,* vol. 6, November 1929, pp. 1-40.

Workman, F. J. "Sixty Years Devoted to the Development of Agriculture." Seven-part series of lengthy articles on W. R. Motherwell's career, Moose Jaw *Times-Herald,* 22-29 July 1940. Written in collaboration with Motherwell.

Wright, George F. "The Wheat Pool and its Problems." Pamphlet reprint of 15 October 1930, speech to Montreal Advertising Club. Passionate defence of the pools' sales policy, by the editor of the Montreal *Star.*

Wright, J. F. C. *Prairie Progress: Consumer Co-operation in Saskatchewan.* Saskatoon: Modern Press, 1956.

Wright, Myrtle Hayes. "Mothering the Prairie." *MacLean's Magazine,* 1 April 1926. Profile of Violet McNaughton.

Yates, Samuel W. *The Saskatchewan Wheat Pool: Its Origin, Organization and Progress 1924-1935.* Saskatoon: United Farmers of Canada (Saskatchewan Section) Ltd., about 1946. Edited by Arthur S. Morton.

Young, Walter D. *The Anatomy of a Party: The National CCF 1932-61.* Toronto: University of Toronto Press, 1969.

Index